HUGO WOLF

THE VOCAL MUSIC

HUGO WOLF

THE VOCAL MUSIC

Susan Youens

PRINCETON UNIVERSITY PRESS

PRINCETON, NEW JERSEY

Library of Congress Cataloging-in-Publication Data
Youens, Susan
Hugo Wolf : the vocal music / by Susan Youens.
p.   cm.
Includes bibliographical references (p.   ) and index.
ISBN 0-691-09145-5
1. Wolf, Hugo, 1860–1903.   Vocal music.   2. Vocal music—
19th century—History and criticism.   I. Title.
ML410.W8Y7   1992
782.42168′092—dc20   91-45446

_____ **_Contents_** _____

Examples and Figures

Examples

Figures

Preface and Acknowledgments

THE LAST decades of the twentieth century have seen a considerable revival of interest in the artistic and intellectual ferment at the end of the preceding century. The success of Carl Schorske's book *Fin-de-Siècle Vienna* (New York: Random House, 1980) made apparent the extent of public fascination with a place and an era to which we trace our modern roots, and the virtual cottage industry of books, monographs, and essays on fin-de-siècle Vienna continues apace. Forms, genres, languages of all kinds—verbal, visual, musical, spatial, philosophical, and others—evolved into something new and modern at the turn of the century, or experienced a final flowering before their demise. From our postmodern aeries or abysses, we can look back to the Viennese caldron in which Romantic traditions underwent evolutionary processes of alteration or destruction, and see at work the forces that overthrew some of what was inherited from earlier generations so that newer and hybrid forms might emerge and flourish.

Among the traditions undergoing change in the final quarter of the century was the Romantic lied, whose greatest fin-de-siècle proponent was Hugo Wolf (13 March 1860–22 February 1903). Although he has been the connoisseur's delight from the time of his first publications, he is sometimes given short shrift in accounts of Viennese artistic efflorescence between 1875 and World War I, crowded out by the proponents of the "gigantic Romantic" and by the Schoenberg-Berg-Webern circle after Wolf's death. Schorske, I would guess, omits Wolf from his "song-cycle" sequence of seven independent but interrelated studies because Wolf accords only awkwardly with the Oedipal overthrow of historicity that Schorske traces through Viennese politics, psychology, and the arts. Despite the famous critic Eduard Hanslick's designation of Wolf as "the Richard Wagner of the lied" (a largely false characterization meant to be pejorative, but with a soupçon of accuracy), and despite Wolf's late-Romantic tonal vocabulary and declamatory melodic manner, Wolf is a faithful conservator of the Schubert-Schumann tradition of lieder composition. He preserves the established boundaries and forms of the lied, its nineteenth-century assertion of a close word-tone relationship (even where the two are antagonistic), and its favorite poets, preferring Goethe, Eichendorff, Mörike, Byron, and folk poetry to his own contemporaries. And yet he was also an innovator, someone who forged his own style out of the stuff of extended tonality at the century's end. Not for him the grandiose, at times grandiosely vulgar, effects of Wagner and Mahler; even the most brilliant of his lieder are marked by a characteristic refinement and delight in nuance. Where flexible vocal declamation cedes to lyrical melody, as in the Eichendorff lied

"Das Ständchen" (The serenade) or his setting of Mörike's "Der Gärtner" (The gardener), he still admits no pandering to a lower common denominator, no sops to singers and listeners unresponsive to subtlety. Although he continually sought and courted a wider audience, he did not write music for what Nietzsche scornfully called "neighbors." He would have nothing to do with sentimental *Trivialpoesie* in accord with popular taste, but instead selected poems such as Goethe's "Anakreons Grab" (Anacreon's grave) that had been passed over by every other lieder composer preceding him. Despite his recognition that music rides roughshod over poetry, obliterating poetic rhyme, rhythm, and form, his determination to do poetry honor in music as compact with gesture and nuance as the works of his favorite poets is the hallmark of his oeuvre. My own delight in Wolf's multiple subtleties has determined the nature of this book: because few composers have converted poetry into music with such finesse and such voracious attention to detail, I have accordingly tried to read the verse he set to music with the attentiveness he obviously felt it deserved, and to limit discussion to only a few works from his large song oeuvre. Excellent summaries of the entire work list already exist, but the pleasure of lingering over individual examples at greater length has been the impelling force behind my labors.

It is now the centenary of a prolonged and extraordinary event in the history of the lied: the spate of songwriting that began on 16 February 1888 and rolled on, checked only by an eight-month lapse of compositional powers in 1889, until the end of December 1891. In those few years, Wolf composed his Mörike, Eichendorff, Goethe, and Keller collections, ranging from six songs to fifty-three in each volume, as well as the *Spanisches Liederbuch* and Part 1 of the *Italienisches Liederbuch*, or a total of 189 songs (seven of the Eichendorff lieder were composed before 1888). More songs and two operas, the second unfinished, followed in 1895–97 after more than three years of excruciating compositional block—possibly the result of syphilis in its lengthy secondary stage of incursion on the brain and nervous system. Surely this is a propitious time to pay that achievement the homage of renewed scholarly attention, perhaps in preparation for observances in 2003 of the centennial anniversary of Wolf's death. David Ossenkop in *Hugo Wolf: A Guide to Research* (New York: Garland Publishing, 1988) has called for a documentary biography, a complete and unexpurgated new edition of the letters, a new life-and-works to encompass discoveries made since Frank Walker's monumental biography, and much else. Already a translation into English—the first ever—by Louise McClelland Urban of the complete letters of Hugo Wolf to his mistress Melanie Köchert has appeared (New York: Schirmer Books, 1991); for those unfamiliar with the prose of the most witty, literate, and compelling composer-writer since Mozart, this book should whet the appetite for more—both the restored German texts in print once again and more English translations.

My book, however, is not primarily biographical, although biographical matters are of importance on many occasions. Rather, I have chosen to examine five aspects of Wolf's music, ranging from the beginning to the end of the composer's creative lifetime, each of which exemplifies hallmarks of both tradition and modernity. It is precisely the way in which Wolf weaves together chosen elements from the preceding glorious century of lieder history and his own musical innovations that constitutes his unique style. If the past weighed heavily upon him on those occasions when the inevitable comparisons with Schubert seemed most galling or when he tried to find poetry not already set to music by his great predecessors, it was also the bedrock upon which his own oeuvre was founded. In his love of older poetry—Goethe, Mörike, and Michelangelo take precedence over modern poets—and his reverence for his predecessors from earlier in the century, such as Carl Loewe, one finds ample evidence of his active involvement with the traditions from which he came. If the five aspects of Wolf's vocal music that I examine in this book seem disparate at first glance, united only in the person of the composer himself, there is nevertheless a connecting thread: each one exemplifies the unique equipoise of tradition and innovation in his compositions, an equipoise differently constituted in the differing genres of ballad, lied, and opera.

Wolf only attained compositional maturity in his late twenties after a protracted period of trial and experiment. During the decade and more from his first teenage efforts to the outpouring of Mörike songs in 1888, Wolf adopted a course common to many composers in the last half of the century: he wrote "under the sign of Schumann," setting texts by Schumann's favorite poet Heinrich Heine in a manner that, at first, echoes Schumann with remarkable fidelity. For a time, he taught himself composition and text setting by writing imitation-Schumann but with traces, first faint and then stronger, of his own style, or what he called "Wölferl's own howl." A small group or *Liederstrauß* (Bouquet of songs) of Schumannesque Heine settings composed in 1878 was the first work Wolf considered fit for publication. "Sie haben heut' Abend Gesellschaft" (They have company this evening), the first and perhaps the most successful song in the *Liederstrauß*, could almost have passed muster as being by Schumann himself; like the endings of *Frauenliebe und Leben* (A woman's love and life), op. 48, and *Dichterliebe* (Poet's love), op. 45, "Sie haben heut' Abend Gesellschaft" concludes with a lengthy piano postlude that extends poetic interpretation into the instrumental conclusion. In my first chapter, entitled "'Too Much Like Schumann': The Apprenticeship of a Lieder Composer," I trace the stages from near-total dependence on prior models to stylistic independence, culminating in the consideration of one of Wolf's first masterpieces, the June 1883 setting of Justinus Kerner's "Zur Ruh', zur Ruh', ihr müden Glieder" (Rest, rest, you tired limbs). Kerner, too, had been one of Schumann's poets, but Wolf found in this single poem—he never set anything else by Kerner—a source of separation from Schumann. Later, in the

Mörike and Goethe songs of 1888–89, he would locate still stronger correspondences to his own musical voice.

Another of Wolf's earliest masterpieces, composed in 1882 before the lone Kerner song, is also his first comic lied—his setting of Mörike's "Mausfallen-Sprüchlein" (Magic charm for mousers). Curiously, Frank Walker, whose biography of Wolf everyone justly describes as monumental, failed fully to appreciate this important facet of the composer's oeuvre, decrying the comic songs as little more than trifles and practical jokes. They were, I strongly believe, much more than that. The numerous subsequent specimens of humor in music that follow "Mausfallen-Sprüchlein" reveal Wolf's taste for what Sigmund Freud would dub "tendentious jokes," in which anger is converted to mock-revenge and discharged as laughter. In full cognizance of the complex mechanisms of humor, Wolf makes no concessions to tonal simplicity in his comic songs. At a time and place when comedy in music was associated with the regressive harmonic style of light opera and operetta, Wolf instead applied every chromatic nuance of his tonal arsenal to comic expression. Poetic jests that were purely literary and verbal become jokes *in* music *about* music—modern music. In songs such as the Mörike lied "Zur Warnung" (A warning), Wolf spoofs the contrast between a regressive diatonic style and the farthest extremes of modern chromaticism. In this way, he could hope to win converts to his unique idiom, to entice listeners to accept a modern tonal language through the agency of laughter—"to draw the one who laughs to his side," in Freud's words. Delighted with his achievement, Wolf once claimed to have invented humor in music—he did not, but he *did* elevate the genre of the comic lied to new heights of complexity, to a new seriousness, if one will pardon the paradox. In my second chapter, "Wolf, Freud, and Humor in Music," I discuss selected comic songs from the *Mörike-Lieder* and the *Italienisches Liederbuch*, especially the songs from the latter anthology in which the poetic persona is a woman. Humor in the Eichendorff and Goethe songs is, not surprisingly, of a different order from the tendentious humor of the Mörike and Italian collections, but I have nonetheless included examples from those volumes both for their instructive contrast with that vein of humor most obviously rooted in anger and in hopes of acquainting readers with a somewhat neglected, and delightful, group of songs.

Wolf did not claim to have invented the ballad, but in this sphere as well he could have pointed with pride to his own considerable and original contributions to the genre. In his, and others', estimation, the ballad "Der Feuerreiter" (The fire-rider) from the *Mörike-Lieder* is among his most brilliant and complex works; even the hostile critic Eduard Hanslick had to sit up and take notice at a performance of "Der Feuerreiter" in Wolf's own arrangement for orchestra, chorus, and soloists. Wolf's loyalty to a tradition of ballad composition that one can trace side-by-side with lieder throughout the nineteenth century is evident from the beginning in his reverence for the master above all others of the German art-ballad, Carl Loewe (1796–1869), and in his early ballads to texts by Nikolaus Lenau and Mörike—his first settings of the latter poet, perhaps the poet most closely identified with him, were ballad settings. If there are no ballads at the end of his compositional life, it is only because the *Italienisches Liederbuch* (Italian songbook), *Spanisches Liederbuch* (Spanish songbook), and the poetry of Michelangelo—his principal text sources in the 1890s—contained either no ballads at all or none to his liking.

But the ballad, by the time of Wolf's youth, was a moribund genre, not yet defunct but in ailing health. Although both lied and ballad are settings of poetry for a pianist and singer, and although nineteenth-century composers often wrote in both genres, the two differ from one another in crucial ways, and the lied had assumed primacy over the ballad by the 1870s. In the 1880s and 1890s, however, the ballad was given a second spring, a new lease on life. A Carl Loewe society was formed in Berlin; the ballads, songs, and even selections from Loewe's failed operas were published in a series of volumes edited by Maximilian Runze; and latter-day ballad composers such as Martin Plüddemann composed new specimens of the genre—eight entire volumes of ballads. Wolf belongs to that second spring, but, typically for him, does so in an idiosyncratic manner. He both borrows recognizable elements and forms from the ballad tradition and adapts them to his own style and predilections in works such as "Die Geister am Mummelsee" (The spirits at the Mummel lake) from the *Mörike-Lieder* and "Ritter Kurts Brautfahrt" (Knight Kurt's bridal journey) from the *Goethe-Lieder*, to cite only two. He does not set the classic ballad texts of Gottfried August Bürger, Ludwig Uhland, Friedrich Schiller, and others, and he diverges significantly from the "pure" ballad in his own works. His liking for ballads in which the poetic persona relates events as he experiences them are unlike the classic texts, in which tales of a distant past are recounted by a narrator who omits far more than he reveals. And yet Wolf paid homage in his own coin both to Loewe's strophic *Balladen in Lied-Form* (a hybrid of ballad and lied) and to the longer, episodic, through-composed works for which Loewe was once so famous, such as "Archibald Douglas," "Der Nöck" (The water-sprite), "Der Mohrenfürst" (The Moorish prince), "Die Heinzelmännchen" (The gnomes), and many others. Because Wolf's tonal language was far more radical in its chromaticism than Loewe's practices, and because Wolf both borrowed from Loewe and introduced his own innovations, he could venerate Loewe without the trepidation caused by the example of Schubert and Wagner in lied and opera, respectively. In the third chapter, "Influence Without Anxiety: Wolf and the Ballad Tradition," I write of the history and nature of the ballad, the ballad revival of the 1880s and 1890s, Wolf's interest in the genre throughout his lifetime, and the differences between his ballads and those by Loewe.

In Chapter 4, "A Spanish Tale: Wolf and His Contemporaries," I have compared several of Wolf's *Spanisches Liederbuch* settings with songs to the same texts by his contemporaries in order better to understand the climate in which Wolf composed, the lieder he knew and heard, and the repertoire that often won more critical approval than his own. The translations of Spanish folk poems by Emanuel Geibel and Paul Heyse published in 1852 were tremendously popular with composers throughout the last half of the century, from Schumann on. These poems, their Spanish derivation guaranteed to appeal to a composer fascinated by Mediterranean themes, elicited from Wolf some of his most tonally adventurous music, in stark contrast with the tamer songs of his contemporaries, even the followers of Liszt and Wagner. Looking at Wolf's songs in company with those by Jensen and his ilk is another way of measuring Wolf's blend of traditionalism and radicalism—one that can perhaps open a window onto a little-known landscape in late-nineteenth-century musical life. Brahms of course was and is famous, the greatest of Wolf's contemporaries to set texts from the *Spanisches Liederbuch*. Wolf, however, despised his Viennese contemporary, whose aesthetic of song composition is very different from Wolf's. Ironically, Brahms too began by imitating Schumann's songs and he too revered Schubert, but tradition and innovation are differently constituted in his lieder, the contrast an instructive one.

Wolf chafed against the designation as "merely" a song composer and yearned, like Schubert and Loewe, to make his mark in the larger word-tone realm of opera. Plans for operas and the quest for a libretto span his entire creative life: his first known operatic project dates from his sixteenth year, and the longing became a monomania in adult life, a true pathological obsession. It was not until 1895 that he rediscovered a libretto he had formerly rejected and began to compose *Der Corregidor*, based on the short novel *El sombrero de tres picos* (The three-cornered hat) by Pedro Antonio de Alarcón; another novel by the same writer, *El niño de la bola* (The boy on the globe [the Christ child]), is the basis for Wolf's second opera, *Manuel Venegas*, left incomplete when Wolf entered the insane asylum. First operas are seldom free from flaws, and the virtues and dramatic vices of *Der Corregidor* have provoked differing responses, pro and contra, from the beginning.

The tale of Wolf's quest for opera is inseparable from the tale of Wagnerian influence in fin-de-siècle Europe. For Wolf, the already daunting difficulties of opera were rendered all the more difficult by the specter of Wagner, his "Obergott" or "Lord above all," the composer he most revered. For a time in his early twenties, he doubted whether he could compose at all in Wagner's wake, whether anything remained for later composers to accomplish. Once that despair had abated and the flood of song composition had begun, Wolf was determined to devise opera distinct from the Wagnerian model—comedy instead of messianic tragedy, and comedy, furthermore, with no taint of Schopenhauer or any hint of redemptive themes. In *Der Corregidor*, he attempted to create "psychological opera" in which the multiple musical refinements of characterization evident in the songs find a new framework in opera—opera for connoisseurs, without concession to the stage spectacles Wagner so masterfully invented. Most who listen to the opera and study the score would agree that there is much to delight the musical epicure, but the work's success as music drama is less assured. For example, Wolf's scorn for the "endless" repetitions of the text in operatic choruses and ensembles and his obdurate refusal to do likewise means that musical numbers in *Der Corregidor* sometimes run their course with startling velocity. In the fifth and final chapter, "Wolf and the Dream of Opera," I recount Wolf's quest for an operatic text to suit his vision, venture once more into the breach on the question of dramatic credibility in *Der Corregidor*, and lament the unfinished torso of *Manuel Venegas*. What little he managed to write—five scenes of the first act—before the onset of insanity is evidence that he had learned from the experience of composing his first opera, and the austere, classicizing grandeur in such passages as Manuel Venegas's aria "Stadt meiner Väter" (City of my ancestors) makes one regret the loss of a second complete Wolf opera all the more keenly.

Whatever the critical debates about Wolf's operatic ventures, few would deny that he created a remarkable body of songs. Stravinsky, the persistent naysayer, was among those detractors who believed Wolf to be overrated and deficient in compositional technique, although he was sufficiently interested in his predecessor to orchestrate "Herr, was trägt der Boden hier" (Lord, what does the ground here bear) and "Wunden trägst du, mein Geliebter" (Thou art wounded, my beloved) from the *Spanisches Liederbuch*. Despite Wolf's strong strain of conservatism, he did not merely defend and preserve the traditions of nineteenth century lied, but devised an original aesthetic of song composition whose complexities are of the era. He was too preoccupied with composing, searching for song texts and librettos, publicizing his music, and enduring the periods of compositional drought to set down on paper an explanation in prose of his approach to vocal music, beyond a few telling comments in his letters. In the comparative lack of didactic impulse, as in much else, he is distinct from his idol Wagner. But the songs are ample testament to his ideals—to his Protean ability to convey a variety of personas in music; to his modernist love of psychological depiction; to the ways in which the musical architecture underscores aspects of the poetry; and to his increasing reliance on the piano as thematically independent from the voice, the culmination of a trend traceable throughout the century. In his unparallelled concern for the verbal dimension of lieder, he lavished great care on prosodic matters; he had the hard-won ability to set words according to refined declamatory principles without hampering the operations of musical structure. His declamation is a constant compromise, handled with consummate skill, between the observance of textual rhythm and accentuation on the one hand and pure melodic design, regular periodicity and phrasing on the other. His musical characterizations are always detailed beyond the wont of other composers, three-dimensional depiction within a small frame: in every aspect of harmony and motivic variation, Wolf tells us in music that "Agnes" (from the *Mörike-Lieder*) is on the verge of madness, her reason barely contained within the straitjacket of strophic form and traditional phrasing. In sum, this is a repertoire of great richness and variety, one that will no doubt continue to attract musicians and scholars well into a second century of performances and prose.

A FEW concluding words about the nature and format of this book are in order. Reproducing the entire score of each song by Wolf that I discuss, or even extensive examples from those songs, would be prohibitive. Therefore, I have assumed that this book will be read with readily available editions or the *Sämtliche Werke* close at hand. However, Wolf's sketches and the unfinished fragments discussed in Chapter 1 are reproduced in full, along with numerous examples from the piano-vocal score of his one completed opera, *Der Corregidor*, in Chapter 5. Both the orchestral score and the piano-vocal reduction of *Der Corregidor* have been long out of print, although Leopold Spitzer's edition for the *Sämtliche Werke* is awaiting publication. (The recent recording on the Schwann record label with Helen Donath, Dietrich Fischer-Dieskau, Kurt Moll, and the Berlin Radio Symphony Orchestra with Gerd Albrecht conducting has served to acquaint more people with this work.) Furthermore, I have taken pains to include examples from songs that are also long out of print and have no immediate prospect of new editions, such as the ballads by Martin Plüddemann discussed in Chapter 3 and the lieder by Adolf Jensen, Wilhelm Taubert, Leopold Damrosch, and Anton Rubinstein discussed in Chapter 4. Where works are available but only in complete, and therefore expensive, editions, such as Peter Cornelius's "Preziosens Sprüchlein gegen Kopfweh" (Preciosa's charm against headache) or some of Loewe's ballads, I have considered it advisable to print those examples as well.

I owe a great debt of gratitude to various people and institutions who have aided and encouraged me during the years of work on this book. The National Endowment for the Humanities generously awarded me a grant in 1987–88 so that I might do research in Vienna. There, the Music Division of the Vienna City Library (Stadt- und Landesbibliothek) and the Music Collection of the Austrian National Library (Österreichische Nationalbibliothek) allowed me unrestricted access to all of the manuscripts and printed material I wished to consult. The Institute for Scholarship in the Liberal Arts at the University of Notre Dame has twice given me summer grants to pursue research on this project in Boston, New York, and Vienna, and has also absorbed the cost of producing camera-ready copy of many of the music examples; I am grateful for their unstinting support of faculty research and publication. Thanks are also owing to Professor Jürgen Thym of the Eastman School of Music, to Hochschulprofessor Mag. Leopold Spitzer in Vienna, and to Dr. Hans Jancik, the editor of Wolf's *Sämtliche Werke*, for their helpful suggestions and inspiring example. Brae Korin has been my collaborator in the German translations, and Professor Ethan Haimo of the University of Notre Dame read the manuscript in several incarnations with his customary brilliant insight and attention to detail. The initial pages of Chapter 5 are based upon my article "Hugo Wolf and the Operatic Grail," in the *Cambridge Opera Journal* 1, no. 3 (November 1989): 277–98 and are reprinted with permission from Cambridge University Press, while the section on the "Cophtisches Lied I" (Coptic song I) in Chapter 2 is based upon my article "Charlatans, Pedants, and Fools: Hugo Wolf's 'Cophtisches Lied I,'" in *Studies in Music* 8, University of Western Ontario (1983): 77–92, reprinted with permission from the Faculty of Music, University of Western Ontario. Professor Walther Dürr, the editor of the *Neue Schubert-Ausgabe*, and Bärenreiter have graciously granted permission to reproduce Examples 10a (Schubert's "Suleika I," D. 720) and 14b ("Geheimes," D. 719), and Gregg International Publishers has given permission to reproduce Examples 18a, 19a, 20b, 21, and 23a from its reprint of Max Runze's edition of Loewe's ballads and songs. Most of all, I warmly thank Dr. Hans Jancik, the editor of Wolf's *Sämtliche Werke*, and the Musikwissenschaftlicher Verlag in Vienna for permission to reproduce Examples 1a, 2, 6, 7, 8, 10b, 11a, 11b, 13, 14a, 18b, 20a, and 28.

This book has been sponsored by two different presses in succession. UMI Research Press had agreed to publish the book until its regrettable demise in 1989, and I am grateful to Professor George Buelow, the editor of its musicology series, for his support of this project and his reassurances that it would indeed find another home after UMI Research Press had ceased to exist. That other home is, of course, Princeton University Press, where Elizabeth Powers has been an exemplary editor and advocate. She, Lauren Oppenheim, and everyone at the Press constitute the kind of publishing enterprise with whom scholarly authors dream of working; I am enormously fortunate to have that dream become reality.

Finally, I owe a special debt of gratitude to two people. My twin sister, Laura Youens Wexler, has patiently listened to untold hours of discourse, sometimes temperate, sometimes not, about lieder in general and Wolf in particular, and has proofread portions of the manuscript—an unpaid labor of love. Most of all, I am indebted to my mentor and dearest friend, the Viennese-born composer, musicologist, critic, and teacher extraordinaire Paul Amadeus Pisk, who died on 12 January 1990 after a long and remarkable life. It was he who suggested that I write this book, and then read and corrected the early drafts of Chapters 1 and 2. He did not live to see its publication, but he knew before he died that it would be dedicated to him. Indeed, I consider everything that I have written an inadequate testament to his example and a monument to my love for him.

South Bend, Indiana

HUGO WOLF

THE VOCAL MUSIC

CHAPTER 1

"Too Much Like Schumann":
The Apprenticeship
of a Lieder Composer

COMPOSERS in their youth must struggle with the competing claims of tradition and innovation in a manner more fraught with conflict than at later periods in their lives, although the battles with past creative wealth endure in changing guises throughout the life of any great artist since the Enlightenment. The craft of composition is conveyed in part through masters, both older teachers and the music of previous composers whose works fledgling composers study in order to learn the workings of their art, but beyond the rudiments of craftsmanship is the more profound necessity of forging a style of one's own, distinct from one's musical ancestors.

The competing claims of tradition and innovation and the struggle for identity are especially interesting to observe in the music of Hugo Wolf because he lived and composed at the end of the nineteenth century, in the wake both of several great lieder composers and of Wagner, "this red specter,"[1] a baleful presence for many fin-de-siècle composers. Wolf initially responded to Schumann's songs—the model of choice for young composers in the last half of the century—by echoing them, with only minor divergences, and even setting the same poems that Schumann had earlier set to music. Unable in his creative immaturity to do otherwise, he mimics the famous strains from 1840. But as time passed, the revisionary maneuvers, the divergences that warp the models in Schumann (and later, Schubert), increase in number and strength until, finally, Wolf stakes out a territory of his own. To make matters more complex, he was largely an autodidact throughout his lengthy apprenticeship of thirteen years or so. Although he enrolled in harmony and composition classes at the Vienna Conservatory, Wolf was expelled in the fall of 1876 for his impertinent assertion that his composition teacher, Franz Krenn, was actually retarding his progress.[2] Thereafter, his principal teachers spoke to him from scores, not from the harmony and composition classes of academic instruction.

On 4 May 1878, the eighteen-year-old Hugo Wolf decided to abandon his setting of Adalbert von Chamisso's "Was soll ich sagen?" just short of its fourth and final quatrain because the lied was "too much like Schumann."[3] (Characteristically, Wolf preserved the unfinished song among his papers, along with other uncompleted works, completed but unpublished songs, and sketches. Although he would on occasion publish songs composed much earlier in company with more recent works, his only reason for keeping a composition that he had no intention of completing was arguably for posterity's sake, so that those who would study his life and works after his death could better trace his stylistic development—another instance of Wolf's faith in his artistic worth.[4]) By continuing to experiment with the possibilities of late-Romantic tonality and by imitating his predecessors, Wolf was able to overcome the glaring errors of his earliest works, the awkward voice leading, maladroit prosody, and daring but inept experiments with chromaticism.[5] "Wölferl's own howl," as the composer dubbed his style, is not entirely lacking, even in the songs most like Schumann, but Wolf nevertheless attained mastery in part by becoming, for a time, a disciple of Schumann. The process is fascinating to observe both because Wolf did it so well and because he ultimately rejected Schumann's favored poets—Heine and Chamisso—as well as Schumann's approach to text setting. Influence is a two-edged sword: imitation, paraphrase, copies, and borrowed traits are all time-honored means of self-instruction, but eventually the echoes from elsewhere must be assimilated into one's own voice and used to forge new means of expression. The apprenticeship past, Wolf's mature style and literary preferences proved to be incompatible with Heine's subjectivity, even those poems not previously set to music by Wolf's great predecessors. For better or worse, Heine's personality is present in every word he ever wrote, and this was not to Wolf's taste.[6] And yet, Heine's youthful poetry was such a basic source for lieder composers that Wolf periodically returned to it until early 1888. The result was either credible imitation-Schumann or mediocre Wolf each time, and eventually, Wolf abandoned the sporadic attempts to manufacture an affinity between his music and Heine's verse.

At the same time that Wolf was composing lieder "under the sign of Schumann," he was also studying Wagner's operas intensively. The experience of learning *Tristan und Isolde* and *Parsifal* brought to life the desire to compose opera (but how, in Wagner's wake?) and may have helped to steer him away from the Schumann model of song composition. In this Pilgrim's Progress, Wolf was following a path taken by other composers of his generation as well. Surveying the lied both before and after Wagner in his 1898 essay "Das deutsche Lied seit dem Tode Richard Wagners" (The German lied since the death of Wagner), the musicologist and conductor Hermann Kretzschmar (1848–1924) pointed out that the great majority of songs composed in the twenty-five years before 1880 were influenced by Schumann. With the advent of the Wagnerian revolution, song composition was affected, in his analysis, in three ways: attempts to expand the lied beyond its traditional limits, thereby renouncing the folk-song influence so important in the history of earlier nineteenth-century German song; the predominant pathos of the new lieder; and the heightened focus on the instrumental part. The voice, he writes, becomes the accompaniment and provides the explanatory or clarifying word to the piano part. Kretzschmar was not entirely happy with the Wagnerian school and decried the primacy of "dry declamation" over more traditional melodic styles, but he also believed that Wagner's influence had mitigated the worst elements of late-Romantic sentimentality and subjectivity in the works of the many Schumann imitators.[7] For a composer born in 1860 and just beginning to come of musical age in the late 1870s, it was only natural, were he at all modernist in his predilections, to begin with Schumann and establish a style in part through the influence of Wagner. Kretzschmar does not mention the possibility that Schumann himself, in such works as the Mignon songs, might have been influenced by the declamatory principles and tonal traits of Wagner's operas before *Der Ring des Nibelungen*, but the intriguing supposition alters little, if anything: it was the Schumann of the miraculous "song year" of 1840 who seems to have been the impetus for imitations thereafter.

Wolf chose texts from Heine for lieder composition on five separate occasions in the years from 1876 to 1888, those occasions ranging from plans for two small collections of Heine songs to a single lied in isolation. By then, Heine was a musical monolith, his *Buch der Lieder* (Book of Songs) the "most renowned book of German poetry in the world"[8] and an irresistible lure for lieder composers, although there were exceptions: the balladeer Carl Loewe did not find much in Heine to his taste, and Gustav Mahler avoided the poet altogether.[9] In the fifty-one years between the first edition of "mein Hauptbuch" (my most important work), as Heine once called it,[10] and Wolf's first Heine lied, several thousand songs had been composed to these verses, in which unrequited love grapples with misogynistic contempt, the dreamworld with reality, the irrational with the rational order of poetry, and the divided self with its warring constituents. Whether composers understood that Heine, the ambivalent heir of Romanticism, often attacked its images and habits of thought with its own language, they could and did find musical inspiration in the vivid imagery. Not even the Victor Hugo craze among composers in France could equal the Heine juggernaut in nineteenth-century musical life.

By Wolf's day, however, composers and critics alike had begun to question the reliance on a past poetic repertoire. Peter Cornelius (1824–74), in a letter written in 1870 to a young musician, asked if Heine's lyric poetry, for all its greatness, was not "somewhat out-of-date [tempo passato],"[11] and, on the other side of the Wagnerian divide, the Viennese critic Eduard Hanslick also criticized the hegemony of Heine lieder. In a discussion of the Austrian diplomat and composer Johann Vesque von Püttlingen's feat in setting all eighty-eight poems of Heine's "Die Heimkehr" (The return home) from the *Buch der Lieder* to music, Hanslick wrote that Heine's mixture of assumed naiveté and heightened self-consciousness and his ironic negation of noble sentiments were largely inaccessible to music.[12] Vesque von Püttlingen's attraction to Heine's sarcastic wit for song composition was all the more notable because of what Hanslick considered to be the musically intractable nature of the texts. Poems such as "Mir träumt, ich bin der liebe Gott" (I dreamed I was the Lord God) were, in his opinion, curiosities, and his friend's music could only transform them into aurally witty curiosities. Even Schumann's setting of Heine's "Ein Jüngling liebt ein Mädchen" (A youth loved a maiden) was, he felt, a mésalliance of music and poetry "that will have nothing to do with music, that thrusts music away."[13] The inherent poetic melodiousness that Hanslick acknowledged in Heine was countered, in his opinion, by the incompatibility of irony and music—the debate on that issue has had a long and acrimonious afterlife. Hanslick is, unusually, too tactful to say so directly, although he implies it, but Vesque von Püttlingen's musical gifts were not sufficient to his self-appointed, gargantuan task. (The diplomat-composer published his works under the pseudonym "J. Hoven," or half of Beethoven. In this ostensibly humble gesture, he was, nevertheless, claiming too great a kinship to his predecessor.)[14]

Furthermore, it became increasingly difficult after the midcentury mark for composers to set certain poems from the *Buch der Lieder* without invoking the prior settings by Schubert and Schumann. One anecdote can illustrate the dilemma. In his old age, Brahms told a correspondent that in his youth he had set almost all of Heine's and Eichendorff's poetry to music (a tongue-in-cheek exaggeration?), but, recognizing the inferiority of the works, later destroyed them.[15] The few that were published reveal at least one reason for the impulse to mass destruction. His op. 5, no. 3 setting of Eichendorff's "In der Fremde" (In a strange land) is closely related to Schumann's *Liederkreis*, op. 39, no. 1, although the hemiola near the end, the subdominant harmonies in the final cadence, the chord doublings in thirds and octaves, and the third-related modulations to A major and D major bespeak the true Brahms. After he came of age musically, Brahms almost entirely shunned Heine, and so too did Wolf. It is ironic—and a sign of the times—that these two composers who detested one another both began song composition as Schumann-imitators and then forged opposing conceptions of the lied. Wolf, fortunately, left posterity a record of his apprenticeship that is far more complete than Brahms's. In the numerous songs he composed during his adolescence and early manhood, one can trace over a span of thirteen years the progression from slavish echoes of famous Schumann songs to uncannily exact assimilation and finally to maturity and a manner of his own.

WOLF AND HEINE IN 1876

Wolf's first three songs to texts by Heine were composed within a five-day span in December of 1876: "Mädchen mit dem roten Mündchen" (Maiden with the little red mouth) on Sunday, 17 December; "Du bist wie eine Blume"

(Thou art like a flower) on Monday, 18 December; and "Wenn ich in deine Augen seh'" (When I look into your eyes) on Thursday, 21 December.[16] All three poems had found ample favor with other song composers, although, significantly, there were no authoritative models for the first of Wolf's Heine songs. Schumann did not set this text, and of the better-known settings that precede Wolf's, it is unlikely that Robert Franz's op. 5, no. 5 had any influence on the young composer, who dismissed Franz as beneath mention—no wonder, as the elderly Franz once said, "The musical content is the essential thing, not the stress of this or that word," and "I have composed feelings, not words," an aesthetic to which Wolf was opposed with every fiber of his being.[17] (Hanslick's favorable opinion of the conservative Franz must have confirmed Wolf's dislike.) Ernst Challier, in the *Grosser Lieder-Katalog* (Great song catalog) of 1885, lists 45 settings of "Mädchen mit dem roten Mündchen," including one by Emil Kauffmann; Kauffmann, the son of a composer-friend of the poet Eduard Mörike, would become one of Wolf's closest friends in the years between 1890 and 1897. Settings of "Du bist wie eine Blume" and "Wenn ich in deine Augen seh'" were even more numerous. Challier lists 158 settings of "Du bist wie eine Blume" (later listings reach 222) and 54 settings of "Wenn ich in deine Augen seh,'"[18] including Schumann's *Myrthen*, op. 25, and *Dichterliebe* songs. Whether Wolf's choice of those two poems previously set by Schumann was due to youthful braggadocio—a head-on challenge to an earlier master—or to the popularity of the poems or to other factors cannot be known, but he soon reverted to the poetry of Nikolaus Lenau, one of his favorite text sources in 1875–76, and did not return to Heine until May of 1878. He must have realized how closely his settings of the *Myrthen* and *Dichterliebe* poems resembled Schumann's.

Like so many before him, Wolf found his texts in the "Lyrisches Intermezzo" (Lyrical intermezzo) and "Die Heimkehr" sections of the *Buch der Lieder*. "Mädchen mit dem roten Mündchen," the fiftieth poem in Heine's third and final reordering of the poems in "Die Heimkehr," is ostensibly a love song, but the familiar brimstone stench of scorn is quickly apparent. The themes of self-hatred and contempt for the beloved are discernible in the diminutives and the general, almost meaningless adjectives by which the poetic persona characterizes his beloved: "süss" (sweet) appears twice in two lines. The longing for a winter-evening chat by the fireside, the confinement of passion to weeping over her "little hand," have a cozy sentimentality that approaches the parodic and bespeaks the trivalization of desire. Whoever she is, she cannot even inspire a varied rhyme in the third and last quatrain, and the repetition of the words "Deine kleine, weisse Hand" (Your little white hand), with its singsong alliteration of the *ei* diphthongs, is tantamount to jeering at a Romantic cliché of love poetry. The worn-out diminutives imply a littleness beyond size; one waits for the *Stimmungsbrechung* ("breaking the tone," or Heine's device of overturning previous expectations in the final few lines of a poem) that will describe her heart and mind in diminutives as well. The characteristic "mule's kick" is not to be found here, but the alliance of sound and sense throughout the poem tells the reader that this is a contemptibly cute and unreal vision of romance.

> Mädchen mit dem roten Mündchen,
> Mit den Äuglein süss und klar,
> Du mein süsses, kleines Mädchen,
> Deiner denk' ich immerdar.
>
> Lang ist heut' der Winterabend,
> Und ich möchte bei dir sein,
> Bei dir sitzen, mit dir schwatzen,
> Im vertrauten Kämmerlein.
>
> An die Lippen wollt ich pressen
> Deine kleine, weisse Hand,
> Und mit Tränen sie benetzen,
> Deine kleine, weisse Hand.

(Maiden with the little red mouth, with your clear, sweet eyes, my sweet, little darling, I think of you constantly. Winter evenings are longer now, and I'd like to be with you, sit with you and chat in the cosy little room. I would press my lips on your little, white hand, and bedew it with tears, your little, white hand.)[19]

Heine's famous divided self lurks within view. The poet who writes this poem observes his (younger?) naively romantic self, yearning in adolescent moon-calf fashion for his sweetheart's petite charms and inventing illusory scripts for a domestic drama in which *he* is the star and his tears only a stage prop, and jeers.

To find in the poem evidence of divided and multiple selves is one possible reading. Wolf's song is another, the poet's personas not entirely congruent with the composer's. The sixteen-year-old Wolf ignores the darker shadings of the poem and instead depicts a happy *naïf* with no knowledge of genuine passion, someone who sings in the most unclouded of eighteenth-century voices—this is all surface and no depth, a choice that is itself a shrewd derivation from the poem. The sentimental self-dramatization of weeping over the sweetheart's hands does not in the slightest alter the prevailing spriteliness of this lively (Lebhaft) lied in F major and does not impel from Wolf a hint of lachrymose sentimentality, unlike either Franz's, Vesque von Püttlingen's, or Leopold Damrosch's settings; Damrosch (1835–85), whose song oeuvre is discussed in Chapter 4, endows *his* poetic persona with the capacity for outright passion (Examples 1a, 1b, 1c, and 1d). Not so Wolf—details of the musical structure, with its unclouded diatonicism and textural clarity in the

Example 1a. Hugo Wolf, "Mädchen mit dem roten Mündchen," measures 1–12

first stanza and postlude, confirm the quiet merriment pervasive throughout. The folk-song heaviness of the trochaic rhythms is emphasized still further by the metrical regularity of the lied, and the intervallic leaps and skips outline conventional triadic contours in all three voices. Within the framework of a classicizing musical style, the young Wolf already displays his responsiveness to details of poetic interpretation, such as the "chatty" flow of sixteenth-notes in the bass; the reverential fermata on the half-cadence at the words "[bei dir] *sein*" in measure 16; the alteration of Heine's trochees to melodic iambs in order to place prosodic emphasis on the repeated word "dir" in the succeeding line, "bei *dir* sitzen, bei *dir* schwatzen"; the withholding of the tonic chord at "Kämmerlein" in measure 20 to signal that the music and the illusion continue still further; and the harmonic-dynamic-melodic decrescendo throughout the

Example 1b. Robert Franz, "Mädchen mit dem roten Mündchen,"
Op. 5, no. 5, measures 1–4

final phrases of text. But this is not comic music, although Wolf was later rightly proud of his gift for musical humor, and it is an incomplete reading. Wolf does not in any way subvert the persona articulated in the music. He does not suggest via dissonance treatment or rhythmic gestures or repetition or any other means that this is a fool speaking, a candidate for imminent disillusionment. The classical formulas of two-, four-, and eight-bar phrasing, broken chordal figuration, and the like are not treated in any fashion suggestive of self-mockery, such as distortion, simplification, exaggeration, or disruption by nonclassicizing references. Wolf's persona is all of a piece, whereas Heine's is not. If it is a considerable achievement for a composer only sixteen years old to reject any impulse to sentimentality, to capture the superficiality of the fantasy, it is an achievement realized by amputating from the music (not from the text that the singer sings) the presence of the Poet, whose implied judgment on his own creation is so harsh and unsparing. Dare one suggest a certain irony in the discrepancy?—a composer later famous for his sense of

Example 1c. Johann Vesque von Püttlingen, "Mädchen mit dem roten Mündchen" from "Die Heimkehr," measures 1–24

obligation to his chosen poets eliminates the controlling poet from this lied almost entirely.

Schumann did not set "Mädchen mit dem roten Mündchen" to music, and Wolf's harmonically conservative song is therefore not a copy of a prior setting. Schumann is, however, an unbanished ghost behind every note of Wolf's "Du bist wie eine Blume." Frank Walker has suggested that Wolf

Example 1c, continued

klar,   du __ mein lie - bes, klei - nes Mäd - chen,

dei - ner denk' ich im - mer - dar;

might have deliberately modeled his setting on that of Schumann as a compositional exercise,[20] echoing in the process his predecessor's approach to a singularly nasty but artful text. Heine's surfaces are not to be trusted: the seeming sentimentality and mannered naiveté are the instruments of misogynistic contempt. S. S. Prawer has pointed out that songs of hate dominate the *Buch der Lieder*,[21] whose fictive personas consider women to be irritating or boring when not in bed, but the anger originates in frustrated idealism. Because love has a quasi-religious function in the *Buch der Lieder*, because it alone is an anchor in the darkness of existence, the poet savagely lashes the beloved with whips made of words when she fails to meet his ideal image in the mind. Elsewhere and often in the anthology, sexual attraction to such inferior matter provokes a riot of self-hatred, but in "Du bist wie eine Blume," the poet concocts a defense by which he both flaunts his male superiority and evades the psychological flagellation evident in other poems. The empty adjectives "hold, schön, rein" (noble, beautiful, pure) are arranged in the heaviest of iambs, the rhythmic emphasis a means of conveying that the compliment is cynical deception, a trap for the simpleminded (or so he thinks) woman to whom he speaks, while the imagined gesture of laying his hands on her head

Example 1d. Leopold Damrosch, "Mädchen mit dem roten Mündchen,"
measures 43–66

and praying that God shall maintain her in that state implies that no such miracle is possible. Infidelity and degeneracy are all one can expect of women, an assumption that serves as protection against suffering. By dint of arrogance and disdain, he rescues himself from any pain that she might have caused him. Ultimately, the pose of speaking "aus tiefem Gemüt," with deep feeling, is just that—a pose and a barb aimed at the language and sentiments of Romantic poetry as well. "Du bist wie eine Blume" is a twofold sneer at women and at outworn words from a poet for whom the Devil was Flesh. The

Example 1d, continued

dei - ne klei - ne, wei - sse Hand.

Mäd - chen mit dem ro - then___ Münd - chen,

underlying misogyny is repellent, the poetic control absolute. Heine kept the poem unchanged through seven editions of the *Buch der Lieder* and spoke well of it in later life, after he had repudiated the "lunatic visions" of his youth.[22]

By the 1870s, Heine's poem was doubly a barbed-wire trap for the unwary. Famous poems, and this is one of the most famous in European literature, acquire over time a baggage train of associations and dispute over differing interpretations, also an aura of importance that makes musical assault more difficult. At the century's end, "Du bist wie eine Blume" was a text colonized by many composers, especially Schumann in the cycle *Myrthen*, op. 25, no. 24. A comparison of the two songs shows that Wolf retained most of the principal elements of Schumann's lied in slightly varied guise, the differences both reflective of dependence on the prior model and indicative of another musical mind at work; the visual resemblance when the two settings are placed side by side is striking. The result was not Wolf's own "howl," not an independent reading of the poem, but that was probably not its purpose. Rather, the young composer was teaching himself principles of text setting and chromatic harmony from the source that he, and others like him, most trusted in the 1870s. According to an anecdote in Edmund Hellmer's *Hugo Wolf, Erlebtes und Erlauschtes* (Hugo Wolf, witnessed and overheard) of 1921, Wolf may have used his close study of Schumann's lieder in part as a means of learning good text declamation after the glaring prosodic sins of his earliest extant songs. Hellmer, the sculptor of Wolf's tomb monument in Vienna's Central Cemetery, regrettably does not supply dates or the full context for the incidents and opinions he reports, nor are the reminiscences organized in chronological, or any other, order, but he is the sole source for several particularly intriguing reminiscences of the composer. In one instance, Hellmer went to Wolf with what he considered to be faults of declamation in Schumann's Heine ballad "Die beiden Grenadiere" (The two grenadiers). Wolf shook his head in disbelief and dissected the song "word for word, note for note" in order to prove to Hellmer that there were no such faults in the ballad. "Schumann—bad declamation?" he asked.[23] He would later devise his own methods of declamatory vocal writing constituted differently from Schumann's, but in his youth, Schumann was the foremost model for declamation and much else besides.

In "Du bist wie eine Blume," Wolf apes Schumann's nonlegato succession of chordal harmonies in the accompaniment; sets the lied in E♭ major, closely related to the A♭ major of Schumann's setting; duplicates the length (twenty bars) and formal design of his model; and writes an initial vocal phrase that seems a simplified variant of Schumann's, without the triplet-figure oscillation on "eine" as the anacrusis to "*Blu*-me," the apex of the line. In a foreshadowing of Wolf's later songs, the vocal part is surrounded by the accompaniment—not the deeper registers of Schumannesque *Innigkeit* but a higher, more ethereal tessitura. Later, Wolf would use similar nonlegato chordal writing to accompany the gentle laughter of the stars in Mörike's "An die Geliebte" (To the beloved), the heavenly miracles following a saint's martyrdom in the Goethe song "St. Nepomuk's Vorabend" (St. Nepomuk's eve), and the apotheosis of a humble peasant woman, newly arrived in heaven, in Gottfried Keller's "Wie glänzt der helle Mond" (The bright moon gleams). But Wolf's changes of register and meter, $\frac{3}{4}$ rather than Schumann's $\frac{2}{4}$, and the prosodic variations—unlike Schumann, Wolf observes the poet's punctuation in the line "betend, dass Gott dich erhalte," obliterating the dactyls by which

Heine mocks the prayerful gesture—seldom constitute skeptical divergence from the song composed thirty-six years earlier.

Where Wolf's nuances differ from Schumann's, the result seems an uneasy alternation between the outward pose, in which the poetic persona pays compliments to a beautiful woman, and the underlying pessimistic mockery. The argument about Schumann's understanding of Heine's irony notwithstanding, the ploy for seduction, the wooer's address, predominates in the *Myrthen* song. The unpleasant implications live on in the words, if anything, heightened by the contesting implications of text and music. Wolf, however, allows the dark underside to show through in his setting of the mock-papal prayer of disbelief, when the prevailing lyricism cracks open and a hint of menace underlies the transposed, varied recurrence of the initial vocal phrases. The act of looking at the flower-women ("Ich schau dich *an*") is the catalyst, the moment of awareness in which the beginning of another four-bar phrase in Eb is interrupted by a mediant shift to the dominant of C minor, anticipating the more prolonged reference to C minor that follows. (Schumann makes "Wehmut" the harmonic event of the first stanza, not the preceding glance.) The forte dynamics throughout the benediction, the starkness of the octaves at the common-tone transition (measure 9), and the massive right-hand chords of measures 10–12 bring bombast to the surface, more overtly than in Schumann. And yet, the end of that phrase, the resolution of the Eb cadence in measures 12–13 ("Haupt dir legen sollt"), is weak, the piano absent altogether from the expected tonic harmony. "'Should' indeed," Wolf seems to say and deprives the word of its foundation; not until the final tonic harmonies of the postlude does one hear the bass Ebs in the register denied in measure 13. With the return to Eb major, any skepticism before the text ends. The accompaniment ascends back to the higher register via sequential statements of the "Blume" figure, variants of the initial vocal phrase, and the calm of the beginning is reestablished. Wolf even maintains the tonic chord throughout the verb "er*halte*," unlike Schumann's transposed, elided echo in the piano (redoubling the prayer and denying it simultaneously, the motion antithetical to the sense of "erhalten"?), and the later composer's postlude is far simpler than Schumann's (Example 2).[24]

For his third Heine song of 1876, Wolf tried another way of learning from his chosen mentor, this attempt bolder than the slavish Siamese-twin relationship between the two incarnations of "Du bist wie eine Blume." To select a poem from Schumann's *Dichterliebe* was to make difficult or impossible a musical reading of one's own. Wolf, not yet ready for a declaration of emancipation from an apprentice's copy work, still produces mock-Schumann but not a facsimile of Schumann's "Wenn ich in deine Augen seh'." Only twice does Wolf echo—in spite of himself?—the vocal line of the earlier setting, at the words "so werd' ich ganz und gar gesund" and again at the line "doch wenn du sprichst: Ich liebe dich," both phrases reminiscent of the prior model (Example 3). With those two exceptions, Wolf seems to have been deter-

Example 2. Hugo Wolf, "Du bist wie eine Blume," measures 1–9

Example 3. Settings of "Wenn ich in deine Augen
seh'" by Robert Schumann, Op. 48, and by
Hugo Wolf

mined not to compose a variant replica of the *Dichterliebe* song. He avoids the
block chords of his predecessor and composes a piano introduction that consumes four bars of a twenty-two-bar song. The piano part wends a seamless
course until the words "Ich liebe dich," and its arpeggiation for the right hand,
combining a melodic line with a subordinate accompanimental voice in a single stream of successive pitches, is familiar both from Schumann's piano
works and from the songs. The vocal line is not an additional melodic voice
but a doubling of the right hand melody an octave lower, dependent upon a
curiously fixated accompaniment. Wolf tried to synthesize the unifying development of a single principal motive with symmetrical four-bar phrase structure based on literal repetition of that motive, and the result is not a happy
one—since he repeats the piano introduction unchanged as the first two
phrases of texted music, we hear measure 1 four times in eight bars, the recourse to saturation unmotivated by anything in the poetry. The vocal part
shares with the piano its frequent dotted rhythms, overriding syntax and
meaning with a series of inappropriately heavy stresses on the accented syllables of successive iambs. Was Wolf trying to avoid Schumann's declamation
on repeated pitches? And yet, Wolf acknowledges the poetry in the worst way
by refusing to break the poem down into musical prose, by setting each line
of verse as a discrete unit. Each line/phrase is the same length, and each one
is a variant or repetition of the same motivic figure—"too much of a much-
ness" in all. The listener inevitably recalls Schumann's sensitive reinterpretations of a unitary motif, his elided phrase relationships between the vocal line
and the piano part, and recognizes the superiority to the later work composed
in its shadow.

In Heine's poem, the sensual pleasures of lovemaking, enumerated along a
line of increasing eroticism (gazing into the woman's eyes, kissing her mouth,
lying on her breast), are wholly satisfactory, health-giving and healing until
she utters the words "Ich liebe dich." Then he is impelled to weep—*"muss* ich
weinen," or "I must weep"—the reason for his sudden grief undisclosed. Either the poetic persona does not know what has provoked his tears or is too
pained to say it, but whatever the cause, it is denied access to words.
Nietzsche's later proclamation that assent to a single desire is simultaneously
assent to an entire world of pain is implicit in "Wenn ich in deine Augen seh',"
if only as a realization suppressed from utterance. That Schumann agrees with
the strategy of suppression and Wolf does not is possibly a by-product of
context: Schumann's song is placed near the beginning of *Dichterliebe*, while
Wolf's setting is an isolated event, without the background or future tense of
lieder that precede and follow it. In both, the end is inherent in the beginning,
the music for the final words "so muss ich weinen bitterlich" derived from
what precedes it, but the correlation between the tears and the restorative
benefits of eros is differently calculated. Wolf makes of cause and effect
something all too obvious. The descending chromatic inflection that ends the

principal motive on its frequent occurrences throughout the catalog of erotic joys becomes somewhat melodramatically set apart from the climactic words "Ich liebe dich," the stuff of tears, while the B♭-minor tonality at the close is prepared, first, in the D♭s of the recurring diminished-seventh chord on the raised fourth degree and, second, in the C♯s of both the brief, unstable references to the mediant tonality of D major and the augmented-sixth chord to which Wolf sets the beloved's words "Ich liebe dich." In the same spirit of anticipating words not yet sung, Wolf also elides the end of the phrase/line "Kommt's über mich wie Himmels*lust*" with the chromatic push in the accompaniment to the climax, the deceptive motion depriving *Lust* of sure tonal ground and signaling, in its clichés of heightened tension, an uneasy denouement to follow. To make the verb "liebe" the principal harmonic event near the end of the lied is less subtle, more sentimental, than Schumann's locus of greatest uncertainty at the word "sprichst," but then, comparisons are perhaps unfair, even though Wolf invites them. For a compositional exercise by a sixteen-year-old, it is an impressive hint of better things to come. Whether consciously calculated or not, it is also another strategy in a course of self-instruction. If he could not yet do other than compose "under the sign of Schumann," he would at least avoid the procedures Schumann had used in setting that same text.

THE UNFINISHED SETTING OF "WAS SOLL ICH SAGEN?"

After the Christmas season of 1876, Wolf did not return to Heine's *Buch der Lieder* for a year and a half. Within that time, he planned and composed part of his first opera, a bloodthirsty tragedy entitled *König Alboin* (King Alboin), about a fifth-century Lombard conqueror named Alboin and his wife, Rosamund,[25] and wrote songs to texts by Lenau, Theodor Körner, Friedrich Rückert, Johann Matthisson, and the minor poet Karl Herlossohn. Before the next batch of Heine songs in late May of 1878, he worked from 1 April to 4 May of that year on a setting of Adalbert von Chamisso's "Was soll ich sagen?" (What should I say?) but abandoned the song after thirty-one bars.[26] "Was soll ich sagen?" had been set to music earlier by Schumann, and Wolf knew the lied. Seemingly unable to escape the pitfalls of stylistic imitation, he gave up and left the song unfinished. Later that same month, still under Schumann's influence and still interested in the *Buch der Lieder*, he took pains to avoid Schumann's textual choices.[27]

Walker describes Chamisso's poem as the inverse of *Frauenliebe und Leben*: instead of a young bride abasing herself in awe and wonder before the older man she loves, it is the older man who abases himself before his young sweetheart. Acutely aware of the difference in age, he tries at her command to say what he feels and fears but shortly ends his plaint in wordless trembling. The near-muteness proclaimed at the beginning of "Was soll ich sagen?" cannot find relief in the masochistic catalog of physical comparisons, age to youth. Choking on the humiliation of his enslavement—whatever she desires shall be done—and an underlying resentment that becomes more overt with each stanza, he finds himself at poem's end unable to continue compliance with her wish that he speak. The sequence of minimal declarative statements is obsessional in nature, the expressivity so restricted because the obsession is unbearable. Shame and misery are at first a partial barrier to speech and finally a total obstruction. Metaphor, symbol, simile, any luxuriance at all in poetic means are absent and indeed are interdicted. So is any mention of context or the external world; the poem takes place within an unhappy mind too consumed by awareness of a December-May contrast to see anything else.

> Mein Aug' ist trüb,
> Mein Mund ist stumm,
> Du heissest mich reden,
> Es sei darum!
>
> Dein Aug' ist klar,
> Dein Mund ist rot,
> Und was du nur wünschest,
> Das ist ein Gebot.
>
> Mein Haar ist grau,
> Mein Herz ist wund,
> Du bist so jung
> Und bist so gesund.
>
> Du heissest mich reden,
> Und machst mir's so schwer.
> Ich seh' dich so an—
> Und zittre so sehr.[28]

(My eyes are sad, I am mute. You have bidden me speak, it shall be so! Your eyes are clear, your mouth red, and whatever you wish is my command. My hair is gray, my heart wounded, you are so young and sound. You bid me speak and that sorely oppresses me. I look at you—and tremble.)

"Was soll ich sagen?" is an odd and challenging choice for a song composer because it is a paradox in rhyme, poetry about the defeat of language in the confrontation with shame. It implies in its cramped form, limited vocabulary, and syntactical sameness that the poem is only the tip of the iceberg, with murkier depths unexpressed and inexpressible, but the sense of concealed matter is not in this case equivalent to compensatory expressivity for the composer. To give voice in music to whatever emotional compound has restrained and then shut off speech is to traduce the few words there are, to suggest that the fullness of expression is closer to the surface, more capable of realization, than Chamisso would have us understand. Without lending the poetic persona "the notes to say it," if not the words, what is left is powerlessness with an additional element of the ignoble, an element of which the poetic protagonist is horribly aware. The composer who desires congruence of some sort between the poetic content and his compositional choices must, it would seem, bar from his setting of "Was soll ich sagen?" melodic beauty and lyric expansiveness, power, harmonic and tonal adventurousness, a generous vocal range, and motivic variety. The poetic persona's dilemma—"What should I say?"—becomes the composer's dilemma—"What should I compose? What remains for me to write after I have honored the restriction, or rather, constriction, at the heart of this text?" An alternative solution is to criticize the words by having music contend with text in overt strife, by writing music that questions the poetic content in some way, but Schumann did not do so in this instance and Wolf never got that far.

Schumann's setting, op. 27, no. 3, although a product of the 1840 *Liederjahr*, is little known and seldom performed; only the Rückert lied "Jasminenstrauch" (The jasmine bush) from this opus is familiar to singers and audiences. The austere, unharmonized motive at the beginning of the piano introduction is to present-day listeners a premonition of Brahms's later socalled Death motive of descending thirds, here in the context of tonal indecision concomitant with the poetic persona's weakness of will. The accented fifth scale degree of E major in measure 1 is altered, raised to B♯, and the culmination of the slow, sinking bass is E♯, the raised "tonic" degree as the root of a diminished-seventh harmony—"Where to turn? what to say?" spelled out in harmonic terms (Example 4). A clear sense of tonal location is delayed until the E-major cadence at the proclamation "Es sei darum!"—resolve stated as resolution that is heralded, even impelled, by the soprano E in the right hand (measures 6–7), her commandment from on high. His initial admissions of inadequacy and depression ("Mein Aug ist trüb, mein Mund ist stumm") are tellingly set above a rising sequence of diminished-seventh chords resolving to the supertonic and mediant harmonies of the eventual E major, each harmony in inversion and lacking a bass line until the words "du heissest mich reden." The strength and clear directionality of the bass line in the dominant B major beneath the words that establish her youth ("Dein Aug' ist klar, dein Mund ist rot") is in stark contrast with *his* multiple indices of weakness. "If you only wish it, that is a command," the lover says, but the deceptive cadence at "Ge-*bot*" in measures 11–12, with the return of the previous diminished seventh on E♯, is a signal, one foreshadowed from measure 4, that he will not be able to fulfill her commandment. Even though the repetition of

Example 4. Robert Schumann, "Was soll ich sagen?" Op. 27, no. 3,
measures 1–8

those words to resolution on the dominant follows right after, the startling disjunction between the word-associations of "Gebot" with fixity and firmness and the destabilizing force of that harmony in this context hints that, law or no law, he cannot comply. The single melodic attempt at lyrical expansion in the vocal part occurs at the verb "wünschest," the wish or desire reaching up to the same high E as the command in measures 6–7, before falling back down again to the more tepid and characteristic low-middle register.

As the self-lacerating list of his physical and emotional debits continues ("Mein Haar ist grau, mein Herz ist wund"), B major becomes dominant of E minor with B in the bass, a weaker, darker, more melancholy retention of her tones. (The prolongation of the repeated adjective "mein"—not the eighth-note anacrusis one might expect but a quarter-note duration—underscores the wounded self-consciousness and the sense of polarized contrast at the core of the poem.) The statement that she is "so young and so healthy" is his defeat, one that Schumann establishes in the instrumental accompaniment beyond the point where the C♯ and V^7/V at "ge-*sund*" conspicuously fail to press upward to E in measures 17–18. Rather, the music collapses to a bare, unharmonized B, elided with the return of the piano introduction and the music for stanza 1. The repetition is tantamount to an admission of incapacity, the poetic persona returning beaten to the same sounds that accompanied his initial revelation of near-muteness. A bleak poem becomes bleak music whose elisions, repetitions, and descending figures are all-too-apt parallels to the text they envelop.

Why Wolf was drawn to this particular poem—as compositional exercise, as an alternative reading and therefore a challenge to his predecessor?—is a mystery and will probably remain one. Whatever the reason, his unfinished lied is both too much like Schumann in some aspects and not enough like him in others, principally, the level of musical invention (Example 5). Unlike the Schumann setting, there is no piano introduction and no contrast between

Example 5. Hugo Wolf, "Was soll ich sagen?" (fragment)

Example 5, continued

descent into the low bass and the lack of bass foundation altogether, but Wolf too, like Schumann, composes tonally indeterminate, harmonically shifting opening measures. The tonality is unclear until the end of the first stanza at the words "Es sei darum!" and the soprano motives are related, both inversionally and directly, to the vocal part of op. 27, no. 3. Other traits are recognizably Schumannesque as well: the doubling of the vocal line in the accompaniment, the prominence of the piano interlude in measures 4–6, and the repeated chordal figuration in the *B* section, reminiscent of songs such as "Widmung" (Dedication), from the *Myrthen* cycle. Schumann, however, reserves unalloyed

Example 5, continued

chordal texture, voice and accompaniment in exact rhythmic accord, for the central words "Du bist so jung und bist so gesund." No competing claims of rhythmic differentiation by the piano are allowed to distract attention from the final statement of the cause for the poetic persona's anguish; furthermore, the sweetheart's wholeness and soundness, perhaps also the simplicity of youth, are symbolized by the chordal texture. Did Wolf perhaps resort to the familiar device of repeated chords and the accompanying change of tonality and meter in order to distinguish the sweetheart's traits ("Dein Aug' ist klar") from those of the poetic persona in stanzas 1 and 3, only to realize that the lines "Du bist so jung und bist so gesund" in stanza 3 should not be repeated to the music of stanza 1? It is at this point that the lied breaks off.

The "Was soll ich sagen?" fragment is a curious mix of Schumannesque lied and Wolfian experimentation with modulation, enharmony, and key relationships by a composer who had left the conservative idiom of "Mädchen mit dem roten Mündchen" far behind. Walker recounts an anecdote of the fifteen-year-old Wolf, newly arrived in Vienna and keenly aware of the deficiencies in his compositional training, inventing chord progressions at the piano in his sister's parlor and calling to her in jubilation whenever he found a new way to modulate from one key to another.[29] The *B* section of "Was soll ich sagen?"

would seem a continuation of the same practice at a higher level, influenced by textual considerations. For example, in his setting of stanza 1, Wolf suggests a correlation between the poetic persona's wavering resolve, his reluctance to speak, and the alternation between G minor and B♭ major, neither one very resolutely stated until repetition of the words "Es sei darum!" and the cadence on B♭. No sooner is the cadence achieved than Wolf shifts venue immediately, hinting both that the lover scrambles to do what his beloved commands and that she exists on a different plane or level from his. He must sing of her in a key not his own. The means of arrival are noteworthy for their relationship to a tonal plan characterized by instability; no key is well grounded, nothing stays for long, and there is no security to be found anywhere. Rather than use the common tone B♭ as the most familiar means of swift transition to a third-related key B♭–G♭, Wolf restates and varies the chromatic inner voice leading of the B♭ cadence in measure 6. The reinterpreted D as the pivot tone for modulation is premonitory both of the VI/F♯ at the word "wünschest" in measure 14, underscoring the importance of her wishes, and of the D-major end of this chain of descending major-third relationships B♭–G♭/F♯ major and minor–D major. The word "Gebot" is each time (Wolf repeats lines and words in the early songs, a practice he would later renounce) conspicuously *not* the point of cadential completion, the poetic persona's unease conveyed in the refusal to equate "commandment" with tonic surety, however temporary. Perhaps the appeal of this text was precisely its invitation to instability and experimentation with frequent modulation—in this instance, the chain-of-thirds pattern found so often in his mature songs. But if the harmonic schema is Wolfian, virtually everything else is borrowed from Schumann, the result neither good early Wolf nor good imitation-Schumann. The fragment is certainly valuable for what it reveals about assimilating an earlier master's style, but one does not regret its unfinished state.

THE DAYS OF LODI AND THE *LIEDERSTRAUß*, VOLUME 1

Ten years later, during the composition of the *Mörike-Lieder*, Wolf told a friend that 1878 had been his first "days of Lodi," a time of great compositional productivity. The "days of Lodi" in 1878 actually began after the abandonment of the Chamisso song with Wolf's plan to assemble a cycle, a *Liederstrauß* (Bouquet of songs) to texts from the *Buch der Lieder*. This time, although he once again chose poems from the "Lyrisches Intermezzo" and "Die Heimkehr," he stayed away from the *Dichterliebe* texts or any other poem previously set by Schumann. The challenge on this occasion is to Schubert, a setting of "Ich stand in dunkeln Träumen," but in a Schumann-derived style. All eight of the Heine poems composed that summer of 1878 had, inevitably, been set before by numerous composers now sunk into obscurity,[30] but none of them mattered much to Wolf or had any perceptible influence on his apprenticeship.

(DH = "Die Heimkehr"; LI = "Lyrisches Intermezzo")

1. "Sie haben heut' Abend Gesellschaft" (They have company this evening), 18–25 May (DH, no. 60)
2. "Ich stand in dunkeln Träumen" (I stood in dark dreams), 26–29 May (DH, no. 23)
3. "Das ist ein Brausen und Heulen" (The heavens storm and thunder), 31 May (LI, no. 57)
4. "Aus meinen grossen Schmerzen" (Out of my great sorrows), 5 June (LI, no. 63)
5. "Wo ich bin, mich rings umdunkelt" (Where I am, darkness surrounds me), 3–4 June (LI, no. 63)
6. "Mir träumte von einem Königskind" (I dreamed of a king's daughter), 16 June (LI, no. 41)
7. "Mein Liebchen, wir sassen beisammen" (My love, we sat together), 22 June (DH, no. 74)[31]

Wolf began composition of another Heine song, "Manch Bild vergessener Zeiten" (Many an image from forgotten times; LI, no. 38) on 24 June, but abandoned the setting after thirty bars. Of the eight completed songs, he chose seven for publication, omitting the uninspired "Wo ich bin, mich rings umdunkelt" (Where I am, darkness surrounds me) as below the standard of the others, and offered the group both to Breitkopf & Härtel and to André. Both firms replied with rejections. In January of 1881, Wolf decided to try once more and sent the *Liederstrauß* to Kistner in Leipzig. He evidently expected their approval or else wanted the songs to be published so badly that he fantasized their acceptance, telling Henriette Lang on 26 January 1881, "You may be interested to know that my songs (seven settings of Heine) will shortly be published by Kistner in Leipzig."[32] Kistner too rejected the Heine cycle, which was not published in Wolf's lifetime.[33] He did on occasion include lieder composed before 1888 in his later publications, but it is probable that he would not want compositions written in someone else's manner offered to a public that knew him differently. At the time, however, he could and did take pride in the enterprise, as well he might. Given the currency of Schumann-inspired lieder, he had every reason to expect that the style would find commercial success and thereby launch his career as a composer.

The songs of the *Liederstrauß* are not musically bound to one another in the fashion of the *Dichterliebe* or the Eichendorff *Liederkreis*, op. 39, and the selection and ordering of the seven texts do not imply any narrative thread. Wolf was never drawn to cycles (were cycles perhaps too reminiscent of both

Schubert and Schumann?), although he does pair songs frequently, and there is nothing definable as cyclic in the Heine collection. There seems to be, however, a conscious ordering of the songs in the collection, a foreshadowing of his later practice with larger volumes of lieder. He begins the *Liederstrauß*, for example, with the longest and most substantial song of the set, ends with a blaze of trumpet fanfares, and varies the tempi and musical material in between. Each of the extant autograph manuscripts is entitled not with the first line of Heine's untitled poems but with the Roman-numeral designation of its placement in the cycle.[34] Given his probable resolve to avoid Schumann's choices from the "Lyrisches Intermezzo" and "Die Heimkehr," Wolf selected poems each of which represents a different aspect of Heine's obsessions— unrequited love and the art of poetry—in the *Buch der Lieder*: jealousy ("Sie haben heut' Abend Gesellschaft"), grief for a lost love ("Ich stand in dunkeln Träumen"), guilt-ridden wonder about the beloved's whereabouts ("Das ist ein Brausen und Heulen"), suicidal melancholy ("Wo ich bin, mich rings um- dunkelt"), a complaint about the ineffectuality of "tinkling" little songs as messengers to the woman he loves ("Aus meinen grossen Schmerzen"), a dream of love and death ("Mir träumte von einem Königskind"), the fantasy of a visionary island-realm unattainable to the poetic persona and his beloved ("Mein Liebchen, wir sassen beisammen"), and a sardonic variation on the old themes of love as warfare and the erotic appeal of soldiers ("Es blasen die blauen Husaren"). Heine does not make available the range of different themes, moods, and voices that Wolf would subsequently find in Mörike and Goethe, but within the limits of the *Buch der Lieder*, Wolf culled as much variety as he could.

The imitation of Schumann attains new levels in these songs. It is not until the *Liederstrauß* that Wolf uses the frequent fluctuations of tempi and the phrases or sections in quasi-recitative style evident in certain Schumann songs, also the lengthy piano postludes that rewrite the poem in some way, that end the lied in tones other than the poet's. Instrumental music is given the last word. The usurpation of authorial control by the composer is quite bald in these instances, and Wolf would subsequently reject the practice, but in the first song of the *Liederstrauß*, he tries his hand at it for the first and only time—never again does one encounter in Wolf a piano postlude occupying one-quarter of the song, 27 bars of the total 104—and succeeds. Other Schu- mann masquerades follow "Sie haben heut' Abend Gesellschaft," but none other in which the tail wags the dog to this extent. The song leads to and culminates in the instrumental postlude.

What Wolf makes overt and the poet prefers partially to suppress is another of Heine's resentful accusations of the beloved for her lack of understanding. The exaggerated tone of his reproaches is typically compounded by both self- persiflage and real grief. The sweetheart's seeming perfidy is the occasion for reproach directed at the Poet's own "heart of darkness," at a feverishly overheated Romantic imagination that he finds repugnant and mocks—painfully. The old notion that the *Buch der Lieder* was autobiography, a versified retelling of Heine's love for two cousins in Hamburg, has long since been discounted, but the poems are indeed *Erlebnisgedichte* (poems drawn from experience, from life) in a sense. A Romantic who despised Romanticism—especially its vein of hallucinatory fantasy—both indulges his own nocturnal world and subjugates it with the controlling devices of poetry. Poems become cages for the fauna spawned by the Romantic mind. In a letter written from Hamburg in early 1821, Heine describes, with pained distaste and a controlling artistry as evident here as in the poems, how he dreamed himself into a frenzy beneath his current Dulcinea's window, the scenario closely resembling "Sie haben heut' Abend Gesellschaft": "All the madhouses had let out their crazy images and heaped them on my head. This accursed throng held its Walpurgisnacht in my head, my teeth chattered the dance music for it, and my heart's blood poured out of my breast." He thought for a moment that he could see her shadowy image smiling down at him, but tore himself out of the illusion to discover that his imagination had once again made a fool of him.[35] By means of the self-mockery in the letter and the stylization of the poetry, both Heine and his poetic alter ego objectify an undignified grief.

> Sie haben heut' Abend Gesellschaft,
> Und das Haus ist lichterfüllt.
> Dort oben am hellen Fenster
> Bewegt sich ein Schattenbild.
>
> Du schaust mich nicht, im Dunkeln
> Steh' ich hier unten allein;
> Noch wen'ger kannst du schauen
> In mein dunkles Herz hinein.
>
> Mein dunkles Herze liebt dich,
> Es liebt dich und es bricht,
> Und bricht und zückt und verblütet,
> Aber du siehst es nicht.

(They have company this evening, and the house is brightly lit. Up above, at the lighted window, a shadowy image is moving. You do not see me; in the darkness, I stand here down below, alone. Still less can you see into my dark heart. My dark heart loves you, loves you and breaks, and breaks and quivers and bleeds, but you do not see it.)[36]

Throughout the *Buch der Lieder*, the Romantic poet's guilty otherness, the sense of being set apart from other people and the "real" world, is expressed in terms of unrequited love and the impossibility of "seeing and being seen" through the chaos of one's own incommunicable inwardness. Against the backdrop of a brightly lit social world to which his sweetheart belongs, in which she is at home and he is not, the narrator laments and mocks. The hyperbole of multiple verbs conveys the conundrum of his "dark heart" and its capacity for emotional excess. The real world is only minimally present for a poetic persona who sees shadows rather than people and cannot himself be seen (Heine uses the verb *sich schauen*, "to perceive"; by extension, "to know"). As the external world recedes, clear consciousness encounters chaos within the soul and records the encounter in verse whose lilting rhythms underscore the self-mockery.

In his setting of "Sie haben heut' Abend Gesellschaft," Wolf for the first time creates music in which sounds from the outside world are altered by the narrator's perceptions. Music initially identified and presented as coming from a source external to the poetic persona is recomposed along the way by the persona's emotions and memories. Walker writes that the Eichendorff song "Rückkehr" (Return), composed in 1883, foreshadows the composer's later predilection for conflict between the vocal line and the accompaniment,[37] but the distinction between the singer and the piano as different musical personas first appears five years earlier in the Heine songs. Actually, the phrase "conflict between voice and piano" is perhaps not the most apt summation of what happens in "Rückkehr," the Eichendorff song "Das Ständchen" (The serenade), "Mein Liebster singt am Haus im Mondenscheine" (My lover sings outside the house, in the moonlight) from the *Italienisches Liederbuch*, and others. At first, the singer joins in accord with music from another source, the vocal line congruent with the strains of a serenading lover or a band of itinerant musicians or waltz music represented in the accompaniment. As the poetic persona reacts to the music, he appropriates it, makes it his own, so that the tonal, rhythmic, melodic, and harmonic gestures of what began as background music reflect the singer's inner world more than the outward context. Development and recurrence in the lied reflect the ebb and flow of awareness, the singer's internalization of the external sounds. Eichendorff in "Das Ständchen" beckons the composer to write a lied about the interplay between the objective reality of music and its subjective metamorphoses in the listener's mind, but Heine does not invoke music in his opposition between inner and outer realms. Uninvited by the poet, Wolf invents salon music for the entertainment of the shadowy company inside and then subjects the party-music pleasantries to the convolutions of a solipsistic mind, the result a dark precipitate of the earlier graceful trivialities.

There are actually two contrasting themes that are transformed into darker versions of themselves in the course of the lied. Wolf found in Heine's despairing lover a vein of anger—the narcissistic rage caused by imagined rejection—apparent from the beginning in the piano introduction, the first of the two themes and one reserved solely for the piano. This introduction, which leads seamlessly into the body of the song, is marked "Lustig, etwas breit"

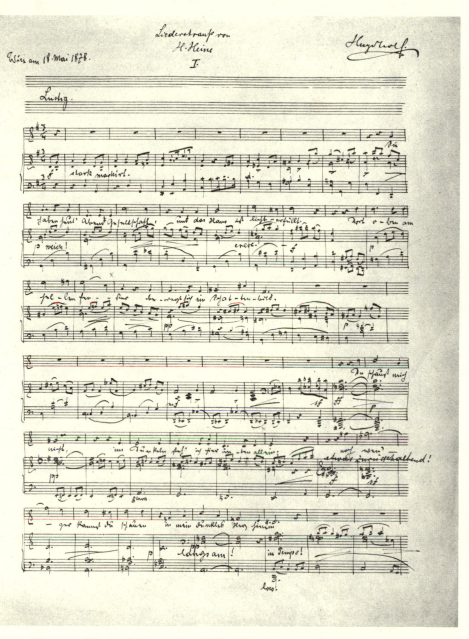

Figure 1. Autograph manuscript of "Sie haben heut' Abend Gesellschaft" from the *Liederstrauß*, vol. 1

(merry, somewhat broad) and has a jaunty quality that comes from the dotted rhythmic figures and the traditional horn-call motive (a rising or falling scale-wise third with an open fifth as the passing harmonic interval), and yet the capacity for anger that breaks out in full fury at the end is also evident: in the accents on every beat and pitch of the anacrusis and throughout measure 1,[38] in the directive "stark markiert" (strongly accented), the forte dynamics, the weak-beat accents of measures 5–6, the sforzando markings in measures 7–8, the dominant-tonic bass figures entirely on the weak second and third beats in measures 1–2, and the chromatic pitches (E♭, F, A♯) that foreshadow later harmonic and tonal events. The most telling signal of incipient rage, however, is in the phrasing near the end of the introduction. Wolf composes a conventional antecedent-consequent pair of four-bar phrases, except that the final two bars of the consequent phrase are a further development of the preceding motive, heightened in intensity—the bass line moves toward resolution, but the rising sequential motives in the right hand suggest just the opposite. The last-minute descent in measure 8 does not resolve the soprano F♯, but instead drops down in measure 9 to the second theme, the waltz, elided with the close of the introduction. Wolf nips the phrase extension in the bud before it can surpass the boundary marker of the fourth bar, but the suppression is not final, merely delayed. At the end of the song, the angry continuation denied in the introduction blazes forth *ff wild*, hammering away at the same ♭6–5̂ progression in a fury beyond words.

Wolf adapts Heine's anapests and iambs in stanza 1 to a Chopin-like waltz, complete with descending scalar anticipation-tone figures in the accompaniment between the vocal phrases and neighbor-note decoration of the dominant pitch on the weak beats, but "her" music does not last long before becoming the instrument of the narrator's emotions. The piano interlude between the second and third vocal phrases, with its forte accented octaves in the bass and the unharmonized descent into the lower register, is the first such outburst, again quickly supplanted by a return to the waltz melody. Other outbursts, longer and more fully developed, soon follow. At the end of the first stanza, Wolf modulates abruptly, via the common tone F♯, to the mediant harmony B major at the words "bewegt sich ein Schattenbild," the change of tonal place emblematic of the plane on which shadow figures move. It is as if a door opened briefly to show an alternate reality and gradually closed again, returning to the dominant of G in the lengthy ten-bar interlude between stanzas 1 and 2 (measures 23–33). In that interlude, motion is arrested on the dominant in measures 29–32, and ornament becomes principal motif and menace, as the neighbor-note figure from the waltz shrinks to a half-step and descends to the bass, the flatted sixth degree emphasized in octave displacement on the weak third beat. What was light and high is now heavy and low, conviviality converted to menace (Example 6).

Example 6. Hugo Wolf, "Sie haben heut' Abend Gesellschaft,"
measures 23–33

The interlude also exemplifies obsessive repetition as a paradoxical element of Romantic instability, the denial of any possibility of resolution. The more we hear the ♭6̂–5̂ figure, the less we expect tonic to follow. Rather, the frustrated grinding of teeth in a single spot impels a breakaway, a search for relief in reproaches couched as "direct address" to one who cannot hear or see or know. One thinks irresistibly of the final song in *Frauenliebe und Leben*, in which lamentation, unable to reach a resting point or come to an end, is extended via deceptive motion and prolongation, the chords in evenly measured, funereal succession. Schumann, of course, devises the famous consolatory postlude, but within the confines of the poem, no such consolation is possible and must be deferred until Chamisso's contribution to the lied is ended. For Heine's persona, however, there is no prior memory of fulfillment, only frustration and lack of closure, each uncompleted statement leading to the next in a search for sure ground that is not there. The tonal instability and the reiterations of the semitone motive merge into the recurrence of the waltz as the singer turns from the darkness within and "speaks" to the sweetheart. The elisions of harmonic progression, phrase, period, and section are the concomitant in sound to a volatile self-reflexivity that does not admit repose. The renewed instability at the word "hinein" (in mein dunkles Herz hinein") makes clear the fact that the *Blick nach Innen*, the gaze inward, merely sets the wheels of obsession turning once more. The neighbor-note motive appears in company with a descending chromatic inner voice that repeats the preceding vocal pitches F–E–E♭/D♯ an octave lower, and continues downward until it joins the recurrent waltz, "resolving" into momentarily renewed awareness of the outside world. Stability, where it occurs, is borrowed briefly from the outer realm and becomes almost immediately susceptible to the distortions imposed by an alienated ego.

The conflict between external and internal realms, dark self and desired other, is differently developed in the final stanza, the proclamation of love and heartbreak. "*It* loves you," Heine has the poetic persona say, in resentful understanding that it is his dark heart, the passions, Plato's black horse, that loves her. The agon becomes a brutal, quick-paced alternation in the accompaniment between the waltz—the singer "listens" to it for four bars before the struggle begins—and transmutation of the graceful descending scale figures from measures 11–12 into heavier syncopated octaves in the right hand, still recognizably a rhythmic and melodic figure from the dance repertoire but emphatic in a way that shortly bursts the bounds of gentility. Furthermore, the three-bar vocal phrases are joined to the phrase structure in the piano, two bars of waltz melody alternating with two bars of the syncopated figure, such that the syncopation underscores and intensifies the verbs at the end of lines 1–3 ("liebt dich," "bricht," "ver-blutet") and the negation, "nicht," at the end of the entire poem. But these angry emphases and the brief flight from G major into tonal turmoil, in unresolved references to the submediant and diminished-seventh harmonies (measures 63–68), collapse in defeat and a passive return to *her* waltz and *her* tonality. Wolf has the despairing lover flagellate himself with the final admission of futility, whatever the heartfelt convulsions, by repeating the last line of verse, "Du aber siehst es nicht": each time, the waltz, not to be banished, recurs. The end of the last vocal phrase, avoiding closure on the tonic root G, is elided with the beginning of the dance from the outside world at the original pitch level. For a moment, as the singer falls mute, the waltz asserts its pristine inviolability from his attacks.

Defeat turns to anger when the words cease. Wolf adds another act to the miniature psychodrama in the instrumental postlude, after Schumann's model, but reverses his predecessor's psychology. In many of the poems from the *Buch der Lieder*, the poetic persona either leaves in anger or seems on the verge of doing so. Wolf takes the fury that is the by-product of futility and gives it free rein at the close, after the poetic control exercised in words has concluded. In contrast, the poet-musician of *Dichterliebe* looks back wordlessly, after the self-mockery in "Die alten bösen Lieder" (The old, evil songs) is over, and "hears the song resound" in the postlude variant of "Hör' ich das Liedchen klingen" (When I hear the sound of the song)—the most potent reminder of many in the cycle that experience metamorphoses into music. Wolf only allows the waltz at the beginning of the postlude four bars of recurrence in its original guise before the frustrated lover's brooding mind intrudes once more, destabilizing the tonic key with the diminished-seventh chord on the raised tonic pitch previously heard in measures 33–34 ("Du schaust mich nicht") and repetitions of the neighbor-note motive. The inability to go anywhere else and the refusal to allow resolution on G become a series of hesitations and chromatic evasions, most telling in the isolated prolongation of the dominant ninth, with the motivically important E♭–D semitone in the bass (Example 7). Wolf then brings back the exaggeratedly jaunty, "Lustig" strains from the introduction, the lover both whistling loudly in the dark (metaphorically speaking) and attempting to assert the primacy of his own music over hers, but that ploy only leads to near-hysteria and a further delay of closure. The right-hand motive denied further extension in the introduction is repeated insistently over the E♭–D bass figure, and it is only with a violent wrench that the tonic "resolution" happens at last, first on the weak third beat and then, correcting the imbalance, on the strong first beat. The chromatic tensions endure to the close. The penultimate cadential harmony is the diminished-seventh chord from measures 67–68 ("verblutet"), and the relief one feels when it is all over, when one is no longer compelled to hear the music of pleasure turned into pain beyond resolution, is immense. Heine's word and phrase repetitions, the redundancies compacted into so short and tight a poem, convey obsession in every quatrain, but Wolf goes beyond the constraints imposed in verse to suggest impending disaster in the loss of selfhood. The listener, spared the spectacle of a breakdown only at the last minute, breathes a sigh of relief; the ultimate goal of the musical form is the catharsis experienced in the silence following the last chord.

"Sie haben heut' Abend Gesellschaft" is a remarkable achievement, especially when one remembers that not two years earlier, Wolf had to struggle with basic elements of compositional craft and could not, in "Wenn ich in deine Augen seh'," devise musical patterns congruent with the unfolding of the poem. The style is obviously derivative, but the assimilation, indeed the internalization, of Schumann's model is so complete as to allow, paradoxi-

Example 7. Hugo Wolf, "Sie haben heut' Abend Gesellschaft,"
measures 77–104

cally, the heightened ability to invent Schumannesque gestures in accord with the poem ("nach dem Sinn des Gedichts," or "after the sense of the poem," Schumann's initial directive for "Mein Wagen rollet langsam," or "My coach rolls slowly along"). For the first time, Wolf understood the possibility of stretching musically the boundaries of the poem, making more explicit the abnormal psychology of the fictive ego. In Heine's text, the constraining artistry of word arrangement asserts control of the same pathological despair it expresses. Chaos is held at bay with iambs and stanzaic structure. Wolf, however, discovered a different but parallel formal principle that makes audible the attempt to find stability outside the self and the failure to do so, as the instability within attacks and breaks down what it has borrowed.

"Ich stand in dunkeln Träumen," the second song in the *Liederstrauß*, is a setting in Schumannesque style—Wolf even borrows a characteristic tempo marking, "Innig, ziemlich langsam"—of a text inevitably associated with Schubert's *Schwanengesang* lied. The listener subsequently has the eerie experience of juxtaposing the memory of Schubert's song against Wolf's different stylistic model and interpretation. The spare texture and the contrapuntal imitation and development of a chromatic motive in the piano introduction are reminiscent of such Schumann works as the late song "Herzeleid" (Heart's sorrow), the beginning of "Zwielicht" (Twilight) from the Eichendorff *Liederkreis*, or the postlude of "Am leuchtenden Sommermorgen" (On a gleaming summer morning), but there is also something of late Liszt about this parenthesis for piano that encloses the song on either side and is reserved solely for the pre- and post-words moments. Wolf inflects so many of the diatonic pitches with their lower chromatic neighbors that eleven of the twelve tones appear in the first three-and-a-half bars, the harmonic implications of a progression filled with secondary dominants enshrouded in localized chromaticism. The tonal and metrical uncertainty of the beginning gives way to clarity with the arrival of the voice: a corridor of relative mystery, its saturated chromaticism reminiscent of Liszt, leads both to and away from the body of the song. Wolf had been introduced the year before into Viennese cultured society by the wealthy poet-composer Adalbert von Goldschmidt (1848–1906), a fervent disciple of Liszt, and Wolf would therefore have had ample opportunity to learn of Liszt's works and Goldschmidt's derivative homages to his master; the influence of Liszt's songs, including Liszt's many settings of Heine, on Wolf has not been sufficiently explored.[39] But Schumann still predominates.

Wolf probably knew Robert Franz's famous setting of "Aus meinen grossen Schmerzen," op. 5, no. 1.[40] It is unlikely, however, that the earlier lied would have disturbed him in the course of composing his own version, so widely divergent were the two men's views of song composition—Wolf characterized Franz as "dull."[41] Hanslick had praised the curmudgeonly Franz, who had made his limitations a matter of ungenerous pride, as one of the lieder composers most sensitive to the ebb and flow of a poetic text, most attentive to "every nuance of every mood."[42] Franz himself defined his mission as the restoration of Bach's kingdom to the modern lied, a cross-pollination of Bach's polyphonic voice leading with folk-song simplicity, a curious combinatorial endeavor. In a letter to Hanslick in 1871, Franz inveighed against "homophony with its despotism by melody" in recent song composition and declared that "poetry by Heine, in which the criss-crossing veins and arteries of subtlest feeling show clearly through the surface, can never be satisfactorily set to music as a cantilena, no matter how expressive . . . only in continuous voice-leading, in polyphony, is this possible."[43] But in practice, Franz ignores the poetry of "Aus meinen grossen Schmerzen," bypassing imagery and content in the service of his compositional aesthetic. For those who know Franz's gently melancholy song, there is a certain malicious pleasure in noting how much more perceptively Wolf read Heine's poem, how much more concerned he truly was with the interpretation of his chosen poetry (Examples 8a and 8b).

As happens often in the *Buch der Lieder*, the poem has as much to do with poetry as with love—here, a complaint about the discrepancy between experience and the poetry it inspires. All the poet can make of his great griefs are small songs that flutter and tinkle, implicitly a devaluation of the sorrows that are the source of his poetry and an expression of wittily ambivalent artistic dissatisfaction: the criticism of "small songs" in the form of yet another example of the genre. Carrier pigeons in words, creatures animated by the creator-poet, the poems take flight to the beloved but can only complain upon their return. Heine fancifully implies that they are separate entities with the volition to refuse disclosure of what they have seen and he cannot. It is they, not the poet, that lament whatever unnamed perfidy they have found in the sweetheart's heart (the repetition of the verb "und klagen, / Und klagen" insinuates that she must indeed be blameworthy)—he is spared unwelcome knowledge through their kind agency. In a conceit that goes beyond the sublimation of experience into art, the poems become servants of their master's bidding and assume at least some of the painful job of living for him, insofar as such inconsequential beings are able. The familiar reproaches to an unworthy lover become the instrument for a fantasy about the relationship of poem to poet, the nature and limitations of small-scale lyric songs forged from such subjective matter, and the disturbing disproportion between the raw material and the completed work.

> Aus meinen grossen Schmerzen
> Mach' ich die kleinen Lieder,
> Sie heben ihr klingend Gefieder
> Und flattern nach ihrem Herzen.

Sie fanden den Weg zur Trauten,
Doch kommen sie wieder und klagen,
Und klagen und wollen nicht sagen,
Was sie im Herzen schauten.

(Out of my great sorrows I make small songs. They lift their tinkling wings and flutter off to her heart. They make their way to the beloved and then return and lament, lament and will not say what they have seen in her heart.)[44]

Heine creates two distinct personas or voices—the poet's and that of the small songs. In Wolf's conception, the small songs have their own musical identity: graceful, sweet, fluttering, lacking in profundity, separate from the author who narrates their actions. The result is salon music for the piano, its palpitations set apart at all times from the poetic persona in the vocal line.[45] Wolf writes an accompaniment that seems a *moto perpetuo* variant in minor mode and duple meter of the sweetheart's waltz in "Sie haben heut' Abend Gesellschaft," but without the powerful, warping, distorting effects of the first song. The narrator, adopting a more distanced stance, does not intrude, and the elegant salon strains go their way undisturbed. The ornamental accompaniment, virtually an independent small-scale piano piece, steals the show almost entirely from the singer, whose part is drier and more restricted by far. Wolf banishes all hints of "great sorrows" or even melancholy from this rather neutral vocal line, with its rhythmic-prosodic sameness and the narrow range of each phrase. Only at the words "Und klagen und wollen nicht sagen" does the singer permit himself a touch of indignation and emphasis. The first lament is followed by an immediate return to the prevailing objective tone and the music from measures 17–20, the recurrence underscoring the futility of the mission. The start of the brief journey, "Sie flattern nach ihrem Herzen," with the destabilizing diminished-seventh chord and B♮ at "Herzen," recurs at the end ("Was sie im Herzen schauten"), no different, no wiser than when the poetic messengers set out. And the "small songs" in the accompaniment, for all the constant motion and the chromatic inflections, are essentially unadventurous creatures, the texture always the same and the tonal design limited, straying only briefly from tonic G minor. The frailty of lyrical poetry—unable, for all its grace, to plumb the depths of feeling—is symbolized by tonal timidity, by music that does not travel far from home.

Given his avoidance of Schumann's choices, Wolf in general selected wisely and well from what remained, but "Wo ich bin, mich rings umdunkelt" is his one mistake of judgment. The misery of rejected love becomes leaden, devoid of the stylized rancor that gives many of these poems their venomous life, and Heine resorts to tired images tiredly ordered. The beloved's eyes no longer light the poet's darkened world; the golden glory of love's starlight is

Example 8a. Hugo Wolf, "Aus meinen großen Schmerzen," measures 1–12

Example 8b. Robert Franz, "Aus meinen großen Schmerzen," Op. 5, no. 1, measures 1–9

extinguished; an abyss yawns at his feet; and he longs for the ultimate darkness of death to envelop him. The same theme—the dark night of the soul,
caused by the beloved's absence—occurs elsewhere in the *Buch der Lieder*,
notably, in "In mein gar zu dunkles Leben" (In my all-too-dark existence) at
the beginning of "Die Heimkehr," but there Heine invokes it in order to reflect
once again and more powerfully on the relationship between subjective experience and lyric poetry as objectification and control. A small child afraid of
the phantoms conjured up by his imagination will sing shrilly to combat his
fear; so too the poet attempts to relieve the darkness created by love's loss
with song. The result may not be entertaining for others, writes the poet
(aware, as ever, of his audience), but it is cathartic for the true poet, the being
whose vocation is poetry and whose imagination is populated with phantasms
from inner realms. The speaker in "Wo ich bin, mich rings umdunkelt," however, is beyond caring about such things as the raison d'être of lyric verse,
beyond awe or terror, beyond all but the motions of poetry. He is too close to
desired extinction to do more than observe the spread of darkness and implore
eternal Night to enfold him.

Wolf responds to the lesser poetic quality with music below the level of the
other six Heine songs from the summer of 1878. Exceptional for the *Liederstrauß* songs, there is neither piano introduction nor postlude, and the accompaniment is as "dumpf und dicht" (torpid and heavy) as the poem. The only
exception to the plodding succession of chordal harmonies is the elision of the
cadential phrase for the voice in measures 7–8 ("Liebste, deiner Augen
Licht") with its variant downward extension in the accompaniment, a cliché
"salon music" bridge to the second of Wolf's three sections:

> 1. Verse 1 (measures 1–8) is set in E minor with a constant quarter-
> note tactus in the bass and each chord divided between the hands. There
> is no pause—pervasive darkness?—and the prosody is unusually poor for
> the Heine songs, with "Wo" and "rings" prolonged beyond their due,
> "mir" insufficiently stressed in the phrase "seit mir nicht mehr," and no
> notice taken of the commas that separate syntactical units in the poem,
> such as "Finsternis, so dumpf und dicht" or "Liebste, deiner Augen
> Licht." Worse yet, the harmonic articulation of two consecutive two-bar
> phrases in the piano (measures 1–4) cuts through the enjambment of
> "rings umdunkelt / Finsternis"; the vocal line, even though it continues
> without a break, reflects the underlying harmonies with their implicit
> division (probably because the song was not offered to publishers in
> Wolf's lifetime, the manuscripts lack the full battery of slurs, articulation
> markings, and dynamic indications that one finds in the other Heine
> songs).
>
> 2. At the beginning of the second section (measures 9–12), the ex-
> pected E-minor resolution is displaced by deceptive motion to C. The

enjambed first half of stanza 2 appears twice, set as a sequential ascent in a constant eighth-note harmonic rhythm, leading to the "Abgrund" of the final section.

3. The third segment (measures 13–20) is marked by still more chordal plodding, this time in a half-note tactus with frequent Neapolitan chords.

In its own way, this is an accurate rendition of a deadening poem. The concept of the light of love extinguished, the resulting despair blacking out the world and life itself, need not produce either uninspired verse or leaden music, but both are visible and audible in this song.

Dream sequences are a frequent occurrence in the *Buch der Lieder*, but dreams in Heine have a special meaning. "They are not so much dreams as dramas of the ordered imagination,"[46] one scholar writes, and they lack therefore the discontinuities, the symbolically encoded hidden meanings, of genuine dreams, nor are they concerned with mystical or transcendant realms beyond the Self. The frequent *Traumbilder* in Heine's early verse can be understood in one sense as an attempt at self-purgation, evidence of the poet's increasing desire throughout the 1820s to be "absolute lord of the dream-world," to rule over dreams and not be ruled by them, to free himself from his fascination with the uncanny and unknowable.[47] The control is manifest in the narrative order of events: "Mir träumte von einem Königskind" could be a scene from a ballad, reduced to its most miniaturized essence and given a unique psychological twist.

> Mir träumte von einem Königskind,
> Mit nassen, blassen Wangen;
> Wir sassen unter der grünen Lind,
> Und hielten uns liebumfangen.
>
> "Ich will nicht deines Vaters Thron,
> Und nicht sein Zepter von Golde,
> Ich will nicht seine demantene Kron,
> Ich will dich selber, du Holde!"
>
> Das kann nicht sein, sprach sie zu mir,
> Ich liege ja im Grabe,
> Und nur des Nachts komm ich zu dir,
> Weil ich so lieb dich habe.

(I dreamed of a king's daughter with moist, pale cheeks. We sat under the green linden tree and clasped one another lovingly. "I do not want your father's throne nor his gold scepter. I do not want his diamond crown; I want only you, thou noble one!" "That cannot be," she said to me, "I lie in the grave and will come to you only at night because I love you so much.")[48]

There is no prehistory or background; the dream begins in medias res with the poet and his princess-sweetheart intertwined under the linden tree, the traditional rendezvous of lovers in German lyric poetry since the Minnesingers. She has not the customary rosebud mouth, lily-white hands, blue eyes, and blonde hair of the princesses in folk and fairy tales, but "nassen, blassen Wangen," an alliterative clue to the ectoplasmic-necrophiliac conclusion of the dream. The poet-suitor swears his devotion to the pallid apparition by renouncing any desire for her father's throne, scepter, and crown, any claim to her kingdom; even in the thrall of love, he does not forget that the scepter is made of gold and the crown diamond-encrusted, the emblems of wealth and power. As in the horror ballads of the eighteenth and early nineteenth centuries, the living dramatis personae do not discover that the beloved is dead until the denouement, but here, the traditional *frisson* of the ending is deepened by the doubly spectral—a ghost in a dream—sweetheart's promise of recurrent nocturnal visitations. Reciprocated love becomes a horror, a rêve d'amour turned nightmare. The power of this small poem is due in large measure to Heine's refusal to end the dream, to have his poetic persona either wake up or respond in word or gesture to the revelation. We are denied knowledge of what happens next. The poem is a self-sufficient, independent entity that can and does stand alone, but within the larger context of the *Buch der Lieder*, it acquires an additional resonance. The object of desire who is derided and reviled in life exacts her revenge when she becomes a ghostly leech, her vows of love tantamount to a threat of continuing horror.

The poem poses to the composer the problem of inventing a musical structure concordant with its premises (or skeptically dissonant with them—not Wolf's wont in 1878), although that did not keep twenty-five other composers from tackling the text by 1885, including Wolf's good friend Oskar Grohe.[49] The linear progression of the narrative and the changes of speaker invite through-composed balladesque treatment, and yet the dimensions are much smaller than those of an extended horror ballad in Loewe's style. If the poem orders and rationalizes the dream, it also manifests in its brevity and compression the horror of enclosure within the small prison cell of three quatrains. Too great a musical expansion of such restrictiveness would be counter to the mental claustrophobia Heine has devised. Unlike "Sie haben heut' Abend Gesellschaft," Heine gives the composer no grounds to imagine an exit from the scene beyond the last words, no justification for a musical change of mood after the dead princess's declaration of love. Wolf, alert both to Heine's proscriptions and to the sense of murky psychological depths beneath the Märchen surface, sets each stanza as a different episode in a continuing tale, airless and unbroken to the end, with transitional passages for the piano as the bridges between episodes. Where there is such a radical gap between the semblance of love and its underlying horror, the accompaniment, as is the rule in the *Liederstrauß*, is given the lion's share of the suggestive burden from the poet.

Figure 2. Autograph manuscript of "Ich träumte von einem Königskind" from the *Liederstrauß*, vol. 1

The beginning of the song is clearly modeled on Schumann's "Ich hab' im Traum geweinet," the two songs sharing a common $\frac{6}{8}$ meter, declamation on a single repeated pitch at the start of the vocal line, the lack of a piano introduction, and motivic similarity in the accompaniment. But once having acknowledged the identity of his model, Wolf tailors the borrowed mantle to his own requirements, revealing in the process hints of his own future style coexistent with the *Dichterliebe* influences. Two aspects in particular of the first section, the setting of stanza 1 in measures 1–8, foreshadow the eventual development beyond the need for creative copies of Schumann: the distinction between vocal line and accompaniment as the signifiers of conflicting orders in the poem and the chain of third relationships compressed into the consequent phrase, measures 5–8. Wolf takes his cue from Heine, who immediately subverts the folk-tale beginnings with hints of death, by writing an entirely diatonic vocal line for the initial phrase set to a chromatic progression in the piano. In this way, the listener is told right away that beneath a placid, sunlit surface, something dark and unsettled is moving about. Wolf actually begins and ends the phrase with the conventional tonic-dominant frame, but the interior elisions and chromatic alterations are far less conventional and the progression to V in measure 4 resolves *after* the G in the voice, producing a dissonant A♭–G clash between the soprano and bass voices. Even Wolf's choice of C major seems calculated for the maximum display of Otherness, of polarity between diatonic and chromatic, light and dark, serene and disturbed, overt and hidden, joy and menace. The subterranean, nonmodulatory chromaticism of this first phrase is succeeded by a chain of rising third relationships in the consequent phrase, beginning with the flatted mediant E♭ major and progressing through G major to B major. Each brief tonal reference, the E♭–G–B progression foreshadowed in the accompaniment of measures 1–4, is "pure," "diatonic" within its one- or two-bar boundaries. The sweetness of the tale at this point is mirrored in the simple triads and dominant sevenths and in the right hand's ascent to a higher register than that of the first phrase.

With the piano interlude in measures 9–10, Wolf returns to C major for the second stanza, the poet-suitor's declaration of love. The renunciations of royal wealth and the proclamations of love are couched in balladesque terms similar to those Wolf would later use more powerfully for Goethe's "Der Rattenfänger" (The rat-catcher). In both songs, the root-position harmonies and the blatant parallel fifths in the arpeggiated bass chords invoke a fairy-tale realm in which the primary chords tell of otherworldly powers. The dream-protagonist's vaunted energy and resolve are expressed in the way Wolf strengthens the principal chords of the key with their secondary dominants and through the doubling of the vocal line by the accompaniment, without the disjunction between the two that is so marked a feature of the first stanza. The poet, with his eagle's-eye command of the entire tale, foreshadows the turn to nightmare at the beginning and then pretends to step aside in order to allow the poetic persona his "direct" address in the central stanza; the composer does likewise by abrogating almost entirely the chromaticism of "nassen, blassen Wangen"—"almost" because the harmonies of measure 16 at the words "demantene Kron" can perhaps be interpreted as Wolf's ironic questioning of the suitor's renunciations, the protagonist weakening slightly at his own invocation of diamond-encrusted crowns.

Wolf evidently contemplated two different musical approaches to the interior verse. Accompanying the photocopied autograph manuscript in the Austrian National Library is a separate half-sheet with a variant, marked "vi-de," of the second stanza. When the composer returned to the *Liederstrauß* in 1881 in order to prepare the manuscripts for review by other publishers, he wrote down a variant of the same measures, possibly a sketch for a revoiced version of the previous "vi-de" variant (Vienna City Library M. H. 6680/c, dated 20 January 1881 and entitled "Variante zu N° 5 aus der Liederstrauss von H. Heine 'Mir träumte von einem Königskind'").[50] For both of the related *Varianten*, Wolf retains only the vocal phrase for the final line of the stanza "ich will dich selber, du Holde!" from the autograph/published version, and replaces everything else with music derived from both the first and third stanzas of the setting. There is no longer a sharp contrast drawn between the singer-suitor's proclamation and what precedes and follows it. Instead, Wolf in the 1878(?) variant develops a semitone bass figure, one of Wolf's frequent Baroque reminiscences—this could be a snippet from the continuo line of a Bach aria—in the first two bars of the stanza. In 1881, he anticipates the stepwise descending bass line from measures 26–28 at the princess's words "ich liege ja im Grabe" and uses a similar scalar descent for the first and third phrases of the vocal line and for the bass line of the second stanza, in particular, the march downward in the bass beneath the first two phrases of text. The preparation for C major in measures 9–10, the interlude between stanzas 1 and 2, does not resolve in measure 11 to C, as before, but moves elsewhere by deceptive extension and elision, the resolute words "ich will nicht . . ." weakened, even negated, by the denial of an equivalent tonal firmness and surety. In other words, Wolf both undermines the protagonist's proclamations harmonically and anticipates the forthcoming revelation of death. The suitor's sentiments are no longer permitted to be what they seem on the surface, but are contradicted by conflicts engendered in the accompaniment, the composer "showing his hand" far more openly than before in order to tell the listener that not all is well in this dreamland. Even the suitor's last bold line—"ich will dich selber, du Holde!"—is denied the rhythmic straightforwardness and C-major resolution, however momentary, of the original version. Instead, Wolf brings back the syncopated G's in the bass of measures 9–10 and therefore begins the extended dominant of C for the interlude earlier than before. The concerns that produced this variant would thus seem twofold: the greater musical unification of the miniature ballad and the continuation of a sense of conflict between the poetic personas and their author-composer. It is not the bold lover who articulates such shifting unease and instability but his creator, and the latter's presence is made much more apparent in the revisions. Where Wolf in the autograph takes the lover at his word, giving him the serenader's gestures and heroic postures to which the dream figure lays claim verbally, he interjects his own, and Heine's, foreknowledge of the denouement in the variant versions.

Wolf was evidently dissatisfied with the 1881 variant and did not complete or refine the fragment, written on a torn-off scrap of music paper, although he preserved it among his other manuscripts of uncompleted songs and sketches. The last half of the fifth measure lacks the inner voice, and there are no indications of phrasing, dynamics, accents, or articulation of any kind, atypical for a composer whose characteristic refinements of nuance are already apparent in the *Liederstrauß*. The vocal line is clearly derived from that in the autograph, but the melody is gutted of much of its former sturdiness. 1881 was not a "year of Lodi": the six *Geistliche Lieder* for mixed chorus to texts by Eichendorff and a single completed Eichendorff lied are the only products of the time in which his love affair with Vally Franck came to an end, the beginning of what Frank Walker has dubbed "the years of indecision."[51] Although the conception given tentative shape in the "Variante" is an interesting one—the use of music to undermine, weaken, even contradict what the words purport to say, the original reading is the more effective. The bravado of the arpeggiated chords and bass octaves is sufficiently overdone to signal an imminent disillusionment.

The piano figuration in "Mein Liebchen, wir sassen beisammen" recalls the piano figuration in Schumann's "Aufträge" (Messages), no. 5 of the *Lieder und Gesänge*, op. 77, to a text by Charles L'Égru. It is also another reminder of Wolf's liking for Chopin. The young Wolf enthusiastically recommended Chopin's songs to his friends and would later defend Chopin against those Viennese Wagnerites who dismissed him as a mere purveyor of salon music.[52]

> Mein Liebchen, wir sassen beisammen,
> Traulich im leichten Kahn.
> Die Nacht war still und wir schwammen
> Auf weiter Wasserbahn.
>
> Die Geisterinsel, die Schöne,
> Lag dämmrig im Mondenglanz;
> Dort klangen Liebe Töne
> Und wogte der Nebeltanz.
>
> Dort klang es lieb und lieber
> Und wogt es hin und her;

Wir aber schwammen vorüber
Trostlos auf weitem Meer.

(My love, we sat together trustingly in the light boat. The night was still, and we drifted on the broad seaway. The spirits' island, the beautiful one, lay gleaming in the moonlight. Sweet music rang out and the mists danced with it. Sweeter and sweeter it sounded and swayed to and fro, but we floated forlornly past on the broad seaway.)[53]

The lovers drift helplessly by the beautiful island, unable to attain its shores, and the sight leaves them bereft. Before they see its misty outlines and hear its unearthly music, they were "traulich im leichten Kahn," afterward, "trostlos auf weitem Meer." The sounds they hear are a fantasy of the poetic imagination "sweet and more sweet" beyond the realm of human compositions ("Da klingt es und da singt es / Von einem Zauberland," or "There is singing, and there are sounds of a magical land," Heine writes in "Aus alten Märchen winkt es" [From old tales someone waves]), and once heard, it robs even reciprocated love—a rarity in the *Buch der Lieder*—of all joy. Elsewhere in Heine's poetry, in "Frau Mette" and "Ich weiss nicht, was soll es bedeuten," the music of magic is an instrument or an omen of death; those who follow its strains and partake of its enchantment die. The lovers in "Mein Liebchen, wir sassen beisammen" live on, but in the desolate knowledge that the island realm of Faerie is beyond their grasp. The love that has brought the pair within sight and sound of the spirit world of the imagination cannot bring them to its shores, and they are cast adrift in the wide seas that so often symbolize temporality, eroticism, that which is elemental and unknown.

The better to suggest unearthly music with earthly sounds, Wolf sets "Mein Liebchen, wir sassen beisammen" in the uncommon tonality of F♯ major with incessant rising and falling, black-key "wave" figuration in the right hand throughout the song, often ascending above the vocal register with the individual waves of arpeggiated sound. At the invocation of the *Geisterinsel*, F♯ major becomes its enharmonic twin G♭ major for five bars only (measures 11–15). This change of tonality at the beginning of stanza 2 was probably made for orthographic reasons: Wolf modulates briefly to the mediant tonality of B♭ major at the words "dämmrig im Mondenglanz," and the short-lived moonlight dazzle, the transport to another and special place before returning to the F♯ major ocean, is easier to notate in B♭ than in A♯ major, but the enharmonic alteration can also be interpreted, perhaps a bit fancifully, as symbolic. So near and yet so far—the lovers' closeness to the desired and ghostly beauty and yet its difference and distance from them are signified by a purely visual image on the page, a private symbol for the performers' and score-readers' delectation. Nowhere else in the small song (thirty measures) does one find a change of tonal place—only in the second stanza, with its progression from $\hat{3}$ to $\hat{5}$, the extension of the tonic triad. For all the coloristic harmonies, the changing shapes of the individual waves, much of the song is a "drifting in place."

The wave figuration in the accompaniment unifies a through-composed lied in three sections corresponding to Heine's three stanzas, through-composed, however, in a schema in which the first and third sections/stanzas in tonic F♯ major-minor frame the mediant and dominant references in the middle. The first is organized around a simple I–V–I progression in which the appoggiatural B♯s in the bass both emphasize the dominant and pave the way for the more emphatic diminished seventh/V–V progression in the final stanza ("Wir aber schwammen vorüber," measures 24–25). Only the momentary inflection to parallel minor and its submediant in measure 8 prepares the forthcoming passage through B♭ major and anticipates the mixed modes of the ending. In the second stanza, Wolf counterbalances five bars of G♭–B♭ with four bars of motion to the dominant, the bass pattern animated for the "liebe Töne" and "Nebeltanz," while the final stanza remains in tonic throughout, the accented repeated tonic pitches the analogue of insistent hypnotic sound, perhaps even an element of angry emphasis as the protagonists are helplessly carried away from the beauty seen and heard so nearby. Wolf was as yet far from devising the heightened declamation of his later songs, and the vocal line—entirely harmonious with the accompaniment, without a trace of differentiation or conflict between the two—closely reproduces in its own coin the symmetries of Heine's verse structure. Dissolving the poem into musical prose and disregarding the stanzaic, or even the line, divisions was still to come in Wolf's later songs.

The final song of the *Liederstrauß*, volume 1, "Es blasen die blauen Husaren" (The Blue Hussars blow their bugles), is the first of Wolf's military march–songs, a foreshadowing of "Sie blasen zum Abmarsch" (They are blowing the bugles for departure) from the *Spanisches Liederbuch*, and the comic song "Ihr jungen Leute" (You young folk) from the *Italienisches Liederbuch*. "Es blasen die blauen Husaren" is actually the second of a pair of poems, nos. 73 and 74 in "Die Heimkehr," in which the Blue Hussars ride in ("Es blasen die blauen Husaren, / Und reiten zum Tor herein") during the first poem and ride out again (". . . und reiten zum Tor hinaus") in the second. Wolf chose the less overtly sensual of the two poems, Heine's cynical version of the old analogy between love and war. Although Wolf's text can be understood on its own, the context is all the more clear when one knows the preceding poem, "An deine schneeweisse Schulter" (On your snow-white shoulders). There, the poet, lying in his mistress's arms, hears the bugles that announce the Blue Hussars' arrival and realizes that she will leave him the next day for erotic conquests among the elite regiment. Resigned to the inevitable, he consoles himself with the thought that she is, for the moment, his and even resolves to be doubly happy in her embrace because one who favors such military heroes deigns to give him her body. In the second poem of the pair, the Hussars ride away, and the poet immediately seeks her out once more, bringing the conventional suitor's bouquet of roses. But anger at her perfidy and his humiliation breaks out uncontrollably in sarcasm: her "dear little heart," the diminutive again a term of contempt, has become a barracks-whorehouse in which war, plague, and their instigators are encamped. The juxtaposition of "viel" (many) and "*Ein*quartierung," a billet the poetic persona imagines to be plural rather than singular, was not one Wolf would later miss. However, he and almost everyone else, except the indefatigable Vesque von Püttlingen,[54] passed by the combined eroticism, misogynistic condemnation, and self-hatred of the first poem. Wolf would later set decidedly sensual poems to music, such as "Geh', Geliebter, geh' jetzt" from the *Spanisches Liederbuch*, and would express in letters a Nietzsche-influenced view of morality in sexual matters, but Heine's insatiate women and scenes of intimate contempt were not to his taste, either in 1878 or thereafter.

> Es blasen die blauen Husaren,
> Und reiten zum Tor hinaus;
> Da komm ich, Geliebte, und bringe
> Dir einen Rosenstrauss.
>
> Das war eine wilde Wirtschaft!
> Kriegsvolk und Landesplag!
> Sogar in deinem Herzchen
> Viel Einquartierung lag.

(The Blue Hussars blow their bugles and ride through the gate and away. Then I come to you, beloved, and bring you a bouquet of roses. That was a wild company! Soldiers and the land's plague! Even in your little heart there was much quartering.)[55]

The song is a miniature series of variations on a military tattoo: the bugles that sound as the Hussars leave town never cease resounding in the angry poet's mind. As in "Sie haben heut Abend Gesellschaft," music from an external source is appropriated by the poetic persona and altered in accord with his emotions, pained and vengeful sentiments once again, before returning to the source. The opening fanfares mimic the diatonic simplicity and emphatic rhythms of military music, the singer echoing the bugle fourths and fifths in his vocal line, but even as the Hussars ride away, Wolf introduces in the accompaniment—not yet the vocal line—the chromatic pitches premonitory of the "wilde Wirtschaft" and the angry second verse (E♯/F♮, A♯, D♯). When the poet presents his bouquet, the fanfares are muted, no longer echoed in the bass, and lead *through* the half-cadence rather than resting there in momentary emphasis on the dominant, as before. The continued harmonic motion through the cadence seems a concomitant to the mental turbulence that puts an end to the "leicht" and "zart" variants of the fanfare, bursting out instead in offbeat accents and a descending harmonic sequence, from E minor to C major (fore-shadowed in measure 7 with the chromatic passing tone in the bass and the resulting II^{b5} harmony that inflects and underscores the word "Geliebte").

Wolf would later abjure any textual repetitions not already present in the poetry, but in 1878, he had not yet converted to that view. By repeating the final two lines—the punch line of the poem—Wolf both extends a small text and opens it up to a musical display of the anger and obsession that rankle just beneath the surface. Where the poet compacts his fury into two short, swift quatrains, the composer exposes and expands the obsessiveness at the poem's core, demonstrating in the permutations of the fanfare figure that the poet too harbors a "wilde Wirtschaft" within his breast. The fanfares go beyond the recording of external fact to become properties of a brooding, near-pathologi-cal mind, the brisk figures in accord with the hatred that accompanies the rose bouquet. When Wolf deflects the expected cadential resolution in the domi-nant tonality at the poet's last word, "lag," to its mediant, G♯ major, thereby creating a structural analogy with the G♯ in the bass at the end of the first stanza (measure 10) and extending in enharmonic reinterpretation the chro-matic pitches G–F✕ and B♯–C♮ from the second stanza, he makes especially apparent the way in which the fanfares haunt the persona's consciousness. Here, as throughout the lied, the bugle tune preserves its identity as an Other, emblematic of an outside world not the poet's own, but his rage can and does send it veering in tonal directions far from the point of origin, rather like a wind shear. Nor is the return to tonic A major and the fanfares in their original guise experienced as relief—quite the contrary. Although the reestablishment of tonic is structurally necessary after the "wild riot" in the second stanza, Wolf ensures that there will no cessation of tension by harping on the A-major fanfare, by repeating it over and over again. Its limitation to tonic and domi-nant harmonies only is in stark contrast to the harmonic goings-on of the music just preceding it, equivalent in length, and the repetitions, entirely lack-ing tonal or harmonic variety of any kind, sound suspiciously like a broken record. No longer does he *use* the external music for his own purposes, for the presentation of the flowers and the expression of condemnation, but, rather, he hears the bugle calls echo until the listener, forced to participate in such pathological anxiety, begins to wonder when and how it will all end. As in "Sie haben heut Abend Gesellschaft," it ends with the brandishing of a clenched fist, the sudden resolve to call a halt to the obsessive repe-titions. With the final fortissimo cadential chords, the fanfares are cut off at last.

Two days after the composition of "Es blasen die blauen Husaren," Wolf began work on another song for the *Liederstrauß*, but abandoned it after thirty bars. This time, he chose a somewhat longer poem in six quatrains, "Manch Bild vergessener Zeiten," with the famous lines "Ich und mein Schatten selbander / Wir wandelten schweigend umher" (I and my shadow, we wander about silently), a poem on the same theme of *Doppelgängertum* and remembered lost love as "Der Doppelgänger."[56] In "Manch Bild vergessener Zeiten," the poet, overcome by memories of past happiness in love, wanders the streets by day and night until he reaches his sweetheart's house and remembers when he stood there in the past. The image of the poet as if turned to stone in the moonlight is beautifully vivid, but Wolf recognized that his setting was in too much compositional difficulty to salvage well before he reached the evocative scene at poem's end.

The manuscript is entitled, after Wolf's usual practice for the *Liederstrauß*, "Aus dem Lieder-Cyklus von H. Heine XI." and dated 24 June 1878 (Vienna City Library, M.H. 6668/c). The numbering is peculiar, as both another no. XI ("Sterne mit den golden Füsschen") and a no. IX, the two elements of the Roman numeral transposed, exist in the later Heine settings. The problems with the lied are evident from the beginning in the lengthy piano introduction, twelve measures of $\frac{4}{4}$ meter in a very slow tempo ("Getragen"), in which Wolf seems to be fishing for the most desirable right-hand figuration and rhythmic disposition for a harmonic sequence in two-bar units, a *Wanderung* through the extended dominant of tonic C♯ minor before arriving at the sweetheart's house and the tonic chord. Each of the two-bar segments in measures 1–6 ends with the cliché of an appoggiatura sighing figure and a pause before the music can wend its weary way further, and with each segment, the rhythmic motion in the piano increases; one is more aware of literalism in the transfer from poem to instrumental narrative than of musical invention at a high level. The cadential progression that follows in measures 7–10 is straightforward and unexciting, even with the Schubertian Neapolitan sixth in measure 11—and Schubert, especially the Schubert of "Der Doppelgänger" (The ghostly double) seems to be the specter haunting "Manch' Bild vergessener Zeiten." There is no ground-bass pattern and nothing of Schubert's distinctive voice leading or chromatic tensions, but the quarter-note chordal tread in measures 13–19 and the predilection for declamation on repeated pitches appear as variant latter-day descendants of the earlier masterpiece. But Wolf, his ingenuity flagging at this point, takes the moonlit protagonist's meandering too literally and fails to direct the tonal and harmonic motion in clearly audible paths (Example 9). Another four quatrains of chromatic apathy must have seemed unworthy of further pursuit, and the manuscript breaks off, one bar after a descending melodic sequence whose interpretive connection with the text ("Die Leute verwundert mich ansah'n / Ich war so traurig und stumm") is mysterious at best. The burst of inspiration that fuelled the composition of the summertime Heine settings had run out, at least for a while. The next song Wolf would attempt after "Manch' Bild vergessener Zeiten"—Friedrich

Example 9. Hugo Wolf, "Manch Bild vergessener Zeiten" (fragment)

Example 9, continued

an - sah'n,   Ich   war   so   trau - rig und

stumm.

Rückert's "Frühling, Liebster" (Spring, beloved)[57]—was also never completed, and Wolf did not resume his Heine collection until October.

THE *LIEDERSTRAUß*, VOLUME 2

In October of 1878, Wolf returned to Heine's poetry and composed four songs
in the span of two weeks: "Es war ein alter König" (There was an old king) on
4 October; "Mit schwarzen Segeln" (With black sails) on 6 October; "Spätherbstnebel" (Late autumn mist) on 7 October; and "Ernst ist der Frühling"
(Spring is grave) on 16 October, actually notated on 17 October.[58] The numbering system for the *Liederstrauß* becomes confusing with the later additions. There are two songs designated as no. VIII in the series, "Es war ein
alter König" and "Spätherbstnebel," while "Mit schwarzen Segeln" is no. IX.
"Ernst ist der Frühling" is the only completed no. X, although another undated
manuscript contains the heading "Aus dem Liederstrauss / von H. Heine /
'Neue Gedichte' / X. Hugo Wolf" and a single three-staff system with a key
signature of three flats and a $\frac{12}{8}$ meter indication—"Ernst ist der Frühling" is
in A♭ major with a $\frac{6}{4}$ meter. Well after the "days of Lodi" and the parting from
Vally Franck, Wolf added two more poems from Heine's *Neue Gedichte*

(New poems): "Sterne mit den goldnen Füsschen" (Stars with the little golden feet) or no. XI, composed 26 November 1880, and "Wie des Mondes Abbild zittert" (How the moon's image trembled) or no. XII, composed 13 February 1880. If there ever was a no. XIII, it is now lost, but on 7 December (of 1880?—the year is not indicated), Wolf composed eight measures, no more, of no. XIV, "Das gelbe Laub erzittert" (The yellow leaf shuddered) from the supplement to the *Neue Gedichte*. Looking at the manuscript, one can see at the end of measure 7 and throughout measure 8 where Wolf took up a fresh pen to continue the composition but evidently decided against it.

For the continuation of his Heine collection, Wolf left the *Buch der Lieder* altogether and turned to the *Neue Gedichte*, written in the early 1830s at the start of Heine's self-exile in Paris. The poems closest in manner to the *Buch der Lieder* had also, like the earlier volume, attracted considerable attention from composers. Challier lists a total of seventy-three settings of "Es war ein alter König" composed before 1896,[59] including those by Ferdinand Hiller, Anton Rubinstein, and Heinrich Marschner, whose opera *Hans Heiling* Wolf admired. "Mit schwarzen Segeln" follows with twenty settings, while there are fourteen prior settings of "Sterne mit den goldnen Füsschen" and ten of "Wie des Mondes Abbild zittert." Franz set all three. "Spätherbstnebel," however, seems to have escaped musical appropriation altogether until Wolf's day, and Hans von Bülow's op. 1, no. 3 is the only other nineteenth-century setting of "Ernst ist der Frühling" that I have been able to locate.[60]

Heine was already complaining about "small songs" within the *Buch der Lieder*; clearly, change was imminent and followed shortly thereafter, with the prose of *Harzreise* (Journey in the Harz Mountains) and *Ideen: Das Buch LeGrand* (Ideas: the book of LeGrand). The poems of the *Neue Gedichte*, though, are a heterogeneous lot that includes both the reprise of old themes—a reprise in which "the poetry of unrequited love consumes and destroys itself"[61]—and a newly coarse treatment of sensual satiety. The first section, deceptively entitled "Neuer Frühling" (New spring), consists mostly of poems in which Love is not only bitter and degrading but inconsequential, a waste of time and energy that removes one from spheres of action. In the "Prolog," for example, a knight is bound captive in flower garlands woven by amoretti while others fight "in the great fight of the age." Throughout the section, an ambiguous spring turns progressively more somber, desolation and ennui pervade, and autumn sets in with no intervening summer of the spirit. In the "Verschiedene" (the word denotes simultaneously the past participle of "verscheiden," meaning "deceased, dead, departed," and the adjective "different, sundry, diverse"), or cycles each of which centers on a particular woman, unrequited love largely vanishes from the scene and is replaced by a series of erotic episodes, a celebration of sensuality that ranges from playful Anacreontic moods to cynicism about creatures he no longer expects to be anything other than dissipated. The poet's disgust with his Baudelairean hell of sensuality approaches the puritanical: if God is no longer alive, Heine implies, Venus is, and she is not a beneficent goddess.[62] One remembers Baudelaire asking, apropos of Heine, why a poet should not be someone who concocts poisons as well as candy ("un broyeur de poisons aussi bien qu'un confiseur").[63] Wolf chose only one poem from the "Verschiedene," and it is not among the more cynical and erotic; "Mit schwarzen Segeln" from the Seraphine cycle sounds the familiar theme of accusation against the woman for her cruelty to him and might, Walker suggests, have appealed to Wolf in part because of his sufferings over Vally.

Two examples from the later songs can serve as indices of a swift progression away from Schumann's influence and increasing evidence of Wolf's own mature style to come. The autumn mists that arise and envelop the landscape in "Spätherbstnebel" suggested to Wolf a recurrent figure in the accompaniment reminiscent of Schubert's evocation of the East Wind's arrival in "Suleika I," D. 720, a figure that Schubert reserves for the introduction only (Examples 10a and 10b). Even the unharmonized measured bass "trill" in "Spätherbstnebel," an intensification of the dominant before the descent back to tonic in measures 4, 8, 16, and 27, recalls Schubert's use of a similar measured trill in "Im Dorfe" (In the village) from *Winterreise*, or the unharmonized figures that serve as corridors, as stark transition passages from one section of a song to the next in that same cycle. The division of the song into sections in parallel minor and major modes, the latter thoroughly anticipated by the chromatic procedures in the former, is also famously Schubertian. And certainly Heine's poem, a variation on the familiar theme of *paysage* as soulscape, with the autumn desolation symbolic of the poet's being and the single evergreen emblematic of "her" image in his heart, might remind some of Wilhelm Müller's more original permutation of nineteenth-century connectives between Nature and humanity in "Letzte Hoffnung" (Last hope), with its autumn trees swiftly stripped of their last remaining leaves. But if the lineage stems more from Schubert than from Schumann (generally speaking, the Hoffmann von Fallersleben settings that come between the first and second installments of Heine lieder are the transition from one model to the next,[64] although such matters are never clear-cut, and the hallmarks of Schumann's influence do not vanish from the scene in the autumn of 1878), there is ample indication of Wolf's own present and future predilections, especially in the prominent mediant "markers" for the lost beloved's green, "unentlaubt" tree. The passage through C major–A minor/A major–C♯ major and hence into the concluding section/stanza in the major mode, incorporating the mediant of both modes, once more features the third relationships toward which Wolf had already demonstrated an inclination. It is tempting to find a trace element of Wagner in the fortissimo deceptive motion at the end of the vocal part, the elision past the "vielgeliebte schöne Frau" to conclusion in the accompaniment, the entire lied actually directed beyond the words, into futility and the resumption of focus on the rising mists.

Example 10a. Franz Schubert, "Suleika I," D. 720, measures 1–5

Example 10b. Hugo Wolf, "Spätherbstnebel," measures 1–6

Spät - herbst - ne - bel, kal - te Träu - me,

Of all the Heine settings, the clearest index of "Wölferl's own howl" is heard in "Ernst ist der Frühling," which seems in retrospect a study for the Mörike lied "Im Frühling" ten years before the fact. One wonders if Wolf remarked the resemblance when he came to compose the later masterpiece. The two songs share the same $\frac{6}{4}$ meter, the similar interplay of triple and duple divisions of the measure, and, most notably, the interwoven motion of the individual melodic lines in the piano and the vocal part, the instrumental melodies and the singer's part of equal importance over a bass foundation in even dotted half-notes (Examples 11a and 11b). "Ernst ist der Frühling" is, not surprisingly, the less complex of the two lieder, the setting of a simpler poem. Here, Heine wishes that his beloved's laughter might turn to tears that will both match the melancholy springtime and provide him the erotic pleasure of kissing them away, a far cry from Mörike's compound of elements: a yearning for an "all-einzige Liebe" (all-unifying love), a mysterious sense that Nature desires something of him, and a meditation on memory. Wolf does not sustain the melodic interplay throughout the Heine song as he does so beautifully in the lengthier later work, nor does he counterbalance so many different voices; in 1878, the contrapuntal texture of the beginning gives way at times to repeated chordal figuration and the doubling of the vocal line in the piano. But

Example 11a. Hugo Wolf, "Ernst ist der Frühling," measures 1–8

Example 11b. Hugo Wolf, "Im Frühling" from the *Mörike-Lieder*, measures 1–9

the seamless motivic development throughout much of the accompaniment foreshadows the similar, more extensive melodic designs of "Im Frühling," and the enharmonic pivot at the imperative, "O weine lieber!"—at which tonic A♭ is respelled as G♯ leading to A major—is an extraordinarily effective gesture by which to heighten the lover's longing for shared sensual sadness. The arpeggiation in the postlude and the prominence of the flatted sixth degree within the context of major mode seem also a clear precursor of the postlude to Eichendorff's "Verschwiegene Liebe" (Silent love), composed in 1888. Hearing such marked omens of Wolf's later songs in "Ernst ist der Frühling," rather than echoes of *Dichterliebe*, one realizes how swiftly the apprenticeship immersion in Schumann's style had progressed. The reliance on models and the accession to compositional maturity did not conclude overnight with the composition of this song, or even the more premonitory settings of Mörike's "Mausfallensprüchlein" and Justinus Kerner's "Zur Ruh', zur Ruh'" in 1882 and 1883 respectively, but the hints of future independence and mastery are quite strong.

WHEN THE *Liederstrauß* reached an impasse and an end with the fragmentary "Das gelbe Laub erzittert" (Example 12), so too ended Wolf's attraction to Heine for song composition. Only once more, on 24 January 1888, ten years later, would Wolf return to Heine and set a single poem to music, "Wo wird einst der Wandermüden" (Weary of wandering, where will I find my final rest?), and the difference in musical quality between it and the outpouring of Mörike songs that followed just three weeks later is a revelation of poetic tastes entirely changed in the interim. However objectively controlled, whatever the poetic distance, Heine's own subjective experience is the source of the entire *Buch der Lieder*; Heine himself said that the collection was a psychological portrait of its author ("diese Buch wurde mein Hauptbuch sein und ein psychologisches Bild von mir geben"[65]). When he wrote to a friend in 1822 to describe the critical furor that had already arisen, he was obliged to qualify the distinction between poet and poetry: "Everywhere I look, I perceive how much they grumble about me (as a poet) and will continue to do so."[66] The defensive nature of the verbal strategem is revealing. Wolf, who extolled "rigorous, harsh, and inexorable truth" as the sovereign principle in art,[67] would later praise the literature that pleased him most for its psychological insight, but such insight was, for him, the product of artistic detachment from the purely personal. The poetic voice, half sarcastic, half self-pitying, that could write "Out of their sleep I shook every tree; they nodded their heads in pity for me"[68] was ultimately not to Wolf's taste, but the instinct that brought Wolf to Schumann as a model for musical self-education entailed a corresponding immersion, for a time, in Heine's poetry.

Wolf was well aware of his dependence on Schumann. When a musician in Graz—one Friedrich von Hausegger—characterized four of Wolf's early songs as "Mendelssohnian in character," the composer reacted angrily, admitting, however, "A strong Schumannian trait runs through the songs, especially in the 'Traurige Wege' [Sorrowful paths], but Mendelssohn?"[69] Wolf even undertook to pass off some of his own imitations of Schumann as the genuine article at a recital given by the Austrian Alpine Society, probably in 1882, but the master of ceremonies gave away the hoax by his manner of

Example 12. Hugo Wolf, "Das gelbe Laub erzittert" (fragment)

introduction, and the infuriated Wolf ran off the stage and disappeared.[70] Anecdotes aside, the songs, completed and uncompleted, reveal an impressive autodidactic process by swift stages, from close echoes of a famous Heine-Schumann lied to assimilation and beyond. But despite the importance of the Schumannesque lieder in the composer's growth to compositional maturity, he would later choose to publish only the last of the lot in his 1897 *Vier Gedichte nach Heine, Shakespeare und Lord Byron* (Four poems after Heine, Shakespeare, and Lord Byron). If "Wo wird einst" is not Wolf at his best, at least it is Wolf, not imitation-Schumann.

Wolf's apprenticeship years did not end with the Heine *Liederstrauß*. Heine no longer being his man, he transferred his allegiance to Eichendorff, composing "Erwartung" (Expectation) and "Die Nacht" (The night) in early 1880, "Nachruf" (In memoriam) in the summer 1880, and the *Sechs geistliche Lieder nach Gedichten von Eichendorff* (Six sacred songs to poems by Eichendorff) for mixed chorus in 1881. In June of 1881, he began composition of the first lied in another small set of songs collectively entitled *In der Fremde* (In a strange land), the second and third songs following two years later in 1883. Wolf had earlier planned to compose a group of Eichendorff ballads; a title page dating perhaps from 1878 in the Vienna City Library lists three *Romanzen von J. von Eichendorff*, settings of "Der Kehraus" (The last dance), "Das zerbrochene Ringlein" (The broken circlet), and "Der traurige Jäger" (The sorrowful hunter) that were subsequently lost.[71] From the beginning, Wolf avoided the specific texts already set by Schumann, although the poems Wolf chose for the *In der Fremde* lieder—"Da fahr' ich still im Wagen" (I journey, silent, by coach), "Ich geh' durch die dunkle Gassen" (I go through the dark streets), and "Wolken, wälderwärts gegangen" (Clouds, departed for the forest)—exemplify the themes and images for which Eichendorff is best known, the poetic style that had earlier inspired Schumann. Wolf would later reject Emil Kauffmann's suggestion of an Eichendorff prose work as a possible source for an opera libretto, saying that the typical *clair-obscur* of the poet's lyrical landscapes was incompatible with dramatic necessity. The human figures lack clear outlines and psychological delineation; they are dream-phantoms, without physiognomy, without personality.[72] He had an intimate acquaintance with that *clair-obscur* landscape in the songs composed before 1888, before his choice of Eichendorff's "portrait gallery" poems, thumbnail sketches of sailors, students, wandering musicians, blustering mercenaries, and the like, for the majority of his twenty *Gedichte von Eichendorff* of 1889. In those poems, he found the clarity of outline and vivid human depictions he had come to recognize as most suited to his musical tastes.

The early Eichendorff songs represent an interesting later development in the course of Wolf's apprenticeship because he remains true to the textual choices of the Schumann disciples but is no longer able to sustain the enterprise. Walker says of the two 1883 *In der Fremde* songs that they "seem to show Wolf endeavouring to revive, without much conviction, the subjective romantic manner of four or five years earlier . . . the impulse which had then driven him on to exalted and passionate lyrical expression was no longer with him; the new songs cannot compare with the best of the Heine and Lenau settings of the earlier period."[73] The three texts of the *In der Fremde* set come from a cycle of six poems collectively entitled *Der verliebte Reisende* (The wanderer in love), and Wolf seems to have tried unsuccessfully to apply Wagnerian symphonic voice leading in the piano accompaniments to all three. There is never any pause in the constant motion of all the instrumental voices in "Da fahr' ich still im Wagen," perhaps inspired by the *gehendes Bewegung* of the coach, but lacking a sense of inevitability and ease. The awkwardness of the text-derived harmonic details is especially notable. The series of enharmonic changes, one after another, in measures 18–22 of the same song— perhaps to differentiate between the "beautiful, deep valleys" and the "larks high in the breezes"?—show Wolf experimenting once again with chord progressions, but in a forced manner.

Egon Schwarz writes of Eichendorff that no other poet uses so restricted a vocabulary, a language of symbolic hieroglyphs in which the recurrent words "forest, wells, moon, flower, rustle, streams, night, still, dream, valleys, stars, bushes, sun, birds, ground, trees," and so on, acquire a singular and near-mystic meaning.[74] (The language in which Wolf describes Nature in his letters shows the marked influence of Eichendorff.[75]) The images from Nature constitute a symbolic picture book of the poet's inner realm, more the interior creations of the poetic mind than external description. "The wide world" is a mode of being, not a place; the darkness or floods of light are spiritual states; the gardens with their rushing streams and profusion of flowers are the poet's workshop, fictions of the poetic imagination. The repeated motifs can have either a negative or positive connotation, can be emblematic of the world and the individual ego (beautiful and treacherous, a prison of subjectivity) or of the spiritual realm. The entire structure of the *Hieroglyphensymbolik* is based on the proposition that poets are impelled either toward or away from the highest love; the verbs "ziehen" (to pull, draw, drag, move, etc.) and "treiben" (to drive, push, force, impel, urge on, set in motion, etc.) abound. The dozens of poetic personas in Eichendorff's verses who hear the post horn, the hunters' horns in the forest, or unknown singers are compelled to follow the sounds, music thus a call to poetry and the eternal striving toward higher love. Wolf would not master this particular strain of Eichendorff's poetic magic until his setting of "Nachtzauber" (Night enchantment) on 24 May 1887, published in the *Eichendorff-Lieder*. Three other early essays at mastering Eichendorff that were originally published in the Eichendorff volume but omitted from the second edition were "Erwartung" (26 January 1880), "Die Nacht" (3 February 1880), and "Waldmädchen" (Forest maiden; 20 April 1887).

IF THE songs of *In der Fremde* are failures within the youthful repertoire, others anticipate the mature style of 1888 and beyond. Before the compositionally arid years as a music critic from 1884 to 1887, he composed two songs that are especially premonitory of "Wölferl's own howl"—the 1882 setting of Mörike's "Mausfallen-Sprüchlein" and Justinus Kerner's "Zur Ruh', zur Ruh', ihr müden Glieder!" (To rest, to rest, you tired limbs) of 1883. In "Mausfallen-Sprüchlein" (Magic charm for mousers), Wolf for the first time taps a vein of humor in music that would become a special province of his art (see Chapter 2),[76] while "Zur Ruh', zur Ruh'" demonstrates a greater command of the chromatic idiom he handled less skillfully in the two Eichendorff songs for *In der Fremde* composed that same year. The text by Kerner (1786–1862) is a unicum in Wolf's works, the only song to poetry by this minor poet and friend of Eduard Mörike. It is possible that the poem appealed to Wolf for musical setting in part because it depicts the hour of death from a stance other than Christian; Wolf may have already abandoned the Catholic observances of his pious mother. Distraught over the end of his love affair with Vally Franck in 1881, he had set the Eichendorff choruses to texts about death, farewell, and resignation to God's will, within the framework of Eichendorff's Catholic beliefs; he found in Kerner's poem a similar concern with last things but without mention of God or Christ. Whatever drew him to the text for musical purposes, the song marks a significant point in Wolf's early works because it harks back to the model of Schumann—in particular, to that composer's "Zum Schluß" (In conclusion) at the end of the *Myrthen* cycle ("Zum Schluß" and "Zur Ruh', zur Ruh'" share the same A♭-major tonality)—and yet the musical language is modern and his own.

Kerner was an interesting eccentric, a physician and occultist fascinated by what he called "the night-realm of Nature." Could Wolf have known in 1883 that "Zur Ruh', zur Ruh'" is the poetic expression of ideas contained in Kerner's best-known prose work, *Die Seherin von Prevorst* (The seeress of Prevorst), an account of the "magnetic powers" of one Frederike Hauffe? It is unlikely, but he would later avidly read secondary literature about Mörike and his other favorite poets and comment excitedly on his discoveries of the genesis of Mörike's "Auf eine Christblume I" and the biographical inception of the same poet's Peregrina songs. Kerner introduces his treatise with "disclosures concerning the inner life of man," in which he distinguishes between external life and the inner self:

> This external life is the dominion of the brain—the intellect which belongs to the world—while the inner life dwells in the region of the heart, within the sphere of sensitive life, in the sympathetic and ganglionic system . . . by virtue of this inner life, mankind is bound up in an eternal connection with nature, from which his imperfect external existence can

only apparently release him. . . . it is this secret unseen connection with nature which unites man with the other world, and conducts him on his way towards it.[77]

The seeress, who saw ghosts and fell into a trance each evening at seven o'clock, also describes the distinction between the soul (*Seele*) and spirit (*Geist*), analyzing in detail the relations between spirit, soul, and body at various stages in the process of dying. Thirty years later, Kerner would profess the same conception of inner powers that act as a psychopompos to conduct the soul from life to life-after-death in his last volume of poetry, *Winterblüten* (Winter Flowers) of 1859. "Zur Ruh', zur Ruh'," the final poem in the collection, purports to be the self-address of a dying man who bids first the limbs (the body), then the eyes (sight, the senses) to loose their hold on life so that the inner powers within can lead him away from earthly sorrows, through night and dreams into the afterlife. For light, or spiritual illumination, finally to be his, the night of death must fall.

> Zur Ruh', zur Ruh', ihr müden Glieder!
> Schließt fest euch zu, ihr Augenlider!
> Ich bin allein, fort ist die Erde;
> Nacht muß es sein, daß Licht mir werde.
>
> O führt mich ganz, ihr innern Mächte!
> Hin zu dem Glanz der tiefsten Nächte.
> Fort aus dem Raum der Erden-Schmerzen,
> Durch Nacht und Traum zum Mutterherzen!

(To rest, to rest, tired limbs! Close tightly shut, eyelids! I am alone; earthly life is vanishing; it must be night for light to be mine. O lead me, ye inner powers! Lead me forth into the glory of the deepest nights. Quickly from the realm of earthly sorrows, through night and dream to the mother's heart!)

Kerner slows the poetic rhythm to a solemn pace at the beginning with the multiple *ts* sounds of "zur," the elongation natural to a succession of *u* vowels in close proximity, and the multiple consonants that render difficult, and therefore slower, the transition from word to word in the line "Schließt fest euch zu." The difficulty of enunciating all those multiple consonant clusters conveys in sound the resolution required to shut out earthly light, to make the passage from life to death.

What forecasts Wolf's mature manner in "Zur Ruh', zur Ruh'" is the combination, fully achieved, of motivic development in abstract terms, chromatic voice leading, carefully disposed prosody, and close attention to the nuances of the text. There is no introduction per se (does this seem so appropriate because the poem tells of the last minutes of life and we are told nothing of what led up to it?). Rather, the string-quartet texture in the instrumental part—a texture that recurs frequently in the later songs—begins the process of sinking to rest, the instrumental and vocal phrases elided throughout measures 1–16, the first half of the song, to produce a continual gentle motion with no stressed resting points that are conjunct for both members of the ensemble until measure 16. The ending of the piano's initial phrase at the beginning of measure 4 and the beginning of its second phrase, a varied restatement of the same progression (a prolongation of the tonic in which the subdominant is emphasized), are elided. The manner in which Wolf develops and varies the melodic sequence in the topmost voice of the piano in measures 7–14 while extending the initial chromatic fragment G♭–F–F♭–E♭ from measures 1–3 in the vocal line of measures 9–12 ("Ich bin allein, fort ist die Erde"), the instrumental and voice parts overlapping, shows the results of his enthusiastic self-tutelage from Wagner. This first half of the song is even somewhat bar line-bound, after the manner of Wagner's rhythmic practice on many occasions. Wolf does not complete the tonic cadence in measures 15–16 in the piano—that is to come later ("werde")—but sounds a soft fanfare on the unharmonized tonic pitch, leading to the enharmonic change of key at the invocation of "innern Mächte." The actual harmonic rhythm is unchanged in the E-major section (measures 17–26), but Wolf maintains a constant quarter-note tactus in all but the topmost voice of the piano, the increased rhythmic activity and marchlike manner indicative of the guiding progression for which the persona pleads. "O führt mich ganz," he prays, and the piano does so even as he speaks. The increasing certainty of safe passage, the presence of guidance, are indicated in the second half of the song in several ways: the doubling of the vocal line in the piano (note the piano's anticipatory stress on the weakbeat B in measure 18 at the word "*ihr* in-[nern Mächte]"), the thicker texture created by the addition of more chord voices, and the inexorable ascent of the bass from low E/D♯ to A♭ (measure 28) an octave and a half higher. The latter transposes and varies the same intervallic gulf one finds between the "night that must be" and the "light to come" in the last vocal phrase of the first half ("Nacht muß es sein, daß Licht mir werde"), with its dramatic leap from one state of being to another. If there is no introduction, there *is* a postlude, an extension of measures 1–2 that sinks gradually downward an octave lower than the beginning. When the words cease, the sinking-to-rest promised in the initial measures is completed in the instrumental part; the final progression reiterates the ♭$\hat{6}$–$\hat{5}$ pitches prominent from the beginning and unfolded in the E-major enharmonic development from F♭. The song is a considerable achievement for one so young, still five years away from the outpouring of Mörike songs in 1888.

To achieve a style of one's own does not mean that music composed from that time onward excludes music by others and ceases to make use of preexistent structural procedures, formulas for harmonic prolongations, motives, melodic contours, accompaniment patterns, and the like. Christopher Hatch demonstrates Wolf's use of fragments taken from earlier *Wanderlieder*, including several by Schumann, in the Mörike song "Fussreise" (Journey on foot),[78] and similar mosaic chips from Wagner, Schumann, Schubert, and lesser lights are to be found in other Wolf songs as well. Rethinking and reworking the ideas of others is something composers past their apprenticeship do as well as those learning the trade, but the materials not invented de novo tend to be more obtrusive, less skillfully interwoven into the whole structure, in the youthful works. Dependence on models is more overt then. By February of 1888, Wolf no longer needed to rely so heavily and in such conscious awareness on models, on Schumann in particular. One wonders what he thought when he looked through the early, unpublished manuscripts; perhaps he remembered the lines from Eichendorff's "Wolken, wälderwärts gegangen" that he had set while still an apprentice in the craft of composition:

> Manches Lied, das ich geschrieben
> wohl vor manchem langen Jahr,
> Da die Welt von treuem Lieben
> Schön mir überglanzet war,
>
> Find ich's wieder jetzt voll Bangen:
> Werd ich wunderbar gerührt,
> Denn so lange ist vergangen,
> Was mich zu dem Lied verführt.[79]

(Many a song that I wrote many a long year ago, when the world was brilliantly illuminated for me with faithful love, I revisit now full of fear—then I am strangely moved, because what led me to the song is so long vanished.)

CHAPTER 2

Of Wolf, Freud, and Humor in Music

> Today I have composed the "beautiful, hungry Toni" ["Ich liess mich sagen" or "I inquired and was told" from the *Italienisches Liederbuch*]—how? That is impossible to describe. I only know one thing, that humor in music has for the first time entered the world in this song. I myself am speechless over it and ask myself: have you, *you*, really found this music? Heaven only knows who gave me these tones. Today I am (a glorious day) so much in the mood to write that I will probably compose a second song as well.[1]

THIS PASSAGE from a letter to Melanie Köchert[2] was written on 28 March 1896, only three days after Wolf began once more composing songs to poems from Paul Heyse's *Italienisches Liederbuch*, an anthology of Italian folk poems in German translation.[3] Wolf often announced new compositions to his friends in a hyperbolically exuberant tone, toward the end of his creative life disquietingly close to mania,[4] and his jubilation in full creative flood tide must be taken with a grain of salt. "Ich liess mich sagen" is not the first example of humor in music; it is not even the first instance in Wolf's own lieder. But if the claim is untrue at one level, it is accurate at another. Wolf *did* in fact create something new by turning the resources of the late-Romantic tonal language to comic use, by harnessing the chromatic alterations of post-Wagnerian compositional craft to humor of a psychologizing kind, imbued with all the complexities of nuance that one finds in the lyrical or serious songs. The under- and overtones of comedy, its origins in and transformation of rage, envy, hatred, and spite, were no news to literature, but comic ambivalence and complexity had been largely filtered from the lied until Wolf (Vesque von Püttlingen's settings of Heine are among the few exceptions, and his musically puerile songs are not part of the standard repertoire). The comic songs are also definable as Oedipal victories. In the early 1880s, Wolf lamented on several occasions that he was born too late, that there was nothing remaining for composers to do after Wagner, except possibly in the fields of lied and comic opera—genres that Wolf promptly claimed as his own.[5] In songs such as "Wie lange schon war immer mein Verlangen" (How long I have yearned) from the *Italienisches Liederbuch*, Wolf has the last laugh, as a Wagnerian leitmotif for Desire and a series of enharmonic reinterpretations of that figure, both the melodic figures and the transformative process born of *Tristan*, become a laughing matter. The weak-beat accent and the prolongation of the tonic pitch across the bar line, as well as the languishing, drooping profile, would, in an operatic context, have spurred the Wolzogens of the world into a naming frenzy. And yet the joke is Janus-faced, and its other side is Wolf's partisan allegiance to the Wagnerians and the avant-garde. The inept, "peaches and cream" musician who makes his entrance at the end plays regressively diatonic music, no match in intensity for what precedes it.[6]

Wolf had a penchant for comic songs and wrote more of them than any other significant lieder composer in the nineteenth and early twentieth centuries. It seems hardly coincidental that his first comic masterpiece, one of the earliest songs to evince Wolf's mature style before 1888, is also his first non-balladesque choice from the poetry of Eduard Mörike (1804–75): "Mausfal-len-Sprüchlein" (Magic charm for mousers), composed 18 June 1882. By then, Wolf understood his dual dependence both on good poetry and on verse not previously claimed by his great predecessors, unless he felt that the earlier setting was flawed in some way. Wolf would not set Mörike's more profound poems until six years later, but the rapidly changing poetic meters and line lengths of this magic charm for mousers, its colloquial tone and the vivacity of its brief phrases, were new to Wolf's songs. Not only were the whimsy and malice of Mörike's text perfectly to Wolf's taste, but the poem does not invite echoes of Schumann, Schubert, Wagner, or Loewe. Notably, it was while studying *Parsifal* and while following a Wagnerian vegetarian diet (the sausage-loving composer did not stay on it for long) that Wolf invented so delicate a species of musical humor. Freed by his choice of verse to rely on his own devices, Wolf composed a blueprint for the comic songs to follow. Recognizing its merit, he later selected "Mausfallen-Sprüchlein" and five other early songs, all composed between 1877 and late 1882, for inclusion in the *Sechs Lieder für eine Frauenstimme* (Six songs for a woman's voice) of 1888, his first publication.[7]

A first blueprint, perfectly executed, deserves examination.[8] What marks the humor as uniquely Wolf's is a combination of factors, in particular, the multiple pictorializing figures—Wolf was never content merely to establish a general atmosphere—and the sophistication with which elements of melodic invention, tonality, harmony, voice leading, and rhythm are calibrated to the text. The poem too foreshadows Wolf's later choices of comic verse in its vitality, strong spice of malice, and psychological realism. Like all children, the child who issues this enticing invitation to revelry in the rodent world has a streak of cruelty. She knows the fatal coda even as she sings of "little guests," of closing the door carefully lest tails be nipped, of dancing in concert around the table, and she anticipates the denouement with glee. Her vitality and naive malice are inseparable.

> (Das Kind geht dreimal um die Falle und spricht:)
> Kleine Gäste, kleines Haus.
> Liebe Mäusin oder Maus,

Stell dich nur kecklich ein
Heut Nacht bei Mondenschein!
Mach aber die Tür fein hinter dir zu,
Hörst du?
Dabei hüte dein Schwänzchen!
Nach Tische singen wir,
Nach Tische springen wir
Und machen ein Tänzchen:
Witt witt!
Meine alte Katze tanzt wahrscheinlich mit.[9]

(The child walks three times around the trap and says: Little guests, little house, dear Miss or Mister Mouse, come out boldly tonight into the moonlight! But close the door behind you very carefully, do you hear? Beware for your tiny tail! After dinner we'll sing, after dinner we'll spring about and do a little dance: Witt, witt! My old cat will probably join us in the dance.)

Wolf translates the childish malice beneath the overt sweetness (the accompaniment is marked "Sehr zart" or "very sweet" at the beginning) into tension between the voice and piano, the kind of conflict characteristic of his mature songs. The dissonant tritones and sevenths between the outer voices and the cross relation in measure 6 of C♮ and C♯ result from clashes in voice leading between the diatonic motive in measures 1–10 of the right-hand part, with its tapping repeated notes and grace-noted intervallic leaps evocative of prancing mice; the largely diatonic vocal line, appropriately consonant with the right-hand part; and the "bass" and "tenor" voices in the left hand. Mörike directs the child to walk three times around the mousetrap before singing, and Wolf continues the miniature compass around the tonic note in the bottommost voice, taking suitably small semitone steps. Most of the chromatic pitches, especially the F♯ and G♯ passing tones and appoggiaturas, foreshadowing the later mediant regions, lurk suitably at the bottom of the texture, like the intent to do mischief, until the turn to the mediant A minor in measures 8–11. (Was Wolf indulging in a musical pun of sorts in measure 6, with undisguised parallel fifths to match the adverb "kecklich"?) The mediant (extended tonic) has the effect of removal to a genuinely enchanted sphere, such that the voice-piano conflicts disappear; the bass line actually doubles the voice an octave lower, rather than clashing with it.[10] With the child's injunction to close the door carefully, the soprano-bass dissonance returns, and so does the tonic key.

Comedy is in the telling: "Mausfallen-Sprüchlein" is filled with "special effects," including mimicry or echoes between the voice and piano, and extravagant leaps from one register to another. However, the comic clichés, such as the stream of descending parallel sixth-chords in measure 24—ballroom dancing gestures—and a laughably simple Alberti bass in measures 25–28, are incorporated into a unified structure. For example, at the declamatory warning "Mach' aber die Tür fein hinter dir zu" in measures 13–15, Wolf brings back the bass motive from measure 1 as a rhythmically augmented trill figure whose rising melodic chromaticism spoofs the menace beneath the small hostess's seeming concern. The repeated motive of a rising third for the mouse-and-child festivities in measures 25–29 is derived from the grace-note figures in measures 3–10. The prominent flatted sixth degree of F or Db for the threat of feline company in measures 32–34, the comic effect augmented by the unison figures and consecutive augmented triads associated with high drama and menace, recalls and reinterprets the preceding third scale degree of A major and the sixth scale degree of E major earlier in the song. In principle, this is little different from Wolf's serious songs in which text-derived details are part of a coherent musical structure, but the extra élan vital of Wolfian comedy comes as well from the delight in emphasis of all kinds: a plethora of trill figures and grace notes; abrupt and frequent registral contrasts; numerous offbeat accents and rhythmic displacements that accentuate mockery and playfulness; and prosodic stresses. Wolf both accents the first syllable of "*wahr*scheinlich," hinting broadly that probability is really certainty, and sets the syllable to a weak-beat D♮, reestablished after the D♭s of the preceding phrase. The invocation of the "old cat" is then elided with the repeated injunctions "Hörst du?" (Wolf's repetitions, not Mörike's) in a single $\frac{5}{8}$ measure, the metrical singularity heightening the mingled piquancy and malice. The nervous intensity that results from a combination of these factors—multiple means of emphasis, the delicate spoof of musical clichés, the refusal to equate childlike humor with lack of tonal sophistication—is new to comic song and, somewhat miraculously, appears full-fledged with Wolf's first entry in the lists.

WOLF AND FREUD: TENDENTIOUS HUMOR IN SONG

After "Mausfallen-Sprüchlein," Wolf wrote few comic songs, indeed, few songs at all during the lean years until early 1888. By that time, he had suffered several crushing professional disappointments, especially the humiliating premiere of his symphonic tone poem inspired by Kleist's *Penthesilea*,[11] and knew what it was to be bitterly angry at the power-mongers and Philistines who stood in his way, including enemies that "the wild Wolf" had made during his four-year stint as a music critic for the *Wiener Salonblatt* from 1884 to 1887. When he returned to Mörike and comic songs once again in 1888–89, he chose poems in which a momentary revenge was possible—poems in which critics, poets and half-poets, composers, lovers, and other denizens of the adult world were his targets. Those familiar with late-nineteenth-century investigations into the psychic mechanisms of comedy, especially Theodor Lipp's *Komik und Humor* (Comedy and humor) of 1898 and Freud's 1905 study *Jokes and Their Relation to the Unconscious*, might be struck by the applicability of their analyses to Wolf's favored comedic styles and subjects. In particular, Freud's discussions of "tendentious jokes," originating in resentment, rage, hostility, and culminating in the psychic discharge of laughter, can help to clarify Wolf's bent for comic songs: "A joke will allow us to exploit something ridiculous in our enemy which we could not, on account of obstacles in the way, bring forward openly or unconsciously; once again, then, the joke *will evade restrictions and open sources of pleasure that have become inaccessible*" (Freud's italics).[12] The "restrictions" are inhibitions, suppressing impulses that the joke assists in overcoming, and the result is pleasure seemingly disproportionate to the means of attainment. Because tendentious jokes must overcome repressions both within the tale-teller and his audience, Freud designates them as the highest form of joke and points to their unique properties of disarmament, that is, the manner in which jokes block criticism of the thoughts they contain, however socially unacceptable.[13] For example, caricature, a subspecies of the tendentious-comic, begins with anger against persons or institutions who lay claim to authority and respect, such as critics and arbiters of taste and judgment in the arts (Mörike's "Abschied" or "Farewell"). The caricaturist safely retaliates with the comic degradation of his enemy or enemies, rendering them ludicrous by isolating an intrinsically funny trait and by emphasizing physical deformity rather than attacking the spiritual or intellectual realms in which the authority is vested.[14] Resorting to assault and battery in actuality is inadvisable, if tempting, but the enemy *can* be "physically" punished in a joke, however savagely the repressing mechanisms will allow. Critics who wield such power over poets (and composers) are ridiculed in "Abschied" for their arrogance and for the nonsensical grounds on which they make injurious judgments. The fictive poet narrating the poem politely endures—for a while—the presence of an uninvited critic who mocks the poet's nose (Freud would, of course, explain the "nose" as a displaced phallic symbol), but in an obsequiously formal manner. At last, the narrator abandons etiquette altogether and kicks the creature down the stairs. In Freud's terminology, a preconscious thought (criticism of critics) is given over for a moment to unconscious revision and the outcome is at once grasped by conscious perception, emerging as a joke—wish-fulfillment after a manner different from that in dreams.[15] "Oh, if only . . ." evades that which would suppress it and becomes, triumphantly, "It is."

Wolf, of course, did not write the comic verse that he set to music. In his youth, he tried his hand at comic ballads and doggerel poems, but recognized their mediocrity. Rather, Wolf was, first, audience for the joke when he read the poems and then a companion-jokester with the poet when he set the poem to music, one who tells the joke to yet another audience. Because poetry consists of words and meanings, a composer's choice of texts reveals aspects of personal taste, even of personality, and those themes for which the composer has the greatest affinity. The indices are complex because the purpose is musical setting, not self-revelation or confession—but the selection of comic verse is possibly the most indicative of personal concerns. "Where he makes a jest, a problem lies concealed," Goethe once observed: Freud cited this aphorism approvingly and added, "The jest is simultaneously the solution to the problem."[16] Wolf, nicknamed "Fluchu" for the ingenuity and variety of his cursing, was a personality given to extremes; he loved and hated intensely, and his resentments, such as his virulent "anti-Brahmimentum" (Wolf's own term for his detestation of Brahms), were not small. By setting certain comic poems to music, he could safely attack people, institutions, and situations that threatened his well-being, could humiliate and mock critics, pedants, unreliable Muses, bad poets, ridiculous musicians, even revered masters (Wagner the "Obergott,"[17] or "God above all others"—Wolf's designation parodies, painfully, religious veneration for supreme deities) from whose influence the apprentice wishes to be freed, as in the "Gesellenlied" of Robert Reinick.[18] If Wolf could not punish his adversaries as he would have liked ("They shall be roasted in hell's brimstone and immersed in dragon's poison"[19]), he could make them musical targets of malice. Furthermore, and just as important, jokes require an audience that is lured by the pleasure of the experience into agreement with its agent. "To draw the one who laughs to his side" ("die Lacher auf seine Seite ziehen") is, Freud says, a principal purpose of telling jokes. By demonstrating the comic capabilities of late-Romantic chromaticism, Wolf could also hope to attract new converts to his cause with the lure of pleasure.

Freud might have found one group of Wolf's comic songs particularly interesting, the choice of texts overdetermined by poetic and musical factors, by predilection, and, perhaps, by the aftermath of events in the composer's life. The biographical fallacy is rightly condemned when it takes the form of naive parallelisms between life and art, and the mystery of creativity remains just that—a mystery—but neither are the artist and the work entirely separable quantities. Almost one-third of Wolf's *Italienisches Liederbuch* consists of songs for women who revile, dismiss, mock, or reproach their inconsiderate, faithless, and unsatisfactory lovers. In the final show-stopper of the volume, "Ich hab' in Penna," a woman of irresistible verve and ingenuity boasts of her multiple lovers, that is, of her power over more than one man. Ten of these women's songs—no. 10, "Du denkst mit einem Fädchen mich zu fangen" (You think you can catch me with a little thread); no. 15, "Mein Liebster ist so klein" (My sweetheart is so small); no. 11, "Wie lange schon war immer mein Verlangen" (How long I have yearned); no. 12, "Nein, junger Herr" (No, young sir, this just won't do); no. 43, "Schweig' einmal still" (Do be quiet, you wretched chatterer); no. 46, "Ich hab' in Penna einen Liebsten wohnen" (I have one lover living in Penna); no. 26, "Ich liess mir sagen und mir ward erzählt" (I inquired and was told); no. 16, "Ihr jungen Leute" (You young folk); no. 24, "Ich esse nun mein Brot nicht trocken mehr" (I no longer eat my bread dry); and no. 25, "Mein Liebster hat zu Tische mich geladen" (My sweetheart invited me to dinner)—are comic. One reason for Wolf's choice was surely the attraction of a fresh poetic repertoire.[20] The adder-tongued women of the *Italienisches Liederbuch* had not been courted by composers before Wolf. Heyse's choice of folk poems is also a determining factor, as most of the comic poems in the anthology are in a woman's voice. The comic poems for male personas are an uninspiring lot, almost all of them harmlessly irreverent "pope jokes," in which a cardinal, bishop, pope, or priest gives the nod to carnal love so long as the sweetheart is pretty. Whether or not the anticlerical Wolf felt any compunctions about publishing such texts in Catholic Austria, the humor is not sufficiently acute for his taste.[21] But one wonders if some of the women's songs might not also have been an unconsciously directed way of giving Melanie Köchert a musical voice for the tensions of their secret relationship, especially in the aftermath of two crises in 1893 and 1894, between the composition of Part 1 in 1891 and Part 2 in 1896. Heinrich Köchert, Melanie's husband and a generous patron of Wolf's, discovered the existence of Wolf's and Melanie's nine-year affair in 1893, and the following year, Wolf fell briefly in love with the mezzo-soprano Frieda Zerny and broke off his longstanding relationship with Melanie for a short time. Wolf's diaries, Melanie's letters, and Wolf's intimate letters to her were all destroyed, and speculative exercises in psychobiography may have nothing to do with his choices of poetry. Still, the possibility that the women of the *Italienisches Liederbuch* might represent surrogate selves through whom Melanie could reproach the cause of her love and distress is intriguing, if inaccessible to proof.

WOLF'S COMEDIC PRINCIPLES

Mörike's comedy differs from Eichendorff's, Eichendorff's from Goethe's, and Goethe's from folk poetry, but there are certain general principles that one can observe in Wolf's comic settings from "Mausfallen-Sprüchlein" to the end of his life. Emphatic creature that he was, he was always attracted to exaggeration, Rabelaisian excess and comic melodrama, to the laughter that is generated when gestures are more extravagant than the occasion warrants. Second, he sought to compress multiple comic details, musical nuances inspired by the text, into both the piano part and the vocal line, but especially in the piano. Assaulted at every instant and from all sides by comic gestures, the listener cannot help but laugh. And finally, whatever the verbal device, the joke becomes primarily a musical jest. Examples of all three general principles combined in a single song abound. In "Ich esse nun mein Brot nicht trocken mehr" (I no longer eat my bread dry),[22] we seem to hear a full-grown and passionate woman melodramatically lamenting the fact that she does not have a lover, and Wolf accordingly gives her the "grown-up" tonality of E♭ minor; string-quartet texture in the accompaniment; a series of descending whole-tone and semitone figures evocative of falling tears; "adult" harmonies, such as diminished-seventh chords and the Neapolitan sixth that heightens the verb "[nicht] trocken"; a suitably anguished emphasis in the vocal line on the tritone A♭–D within the dominant-seventh chord; and a series of dotted rhythmic patterns whose slurring mimics Scotch-snap rhythm, as if the singer were stumbling through tears. "Ein Dorn ist mir im Fusse stecken blieben" (A thorn got stuck in my foot), she proclaims to a suitably "thorny" chromatic progression in measures 3–4 that both dramatizes the raised sixth degree of the approach to B♭ minor and, in measure 4, begins a literal repetition ("stecken blieben") but does not continue that way. The crescendo to the change of key at the end of measure 4 culminates in a sudden hushed pianissimo for the arrival at B♭ minor and the transposition up a fifth of the previous passage from measures 1–2, the vocal line altered so that its twists and turns, its changes of direction mimic the motions in the text: "Umsonst nach rechts und links blick' ich umher" (In vain do I look right and left). The chromatic hand wringing is sufficiently melodramatic that the listener is all the more amused when the singer is revealed, in parallel major mode, to be about fourteen, the age of the "elderly little man" for whom she longs. The speaker delays the revelation of her true age until the last line, although the naively incongruous reference to an "altes Männlein" is the first hint of a comic conclusion. It is at this point that Wolf shifts to parallel major, to a "Gemächlich" (comfortable, moderate) cheeriness and far too many staccato notes for tragedy. The underlying joke for the cognoscenti is the identification of adult posturing with Wagnerian motivic development and intensive chromaticism and of contrasting childish satisfaction with a more diatonic strain. The contrast between regressive/childish/triumphant diatonicism and chromatic intensity is one that Wolf had already used to brilliant effect in the *Mörike-Lieder,* and it has an underlying didactic purpose we shall discover illustrated most extensively in that collection.

Still another example comes from the realm of grotesquerie, in which horror becomes comic and demons are domesticated as objects of laughter. The creator of comic grotesques uses exaggeration to bring what is fearful to the surface and render it, by overstatement, ludicrous as well as horrific. In "Bei einer Trauung" (At a wedding),[23] Mörike mocks the loveless arranged marriages of the aristocracy with a grotesque wedding scene—the bride weeps fiercely and the groom pulls faces—and a musical pun that Wolf found irresistible. "Der Himmel hängt voller Geigen," or "Things look rosy" (no literal translation is possible), becomes "Die Orgel hängt voll Geigen [the string-orchestra effects of saccharine wedding music for the organ], der Himmel nicht, mein' Treu!" The oath "mein' Treu!" and the repeated adverb "freilich, freilich" in the penultimate line ("Denn leider freilich, freilich / Keine Lieb' ist nicht dabei") are wonderfully ironic choices of wording. Throughout the right-hand part, Wolf repeats different transpositions and variants of the same three-note figure, each of the forty repetitions evocative of a short, sharp grimace above a funeral-march drone bass.[24] These figures are most often contained within the compass of a diminished third, fourth, or fifth; the descending contour formed by the repetitions of these motives in each of the piano interludes between vocal phrases outlines the harmony given in the left hand. (Wolf sets each line of the first stanza as a separate vocal phrase, rather than joining the first two lines—"Vor lauter hochadligen Zeugen / copulirt man ihrer Zwei," or "Before witnesses exclusively from the upper nobility, two of them are getting married"—together as musical prose. In this way, he both heightens the mock-suspenseful solemnity of the narration, especially as the first phrase culminates with the dramatic gesture of a dotted rhythmic leap of a perfect fifth to a normally weak beat, and enacts separation and disjunction—the true situation—in the phrase structure.) One can hear the repeated motives in the piano additionally as a musical metaphor for the forcible uniting of discordant elements: the dissonant nonchord tones are forced into conformity and resolution to chord tones, made to unite with the harmony below, but the conflict between them is all too evident. The lugubrious pedal point throughout the first half of the song seems multiply emblematic of a funeral-march bass, a church organist sustaining a lengthy pedal, and the miserable couple and their guests chained to one spot for the duration of the marriage vows. In the second half, the bass rises by intervals of a minor third (Ab–B–D–F–G♯); the raised fourth degree B♮, forming a tritone with the tonic bass, is important throughout the first half in preparation. Wolf, who used to terrify his sisters with impromptu piano performances of the Wolf's Glen Scene, spoofs the conflict of Good and Evil symbolized tonally by the implications of that harmony, especially since he writes a sequence of augmented triads above the ascending minor thirds in the bass. Augmented chords tend to occur most often as the result of passing motion, but Wolf exploits them here in excess for parodistic ends, for black humor. The off-beat placement and accentuation of the words "she" and "he" in measures 10 and 12 ("*sie* weint ja gräulich, *er* macht ein Gesicht abscheulich!" or "*She* weeps horribly, *he* makes a frightful face") is a delightfully emphatic detail of prosody deployed for comic purposes. The wittiest touch of all may well be the end of the vocal line in measures 16–17: at the word "dabei," the cadence sours abruptly. The singer refuses tonic closure on F and descends a tritone from the dominant pitch C to Gb, grating against the "organist's" F in the bass. There is no harmonious resolution to this dissonant situation, the poet tells us, and Wolf seconds him in his own terms, the negation underscored by the comic prosodic nicety of the sixteenth-note rest after "nicht [dabei]" and the grating dissonance. (Wolf devises a similar instance of tonal humor near the beginning of another Mörike song, "Selbstgeständniss" or "A confession to oneself." When the cheerful protagonist, who confesses to being a spoiled only child, says that the other children "did not show up," or "ausblieben sind," Wolf has the vocal line for that phrase culminate in measure 6 on an "outside" or "ausblieben" chromatic tone G♯.) The postlude ("immer *ppp*") prolongs the F–G♭ dissonance throughout two bars before restoring G♮ and ending the song with a diatonic augmentation of the "shuddering figure," now recognizable as a cliché from the formulaic church music Wolf spoofs in this song. Grotesquerie is a matter of excess, of evocative elements exaggerated to comic effect but without expunging entirely the sense of a true monstrosity— loveless marriages, the social arrangements of the aristocracy—as the point of departure for the poet's whimsy.

Of the three general principles above, the third is perhaps the most important, everything else subsumed within it. Despite his sincere protestations of abnegation before the poet, Wolf knew that the jokes had to become musical as well as verbal, the comedy located in compositional choices of pitch, rhythm, texture, tonality, harmony, voice leading, register, and the like. Ultimately, the comic songs become jokes *in* music *about* music—specifically, contemporary music and the dilemmas of contemporary musicians. Frank Walker has written that the last five songs of the Mörike volume "ask not to be taken too seriously" and "do not amount to much more than the musical equivalent of a practical joke," that "Zur Warnung" (A warning) is "somewhat out of place in cold print,"[25] but Mörike's jokes in fact have a serious substratum. So do Wolf's settings, especially when Mörike's jests about poets and poetry become additionally the fin-de-siècle composer's jokes about composers and modern music. For all the buffoonery in "Zur Warnung" and "Abschied" (these are two of the best encore songs ever composed), the comic rhetoric is meant, earnestly, to persuade, and to do so in the most persuasive way—through the seduction of laughter.

"ZUR WARNUNG" AND "ABSCHIED": COMIC LESSONS IN MODERN ART

Artists have been the butts of their own comedy for over two thousand years. The legendary self-involvement of the artistic ego requires only slight exaggeration, if any, to appear comic, and pretensions to genius, even genius itself, irresistibly invite comic deflation. In comedy, artists can and do make mock of their own predicaments, their reliance on fallible humanity and their own fallible flesh and on the mystery of artistic creativity and the unreliability of creative inspiration. The latter theme is literally ancient. Before the fictive

Euripides and Aeschylus begin their verbal jousting match in Aristophanes' *The Frogs*, Dionysus calls for the chorus and each of the combatants to invoke the Muse or Muses of their choice. Euripides responds with the prayer, "Aether, my Staff of Life! Glib-tongue! Sharp-wit! Critical Prodnose! Guide me truly—*to smash his lines to pieces!*"[26]—malicious indeed. Later, nineteenth-century writers satirized the Romantic Artist-as-Outsider and the cult of genius, the eccentricities and transcendentalizing pretensions of their peers easy targets for laughter. Mörike joins their ranks when he pokes fun at hungover poets and their mocking Muses in this cautionary tale, complete with a moral at the end, but behind the laughter is recognition of creativity's unknowable, untamed being.

The elective affinity between Wolf and Mörike is not entirely susceptible to explanation, but one reason for it is possibly their mutual belief in the Muses, symbolic personifications of creative forces. The Muses are anthropomorphized and named as if they were beings apart from the poet because creativity, like a person other than oneself, is not always present and cannot be understood. Wolf frequently referred to his Muse Polyhymnia in letters to friends, in this way telling them of creativity's presence and frequent, terrible absences. In one of his exultant notes written during the composition of the *Mörike-Lieder* in 1888, Wolf told Edmund Lang, "Should Polyhymnia be sufficiently attentive to threaten me with a third song, I will personally convey to you the dreadful news . . . Despise me! The hat-trick is now complete."[27] During the long compositional drought from 1892 to 1895, Wolf on one occasion conveyed the news of his unchanged condition with the words "Polyhymnia is still sulking,"[28] his pain clearly evident beneath the surface of the witty and (momentarily) stoic phrase. When he fell in love with Frieda Zerny in 1894, he wrote her an extraordinary letter containing a dialogue between the composer and an angel flying about his room, an angel to whom the concept of love letters must be explained.[29] The angel is close kin to his Muse, still in hiding. Wolf had hoped that his newfound love would bring Polyhymnia back to life and quotes, with painful hopefulness, Mörike's "Zur Warnung" in the letter to Frieda: "I am, as artists say, 'in the vein,' or as Mörike once jokingly writes: 'Beinahe poetisch.'" To the end of his creative days, he would hope for the Muse's arrival and rejoice in her presence. In a letter of April 1897, only five months before the onset of insanity, Wolf wrote to his longtime friend Heinrich Werner, saying, "An indescribable happiness fills my entire being. I feel as if transfigured. I hope that the Muse will soon install herself here—I can sense already something of her revitalizing, fructifying nearness."[30]

"Göttlicher Mörike!" (divine Mörike), as Wolf called him, also wrote of Muses, sometimes comically, sometimes seriously but always as figures of great and mysterious power. "Zur Warnung" has a tragic twin in "Muse und Dichter" (Muse and poet), a poem in a single eight-line stanza whose archaizing hexameters underscore the classical associations. Wolf did not set this poem to music, although he surely knew it; perhaps it struck too close to the bone. "Muse und Dichter" is a dialogue poem in which a weakened, sick poet wonders despairingly why his Muse is silent and begs/commands her, "Give me the lyre!" She refuses, saying that "Ruhe," rest and peace, is ordained for him. Although she promises him a garland from her own hand, she will not say whether it signifies creativity and life, the two implicitly synonymous, or death. The poem ends with the poet's plea for continued life and poetry, not the laurel wreath that adorns the cold brow of a dead poet.

> "Krank nun vollends und matt! Und du, O Himmlische, willst mir
>   Auch schon verstummen—O was deutet dies Schweigen mir an?
> Gib die Leier!"—"Nicht doch, dir ist die Ruhe geboten.
>   Schlafe! träume nur! Still ruf' ich dir Hülfe herab.
> Deinem Haupte noch blühet ein Kranz; und sei es zum Leben,
>   Sei's zum Tode, getrost! meine Hand windet ihn dir."—
> "Keinen Lorbeer will dich, die kalte Stirne zu schmücken:
> Lass mich leben und gib fröhliche Blumen zum Strauss!"[31]

("How utterly weak and ill I am now! And you, oh Heavenly One, will you also soon fall silent?—Oh, what does this silence mean? Give me the lyre!"—"Not yet, rest is ordained for you. Sleep! dream on! In stillness I will summon help for you. A garland will yet bloom upon your brow; whether for life or death, be of good cheer! My hand will wind it for you."—"I do not want a myrtle wreath adorning my cold, dead brow! Let me live and give me joyful flowers for my garland!")

The uncertainty at the close—the Muse does not answer—is tragic. Wolf already knew and would rediscover even more painfully four years after setting "Zur Warnung" that Polyhymnia could fall inexplicably silent, her purposes and her return incalculable, and he too equated artistic creativity with life. "When I can no longer compose, they may throw me on the dungheap," he once said, and he compared life without musical creation to "a frog's existence."[32] No wonder that he was drawn to Mörike's comic version of the myth as a matter of hangovers and mockery. Unlike "Muse und Dichter," "Zur Warnung" ends with a celebration of the Poet triumphant over his divine collaborator, who has ostensibly humbled him and taught him a comic lesson. Like old friends, like joshing lovers, the two play tricks on one another. It is even possible for the Poet to have the last word.

Wolf was drawn to comic Muses early. In 1884 when he was sharing rooms at the Trattnerhof with Edmund Lang and the writer Hermann Bahr, his two carousing roommates would return home at a disreputable hour, to be met with Wolf's dramatic readings from Kleist and from Christian Dietrich Grabbe's play "Scherz, Satire, Ironie und tiefere Bedeutung" (Jest, satire, irony, and deeper meaning) of 1822.[33] In Grabbe's comedy, the devil is expelled from hell while his grandmother does the infernal housecleaning. After being captured, caged, and poked by a group of scientists, he becomes involved in a seduction plot and in tweaking a bad poet with pretensions to genius—minor devilry for a post-Romantic Satan whose powers of diablerie have diminished. In particular, the ego-talent discrepancy of self-styled poets and the demon of noninspiration are Grabbe's targets in one of the play's funniest scenes, act 2, scene 2. Grabbe invents an untalented creature named Rattengift, or Rat Poison (for English readers, the cognate "rotten gift" is irresistibly present as well) who tries to compose a sonnet. "Alas for thoughts!" he cries, "Rhymes are there, but alas, thoughts—where are they?" Grabbe compresses entire treatises on the relationship of form and content in poetry into this one wonderfully silly lament. When thought refuses to come, Rattengift decides on a strikingly modern course of action: he will write a poem on the *absence* of thought, not just any kind of poem, but a sonnet beginning, "Ich sass an meinem Tisch und kaute Federn, / So wie —" (I sit at my table and cut quills like —). There, his noninspiration deserts him. After much hemming and hawing, he finally concocts a simile that he enthusiastically declares to be "clever, new, calderonish": "like the lion before the morning dawns chews on the horse, his quick feather," to approximate the scrambled syntax of the German. Presumably, what the mane is to the horse, the feather is to the quill, while the king of the beasts is the egomaniacal poet himself. Delighted with his ingenuity, he breaks out in rhapsodic self-encomium, pointing to the Homeric ring of "eh der Morgen grauet." "I am frightened by my own poetic genius," he concludes, the verb indeed appropriate but not the final noun. Overcome by parodistic narcissism, he runs to the mirror and exults in the spectacle of his large nose (again, Freudian phallic displacement), surely a sign of genius. At this point, the devil enters, and the sonnet is mercifully cut short. Satanic intervention is to be thanked in this instance.[34]

Unlike Rattengift, the poet-narrator in "Zur Warnung" is both the object of mockery and a mocker himself, an ironist in triumphant possession of the last laugh. He is also a far better poet: he actually completes a poem on noninspiration of a different sort—that is, the mistaken identification of a hangover with poetic fervor.

> Einmal nach einer lustigen Nacht
> War ich am Morgen seltsam aufgewacht:
> Durst, Wasserscheu, ungleich Geblüt,
> Dabei gerührt und weichlich im Gemüt,
> Beinah poetisch, ja, ich bat die Muse um ein Lied.
> Sie, mit verstelltem Pathos, spottet mein,
> Gab mir den schnöden Bafel ein:

"Es schlagt eine Nachtigall
Am Wasserfall;
Und ein Vogel ebenfalls,
Der schreibt sich Wendehals,
Johann Jakob Wendehals;
Der tut tanzen
Bei den Pflanzen
Obbemeld'ten Wasserfalls—"

So ging es fort; mir wurde immer bänger.
Jetzt sprang ich auf: zum Wein! Der war denn auch mein Retter.
—Merkt's euch, ihr tränenreichen Sänger,
Im Katzenjammer ruft man keine Götter![35]

(Once, after a merry night, I woke up in the morning feeling strange: I was thirsty, hated the sight of water, felt queasy inside, and at the same time, very sentimental and softhearted, in the poetic vein. Yes, I asked the Muse for a song. She, with disguised pathos, mocked me and gave me this contemptible drivel: "A nightingale sings by the waterfall; and a bird likewise, whose name is Wryneck, Johann Jakob Wryneck. He does a dance near the plants of the aforesaid waterfall." It went on in this way; I became more and more frightened. Then I jumped up: some wine! And that was my salvation. Take heed, you tearful poets: don't call on the gods when you're hung-over!)

Part of the humor is prosodic, the poet's drunken ineptitude rhythmically manifest in Mörike's metrical combinations and changes. The speaker lurches into the poem with a suitably hung-over line consisting of a trochee, two iambs and an anapest, with the first word, "Einmal," set apart rhythmically from the prepositional clause that follows. Each item in the roll call of hangover miseries, "Durst, Wasserscheu, ungleich Geblüt," is given its own foot measure, the number of syllables increasing with each addendum. When postalcoholic grandiosity induces *folie de poésie*, the poet calls for his Muse to dictate a poem in a line that spills over into extra feet and fails to rhyme with anything around it—an unicum that both emphasizes the hung-over poet's presumption and, although comically, indicates that "Lied" is indeed something privileged, a special creative entity. The final line of the first asymmetric stanza, just before the Muse's absurd *dictée*, is in iambic tetrameters, shorter than the preceding lines, as if the mere thought of the "contemptible drivel" to come induces the narrator to break off in disgust. Mörike, a master craftsman who plays with the elements of poetic rhythm, continues the fluctuations of meter and line length throughout the poem, thereby giving Wolf the opportunity for a virtuoso display of prosodic ingenuity.

The Muse begins her wickedly funny drivel with the two most exhausted clichés of Romantic Nature, a nightingale and a waterfall, but she does not treat them very romantically. The nightingale is actually a red herring who disappears from the scene after the initial invocation. The Muse both deceives the poet by leading him to expect a familiar topos, the nightingale as accoutrement and accompaniment to human love, and mocks the reliance on imagery whose former resonance is lost, overused by too many poets "beinahe poetisch." Instead, she ignores the nightingale after the introductory line and replaces it with an ornithological species previously unknown to lyric verse: the *Jynx torquilla*, or Wryneck—the poet Robert Reinick for whom Mörike had little regard? Wolf, who had earlier set several poems by Reinick, might well have enjoyed the pun. With this creature, hilariously pedantic in his proper German names and the legalistic language ("aforesaid," "likewise") used to describe his actions, Mörike pokes fun at the desperation to which uninspired poets were driven by the demon of originality, at the eccentricity of the images they invented in their quest for novelty. The strange bird, ill-equipped for dithyrambic ecstasies, is nevertheless put through the motions appropriate to its surroundings, and communes with Nature in dance. One notices with particular enjoyment the unpredictable poetic meters from line to line, inebriated and inept, and the phrase "tut tanzen." Just so would a bad poet manufacture alliterative opportunities. Furthermore, the verb "tanzt" alone might imply grace or facility, out of place in this Muse's lied. Only considerable poetic technique could produce such a parody of ineptitude.

Comedy exists in order to snatch victory from defeat, to enable the weaker and more vulnerable of two opposing forces to triumph. It rewrites reality's endings in this, not the best of all possible worlds, and makes an absurdity of something potentially tragic. In a comic miracle, the poet of "Zur Warnung" wins a twofold victory over a Muse capable of continuing her torture by rhyme and unreason ad infinitum. The first triumph is explicit, when he banishes her by means of wine (comedy too is an intoxicant), the second implicit but even more decisive: "Zur Warnung" itself, a poem fashioned from the poet's seeming defeat at the hands of his Muse. This is a creation made from creativity's refusal to cooperate. The nonrhyme of "mein Retter" and "keine Götter" underscores the fact that the final victory is human. The poet, while paying homage to the Muse's awesome power, including her power to make a fool of him, actually denies her the omnipotence she claims for herself in this mock-rueful narration. Mörike knew the vagaries of Muses well (he had discovered early, when he left the vicarate for a few months to take a steady writing job, that he could not write on command[36]), and he knew the ultimate value of the relationship between "Muse und Dichter." In this comic scenario, truly the Freudian jest-solution to a problem, Muse and Poet laugh at one another, and a shrewd Poet fashions comic art from the mistaken equation of hung-over sentimentality with artistic profundity.

To translate both a hangover and "schnöde Bafel" into music, Wolf resorts to parody in which the far reaches of enharmony are equated with a hangover while the Muse dictates diatonic nonsense.[37] If the joke is on poets in Mörike's poem, Wolf makes it additionally a jest about modern music and the plight of modern composers in the late nineteenth century. Like other Wagnerites of the era, he had incurred the usual criticisms of musical anarchy and dissonance run riot. One reader for a music publishing firm, rejecting the composer's songs, characterized him as "the extreme left wing of the New German school," and even his close friend and admirer Emil Kauffmann worried about "unresolved dissonances" in the lieder. In reply, Wolf protested that every progression in his music could be justified by "the strictest rules of compositional practice."[38] Here, Wolf enjoys a laugh at both his own expense and that of the Philistine public, to whose unaccustomed ears the century's latest musical offspring must have seemed the aftermath of inebriation. At the same time, the parodistically simple diatonic "Bafel" reveals that this was no solution to the modern hangover. Only further chromaticism, more soberly applied, would do.[39]

On 25 March 1889, after composing "Zur Warnung," Wolf wrote a brief note to a friend, saying "Today two new songs (by Eduard Mörike) have occurred to me, of which one sounds so weird and strange that I am quite afraid of it. There has never been anything like it. God help the unfortunate people who will one day hear it!"[40] The "weirdness and strangeness" are evident in the introduction, five measures of pianissimo queasiness—Wolf considerately spares the hung-over poet-composer any unnecessary noise. The sense of terra firma underfoot is blurred the morning after a spree, and so, analogously, is the sense of tonal location at the beginning. The details of the principal motive and its development are comically appropriate to the context: the motive spans a tritone and moves downward sequentially by whole-tone motion A–G–F–E♭, derived from the A–D♯ span of the initial motivic figure. The slump downward accelerates as it progresses; the built-in accelerando toward the end of the phrase is familiar from classical phrase construction, but in this context also suggests difficulty in holding oneself upright. The lack of a discernible tonal center in the whole-tone descent is the corollary to a spree victim's "verkehrte Welt" (topsy-turvy world) or the disorientation of a hangover, a clever comic reversal of the contemporaneous usage of whole-tone fragments (Example 13). According to late-Romantic theorists, the use of whole-tone progressions, especially quasi-modal successions of pure triads, to evoke a sense of celestial boundlessness had its origin in familiar-style (chordal) passages from sacred works by Palestrina and his contemporaries;[41] passages from the second movement of Liszt's Dante Symphony and Hans Pfitzner's setting of Goethe's "An den Mond" (To the moon) both exemplify this usage. But in "Zur Warnung," each statement of the principal motive culminates in an augmented triad, and the result is not a sense of mystic trans-

Example 13. Hugo Wolf, "Zur Warnung," measures 1–6

port beyond earthly bounds, but "weirdness and strangeness"—otherworldly perhaps, but celestial, no. In tonal music, the augmented triad is not a point of repose, and several in close succession engender extreme tension. Wolf was fond of clustered augmented chords as indices either of great distress or of great distress parodied, and uses the same device in "Bei einer Trauung" and "Abschied" for similar mock-horrific ends.

Wolf was also demonstrating, to excess and with ironic intent, the enharmonic utility of augmented triads in the contemporary idiom, due to their equidistant intervals of a major third. In its equal intervallic structure and its malleability for purposes of modulation, the augmented triad is comparable to the diminished-seventh chord, but the hung-over composer who takes the place of Mörike's hung-over poet goes everywhere and nowhere at once. Rather, Wolf uses enharmony and the cross relations created by the pervasive enharmonic changes as expressive of queasiness.[42] Between measure 1 and measure 3, sharps are replaced by flats, as the "schleichend und trübe" phrase slides lower and into greater darkness. There is actually an implied tonal goal by the latter half of measure 2—a half-cadence on the dominant of Ab minor, but the poet-composer is too befuddled to arrive at the cadence and ends the initial phrase in confusion and on a diminished-seventh chord—hardly very conclusive. The hiccups in measure 3 are Wolf's own Rabelaisian additions to Mörike's poem, precisely the kind of plausible pictorial additions Wolf often made to his chosen texts.

Nothing resolves until the Muse is invoked in Wolfian prosody so detailed as to be a parody of itself. The slight prolongation of the *u* sound of *"Mu*-se" and the exaggeratedly reverential rest before the sacred word "Lied"—the tonic pitch unharmonized, as befitting a mystery—are especially comic. The whole-tone fragments, the queasy wavering between harmonized and unharmonized pitches continue until the poet-composer is at last sufficiently coherent to demand a song. Only then does Eb become D♯ as the raised fourth degree of A minor, Ab turn to G♯ as leading tone to A, and an authentic cadence emerge from the inchoate beginnings. When the Muse appears, she takes over the accompaniment and mocks his whole-tone confusion in the bass of measure 12, within the context of a clearly directed cadential approach to the dominant. If the poet does not know where he is, she does, and her syncopations across the bar line, braying figures, and grace notes suggest her mocking intent before the "schnöde Bafel" begins.

Wolf was surely poking fun at the Beethovenian aspirations of other composers (his favorite target, Brahms?) when he set the Muse's anti-Romantic silliness to a trivialization of Beethoven's Ninth. Wolf mimics the $\frac{2}{4}$ meter and falling perfect fifths of his model, but everything else is different: "Lebhaft (phantastisch)," the parenthetical indication comically redundant, instead of Beethoven's "Allegro ma non troppo, un poco maestoso," and an insistent dactylic-trochaic bass ostinato in place of Beethoven's string tremolandos. The falling fifths, marked "grell" or "shrill," evoke birdcalls; in an antic metamorphosis, Beethoven becomes monotonous, slightly crazed, and very loud chirping, and the vast consequences of the figure in Beethoven's symphony are replaced by the ungifted composer's inability to develop an idea. The monotony is indeed acute. A modern tone poet, with his cadential elisions, substitute harmonies, third relations, and intensive chromatic alteration, receives from his Muse kindergarten diatonicism. Eric Sams has also pointed out the resemblance of the left-hand figures to the motif of Beckmesser's cudgeling in the act 2 finale of *Die Meistersinger von Nürnberg*,[43] the associations with criticism, mockery, inspiration and its lack very much alive in the midsection masterpiece. In addition to the unchanging rhythmic ostinato, the harmonies are restricted to the tonic and dominant chords, mostly incomplete, in A minor. The only relief of sorts comes in the form of dissonance, or wryness, that first appears with the Wryneck, G♯ against the tonic pitch A.

When the bird's full name unrolls, the singer bypasses the previous lower compass of the vocal line on E and lands awkwardly on a dissonant D♯, the tritone formed by the bass derived directly from the opening measures. To make the punishment fit the crime, the Muse concocts a reductio ad absurdum of Beethoven, Wagner, and the narrator's own chromatic hangover.

Not until the narrator resumes ("So ging es fort; mir wurde immer bänger"), summarizing the continued horror of the Muse's song in order to spare both himself and his listeners, does the tonality change and the music begin once more to move. At the word "fort" in measure 37, the Muse's earlier Neapolitan harmony from measure 12 becomes the point of departure for a series of brief references to F major, then F minor. When the narrator can take no more and springs up, the music does likewise—the motion to darker, flat keys is halted, and A♭ once again becomes G♯ in the dominant chord of A major, the raised third degree and the arrival at tonic appearing in conjunction with the moral at the end ("Merkt's euch, ihr tränenreichen Sänger"). The "tearful poets" are a moderately modern lot, given to deceptive motion, to extension by evading cadential resolution, to chromatic suspensions and contrary motion between the moving voices. If they are neither Tristan nor Parsifal, their credentials as modernists are still apparent, and it is they who are most at risk of mistaking emotionalism for creativity and therefore most in need of warning. In one of the wittiest details of the setting, the poet-composer has the last "word," the ultimate victory over his Muse evident in the disposition of the final cadence. Wolf does not allow closure in the vocal line on the word "Götter!" but grants arrival at the tonic harmony to the piano alone, to music rather than to words or the gods.

This is not to claim for "Zur Warnung" more significance than the song deserves. It does not have the profundity of "Seufzer" (Sigh), for example, from the same collection, and Wolf was not placing any serious strain on his listeners' capacity to absorb late-Romantic tonal complications. But the joke does have its serious side. Hanslick himself could not have warned the Wagner epigones of the fin de siècle so tellingly as Wolf did in setting Mörike's spoof of romanticizing, self-indulgent poets, while the equation of enharmony with a hangover is actually persuasion for that which it seems to mock: the chromatic "excesses" of the new generation of composers.

Wolf uses a similarly exaggerated contrast between diatonic and chromatic realms in the last of his *Mörike-Lieder*, the aptly named "Abschied" (Farewell).[44] The lied is better known than "Zur Warnung" because of the rambunctious waltz at the end, but the joke is simpler. The division between diatonic and chromatic styles serves a more obvious purpose—the characterization of obfuscating critics and subsequent rejoicing at their humiliation—having little to do with the larger themes of inspiration, influence, and modernism that one finds in "Zur Warnung." Nevertheless, Wolf's setting of Mörike's pitched battle between Artist and Critic[45] is thoroughly enjoyable, and the musical

means by which he characterizes the critic as grotesque are typically sophisticated.

> Unangeklopft ein Herr tritt Abends bei mir ein:
> "Ich habe die Ehr', Ihr Rezensent zu sein."
> Sofort nimmt er das Licht in die Hand,
> Besieht lang meinen Schatten an der Wand,
> Rückt nah und fern: "Nun, lieber junger Mann,
> Sehn Sie doch gefälligst mal Ihre Nas' so von der Seite an!
> Sie geben zu, dass das ein Auswuchs ist."
> —Das? Alle Wetter—gewiss!
> Ei Hasen! ich dachte nicht,
> All mein Lebtage nicht,
> Dass ich so eine Weltsnase führt' im Gesicht!!
>
> Der Mann sprach noch Verschied'nes hin und her,
> Ich weiss, auf meine Ehre, nicht mehr;
> Meinte vielleicht, ich sollt' ihm beichten.
> Zuletzt stand er auf; ich tat ihm leuchten.
> Wie wir nun an der Treppe sind,
> Da geb' ich ihm, ganz froh gesinnt,
> Einen kleinen Tritt
> Nur so von hinten aufs Gesässe mit—
> Alle Hagel! ward das ein Gerumpel,
> Ein Gepurzel, ein Gehumpel!
> Dergleichen hab' ich nie gesehn,
> All mein Lebtage nicht gesehn,
> Einen Menschen so rasch die Trepp' hinabgehn![46]

(Without knocking, a gentleman comes into my room in the evening: "I
have the honor to be your critic!" Right away, he picks up the candle,
studies my shadow on the wall for some time, steps close to me and then
backs away. "Now, my dear young man, kindly look at your nose from
the side like this! You must admit that it's an excrescence." "It is? Damn
it—so it is! Hell! I never thought, never in all my life, that I had such an
enormous nose!!" The man continued talking about this and that; on my
honor, I don't remember what. Maybe he thought I should confess to
him. At last, he stood up; I lit the way for him. When we got to the top
of the stairs, I felt very merry and gave him just a little kick from behind
on his bottom to send him on his way. Good gracious, was that ever a
commotion, a tumbling and a stumbling! I have never seen its equal in all
my days; never have I seen a person go down the stairs so fast!)

As in "Mausfallen-Sprüchlein" and "Zur Warnung," the poetic form is ingenious. Mörike's rhyming couplets are disposed in varying line lengths, even

within couplets, and are remarkable for a crazy-quilt mixture of meters: iambic pentameters ("Der Mann sprach noch Verschied'nes hin und her"), anapaestic tetrameters ("Das ich so eine Weltsnase führt' im Gesicht!"), trochaic trimeters ("Einen kleinen Tritt"), lines with mixed meters ("Ich weiss, auf meine Ehre, nicht mehr"), and more. Wolf's setting is subsequently a demonstration of the composer's extraordinary prosodic sensitivity, especially when Wolf accepts the poet's invitation to exaggerate still more. He even distorts Mörike's rhythms on occasion in the service of wickedly funny emphasis. At the poetic persona's mock acquiescence to possession of a "Weltsnase," Wolf inserts a hiccuplike rest before the second syllable, "-*na*-se," and then prolongs that syllable over the bar line, a musical alteration of the poet's anapests but one that exaggerates the phallic nose even more—wonderfully apropos. Similarly, Wolf has the singer speed up in excitement at the words "hinten auf's Gesässe mit," at the point where we hear the last reference to the initial tonality of C minor and the beginning of a transition to B♭ major for the waltz. The rude but well-deserved kick puts an end to the critic's pontifications and therefore to his tonality, while the distance between C minor and B♭ major in a tonally progressive song becomes a metaphor for the distance between artists and hostile critics.

"Abschied" is caricature. Wolf accordingly resorts to parallel exaggerations in music—gestures that are larger or longer, voice leading and progressions either more spectacularly resolved or unresolved than usual, heightened contrasts—in order to emphasize the ludicrousness of the colloquy and the animosity of the conflict. Typically, some of the most enjoyable details of Wolf's humor in "Abschied" stem from consideration of tonal clarity or its lack and from conflicts between the voice and piano parts:

1. In measures 26–31, Wolf uses conflicts of phrasing and voice leading to suggest both the poet's confusion at the critic's bizarre behavior and the critic's illogic. As the critic tells the narrator to look at the silhouetted shadow of his nose (critics, Mörike hints, actually insist upon seeing the shadow rather than the substance), the rising sequential repetitions of the figure from measures 1–4, rhythmically diminished, overlap with the vocal phrases, which at times duplicate the unharmonized melodic line in the accompaniment and at times diverge from it. Another instance of the voice-accompaniment conflicts occurs in measures 57–63 ("Der Mann sprach noch Verschied'nes hin und her"), when the vocal line continues in the previous $\frac{2}{4}$ meter, while the accompaniment changes to $\frac{6}{8}$. Although the tension between the critic and the criticized takes the form of a metrical clash, the conflict is not a drastic one—these are not polyrhythms—because the narrator has not yet allowed his anger free rein. Much of the passage is recitativelike, with minimal accompaniment, while the measured trills emblematic of the critic's babbling in measures 57 and 59 do not include the variegated rhythmic patterns that

identify a particular meter. In a third example (measures 70–74), Wolf devises a new variation on the intervallic cell of the ascending semitones from the opening to depict the two characters jostling one another at the top of the stairs (another of Wolf's additions to the poetic scenario), including a wonderfully pungent direct cross relation between F♯ and F at the word "ganz."

2. When the critic says, "Sie geben zu, daß das ein Auswuchs ist" in measures 32–36, Wolf surrounds a continuation of the figure from measure 1 with a harmonic trill on two augmented chords, G♭ with the raised fifth D♮ in the outermost voices and F. The D in measures 39–40 becomes the leading tone to the relative-major tonality of E♭, which is only made clear when the narrator exclaims "Gewiss!" Wolf amusingly has the pianist repeat the last measure of the critic's condemnation (measure 36) for two and a half measures while the narrator in mock-horror checks to see whether the excrescence is really there. The change from continual chromatic instability—a metaphor in music for the critic's shiftiness, or even his ignorance of what he is?—to tonal surety in E♭ is comically abrupt, the tonal version of a pratfall after a long chase scene.

3. The poet's astonishment "dass ich so eine Weltsnase führt' im Gesicht" in measures 47–56 is set in A♭ minor, but without ever resolving to a root-position tonic chord; the passage ends with a half-cadence. The E♭ dominant pitch is extended, unharmonized and fortississimo, in the piano throughout measures 52–56 until it vanishes. The poet refuses concurrence with the critic's pronouncement and does so in tonal terms by refusing resolution.

The waltz at the end of "Abschied" was and is a good local joke in a city that buried its Waltz Kings in the same Grove of Honor with Beethoven, Brahms, Schubert, and, later, Wolf himself. Vienna had been dance-mad for a century and continued to be similarly obsessed in Wolf's day; he would have had ample opportunity to hear the dance music and operettas of the Strauss family, Richard Heuberger, Carl Millöcker, and their numerous imitators. He certainly duplicates the conventions to a nicety in "Abschied."[47] The "Gerumpel, Gepurzel, Gehumpel" tumbling that leads to the waltz consists of motivic variations on the intervallic figures from the beginning, a witty way of pointing out that the critic's earlier audacities have ensured his downfall. The chromatic melee culminates in a childish, that is, unrelievedly diatonic fit of glee, interpreted as a waltz. Amusingly, the singer's words end before the completion of the first sixteen-measure period, implying that physical actions replace verbal expression at the peak of the narrator's triumph. The equation of a Viennese waltz with such an unabashedly childish revenge is, once more, Wolf's addition to Mörike's poem—an equation that connects him to a particular cultural heritage with which he is not usually associated, and does so in a markedly ambivalent way: waltz = pure enjoyment = regressive diatonic simplicity = childishness. Freud, who wrote "What is comic is invariably on the infantile side," who located the comic in childish superiority ("You fell down, and I didn't"),[48] might have enjoyed the additional corroboration in this song for his theories regarding the psychic mechanisms of jokes.

COMEDY IN THE *EICHENDORFF-LIEDER*

Wolf gravitated to an earlier generation of poets as his preferred sources, but that was precisely the poetic repertoire that had been mined for musical setting over and over again. His affinity with Mörike was a godsend, the most fortuitous encounter of his creative life, since his poetic genius encompassed those themes most sympathetic to Wolf's musical style, and many of his poems had not been set to music by important composers before Wolf. In the works of other poets, Wolf consciously sought those poems passed over by his predecessors. Striking a new vein in Joseph von Eichendorff's poetry must have seemed all the more necessary because of the inevitable comparisons with Schumann. Were Wolf to set only the poems most characteristic of Eichendorff's repertory—poems in which symbolically charged landscapes suggest mystic relationships between God, humanity, and nature (*Stimmungsgedichte*)—the living presence of Schumann's op. 39 *Liederkreis* would haunt both him and the audience, and he knew it. He would have to find something other than the Eichendorff of "Mondnacht" (Moonlit night), something more attuned to his own brand of realism and human drama in the lied.

The latter reason was the more crucial one by 1888, since the days of Schumann-imitations were largely over. When Wolf decided to interrupt the spate of Mörike songs for the month between 31 August and 29 September 1888 in order to compile a small volume of *Gedichte von Eichendorff*, he looked for more of Eichendorff's *Rollengedichte*, that is, poems conceived as being spoken by a particular person who characterizes himself or herself through what he or she says.[49] He had first discovered this aspect of Eichendorff in 1886–87 when he set "Der Soldat I" (The soldier; 1887), "Der Soldat II" (1886), "Waldmädchen" (Forest maiden; 1887),[50] and "Die Zigeunerin" (The gypsy woman; 1887), although he also composed a setting of a *Stimmungsgedicht*, the exquisite "Nachtzauber" (Night enchantment), that Schumann had bypassed. To those songs, he now added thirteen others: "Verschwiegene Liebe" (Taciturn love), composed on 31 August 1888; "Der Schreckenberger" (Captain Dreadnought), composed on 14 September 1888; "Der Glücksritter" (Fortune's knight), composed on 16 September 1888; "Seemans Abschied" (Sailor's farewell), composed on 21 September 1888; "Der Scholar" (The scholar), composed on 22 September 1888; "Der Musikant" (The musician), composed on 22 September 1888; "Der verzweifelte Liebhaber" (The despairing lover), composed on 23 September 1888; "Unfall" (Mishap), composed on 25 September 1888; "Der Freund" (The friend), composed on 26 September 1888; "Liebesglück" (Love's happiness), composed on 27 September 1888; "Das Ständchen" (The serenade), composed on 28 September 1888; "Heimweh" (Homesickness), composed on 29 September 1888; and "Lieber alles" (I'll take them all), composed on 29 September 1888. In 1878, Wolf had attempted to set "Verschwiegene Liebe," a *Stimmungsgedicht* with antecedents in the famous Arnim-Brentano anthology *Des Knaben Wunderhorn*, and he returned to it a decade later for one of the masterpieces of his small Eichendorff collection. (Could the budding Nietzschean freethinker have been drawn to this text for its line "Die Gedanken sind frei," or "Thoughts are free"? And without pursuing the biographical fallacy beyond limits of credibility, the composer who was by 1888 involved in a secret affair with Melanie Köchert might have felt an affinity with the silent, hidden, beautiful love in this poem.) Of the remaining twelve songs, all but nos. 4, 8, and 12 are "role" poems, and only a few appear in Challier's *Grosser Lieder-Katalog* in previous settings by other composers.[51] Wolf had indeed discovered something new for song composition, and he was justifiably proud of his discovery. In a letter of March 12, 1891 to his fellow-composer and friend Engelbert Humperdinck, Wolf wrote: "In accord with the more realistic movement in the arts, the Romantic element in the Eichendorff songs almost entirely withdraws into the background. Rather, the composer has preferred the sharply humorous, robustly sensuous side of the poet, which is virtually unknown, and he has drawn some successful features from it. For example: Schreckenberger, Glücksritter, Unfall, Scholar, Soldat I, Seemans Abschied."[52] The reference to realism is telling. By the end of his apprenticeship years, Wolf had discovered his preference for sharply detailed characterization. He was drawn only rarely to the mysteriousness of Eichendorff's metaphysical worlds, preferring instead miniature dramas in song. The same aesthetic demands for psychologically rich depiction pervade both his song repertoire and his troubled search for the ideal opera libretto.

Wolf's Eichendorff volume is smaller than his other song collections in part because Eichendorff provided him with only a limited number of suitable texts. Of the small number of role poems, Wolf selected only those in which a single poetic persona speaks directly, bypassing those poems in which a narrator observes someone and describes the figure, or the dialogue poems such as "Jäger und Jägerin" (Hunter and huntress).[53] He was particularly drawn to Eichendorff's quirky figures outside the bounds of the Philistine bourgeoisie, such as mercenary soldiers, gypsies, and sailors, although his portrait gallery also includes comic Philistines and conventional creatures disinclined to active endeavors ("Der Scholar" and "Unfall"). Wolf, who had little patience for conventional mores and society's strictures, clearly relished the elements of rebellion in his chosen eccentrics.

Role poems—thumbnail sketches of fictive human beings—are different in nature from Mörike's comic jests in which the poet triumphs over the stronger forces of Muses and critics. Only one of the Eichendorff songs is a setting of a comic anecdote in which two antagonists collide, the loser representative of someone—an element of society, a type, a mentality—who had incurred the poet's displeasure. Eichendorff's "Der Landreiter"[54] (The gendarme on horseback), entitled "Unfall" (Mishap) in the edition Wolf used, is a variation on the old theme of mortals who dare to laugh at Cupid and are suitably punished when the little god strikes them down with lovesickness. Wolf would surely have known Mozart's song "Dans un bois solitaire et sombre" (In a dark and lonely forest); here, the poetic persona is not the graceful eighteenth-century swain of Mozart's lovely chanson, but a choleric bachelor who stubbornly refuses to fall in love with anyone. If there is a candidate for sweetheart anywhere on the scene, the angry protagonist does not mention her.

> Ich ging bei Nacht einst über Land,
> Ein Bürschlein traf' ich draussen,
> Das hat'nen Stutzen in der Hand
> Und zielt auf mich voll Grausen.
> Ich renne, da ich mich erbos',
> Auf ihn in vollem Rasen,
> Da drückt das kecke Bürschlein los
> Und ich stürzt' auf die Nasen.
> Er aber lacht mir ins Gesicht,
> Dass er mich angeschossen,
> Cupido war der kleine Wicht—
> Das hat mich sehr verdrossen.

(When I went out one night across the fields, I met a little lad outside who had a gun in his hand and took aim at me frighteningly. Provoked, I rush toward him as fast as I can. But the bold little fellow fires a shot, and I fall on my nose. But he laughs in my face for having shot me. Cupid was the little brat. That made me very mad.)

This is the classic childish comedy of comeuppance taken out of the nursery and made into an instrument of literary revenge in adult matters. In such jokes, the threat of violence is turned at the last minute into lesser bodily harm (falling on one's nose rather than falling dead), but the desired greater vengeance is clearly understood. In this way, the poet, the composer, and the audience can have their cake and eat it too: they can benevolently spare their victim the worst harm and yet reap all the satisfactions of guilt-free revenge.

Just as the poet turns what are supposedly the pawkish protagonist's words against him, so Wolf's music mocks the speaker from within the music. Wolf adopts the balladesque story-telling style, that is, syllabic text setting in

square-cut phrases. However, Wolf winks at the listener in every compositional choice he makes in this song, such that the simplicities of that style are
invested with multiple humorous touches. Even the "Gemächlich" (easygoing, comfortable) tempo is a means to mock a character who is far from
easygoing. The poetic persona, who alternately blusters and whines, begins
his tale of misfortune without any piano introduction in the "tragic key" of D
minor, but a rollicking, staccato walking bass contradicts any hint of true
tragedy. The voice leading in the inner voice that produces D-*major* chords on
the second beat of measures 1 and 5 foreshadows the G♭ pitches of Cupid's
mockery to come, but just as important, it betrays the presence of an amused
composer who cannot maintain minor mode for even a single beat without
hinting that this is comedy. Similarly, the E-minor harmony in measure 3
becomes E *major* as brightness breaks in on the curmudgeon's grumbling.
When the folkish vocal line for that second phrase reaches its final point of
descent, the cadential harmonies in the piano frisk upward, the multiple grace
notes Wolf's standard index of comic emphasis and humorous criticism rooted
in anger. The interval of a fourth, prominent in measure 1 in the piano A–D/
B–E and in measure 3 in the voice, appears clustered in measure 4 in the piano
as the means of return to the music of measures 1–2, or the first phrase. But
if the first phrase can return as the third in a mimicry of folk-song convention,
the fourth phrase in measures 7–8 is a delightful variant of previous figures
and relationships. When the bachelor recounts his fright, "Und zielt auf mich
voll Grausen," Wolf takes the F that was the apex of the first phrase and the
E that follows at the beginning of the second phrase and dramatizes them via
harmonization and octave leaps. As the speaker quakes in fear, the F-major
and B♭-minor chords, with their parallel fifths in the bass (Wolf's signature
gesture for rusticity), are a premonition of the end of stanza 2; the off-beat
placement of the bagpipe figure heightens its comic effect. The gendarme
knows what is to come in this remembered recounting of his humiliation and
foretells it harmonically.

Wolf structures "Unfall" as a through-composed song in three episodes
equivalent in length, the second and third episodes each developed from the
music of the preceding section in cinematic succession. The second section is
the comic confrontation as the gendarme charges the "saucy fellow" and falls
flat on his face. Half of the middle section (measures 9–12) is a variation on
measures 1–4 in which the eighth-notes in the bass are doubled in speed to
sixteenth-notes, no longer "easygoing and comfortable." The charge of the
comic antagonists is depicted in terms of rhythmic conflict, two against three
(Cupid is the higher, quicker right-hand part, while the gendarme lumbers
along in the bass); acerbic soprano-bass dissonances, especially appoggiatura
clashes such as the one in measure 9 that pits D♯ and D♮ on the downbeat; and
the elevated tessitura, the high G at the start surpassing the F of stanza 1. The
straightforward scalar descent that constitutes the second phrase of the first

section returns as the second phrase in the middle section, but transposed such that the cadence is now on the dominant for the first time at the words "in vollem Rasen" (in an utter rage). The foreshadowings of fury occur on V/V, "complete rage" on the dominant itself—yet another instance of Wolf's characteristic gift for assimilating nuances of text interpretation into the harmonic and tonal structure.

Wolf typically unleashes a barrage of musical figures to underscore the denouement of a comic pratfall, and he does so here for the final half of the second section ("Da drückt das kecke Bürschlein los / Und ich stürzt' auf die Nasen," or "The audacious little fellow fired at me, and I fell on my nose"). Not content with a single comic gesture, he concocts one illustrative device after another to extend the joke to its fullest possible length and keep his audience laughing. The transposed variant in the vocal line of the familiar fourths and scalar cells is underscored by the B♭ harmonies from measure 7, this time extended throughout measures 13–18, the dotted rhythms both new and suitably "keck" or saucy. When Cupid's gun goes off to a sforzando dissonant seventh chord on C♭, the protagonist becomes tearful ("weinerlich") and haltingly recounts his fall, the final line of the stanza broken into fragments and couched in an abashed undertone, softer and softer toward the culmination. The passage is filled with the semitone cells or longer chromatic scale figures from earlier in the song: measures 15–18 trace a chromatic G♭–F–F♭–E♭–D♮ descent in the piano, overlaid with the same chromatic line—doubly woeful—beginning with the lamenting semitone at the word "Nasen" (nose) and continuing in the piano. Scale motives spanning a fifth in thirty-second–notes are a Wolfian figure associated with anger ("Was soll der Zorn, mein Schatz" and "Verschling' den Abgrund" from the *Italienisches Liederbuch* are two examples), and a single isolated specimen appears in measure 17, pianissimo and ritardando: the gendarme now recollects his former anger in chagrin. However, when Wolf completes the cadence at the end of the second section on a B♭-*major* harmony in the piano (measure 18), not in the voice, and does so loudly, he deliberately betrays the presence of an amused composer who stands just behind the curmudgeonly "I" of the poem and cannot resist commentary of his own. Within the lied, there is both an ostensible storyteller—the butt of his own tale—and a pair of gleeful second storytellers, the poet and composer.

Just as the setting of lines 5–8 is a development of material from the setting of the first four lines, so the third and final section is largely a further development of what immediately precedes it. Here, Wolf creates a late-Romantic echo of Purcell's laughing witches in *Dido and Aeneas*—malice whose triplet sixteenth-note patterns originate with the triplets in measures 9–12. Wolf distinguishes between the conflicting parties tonally such that the turn to B♭ in the second and third sections is the key of Cupid's violence and subsequent ridicule; not until the peeved gendarme says at the end that he was "exceedingly angry" does G♭ turn back into F♯ and D minor reappear just in time for the postlude. Even there, B♭ pitches and harmonies figure prominently in the final cadence in measures 29–39, its registral contrasts and rhythms a foreshadowing of the end to "Du denkst mit einem Fädchen" from the *Italienisches Liederbuch*.

In the other role poems in the *Eichendorff-Lieder*, the fictive persona says something that vividly encapsulates his personality: an assertion, a bit of braggadocio, a dilemma to ponder. In several of these songs, comedy is an element, but not the point of the enterprise. For example, in his affectionate portrait of the contented student in "Der Scholar" (The scholar), Wolf underscores the youthful pomposity of the words "Frei von Mammon will ich schreiten / Auf dem Feld der Wissenschaft, / Sinne ernst und nehm zuzeiten / Einen Mund voll Rebensaft" (Uncorrupted by Mammon, I will stroll in the field of knowledge, think seriously, and from time to time, savor a mouthful of wine) by means of large intervallic leaps up and down, one after another, throughout the setting of the first two lines. The sequential intervallic cells inch upward by semitones, both the breadth of knowledge and the strolling motion made comically audible. In these role poems, soldiers and young men predominate: a male recitalist putting together a program might want to contrast the group composed of "Der Soldat I," "Der Soldat II," "Der Schreckenberger," and "Der Glücksritter" with a group portraying amusingly callow young men ("Lieber alles," "Der Scholar," "Der verzweifelte Liebhaber"). The poetic persona of "Lieber alles" (I'll take them all) attempts to pick a profession or occupation:

> Soldat sein ist gefährlich,—
> Studieren sehr beschwerlich,
> Das Dichten süss und zierlich,
> Der Dichter gar posierlich
> In diesen wilden Zeiten.
> Ich möcht' am liebsten reiten,
> Ein gutes Schwert zur Seiten,
> Die Laute in der Rechten,
> Studentenherz zum Fechten.
> Ein wildes Ross ist's leben,
> Die Hufe Funken geben,
> Wer's ehrlich wagt, bezwingt es,
> Und wo es tritt, da klingt es!

(To be a soldier is dangerous, studying is very difficult, writing poetry is elegant and delightful. The poet is truly a droll figure in these wild times. I'd like to ride forth into the world, a good sword at my side, a lute in my hand, a student's heart for fighting. Life is a wild horse whose hooves strike sparks. He who honorably dares can conquer it, and where it goes, it resounds!)

The young man begins by recounting all the disadvantages of the few occupations he is willing to consider at all. The quickness of the iambic trimeters and the succession of rhyming couplets—one per profession—are appropriate to this hasty (non)-consideration of the means to make a living. He only invokes those occupations with a tinge of outlawry or wildness, but finds flaws in each. Rather than the substance of any one identity, he wants the attributes and poses of them all: the poet's lute, a soldier's sword buckled by his side, a student's hotheaded inclination to fight. To be a soldier is to place oneself in danger, and studying is hard work, while writing poetry—Eichendorff mocking his own calling—is too dainty a profession for wild times such as these. Eichendorff himself found the "wild times" in which he lived disturbing in their spiritual lawlessness, but the archetypal impatient young man of "Lieber alles," bristling with energy but as yet without purpose, finds them eminently to his liking and wants only to become caught up in the currents of outlaw energy. The context is comic, but the underlying question—"What use poetry in postrevolutionary upheaval?"—is serious.

In the lengthy piano introduction (measures 1–10), a mercurial parade of motivic figures that progress from loud to still louder and then sink to pensive softness constitute a character portrait without words before the singer even enters. By notating a G-major key signature and beginning in G minor, Wolf both indicates an aura of weightiness, even potential tragedy, while hinting that the outcome is brighter than it appears to be at the start. The young man's quixotic nature is evident in the rapid-fire (*Sehr schnell*, or "very fast") succession of motivic fragments in the introduction, each one with its own stamp—he is evidently a creature of extremes. These figures change rhythmic configuration as the poetic persona darts from thought to thought, from the midmeasure chordal accents of the first figure (measures 1–2) to the multiple off-beat accents of measures 3–4, a crescendo to a measure of silence that dramatizes the rush upward to the peak of the introduction in measures 6–8. For all their rhythmic dissimilarities, the motivic figures are actually linked by the rising semitone(s) at the beginning of each one (measures 1, 3, 6, 8–9), and by other intervallic and pitch relationships as well: the descending tritone E♭–A in measure 1 and its consequent cell figure D–F♯, transposed downward and widened, is answered in measure 6 by the leap upward of a minor seventh. In particular, the initial pitches D–E♭ are the motivic glue that holds the introduction together, recurring at the bottom voice in measure 4 and then augmented and reversed, again in the bass, in measures 7–10.

When the impetuous rush of the introduction cools at the end, the stage is set for a more moderate (*Mässig*) presentation of the three occupations under review in stanza 1. Each statement of the disadvantages of this, that, and the other calling concludes with irresolute seventh chords ornamented by descending appoggiaturas, as if the young man were sighing in dismay. Wolf gives each profession its own comic inflection, such as the break or rest, as if in dismay, after the words "Soldat sein—ist gefährlich." The brief reference to studying is marked "zurückhaltend" (slowing down), the dreaded weight of studies dragging at the tempo, while the elegance of poetry elicits a whole series of semitone figures in birdlike, cheeping sequence, a parody of tea-table refinement that Wolf had earlier used in the Heine song "Aus meinen grossen Schmerzen" to characterize the ineffectual, twittering little poems the poet sends to his beloved. As in "Zur Warnung," the poet becomes a composer in Wolf's setting, one who shows off his elegance with a display of contrary motion in the piano, but the display has a wickedly apposite point. According to the hotheaded speaker, poetry has little usefulness in times such as these; the music of Wolf's composer dithers gracefully and delays cadential resolution until the "wild times" bring about the completed cadence on the dominant.

The mercenary soldiers of "Der Schreckenberger" and "Der Glücksritter," blusterers both, are born of Eichendorff's novella *Die Glücksritter* of 1841. The most comic of the two is "Der Glücksritter," with its byplay between Dame Fortune in a temporary fit of pique and her knight, the speaker of the poem.

> Wenn Fortuna spröde tut,
> Lass' ich sie in Ruh',
> Singe recht und trinke gut,
> Und Fortune kriegt auch Mut,
> Setzt sich mit dazu.
>
> Doch ich geb' mir keine Müh':
> "He, noch eine her!"
> Kehr' den Rükken gegen sie,
> Lass' hoch leben die und die—
> Das verdriesst sie sehr.
>
> Und bald rückt sie sacht zu mir:
> "Hast du deren mehr?"
> "Wie Sie seh'n, drei Kannen schier,
> Und das lauter Klebebier!
> 'S wird mir gar nicht schwer."
>
> Drauf sie zu mir lächelt fein:
> "Bist ein ganzer Kerl!"
> Ruft den Kellner, schreit nach Wein,

Trinkt mir zu und schenkt mir ein,
Echte Blum' und Perl'.

Sie bezahlet Wein und Bier,
Und ich, wieder gut,
Führe sie am Arm mit mir
Aus dem Haus wie'n Kavalier,
Alles zieht den Hut.

(When Dame Fortune plays the prude, I ignore her. If I go on singing and drinking, Fortune will take heart and sit with me. But I don't trouble myself: "Hey, bring me another!" I turn my back on her, drink the health of this and that lass—that really annoys her. And soon she comes close to me: "Do you have more of those?" "As you see, three tankards full of beer . . . that won't take me long." Then she laughingly says: "You're a real man!" She calls the bartender, orders wine, drinks to my health and pours out the sparkling wine for me. She pays for the wine and beer and I, once more in good humor, lead her arm-in-arm out of the inn like a cavalier. Everyone tips his hat to us as we leave.)

In life, fortune is not so compliant as she is here, as amenable to proper management by a macho man, but in comedy, such cosmic matters can be and are reversed in our favor. Like the young fellow (a budding "Glücksritter"?) in "Lieber alles," the braggart of this little ballad believes that life can be mastered by refusing to concede defeat. With the proper attitude, so goes this credo, the anthropomorphized forces of fate will come around and grant one the prize of good luck and fortune. Dame Fortune even picks up the tavern tab, the final fillip to her comic alliance with those who refuse to be cowed by her "feminine" fickleness. To those fortunate few, lesser mortals doff their hats and pay tribute.

Wolf begins his musical portrait before the first note of music, with the indication "Keck und etwas gemessen" (Bold and somewhat precise, or strict). The seeming contradiction is in keeping with the depiction of an ideal soldier-of-fortune, someone both recklessly courageous and yet bound by military order. Like "Unfall," "Der Glücksritter" is in $\frac{4}{8}$ meter, march music but in an eighth-note tactus whose quicker pace spells comedy; also like "Unfall," the miniature narrative begins without preamble. Wolf not only mimics the stanzaic sectionalization of the tale in his musical structure but emphasizes it: the end of each of the five stanzas is the occasion for a triumphal cadence, the exuberant peak of the music and all the funnier for the weak-beat resolution to tonic. The knight is so carried away by self-congratulatory exuberance that he cannot wait for the second beat. Each stanza, in proper soldierly drill, follows the same plan but with Wolf's customary nuances specific to each stage of the story. The first four-bar phrase in every strophe is split into a two-bar unison figure, followed by a consequent phrase, fully harmonized and ending with a cadence on the mediant E that is the peak of the first phrase. Wolf embellishes the initial phrases with a sprinkling of ornaments, typical of his comic songs: the accented syllable of Dame Fortuna's name receives a grace-noted emphasis, a miniature drumroll that also restates the motivically important figure of a scalewise rising third C to E, and the downbeat of measure 2 at the word "spröde" is given a trill, a mock-shuddering emphasis on the tonic before the downward fall of a diminished fourth to G♯. That interval is, of course, traditionally associated with lamentation—another of Wolf's inside jokes. And the soldier cannot resist rewarding himself for his clever strategy ("I leave her in peace") with a fanfare that brings E back to the higher register.

When the military swagger begins in measure 5 at the words "Singe recht und trinke gut" (I sing out loudly and drink deep), the two "contrasting" phrases are actually fashioned from the same material reversed, appropriate for a character so adept at turning misfortune into fortune. The scalewise third figure and the diminished fourth recur, the latter transposed to F–C♯ in measure 8, while Fortune's descent in measures 1–2 becomes a series of ascending figures. The doubling in octaves throughout measures 5–12 (and subsequently in the second half of each strophe) and the rocking fourths and fifths in the bass provide the proper "manly" fortification, poised right on the brink of parody, for the beginning of this alcoholic test of wills. At the end of stanza 1, the knight says that Fortune "sits down by me"; what she will say or do is as yet unclear, whether for good or bad, and Wolf milks the uncertainty for a moment in measures 8–10, hinting at D-minor tragedy until the flamboyant cadence on F major in the piano restores and redoubles the previous cheerfulness.

Each stanza has its own comic variations. The conflict between Fortune and her knight is especially tense at the start of stanza 2, when the knight turns his back on her. When the figure from measures 1–2 returns in measures 13–14, beginning on the tonic pitch C, Wolf has the knight/vocal line begin on B♮, and the dissonance on the downbeat sets the clash of the poetic personas in motion. The quiet chords of measure 3 ("I leave her in peace") are no longer appropriate for the knight's loud order—"Hey, bring me another!"—to the tavernkeeper, and therefore the fanfares on E-major harmonies resound earlier. The march too is varied, elevated to A major as the knight lifts his glass high in toasts to other women; here, the dissonances at the end of the stanza underscore just how aggrieved Dame Fortune is, especially the accented clash of G♯ and A at the word "sehr."

Her aggravation does not last long, nor does the tonality of his seeming perfidy and her frustration. With stanza 3, the penitent Dame Fortune sidles up to this master of reverse psychology, and her music in measures 25–30 descends from the A at the end of the previous strophe through G♮ to F♯. Wolf devises a questioning upward inflection for Fortune's question "Do you have

any more?" and extends her wheedling through the "zart" (sweet) piano interlude of measures 29–30, where the G♮–F♯ relationship of this half of the
stanza is repeated twice as embellished high treble figures. Her cavalier maintains both the upper hand and his own separate identity when he raises the ante
from F♯ major to G major in the marchlike second half of the third stanza. In
stanza 4, Dame Fortune's capitulation is complete when she congratulates him
for being a real man ("Bist ein ganzer Kerl!") to *his* fanfares on E major from
measures 15–16 and toasts him to the A-major harmonies with which he had
earlier toasted everyone else but her—stanza 4 is a minimally altered variant
of stanza 2.

According to the knight's successful strategy, she becomes *his* servitor, and
his will prevails, musically as in all else. The voice doubling the piano in
measure 43 ("She calls the bartender") is yet another miniature detail that
makes apparent a concord based on male domination and female approval of
the very techniques that hold them in check. Only when she has signified her
favor by paying the bill does the C-major tonality promised in the key signature from the beginning appear (at the verb "führen," "to lead") and a "simple,
natural" order assert itself. The tonic key is saved for the denouement of the
tale. At the final words of Eichendorff's poem, everyone doffs his hat to the
pair in a sweeping octave leap, although the properly awed onlookers at the
end of the text do not have the last word: it is the knight's/piano's privilege to
complete the cadence. With that, he leads Dame Fortune forth to a march for
piano, another of Wolf's extended piano postludes in which he adds a plausible if unwritten last act to the poem and expounds C major for an additional
sixteen measures. The descending chromatic inner voice and the repetition
an octave lower and more softly (a musical metaphor for increasing distance) foreshadow the kingly exit of the three kings in the Goethe song
"Epiphanias."

Mastery and lordliness assume the form of (male) victory from (female)
defeat. The allegorical scenario hinges on the personification of Fortune—like
the similar personifications of Liberty, Justice, Victory, Fame—as a woman,
the gender least likely to possess such grandiose abstract concepts in actuality.[55] Women in early-nineteenth-century Germany or fin-de-siècle Vienna
were in the main dependent upon men for their fortune or lack of it, as Fortune
herself is dependent upon her knight for her peace of mind. According to the
he-man of "Der Glücksritter," this is the way things should be—primordial
perfection in the primary key of C major. But if the male bluster is comic in
Eichendorff's poem, it is doubly so by the time Wolf is through with it. Wolf,
after all, had recently set to music Mörike's astonishing poem of sexual realism, "Erstes Liebeslied eines Mädchens"[56] (A maiden's first love song) and
would begin setting the women's poems from the *Italienisches Liederbuch*
just a few years later. The librettist for his only completed opera, Rosa Mayreder, was one of Vienna's foremost early feminists, and Wolf, forced to pay

heed to the conventions that bound Viennese women for the sake of Melanie Köchert's reputation, had little respect for the sexual hypocrisies of his time. *His* knight is comically self-satisfied, and Wolf sticks grace-noted pins in his protagonist's pomposity at every turn.

Eichendorff, less Protean a poet than Mörike, gave Wolf fewer opportunities for tendentious humor of the kind he found so appealing. Anger and comic comeuppance are among the principal elements of "Unfall," but even that poem is primarily a witty celebration of all-conquering love. "Der Glücksritter" too is a comic reversal of the usual order, the weak triumphing over the strong, such that humanity wins a victory over Lady Luck or Dame Fortune, and macho posturing is unmasked as comic at the core. But elsewhere in the role poems, Freudian jest-solutions are not the purpose of the enterprise. Rather, the unconventional beings Eichendorff portrays are emphatic creatures whose exaggerated manner of expression impelled from Wolf many of the same musical devices that one finds in the comic songs to texts by Mörike, to similarly delightful effect.

COMEDY IN THE *GOETHE-LIEDER*

Wolf's choice of fifty-two poems for his *Gedichte von Goethe*, composed in a spate that began on 27 October 1888 and ended a year later on 21 October 1889, reveals both his challenging response to texts previously set by Schubert (the Mignon and Harper songs, the odes "Prometheus," "Ganymed," and "Grenzen der Menschheit") and the continuing quest for those texts shunned by earlier composers.[57] Wolf's great advocate Frank Walker prefaces his criticism of the comic ballads "Ritter Kurts Brautfahrt" (Knight Kurt's bridal journey) and "Gutmann und Gutweib" (Good man and good wife) by writing that Wolf "seems to have had to search far afield to find unhackneyed poems for musical treatment, and among the garland with which he returned are some rather prickly, thistle-like growths."[58] Again, he gives short shrift to several songs whose musical wit exemplifies Wolf's statement to Emil Kauffmann that certain poems had to await the development of a post-Wagnerian tonal language before they could be satisfactorily realized in music.[59] Wolf was referring to the odes "Ganymed" and "Prometheus," but the comic songs also demonstrate why the Vienna Goethe Society in 1890 could say, "We must let Wolf explain Goethe to us."[60]

Once again, the species of humor changes with the change of poet. Unlike Mörike's comic-fantastic vein and Eichendorff's role poems, Goethe's comic poems often point beyond the humorous traits of individual characters and traditional genres (balladry, pastoral poetry) to make universal observations about human nature. Even where the poem satirizes a historical personage, that personage dispenses categorical advice about the human condition and in turn exemplifies his own warnings about fools throughout the ages. Goethe is a byword for variety of subject matter and poetic techniques, but a certain breadth of vision that extrapolates the general from the particular, the universal from the individual, is a common denominator among the comic songs. The poetic personas are no less individual in their yawning, love-struck, pontificating, resolutely physical selves, but what they do and say impels recognition of their kinship with humanity who act in similar ways and speak in similar tones, if less brilliantly.

"Cophtisches Lied I"[61] (Coptic song 1) and its pendant "Cophtisches Lied II," both composed on 28 December 1888, are among those poems by Goethe that were shunned by song composers before Wolf. The Coptic songs purport to be moral instruction handed down from a teacher, sage, or prophet to his disciples, but while the second can be taken seriously—the message being that one should decide when young whether to serve or lead, suffer or triumph, be an anvil or the hammer that strikes it—the first cannot be read as anything other than inspired silliness. A charlatan with a severe case of *folie de grandeur* tells his followers that he has conversed with Merlin and spoken with the dead in the depths of Egyptian crypts. These awe-inspiring spirits from the past have all given him the same message: to leave fools to their own devices.

> Lasset Gelehrte sich zanken und streiten,
> Streng und bedächtig die Lehrer auch sein!
> Alle die Weisesten aller der Zeiten
> Lächeln und winken und stimmen mit ein:
> Töricht, auf Bessrung der Toren zu harren!
> Kinder der Klugheit, o habet die Narren
> Eben zum Narren auch, wie sich's gehört!
>
> Merlin der Alte, im leuchtenden Grabe,
> Wo ich als Jüngling gesprochen ihn habe,
> Hat mich mit ähnlicher Antwort belehrt:
> Töricht, auf Bessrung der Toren zu harren!
> Kinder der Klugheit, o habet die Narren
> Eben zum Narren auch, wie sich's gehört!
>
> Und auf den Höhen der indischen Lüfte
> Und in den Tiefen ägyptischer Grüfte
> Hab' ich das heilige Wort nur gehört:
> Töricht, auf Bessrung der Toren zu harren!
> Kinder der Klugheit, o habet die Narren
> Eben zum Narren auch, wie sich's gehört![62]

(Let scholars squabble and dispute among themselves, let pedants and pundits be as strict and circumspect as they like: all the wisest men throughout the ages have smiled and winked and agreed that it's foolish to hope to teach a fool. Children of wisdom, just leave him to his folly, as is proper! Old Merlin, when as a youth, I questioned him in his shining tomb, gave me this same answer: It is foolish to hope to teach a fool. Children of wisdom, just leave him to his folly, as is proper! And in the windswept heights of India and in the deep Egyptian abysses, this alone was the gospel that I heard: It is foolish to hope to teach a fool. Children of wisdom, just leave him to his folly, as is proper!)

The name-dropping sage in the song is an actual historical personage, the self-proclaimed seer and sorceror Alessandro Cagliostro (1743–95). Goethe was fascinated by his charlatan contemporary and included him as a figure in an unfinished operatic project and a prose play, "Der Gross-Cophta." Whether Wolf knew the background of the two "Coptic songs," which were extracted from the unfinished libretto and published separately, is unknown. It is at least probable that he investigated the matter, since the title "*Coptic* songs" might arouse curiosity in those less literarily inclined than Wolf, but that is only speculation. Wolf, after all, only discovered the biographical background to Mörike's Peregrina poems several years after setting two of them to music; he was utterly taken with the tale, but knowledge of it was not necessary for composition. Knowing the genesis of the poetry does, however, give those of us who follow in the composer's wake an additional window into the song.

During the 1780s and 1790s, Goethe's interest in the death throes of the Bourbon dynasty and his desire to write opera librettos briefly coincided, resulting finally in 1787 in the first sketches of a work on the famous Necklace Affair of 1785–86.[63] Goethe had first approached the composer and pianist Philipp Christoph Kayser (1755–1823) in 1784 about an operatic collaboration,[64] but conceived the idea of an opera buffa on the recent scandal only after his trip to Italy.[65] The second sketch, however, is a singspiel libretto written in German and entitled "Die Mystificirten" (The mystification), with indications for arias, recitatives, trios, an arioso, and a duet, the libretto fragmentary and never finished.[66] Instead, Goethe rewrote the work in prose as a five-act comedy, "Der Gross-Cophta" (The great Copt), first performed 17 December 1791 by the ducal theater at the Weimar court.

The character who sings the two Coptic songs in act 1, scene 4 of the unfinished singspiel is Count Rostro, a transparent pseudonym for Cagliostro, who claimed to be one of the greatest of all magicians.[67] His popularity in the most aristocratic circles during the Age of Reason is a pointed reminder that necromancy and superstition flourished right alongside the work of the *Encyclopédistes*. His real name was probably Giuseppe Balsamo, born of poor parents in Palermo. He entered a monastery in his early teens as a matter of expediency and for a time assisted an apothecary there; chemistry and medicine were still closely allied with alchemy at that time. He later claimed in his memoirs that he was born in El-Medina and studied astrology, alchemy, and the Coptic Christian ritual in Alexandria. Although much of the story is false, he did travel for a year or so in Malta, Messina, and perhaps to Alexandria and Cairo. He returned to Italy in 1768 and married a fourteen-year-old siren, Lorenza Feliciani, of a similar amoral disposition. In 1776, on his second trip to London, Balsamo took the name Conte di Cagliostro, and the pair established a salon for sorcery, with the rich and titled especially welcome. In 1780, they moved to Paris as protégés of the Cardinal de Rohan, whose disfavor with Marie Antoinette the sorceror had promised to rectify. Instead, both the disgraced Cardinal and Cagliostro became cat's-paws for Countess Jeanne de la Motte, who schemed to acquire a valuable diamond necklace by trading on the Queen's name. Cagliostro paid dearly for his role as dupe, as he was thrown in the Bastille until June 1786 and subsequently exiled from France. He was imprisoned in 1791 by the Inquisition and died, still in captivity, in 1795.[68]

Goethe's interest in Cagliostro in the 1780s seems inevitable in retrospect, not only because Cagliostro was such a successful charlatan, one who fascinated intelligent, cultured people as well as the easily gulled, but because the two men ironically shared many interests. Both were Freemasons, although Cagliostro's brand of "Egyptian Freemasonry" eventually caused him to be expelled from the society. In particular, Goethe was interested in the apothecary arts, in mysticism, the Philosopher's Stone and alchemy—branches of knowledge to which Cagliostro pretended expertise. Goethe's curiosity was finally so piqued that he traveled to Palermo in April 1787 and paid a visit to the Balsamo family.[69] In the unfinished librettos and in "Der Gross-Cophta," Goethe pokes fun at Cagliostro's absurd rituals, the worshipfulness accorded him by sycophantic disciples, the linguistic babble in which he conveyed spirit messages, and his propensity for grand entrances. (Goethe's fictional courtiers in act 1, scene 2 of the prose play form an antiphonal chorus of fulsome praise when the Count first appears—"What majesty! What power! What a voice! What a man!"—as an envoy of the unknown and unseen Great Copt.) The caricature is more lighthearted in the libretto sketches and the poems than in the play.

In the "Cophtisches Lied I," Graf Rostro, speaking to his disciples, dispenses what passes for both "wisdom" and his divine credentials. He is understandably vague about his sources. Only Merlin, a legend and safely dead, is invoked by name. Even before the first appearance of the refrain, we are told in several ways that it is a fool himself, not a sage, who speaks. Dactylic tetrameters are not the meter to select for serious matters, since they usually sound either fast-paced and driven or, as here, light-hearted, bouncy, and frivolous. There is a comic discrepancy between the poetic meter and the claims to profundity. The charlatan distinguishes between "Gelehrte" (learned men), whom he dismisses as hopeless pedants, and the "Weisesten" (the wisest men) such as himself. The image of sages throughout history clucking together like chickens in a barn, laughing and winking and trading such elderly clichés as the refrain "Töricht, auf Bessrung der Torren zu harren" is wonderfully funny. The Count is understandably obsessed with fools, so the related words "Töricht" and "Torren" appear in the first line of the refrain, while the word "Narren" is repeated in the second and third lines. Those second and third lines are elided in such a way that the concluding tag phrase, "wie sichs gehört," is stressed. This prim colloquialism seems to hail more from some bourgeois German parlor than from an alchemist's chambers; to end a supposed "mystic maxim" with this commonplace and self-satisfied little flourish is one of the best comic touches in the poem. By the end of the third verse, the Count in his grandiloquence compares the nonsensical adage to scripture, "das heilige Wort."

Wolf, who suffered neither pedants nor charlatans gladly, both heightens the multiple verbal clues that the pot is calling the kettle black and adds still others from the musical realm.[70] The song has no introduction; rather, the so-called magician launches into the pervasive dactylic rhythms without preamble. The wit, as always, lies in the handling of the tonal and harmonic materials. The tonal strife and contention appears, with wickedly apposite humor, before the verbs "zanken und streiten" at the first invocation of the "Gelehrte." The E♮ produced by passing motion in the inner voice and by the mock-pathetic diminished fourth in the vocal line produces a conflict-ridden augmented tonic chord in measure 1, en route to subdominant harmonies similarly altered in further depiction of scholarly strife. The E♮ is subsequently reinterpreted, first, as F♭ in the "streng und bedächtig" contrary motion of measure 3, the chord progression in that bar recurring varied and revoiced four measures later at the words "lächeln und winken," the pseudosages' laughter a duplication of their earlier mockery. And yet, one notices that the strophe is divided into neatly symmetrical antecedent-consequent phrases, as square-cut as ever any pedant could devise, with each line of text accorded two bars of brisk dactylic processional rhythm ("not slow and sluggish," Wolf cautions, tongue-in-cheek). One measure later, it is respelled as the E♮ chord tone in the C-major point of arrival, the C–E♮s of the chord voicing in measure 1 given a new harmonic context, and still later, as the unison F♭s used to inveigh against fools and foolishness in the refrain. The "Gelehrte" are thus identified as fools from the start. The refrain approaches slapstick comedy in music, hilariously prepared by the cadence on the dominant E♭ in the upper register just preceding the "mystery motif"[71]—the E♭ cadence the harmonic analogy to the colon at the end of the poetic line ("stimmen mit ein":). The neighbor-note relationship of F♭ and E♭ is dramatized by multiple contrasts, by the major-seventh leap in measure 10, the sforzando initial pitch followed by a sudden hush, the contrast between unharmonized octaves and the return to full chordal texture, all culminating in the triumphal and "proper" cadence.

Wolf honors the enjambment of lines 2 and 3 of the refrain ("Kinder der Klugheit, o haben die Narren / eben zum Narren auch, wie sich's gehört!") by enjambing the chunky two-bar phrases for the first time, the lines bridged by the emphatic D♭ reintroduced at the end of measure 12 and by the overlapping seventh chords. Each time the triumphantly simple cadence recurs, it is preceded by a jaunty dotted rhythm in the vocal line, the only dotted rhythmic figure in the entire song, and ends with the scale degrees $\hat{3}$–$\hat{2}$–$\hat{1}$ in the topmost voice, a repetition of the initial three pitches in the vocal line. Perhaps because the adage is so silly, one hears in the concluding formula an echo of "Three Blind Mice."

The mystery motif at the beginning of the refrain is openly mocked in the four-bar piano interlude that follows the refrain each time, both musical mimicry of the Count and his disciples laughing in concert and a parody of this emanation from Beyond. The ascending major sevenths of measure 10 become descending minor ninths, related in kind to the exaggerated intervallic gestures that bespeak donkeys' braying in the "Lied des transferierten Zettel" (Song of the transformed Bottom) and "Schweig' einmal still" from the *Italienisches Liederbuch*, with the right- and left-hand parts ricocheting in opposite directions and the F♭s of measures 15–17 resolving to the lower neighbor E♭ in another register. Only with the final measure of the refrain does F♭ become a repeated grace note to E♭ in a cadence whose mild dissonances—a jangle of laughter—are absent from the deliberately proper cadence in measure 14. The lack of a strong first beat for the first time in seventeen measures suggests with wicked accuracy a gasp for breath before a burst of derisive laughter, while the grace notes in close succession are a familiar Wolfian index of two-sided comic criticism. The poetic persona mocks *his* target, and the music mocks him.

In the second stanza, Graf Rostro ostensibly travels back in time to his youthful chats with the entombed Merlin, who tells him the same obvious maxim he has just presented in the first stanza. Wolf spoofs both distance and mysticism when he uses enharmonic presto-chango tactics in measure 21 to move suddenly, far, far away from the A♭/E♭ axis to a passage without a strong sense of rooted location as transition to the hilariously varied refrain. The enharmonic time-travel to a briefly and unstably tonicized E♮—the F♭ of the first refrain—returns by measure 24 to the dominant of B♭, prolonged at the word "belehrt" while the disciples wait with bated breath for the revelation. The portentous pause before the mystical "answer," prolonging the suspense like a proper charlatan, is marked by three solemn strokes on F in the low bass, as if issuing from a grave. The dactylic pattern appears here reversed (fast-fast-slow) and in augmentation, its former antic liveliness transformed into mystical gong strokes. The maxim about and by fools now purports to come from Merlin's tomb, a magician more venerable than the Graf, so the pseudomystification deepens. Wolf concocts a delightful visual-musical metaphor for the maxim, that is, for something simple disguised as something complex: a minor triad spelled G♭–A–D♭, the D♭–C semitone in the bass shortly to be reharmonized in the tonic key of A♭.

The third stanza begins as a slightly varied return to the music of the first stanza, set initially in a higher tessitura to match the "heights of the Indian breezes," followed by a plunge downward to suggest the Egyptian abysses (some mention of Egypt is virtually obligatory for Cagliostro, the self-proclaimed inventor of Egyptian Freemasonry). The first-beat emphasis on "und" ("*und* auf den Höhen . . . *und* in den Tiefen") in each instance is a prosodic detail by means of which Wolf wickedly points out the redundancy of this evidentiary roll call. The tonal ambiguity of measures 40–43 at the words "hab' ich das heilige Wort nur gehört" and the sequential repetition a step higher in the piano is the concomitant of mystic indeterminacy of time and space, except for the undeniable fact that the melodic-motivic material of the "Holy Writ" is unchanged from before. The refrain, its dramatic beginning transposed upward for each recurrence, resounds from the heights and the depths simultaneously, over a six-octave span in the accompaniment. The postlude is unchanged from its earlier incarnations—the augmented "profundity" of the mystic refrain provokes the same cackle of laughter as before. And yet, by mingling harmonies borrowed from the E tonal center that stems from the initial chromatic disturbance in measure 1 into the A♭-major fabric of the song, Wolf suggests the genuine complexity of the knowledge, magical or musical, that the Count does not know but on whose grounds he trespasses. Intrinsic in the structure of Wolf's setting is the twofold revelation that the Count knows nothing and is himself a fool and that which he pretends to possess is, in spite of his charlatanry, something profound. The lied does indeed "raise spirits," if not in Cagliostro's meaning.

Walker was no happier with the humorous songs in the *Goethe-Lieder* than he was with the Mörike songs. The "Cophtisches Lied I," he concedes, has a "touch of humor," while "Erschaffen und Beleben" (To create and animate) from Goethe's late Orientalizing collection, *Der West-östliche Divan*, belongs to the "characteristic" type in which "the singer has to be content with a declamatory style that is far removed from the normal conception of a 'song.'" The five songs from the *Schenkenbuch* (The tavern-keeper's book) section of *Der West-östliche Divan*, including the comic song in praise of wine, "Ob der Koran von Ewigkeit sei?" (Has the Koran existed from eternity?), are, he says, difficult to perform and to appreciate.[72] These comic poems do not exemplify tendentious comedy in the same sense, certainly not in the same degree, as the Mörike poems, and Walker seems therefore to have missed many of the comic elements altogether and to have reacted in a tepid fashion to those he did observe. It is a curious dissonance to discover between the composer, who prized his comedic creations and always gravitated to the comic works by his favorite poets, and his best biographer.

Walker does not even mention "Der Schäfer" (The shepherd). Here, Goethe does a comic turn on the pastoral tradition in which Aminta, Tirsi, Clori, and assorted swains languish for love in Arcadia. The poem hinges on the rhymes "Schäfer-Schläfer/Schaf-Schlaf" (shepherd-sleeper, sheep-sleep) and on love's kinship with and difference from other fleshly appetites. A shepherd notable principally for his laziness falls in love and cannot eat or sleep. Wandering about disconsolately by night, he counts not sheep but stars. Unrequited love for a time displaces all other physical needs, but once the sweetheart accepts the "poor booby" ("der Tropf," the poetic narrator's term for the unheroic protagonist) and love is satiated, the bodily appetites flood back in full force. Even the most melodramatic manifestations of love do not change the lover's nature, especially one so strongly defined by its physical needs. The poem is a comic demonstration of a pessimistic point about the unalterability of the human animal.

Wolf marks the song "Träge und schleppend" (sluggish and dawdling) and then makes his music yawn and dawdle in several ways. The introduction, like the introduction to "Zur Warnung," exemplifies Wolf's ability to devise music perceived as comic before words enter to define the nature of the joke. The yawning figures of a major seventh and major ninth, the second yawn bigger than the first, shambles across the bar lines, the shepherd too sleepy to notice them. The shuddering, yawning trills provide rhythmic emphasis on the downbeat, but that pitch is much lower than the anacrusis, a bit of melodic-metrical obfuscation evocative of sleep-dazed bleariness. The music is likewise initially lazy about defining the C-minor tonality of the song. Wolf sets the first stanza as a 2 + 2–bar unharmonized sequence, based on the semitone figures and descending motion of the introduction but not a literal restatement. When the maiden arrives on the scene in stanza 2 and in the treble register, the yawning stops momentarily, replaced by chromatic lamentation. The prolongation of the word "Fort [Appetit und Schlaf]" (Hunger and sleep vanished) is a typical Wolfian prosodic refinement; Wolf uses the same prosodic means at the beginning of the fourth stanza, when the word that pulls the tale forward into the present—"Nun" (Now)—is prolonged across the bar line. Lost repose does not permit cadential resolution, hence the mock-horror cliché of deceptive motion to a diminished-seventh chord at the word "Schlaf." Something similar but even more mock-melodramatic occurs at the end of stanza 4 on the same word, the trill-figure emphases on the pitch A♭ earlier in the song eventually leading to a deceptive cadence on an A♭ chord in measure 34 (but with tonic C in the bass and the voice). In this $A \ B \ A^1 \ B^1$ form, the setting of the third stanza, when the love-struck shepherd is counting stars in the wilderness, is a rhythmic variant of the first stanza; the tick-tock repeated notes evoke monotonous counting and walking motion simultaneously. The musical parallelism tells us that the shepherd who laments by night is the same lazy creature that we met sans sweetheart in the first stanza.

Two of the comic songs from the *Goethe-Lieder*, both in praise of wine, come from *Der West-östlicher Divan*, one of the most renowned German poetic works on the Orient. Goethe, however, had no experience of the Far East: his Orient is what Edward Said calls a "free-floating Orient," a realm of unimaginable antiquity that acted as a form of release for the poetic imagination. Stunned by his discovery in June 1814 of poems by the late-fourteenth-century Persian poet Hafiz in translations by the Orientalist Joseph von Hammer-Purgstall,[73] Goethe declared that he had found, in a distant land and a distant age, the poetic twin to his own late style:[74] rejoicing in life, embracing the eternal from the standpoint of earthly things, mixing together the objective and symbolic realms, often playful in tone, the distinctive playfulness of a few old, wise poets. As Goethe told Zelter in a letter of 11 May 1820, "The Mohammedan religion, mythology, and customs invite a poetry fitting for one my age. Absolute surrender to the inscrutable will of God; the calmly cheerful survey of earthly striving, always moving—, circling—, spiraling back to where it began; love, affection, all swaying between two worlds, everything that is real purified, dissolving into the symbolic. What more could an old man want?"[75] He had studied Judaic, Arabic, and Persian antiquity much earlier in his life (he contemplated a "Mahomet-Drama" in 1773) and read Oriental travel literature throughout his life, but the encounter with a Germanized Hafiz at this period in his life was a fateful one.

Goethe began his Hafiz-like enterprise not with the great mystical poems in the collection but with merry poems in praise of wine. The theme of *Weinseligkeit* ("intoxicated blessedness," or rapture conferred by wine, the German word nicely apropos) recurs many times in Hafiz's poetry, part of a complex of leitmotifs (wine, nightingales, roses, love and the beloved, wistful reflections on time and aging) reminiscent of the Anacreontic poetry prevalent in Germany when Goethe was a young man. "Erschaffen und Beleben" from the *Buch des Sängers* (The singer's book), the first book of *Der West-östliche Divan*, is the first poem Goethe wrote for his *Divan*, the autograph manuscript dated 21 June 1814. It is a comic version of the creation myth, both earthy and effervescent, joined with an encomium to wine. God's infusion of divine spirit is not sufficient to counteract man's derivation from a clump of soil; we are botched creations, uncouthness our inheritance from Mother Earth. The image of the newly fashioned, rough-hewn first man—Goethe turns him into a German peasant lad named Hans Adam—sneezing when God blows the breath of life into his nostrils is Goethe's wonderfully boorish addition to a theme borrowed from Hafiz and transformed.[76] Despite God's best efforts, His creation remains "half an oaf," a lump of unleavened dough, until Noah introduces him to wine, Goethe weaving together two incidents from Genesis in defiance of biblical chronology: the creation myth and Noah's drunkenness. Only strong drink completes the process of bringing man fully to life, awakening and enrapturing the spirit, and if one follows Hafiz's example, one can thereby ascend all the way to heaven. Wine is both wine and the intoxicating excess of that which is Godly on earth, a liquid bridge to God, but the subject is always a matter for merriment.

In "Erschaffen und Beleben," Goethe writes folk song–like quatrains in emphatic iambic rhythms and equally thumping rhymes.

> Hans Adam war ein Erdenkloss,
> Den Gott zum Menschen machte;
> Doch bracht' er aus der Mutter Schoss
> Noch vieles Ungeschlachte.
>
> Die Elohim zur Nas hinein
> Den besten Geist ihm bliesen;
> Nun schien er schon was mehr zu sein,
> Denn er fing an zu niesen.
>
> Doch mit Gebein und Glied und Kopf
> Blieb er ein halber Klumpen,
> Bis endlich Noah für den Tropf
> Das Wahre fand, den Humpen.
>
> Der Klumpe fühlt sogleich den Schwung,
> Sobald er sich benetzet,
> So wie der Teig durch Säuerung
> Sich in Bewegung setzet.
>
> So, Hafis, mag dein holder Sang,
> Dein heiliges Exempel
> Uns führen, bei der Gläser Klang,
> Zu unsres Schöpfers Tempel.

(Hans Adam was a clod of earth that God made into a man, yet from his mother's womb, he brought much that was uncouth. The Immortal blew the divine spirit into his nostrils. Now there appeared to be more to him, and he began to sneeze. But in bones and limbs and head he remained half an oaf until finally Noah found the booby a tonic in a tankard. The boor at once felt his pulses quicken when he had wet his whistle, as dough begins to rise when one adds the leaven. So Hafiz, may your noble song, your holy example, lead us, with the clink of glasses, to our Creator's temple!)

Wolf took his cue from Goethe and translated the poet's bumptious rhythms into the heaviest quarter-note tactus in $\frac{4}{4}$ meter, musical accompaniment for beer tankards hitting a table. The tempo is proper for story telling ("Etwas gemessen, nicht schleppend," or "Somewhat measured, not sluggish"), and the syllabic text setting and quarter-note tactus are folk song–like, but the harmonic excursions are far from folkish. Boorishness is given a sophisticated compound of musical indices, from the forceful (*wuchtig*) open fifths in the piano at the start of the song and the parallel fifths elsewhere (often a sign of peasant, village, or folk life in Wolf's songs), the tritone between the bass and the vocal line in measure 3, and the dissonant cluster C–D–E in measure 6. Hilariously, register is determined by the text in this setting. Wolf places the accompaniment for measures 1–11 entirely in the bass clef, appropriate to a clod of earth; when the Elohim (a designation for God in the Old Testament) appears to blow the breath of divine life into the clump, the right hand swings back and forth for four measures (measures 12–15) between the treble clef and the bass clef, "pumping" motion that raises the clod from his lowly beginnings to a higher level. How Wolf must have laughed when he set those two lines ("Die Elohim zur Nas hinein / den besten Geist ihm bliesen") to the baldest possible tritone in the bass (*diabolus in musica*) in measures 12–15! Just before, the dynamics drop from forte to piano for the admission that God brought forth from Mother Earth much that was crude, as if such indelicate matters should only be mentioned in hushed tones, and the composer begins to dig flats out of the musical earth, mining a new musical symbolism for the enharmonic maneuver. God's breath or no, the uncouthness and therefore the flats persist throughout the infusion of holy spirit.

It is always interesting to see what inspired Wolf in a poem and which elements left him cold. The setting of stanzas 1, 2, and 3 is characteristic Wolfian humor of a high order. When Hans Adam seems to be taking shape at the end of stanza 2, the flats give way to relative major (G major) and a fit of grace-noted sneezing in the piano, the paired sneezes sounding in the higher register as the music expels the last flats for a time. The sneezing also causes the newly created man to lose some of the divine, elevating spirit just bestowed on him, and therefore Wolf reinterprets the uncouth G♭s from before and sets the music down a peg from G major to F♯ major for stanza 3. Goethe arranges the syntax of this stanza so that the alcoholic remedy is delayed until the last words, and Wolf dramatizes the buildup to climactic disclosure even more by musical means. The beer-hall quarter-note tactus continues unabated in the piano throughout the third stanza, but in the vocal line, Wolf sustains each accented syllable of each iamb for three beats across the bar line ("bis *end*-lich *No*-ah *für* den *Tropf* . . ."). The tactic indeed prolongs the suspense: where two lines of verse occupied four bars of music in the previous stanzas, they require eight measures here, while the rising chromatic sequence traced throughout the phrase is a comically unsubtle means to procure added emphasis. But stanza 4, with its image of leavened bread rising, seems not to have engaged Wolf's imagination, and Wolf merely extends the previous F♯ tonal area until the poet turns from Hans Adam to Hafiz in the fifth and final stanza. The initial word of the stanza, "So," is prolonged throughout an entire measure, just as one might prolong that word in speech to underscore

a change of subject or direction, here, to humorously exaggerated grandiloquence evident in wide-spanning rolled chords and a doubling of the narrative
tactus. Wolf returns to the E-minor tonality he left behind near the beginning
of the song, en route to a massive E-major conclusion. The semitone slip
downward from E to D♯ at the words "holy example" is a means of harmonic
emphasis Wolf uses here for the tongue-in-cheek invocation of sanctity, reminiscent of similarly "sacred" gestures in "Cophtisches Lied I." And like the
ending of "Der Glücksritter," Wolf imagines a comic processional in the
piano postlude, replete with plagal harmonies, to accompany a well-oiled
entry into heaven.

THE WOMEN OF THE *ITALIENISCHES LIEDERBUCH*

The comic songs in the Mörike volume are remarkable for elements of the
fantastic, but even these caprices are characterized by a psychological realism
that Wolf admired[77] and that must have constituted part of the attraction to
Heyse's folksong translations.[78] The comic songs in the *Italienisches Liederbuch* are consistent with Wolf's preferences for exaggerated imagery, emphatic tone, and the comedy of hostility. At last he could return to tendentious
humor in music, after Goethe's tolerant laughter—the merriment of an old
man who could, and did, laugh like a child—and the predominantly tragic or
passionate poems of the *Spanisches Liederbuch*.

The anonymous folk poets of the *Italienisches Liederbuch* are preoccupied
almost entirely with love in its different aspects and moods, including the
inevitable episodes of anger at the beloved for his or her shortcomings—primarily his. This is not a world of fantasy and poetry about poetry, but a sphere
where the strong-willed kin of Despina, Serpina, and Susanna keep their lovers in line, upbraid them, dismiss them, complain about them. The depth of
characterization in these songs is the final step in a cumulative process by
which the original Italian folk poems undergo a sea change in Heyse's German translation and then are once again reinterpreted in the musical setting.
The women of "Du denkst mit einem Fädchen," "Mein Liebster ist so klein,"
"Mein Liebster hat zu Tische mich geladen," and "Ich liess mir sagen" become Teutonic types, robbed of their Italian peasant naiveté by a translator
who had hoped to do otherwise and a composer uninterested in folklike simplicities. The ambivalence of humor, its psychological compound of mixed
motives and psychic mechanisms, becomes more marked with each stage
away from the folk-song origins.

Paul Heyse (1830–1914), "the master of the modern novella," was awarded
the Nobel Prize for literature in 1910, but his renown did not endure much
beyond his death. He was a prolific writer, with twenty-four volumes of no-

Figure 3. Paul Heyse (1830–1914), poet and translator of the
Italienisches Liederbuch

vellas, almost fifty verse dramas, novels by the score, a considerable body of
original lyric and epic poetry, and numerous translations from Spanish,
Provençal, French, and Italian sources. He became interested in Italian folk
poetry during his university years in Berlin in the late 1840s, when he befriended the historian Jacob Burckhardt (1818–97) and the art historian Franz
Kugler, who taught at the Kunstakademie and collected Italian folk poetry as
an avocation. Kugler's house was a second home to Emanuel Geibel, Heyse's
collaborator on the *Spanisches Liederbuch*, and to Heyse, who married
Kugler's daughter Margarethe in 1852 and took her to Italy for their honey-
moon in 1852–53. In May of 1854, Heyse went to Munich and became the
organizing force of a poetic society entitled "Die Krokodile" (The crocodiles)
after a humorous poem, "Das Krokodil zu Singapur," by Hermann Lingg.[79]

Lingg and Baron Adolph Friedrich von Schack, along with Heinrich
Leuthold, Wilhelm Hertz, Friedrich Bodenstedt, Geibel, and Heyse were the
principal constituents of "Die Krokodile," which did not produce much, if
any, great poetry on its own merits but did provide lieder composers with a
wealth of material. Several members of the group courted Mörike's friendship
and his advice regarding their works; Wolf, who read and admired Mörike's
letters, might have been amused to find that the older master criticized Lingg's
verse quite sharply in a personal letter to the Bavarian-born army surgeon.[80]
(Brahms set Lingg's "Lied" from the *Gedichte* of 1855 as "Immer leiser wird
mein Schlummer," or "Ever gentler grows my slumber," op. 105, no. 2, one
of the foremost examples of a great lied fashioned from mediocre poetry.)
Heyse and Geibel both fared better with the older master, especially Heyse,
for whom Mörike wrote his "Besuch in der Kartause: Epistel an Paul Heyse"
(Visit to the Kartause: letter to Paul Heyse).[81]

The *Italienisches Liederbuch* was dedicated to Burckhardt and published in
Berlin in 1860. The poems in the anthology are taken not from field research
but from Italian collections of folk verse published between 1829 and the late
1850s and from Kugler's unpublished manuscript collection. Heyse only
translated a fraction of the folk poems contained in his sources, including two
previous German anthologies of Italian folk poetry. In the preface, Heyse
writes that the *Italienisches Liederbuch* was compiled as a continuation of his
German predecessors' accomplishments in the dissemination of Italian folk
poetry, beginning with Herder's *Stimmen der Völker in Gesang* (Voices of the
people in song).

EGERIA. Raccolta di Poesie Italiane Popolari, cominciata da Gu-
glielmo Mueller, dopo la di lui morte terminata e pubblicata da O.L.B.
Wolff, Dottore e Professore.

[Sammlung italienischer Volkslieder, aus mündlicher Ueberlieferung
und fliegenden Blättern, begonnen von Wilhelm Müller, vollendet, nach
dessen Tode herausgegeben und mit erlauternden Anmerkungen ver-
sehen von Dr. O.L.B. Wolff.] Leipzig, Ernst Fleischer. 1829.

AGRUMI. Volksthümliche Poesieen aus allen Mundarten Italiens und
seiner Inseln. Gesammelt und übersetzt von August Kopisch. Berlin,
Verlag von Gustav Franz. 1838.

Wolf would have known Müller (1794–1827) as the poet of the Schubert song
cycles,[82] and Kopisch's name would have been familiar to him from Loewe's
settings of ballads by that poet.[83] Of Heyse's Italian sources, I mention only
those for the poems Wolf set to music.

CANTI POPOLARI Toscani Corsi Illirici Greci raccolti e illustrati da
N[iccoló]. Tommaseo, con opusculo originale del medisimo autore. Vol.

I. II. Venezia. 1841. dalla Stabilimento tipografico enciclopedico di Girolamo Tasso.[84]

CANTI DEL POPOLO VENEZIANO per la prima volta raccolti ed illustrati da Angelo Dalmedico, volume unico, opera che puó continuarsi a quella dei canti popolari Toscani etc. del Cittadino N. Tommaseo. Venezia. Andrea Santini e Figlio. MCDDDXLVIII.

CANTI POPOLARI inediti Umbri Liguri Piceni Piemontesi Latini raccolti e illustrati da Oreste Marcoaldi. Genova, co' tipi del R.J. de' Sordomuti. 1855.

CANTI POPOLARI TOSCANI raccolti e annotati da Giuseppe Tigri. Volume unico. Firenze, Barbera, Bianchi e Comp. Via Faenza 4765. 1856, vol. 2 in 1860.

Heyse does not explain on what basis he made his selection, although he writes of various topics in the introduction: the changeable improvisational art of folk song "that knows of nothing fixed"; the Corsican predilection for death laments; and the relative lack of narrative ballads compared to other European and Nordic traditions. Aware of the pitfalls of translation and, it would seem, anxious to mitigate criticism in advance, he admits the deficiencies to which foreign scholars are prone, pointing out that such as he have not "sharpened their ears to the finest half-tones of a foreign language," have not "imbibed the language with their mother's milk," and therefore cannot possibly say the last word on the folk art of another culture. This, he says, is just the beginning for German readers interested in Italian folk poetry, a foundation on which others can build.[85]

Heyse stated his intent to create in German translation a "middle way" between the directness and naiveté characteristic of Italian folk poetry and the "affected and bombastic" nature of German speech.[86] He tried to preserve the standard eleven-syllable line of the Italian originals wherever possible, even though German poetry is not defined by syllabification, and he attempted literal translation rather than paraphrase on many occasions. But directness, naiveté, and literal translation proved difficult goals to achieve, and the "middle way" becomes in many instances a metamorphosis of Italian peasant maidens into German women with larger vocabularies and greater intensity of expression than their models. Heyse even adds additional lines—further variations on the preceding theme—in "Mein Liebster ist so klein" (My lover is so small), based on a Tuscan rispetto from Giuseppe Tigri's second volume in 1860.

> E lo mio damo e tanto piccolino,
> Che co' capelli mi spazza la casa.
> Ando nell'orto a corre un gelsomino,

Ebbe paura d'una lumaca.
E venne in casa, e si messe a sedere,
Passo una mosca e lo fece cadere.
E lu' si rizza, e ando alla finestra,
Passo un tafano e gli rompe la testa:
E maledisco le mosche e i cugini,
E chi s'innamoro de' piccolini.[87]

Wolf almost certainly did not know the Italian originals. In a letter to Emil
Kauffmann on 23 December 1892, he writes, "A warm heart, I can assure
you, beats in the small bodies of my youngest children of the South, who
cannot, despite appearances, deny their German origins. Yes, their hearts beat
in German, though the sun shines on them in Italian (as with France in 'Der
Tambour')."[88]

The woman who speaks in "Mein Liebster ist so klein," seemingly dis-
mayed over her sweetheart's smallness, resorts to revenge-fantasy in which
the Lilliputian lover is characterized as a mincing, feminine creature; assaulted and beaten by insects; and finally grouped with them as a similarly
plaguey creature. His manhood is multiply impugned: like a woman, he
cleans house; like a woman, he has long hair; like a woman, he goes out into
the garden (in the German translation, a "Gärtlein," or little garden, to match
his own diminutive stature) to pick jasmine, a decidedly unmasculine occupation in those unliberated times. Her frustration is even more pronounced in
Heyse's German.

Mein Liebster ist so klein, dass ohne Bücken
Er mir das Zimmer fegt mit seinen Locken.
Als er ins Gärtlein ging, Jasmin zu pflücken,
Ist er vor einer Schnecke sehr erschrocken.
Dann setzt er sich ins Haus um zu verschnaufen,
Da warf ihn eine Fliege übern Haufen;
Und als er hintrat an mein Fensterlein,
Stiess eine Bremse ihm den Schädel ein.
Verwünscht sei'n alle Fliegen, Schnacken, Bremsen—
Und wer ein Schätzchen hat aus den Maremmen!
Verwünscht sei'n alle Fliegen, Schnacken, Mücken—
Und wer sich, wenn er küsst, so tief muss bücken![89]

(My beloved is so small that without stooping, he can sweep the floor
with his curls. When he went into the little garden to pick jasmine, he
was greatly frightened by a snail. Then, when he sat down in the house
to catch his breath, a fly knocked him over, and when he stepped over to
my little window, a bluebottle smashed in his head. Accursed be all flies,
midges, bluebottles, and whoever has a sweetheart from Maremma!

Accursed be all flies, midges, gnats and all who must stoop so low for a kiss!)

The difference is a matter of emphasis. To be "sehr erschrocken" (greatly frightened) is more emphatic than the unmodified "paura" of the Italian poem; "lo fece cadere" (made him fall) is tamer than "werfen ihn übern Haufen" (knock him over) and "gli rompe la testa" is similarly simpler and less vivid than Heyse's idiomatic expression, "Stiess eine Bremse ihm den Schädel ein."

Heyse extends the poem by two additional lines and alters the ending, countermanding his stated goal of fidelity to the Italian originals. The result, however, is an astute enrichment of the poem. In the folk poem, the woman ends by cursing, first, all pesky insects and those "who love little men." Despite the Swiftian caricature-diminishment to which she has subjected the small-scale lover in her comic fantasy, it is clear that she loves him. Heyse's German counterpart is even more passionate than her Italian model. One teasing curse is not enough for her; first, she heaps invective on those who have a sweetheart from Maremma, where the men are proverbially short of stature, and then curses those who must stoop to be kissed. The word "Schätzchen," "little treasure" or "sweetheart," already tells the reader that the diminutive beloved is not an ex-sweetheart, and the "stooping" at beginning and end is Heyse's pictorializing addition to his Tuscan source. The lover need not bend down to sweep the floor with his Rapunzel tresses, but *she* must stoop down to receive his kisses.

Wolf, with his customary insight into characterization, understood that such intensity does not spring from indifference.[90] In the piano postlude, he does what Heyse had done before him in the translation; that is, he adds an invented image of his own derived from the last line of the poem, and thereby alters the tone of the tale at its end. The singer's last words, "so tief muss bücken," are set as a completed melodic cadence in the parallel minor mode to tonic F major, after invective rendered all the more dramatic by the descending sequence full of augmented triads in measures 54–57 and the Neapolitan harmonies in measures 57–59. But the piano, especially from measures 54–61, keeps delaying arrival at the tonic and at the end of the texted body of the song, rhythmically displaces the expected tonic, as if in tonal analogy to the verb "bücken." With the postlude, there is yet another postponement of tonic but one that ascends from the lower register of the Bb-minor cursing into the upper register. Wolf in this way implies that the lover, more considerate than some in the *Italienisches Liederbuch*, does not want his beloved to stoop down, and therefore strains upward on tiptoe in order to kiss her. The half- and whole steps in the brief motives that have depicted him from the beginning as a mincing, delicate creature widen to thirds and fourths; the "swinging" motion and the bell-like voicing, with prominent intervals of

the perfect fifth, recall similar *Glockenklänge* sounds associated with peace
after travail in the Mörike song "In der Frühe" (At dawn) and suggest reconciliation and an imminent end to the singer's rage. The anger is not forgotten,
however, evident in the retention to the end of the lowered sixth and lowered
second scale degrees prominent from the beginning of the song. The ambivalence of mixed emotions—love and the echoes of recent sarcastic anger—
becomes mixed modal sounds in an ending that supplies an additional vignette
to Heyse's poem.

At the beginning, however, the lover is completely humorous, an effeminate creature in the treble register. The figure repeated in various transforma-
tions throughout the piano part is appropriately suggestive of littleness
incarnate—short-breathed and intervallically restricted. It also seems like a
chromatic reincarnation of similar figuration throughout Schubert's Goethe
lied "Geheimes," D. 719 (Examples 14a and 14b). The association, conscious
or unconscious on Wolf's part, hardly seems coincidental when one realizes
that in both songs love is simultaneously hidden and known, cloaked in secrecy or exasperation and yet assured. The lover in "Geheimes" rejoices that

Example 14a. Hugo Wolf, "Mein Liebster ist so klein," measures 1–10

Example 14b. Franz Schubert, "Geheimes," D. 719, measures 1–10

he knows the code behind his sweetheart's flirtatious glances, knows that they signify loving messages for him alone, while the woman in Heyse's poem cannot, for all her invective, hide her love for the "Schätzchen" from Maremma. When one remembers that Wolf was a small man whose friends at times compared him to an elf, that Schubert was similarly short of stature, that Wolf's love for Melanie was a matter of secrecy and coded messages, that his feelings for Schubert—the "Liederfürst," or "Prince of Song"—encompassed both love and frustration, the motivic connection between "Geheimes" and "Mein Liebster ist so klein" seems, if anything, overdetermined. For all Wolf's anger that he came after Schubert, he could not help but love his predecessor's lieder, and the helpless capitulation to such profound ambiguity exactly parallels the emotional situation in Heyse's poem.

Whatever the link to Schubert's song, the figures become entirely Wolfian in their chromatic-comedic manifestations. In several of Wolf's humorous songs, including "Nein, junger Herr," "Mein Liebster hat zu Tische mich geladen," and "Mein Liebster ist so klein," the introduction is a comic exercise in much ado about very little, or rather, dominant prolongations preceding the initial tonic chord when the singer enters. Here, the lover minces back and forth within a narrow plot of harmonic ground whose enharmonic alterations (C♯ and F♯ for melodic ascent, D♭ and G♭ for descending motion) are further developed later in the lied; for example, the prominent Neapolitan harmonies at the end are implicit in the appoggiaturas to the prolongation of IV$_4^6$ at the beginning—F only appears as a root-position chord when the singer enters. With the woman's first image of the tiny lover and effortless parlor sweeping, we understand the contrary motion between the outer voices in the introduction, the rhythmic displacement created by the appoggiaturas, as the parodistically dainty sweeping movements of the long tresses and the decrescendos through each of the phrase subdivisions in measures 1–6 (1 + 1 + 2 + 2 [+ 1 + 1]) as mimicry of feminine palpitations and airs, and yet the genuine sweetness is evident in the harmonic thirds throughout the right-hand part. The voice leading in all three parts throughout the introduction is restricted to major- and minor-second intervallic relationships, with the harmonic seconds B♭–C exposed at the ends of measures 4, 6, and 7–8 in graphic depiction of littleness. When the singer enters and sings "Mein Liebster ist so klein" to those same intervals, such that the *major* second is expressive of emphasis ("*so* klein"), both the satire and the sweetness are clear. The fact that the motivic seconds of the introduction expand in both directions, but particularly upward in the topmost voice of the piano is especially charming, Wolf thus suggesting that the lover already reaches up to the singer-sweetheart. The high B♭ in measure 17 can be heard both as registral displacement to emphasize the restoration of B♭ after the passing tones/B♮s in measures 15–16—the use of these chromatic passing tones is, of course, a delightful tonal analogy to the verb "fegen," the sweeping motion of the lover's locks—and as the lover overreaching in the attempt to strain upward, perhaps also as a delicate feminine squeal.

Not since Haydn's *The Creation* had a composer so relished the musical depiction of the insect world. Each episode of the lover's tribulations prompts its own variation of the "littleness" figures, its own tonality and tessitura. The vignette of the snail in measures 22–26 produces a higher register and fuller textures evocative of shock and reinterprets the tonic–leading tone pitches of F major as constituents in an implied A-minor mediant region, bringing back the elements of measures 15–16: the D♯–E bass pitches, the B-major seventh chords, and a transposed variant of the vocal line. The ascending leap to F♯, a semitone higher than the initial pitch of the phrase, at its end in measure 25 is an enactment of the motions of fright, typical of Wolf's dramatic bent. (The augmented triad at the end of measure 24 is a favorite harmonic index for extremity, "*sehr* erschrocken.") When the shaken lover returns to the house in measures 27–30, the phrase begins with the same F♮ and E pitches as at the start of the previous phrase but an octave lower and set to an extended dominant of A minor in which the dissonant cross relation between A♯ and A♮ foreshadows the B♭ minor to come and warns that the period of recovery is about to end, that more comic violence is just around the corner. This prolongation of V/III with the 2–3 suspensions is not allowed to "recover," or resolve: before he can recover, measure 31 knocks him headlong harmonically.

The fly buzzes in for the attack with the A–C pitches of the expected resolution but with F as the implied root, followed by a passage in measures 31–34 notable for the neighboring motion around C: the counterpoint buzzes about without going anywhere, quite flylike. The vocal line furthermore is a rearrangement of the same pitches as the vocal part at the beginning, seemingly headed toward the dominant regions. In another delightful instance of tonal wit, Wolf instead brings about a violent turn to the subdominant or B♭ minor, truly a harmonic blow to match the verb "*stiess* eine Bremse ihm den Schädel ein." Here, the B♮s/F♯s of the "fegendes" passing tones in measures 15–16 and of the "fright" in measures 25–26 become the Neapolitan to B♭. The placement of the B♭ chords/unharmonized octaves in measures 42–44 on the second beat of the measure is both an apt detail of text painting (off-beat blows) and a later consequence of the rhythmic displacements at the beginning. One notices, for example, that tonic F in the vocal line of measure 61, at the end of the texted body of the song, is similarly displaced on the second beat and that the root-position tonic harmonies in the postlude are subject to the appoggiatura displacements from earlier.

The twofold cursing is a continued development of the "littleness" figures, the first outbreak in measures 46–49 both a prolongation of the tonicized B♭ minor and an emphatic variation on the descending seconds in measures 3–4. When the singer refers to those "who have a sweetheart from Maremma," one hears those figures from the introduction repeated in the piano but with the continued B♭ pedal in the (treble register) bass; the true foundational tone is the C in the bass of measure 53. The sequential, varied repetition of the curse on the insect horde begins on the A♭s belonging to tonic minor and repeats the descending motives in the piano, this time harmonized with the successive augmented triads that are a familiar stylistic register of anguish and desperation; as the outer voices descend in tenths, different inner voices are delayed and come down at different rates to produce the augmented chords en route. With the postlude, Wolf makes plain that the B♭-minor tonality, the triad outlined here in the outer voices, is subsumed within tonic F; in a charming instance of tonal symbolism, what had seemed separate and even inimical entities are united and have been all along. Ultimately, one understands the entire song as a simple I–IV–V–I structure, but with witty, text-derived decorations, embellishments, delaying tactics, and prolongations.

Yet another woman complains about her lover's deficiencies in "Mein Liebster hat zu Tische mich geladen" (My sweetheart invited me to dinner), but this time, there is no emotional ambivalence at the end. The lover whose ineptitude as a host has inspired the indictments in this Venetian *vilota* will soon become history, if he has not become so already by the time the tirade begins. In Angelo Dalmedico's *Canti del Popolo Veneziano* of 1848, the folk poem has a simplicity that stems in part from the repetitions of the phrases "Ghe manca" and "E nol gavea."

El mio moroso m'a invidato a cena,
E nol gavea casa da menarme.
Ghe manca 'l fogo e ghe manca la legna,
Ghe manca la pignata da tacare.
Ghe manca 'l caratelo del vin bon,
E nol gavea bocal da travasarlo.
Curta la tola e streta la tovagia,
El pan xe duro e 'l cortelo no tagia.[91]

The angry exaggeration is apparent from the first item on the list—was this an al fresco ordeal? Heyse's German maiden embellishes her Italian counterpart's complaints: the pan and wine flask are not missing, but present and broken; the bread is not just hard, but "hard as a rock"; and the knife is completely blunted and dull.

Mein Liebster hat zu Tische mich geladen,
Und hätte doch kein Haus mich zu empfangen,
Nicht Holz noch Herd zum Kochen und zum Braten,
Der Hafen auch war längst entzwei gegangen.
An einem Fässchen Wein gebrach es auch,
Und Gläser hatt' er gar nicht im Gebrauch;
Der Tisch war schmal, das Tafeltuch nicht besser,
Das Brot steinhart und völlig stumpf das Messer.[92]

(My sweetheart invited me to dinner and then had no house in which to receive me, neither wood nor stove for cooking and roasting. The pot was long since broken in two. There was no cask of wine; he didn't have any drinking glasses, the table was narrow, and the tablecloth no better, the bread hard as a rock and the knife completely blunted.)

Even though Heyse is more scrupulous about the regular hendecasyllabic lines than the folk poet, even though he duplicates the *a b a b c c d d* rhyme scheme of the original, the tone is different. Only a self-conscious poet would have crafted the alliterations that emphasize the woman's accusatory exaggerations, such as "Nicht Holz noch Herd," with its alternating *n* and *h* sounds (the brighter sounds frame the syntactical unit, with the darker *o* vowels of "Holz noch" placed in the middle and augmented by the word "K*o*chen" later in the same line). Other examples include the rhyming *g*'s of "Gläser, gar, Gebrauch"; the echoed *st*'s of "steinhart" and "stumpf"; the sizzle of the *z*'s in "Holz-zum-zum"; and the *t* and *sch* sounds of "Tisch, schmal, Tafeltuch"—a preponderance of hard consonants for added emphasis.

Wolf told Edwin Mayser, a high-school teacher in Stuttgart and later the pianist for the Hugo Wolf Verein in that city, that the second part of the *Italienisches Liederbuch* contained more absolute music than the first, that many things in it could be played equally well by a string quartet. Walker agrees that the motivic development in songs such as "Wohl kenn' ich Euren Stand" bears out the composer's assertion, but also points out that Wolf's customary concern for poetic interpretation is still present. In "Mein Liebster hat zu Tische mich geladen," one finds both comic traits familiar from Part 1 and the newer tendency toward more abstract motivic development in the piano part, music less definable in pictorializing terms.[93] As in "Nein, junger Herr," the piano introduction consists basically of a single dominant-seventh harmony, chromatically embellished and with a single repeated "fanfare" figure, while Wolfian onomatopoeia in the brief postlude—hacking at the stale bread with a blunted knife—recalls depictive details in the songs of Part 1. Throughout the piano part, Wolf alternates two distinct figures—a cadential chordal figure in a higher register, which overlaps with its harmonic extension, a livelier figure in a lower register, beginning each time with a dotted pattern followed by staccato eighth-notes. The latter is nearly always marked piano, and the former forte or mezzo-forte, as if the poetic persona were attempting to keep her anger under control, to tell her story in a dignified, but emphatic manner. And yet, the contrasts of register, dynamic planes, rhythmic and motivic character give the amusing impression that the singer is, literally, hopping mad, especially as the livelier motive culminates in rising sequential melodic sixths and the vocal line is of the comic variety also evident in "Mein Liebster ist so klein"—successive intervallic leaps in one direction counterbalanced by leaps in the opposite direction. Not for these women the calm of conjunct motion. Within its small framework, this is archetypal comedy of exaggeration and extremes.

The singer conveys her anger at each unpleasant facet of the dinner by means of an abrupt change of tonal center, beginning with measures 7–8 and the "surprise" turn to A major; the new key has actually been prepared by the chromatic pitches of the introduction (B♮, G♯, F♯), but the brief incursion into the major mediant tonality still comes as a deliberate shock, analogous to the discovery that there is no house. The lack of hearth and wood in measure 9 becomes, even more abruptly, a leap into the dominant, Wolf resorting to his favored procedure of linked third relationships as the tonal embodiment of rising disbelief and fury. The mediant and dominant references are distinguished by their "diatonic" clarity; although each is dissonant to the tonic, both are pure, uncolored by chromaticism from outside their own realms. With measure 11 and the transition from C major to E major, extending the third relationships still farther, that is no longer the case: the degree of chromatic saturation is one index among several of increasing anger. E major is followed in measures 13–17 by E minor, C minor (minor mode is reserved for the second half of the song, as the singer becomes more bitter), E major and C minor once more, via the enharmonic respelling of G♯ as A♭. The song

jumps from one tonal reference to the next without resolving the preceding
cadences—hopping mad indeed.

The motivic variations at the end also tell of quickened anger, an increasingly swift tempo of change. In measures 18–19, the forte figure is rhythmically diminished to half its former durational values, followed by a fragment
of the eighth-note figure. The successive statement of the two figures that
formerly required two bars is now compressed into one, and the previous
rhythmic differentiation between the two motives no longer exists. The loud-
soft terraced dynamic levels are expunged in a uniform crescendo from forte
to fortissimo—the last vestiges of calm have been swept away by the roll call
of indignities—although the registral contrasts continue, emphasizing the deceptive motion and the delays of resolution to tonic. The pitch emphasis on the
connective "und," despite its proper rhythmic placement on a weak beat, is a
prosodic indication of the angry stress on continuation. By the end, the narrator is too angry for closure and completion, and it is left to the piano to vary
her "hacking at stony bread" motif and then end it all with a completed cadence, although the end is left in doubt for an instant longer in measure 22.
Wolf has the right hand sound every pitch of the dominant-seventh chord
except for its root and delays resolution of D♭ to C in the bass. Not only is the
gesture a last comic commentary on the evaded, elided, delayed resolutions
earlier in the song, it has all the resonance of a good swift kick, judiciously
placed.

Papageno in *Die Zauberflöte* announces both himself and his libidinous
interests when he sings "Der Vogelfänger bin ich ja," if one accepts the Freudian interpretation of bird imagery and bird catching in dreams or fantasy. The
woman in "Du denkst mit einem Fädchen" taunts a would-be lover, wrongly
confident of maximum success for minimum effort, with sexualized references to flying and trapping those who fly. Heyse's source for this text is a
rispetto from the section entitled "Non ti fidare" in Niccolò Tommaseo's *Canti
Popolari Toscani Corsi Illirici Greci*:

> Tu pensi di legarmi con un filo,
> Con uno sguardo farmi innamorare.
> Non ti fidar di me quando che rido:
> Che più d'in alto l'ho fatti calare.
>
> E l'ho fatti calar; credilo a mene.
> So' innamorata, ma non gia de tene.[94]

The translation is almost literal, although Heyse transposes the third and
fourth lines for the sake of the German rhyme scheme.

> Du denkst mit einem Fädchen mich zu fangen,
> Mit einem Blick schon mich verliebt zu machen?

> Ich fing' schon andre, die sich höher schwangen,
> Du darfst mir ja nicht trau'n, siehst du mich lachen.
> Schon andre fing ich, glaub' es sicherlich.
> Ich bin verliebt, doch eben nicht in dich.[95]

(You think you can catch me with a little thread, make me fall in love with you at a glance? I've caught others who flew higher; don't trust me if you see me laughing. I've caught others, believe me truly. I'm in love, but not with you.)

Taunting proceeds by overturning expectations, by exaggeration (the taunter's boastful grandiosity used as diminishment of the person to whom she speaks), by the unexpected, and Wolf finds musical analogues for all three in the piano introduction.[96] The ascending motion, the pomposity of the double-dotted rhythms, and the initial B♭-major tonality are all overturned in measure 2, countered by the intervallic plunge in the right hand to the chromatic raised fifth degree, the nonlegato chords suggestive of laughter and echoed by the singer in her first words. The register for the left hand also shifts in measure 2 to the treble, replacing the pseudosolemnity of the first measure, and remains there until the end of measure 6 and the end of the woman's taunting question. That question hangs comically in midair: the passage is set as a harmonic trill in which the German sixth of G minor alternates with the dominant-seventh chord, but never resolves to the new tonal center—the tonal version of erotic teasing, especially since the intervallic cell of the descending sixth from measures 1–2 recurs throughout the question in such a way as to emphasize the motion from C♯ to C♮ and back again. The inverse relationship between intervallic cells in the vocal line and in the right hand-part seems a subversive hint of contradiction; her upward leaps of a G–E♭ sixth are immediately inverted as descending sixths in the right hand, while her rising semitone C♯–D becomes D–C♯ in the piano. By echoed motion in the opposite direction, Wolf seems to imply musically, "What *you* think—the direction in which you believe the matter to be going—is wrong." Taunting often makes use of repetition, from the child's "Nyah, nyah, nyah" to more protracted adult mockery; here, the motivic repetitions also prolong the relative minor so suddenly introduced in measure 2. If G minor, significantly left uncompleted for the moment, is the tonality of the lover's delusions of erotic success, then tonic B♭ is ultimately the locale of comic disillusionment.

The question is left unresolved, hanging in midair, and the taunting continues. When the narrator speaks in measures 7–8 of nabbing other men who had more to offer than the unseen character on the receiving end of this diatribe, the B♭ tonality and the lower bass register return, the bass line doubled in octaves, loud and assertive. These are clearly "real men," as opposed to the feminized, treble-voiced creature she mocks by every means at her disposal.

When she speaks directly to him, "du darfst mir ja nicht trau'n" in measure 9, the music reverts once more to the treble register and the harmonies of measures 3–6, while the repeated taunt, "Schon *andre* fing' ich" brings back the bass register and the octave doubling. At the same time, there are hints that the denouement is close at hand when the C♯ is reinterpreted as D♭ in measure 10, in conjunction with a turn to V/B♭ at the words "siehst du mich lachen." The "last laugh" is on the way.

In his mature songs, Wolf did not usually repeat words, phrases, or lines of text unless the poet had done so, but he makes an exception for Heyse's final line ("Ich bin verliebt, doch eben nicht in dich"), in the spirit of mockery. When the woman first declares "Ich bin verliebt," Wolf sets the phrase as a triumphal proclamation, rendered all the more dramatic by previously unheard A♭ harmonies and the deceptive motion to a comically prolonged diminished-seventh chord. This announcement is followed by the consequent clause of dismissal and rejection, the quick-patter song prosody emphasizing still further the clustered percussive *d*, *b*, *t*, and *ich* sounds of the text. But she is not through with her presumptuous ex-suitor yet. The turn toward B♭ and resolution in the vocal line is followed by a deceptive cadential harmonization elided with the subsequent restatement of the final line of text. At last, the G-minor chord expected earlier appears, but within the context of tonic B♭ and a revelation at odds with the lover's initial expectations.

To torment her listener still more, the singer repeats "Ich bin verliebt" not as a proclamation but as a mimicry of transport into realms of erotic bliss for which the hapless suitor is not responsible, ecstasy translated into a reharmonization of the B♭–C–D motive from measure 1, a prolonged and ornamented cadential $^6_4$ chord, and the rise into the treble register. The visual humor of a fermata over a thirty-second–note rest is a typically Puckish detail. That rest is the result of Wolf's usual prosodic refinement—placing the final *bt* consonants of "verliebt" just after the beginning of the second beat—and the small but effective rhythmic variation in the final clause by which "doch" is set as a thirty-second rather than a sixteenth-note, but one can imagine Wolf's enjoyment of the comic disproportion of a fermata prolonging so small a pause. The final words of dismissal are in comic contrast with the small-scale swoon just preceding, with the full-textured chords succeeded by unharmonized octaves and the bass register returning. Even at the end, the singer still teases: the last word, "dich," is unaccompanied and set to the third degree of the tonic chord, as if hinting at yet another continuation. Only when the piano echoes her cadence in the higher register of her earlier mockery does the root pitch of the tonic chord finally appear, and the mockery end.

Another flirtatious woman ends the *Italienisches Liederbuch* with a virtuoso display of high spirits. The rispetto form is ideally suited to a miniature catalog aria sung by a woman surely in little danger of infernal retribution.

> Ce l'ho un amante alla Citta di Penna,
> E l'altro l'ho al bel porto d'Ancona:
> N'ho uno sul gran pian della Maremma,
> L'altro a Viterbo ch'e terra di Roma:
> Ne ho uno giù pel pian del Casentino,
> Quello del mio paese e più vicino:
> Ne ho uno verso il pian della Magione,
> Quattro alla Fratta, e diece a Castiglione.[97]

Heyse transposes locales for the sake of rhyme, placing the Maremma plains ahead of the "beautiful harbor of Ancona," but otherwise writes a straightforward translation. One would not wish this poem, the essence of lighthearted frivolity, rendered more profound.

> Ich hab' in Penna einen Liebsten wohnen,
> In der Maremmeneb'ne einen andern,
> Einen im schönen Hafen von Ancona,
> Zum vierten muß ich nach Viterbo wandern;
> Ein andrer wohnt in Casentino dort,
> Der nächste lebt mit mir am selben Ort,
> Und wieder einen hab' ich in Magione,
> Vier in La Fratta, zehn in Castiglione.[98]

(I have one lover living in Penna, another in the plain of Maremma, one in the beautiful port of Ancona, to see the fourth I must wander to Viterbo; another lives over there in Casentino, the next lives in my own hometown; I have another in Magione, four in La Fratta, ten in Castiglione.)

There is not much of an introduction: this woman is so delighted with herself, so vivacious, that she can hardly wait to launch into her list of conquests.[99] None of them, one notes, has a name or any particularity: they are integers and geographical locations only, the feminine version of notches on a belt. Rather, the staccato thirds in measure 1 establish a quick tactus; a staccato, chattering backdrop; and an incomplete harmonic interval to be filled in by the voice. The right-hand part in measures 3 and 5 is a co-conspirator with the singer, echoing her figures but transposed and varied. It is tempting to hear these figures and their overlapping repetitions as analogous to the lovers who all belong under the same general heading (Lovers/Motivic Figure) but live in different places and outline different harmonies. Wolf fashions the motivic figure primarily from a rising scalewise third, a descending scalewise fourth or third, a change of direction between the two—this woman can turn on a dime and goes, quite busily, in all directions. One of the most telling details of characterization, though, is the series of secondary dominants, one after another and one per measure, in much of the first section of this small through-composed song. Richer, more complex chromaticism is not called for, as the singer is a self-congratulatory village flirt, not a Peregrina or Agnes, and Wolf wittily suggests her travels within the region, her refusal to stop anywhere for long, and her evident skills at deception by means of unresolved or deceptively resolved dominants in a series. The vocal phrase in measures 8–9 ("zum vierten muß ich nach Viterbo wandern") recalls other passages from Wolf's comic songs in which syllabic declamation and a change of direction up or down with virtually each successive interval are indices of great vitality, especially since the vocal phrase "ends," in a comically graphic depiction of the verb "wandern," with an upward inflection on $\hat{5}$ of D minor and on a weak beat. The final three vocal pitches for the phrase F–G–A are, of course, another instance of the scalewise motive and a recollection as well of measure 1. D minor is one way to complete the harmonic third F–A of the beginning, but not the final way—this is merely a midpoint marker and an amusing hint of minor modal suspense. Given the resolution in the piano to unharmonized D's and the sudden decrescendo from forte to piano in measure 9, the listener wonders, for a millisecond, if we are about to hear that the multiple lovers have discovered one another's existence.

The catalog continues toward a final count that is considerably less than "mille e tre" but more than enough for bragging rights. The rising sequence in measures 10–16 ("ein andrer wohnt in Casentino dort, / der nächste lebt mit mir am selben Ort") traces the ascent in the bass, pricked out in off-beat grace notes, from D to E and, at last, a fanfare-bravura proclamation of F major as tonic. Thus, the D–E[–C–]F in the bass of measures 10–17 and in the vocal line ("dort . . . Ort . . . wie[-der]") is another instance of the rising-third fragment that pervades the song, while the right-hand part, in a series of "Chopsticks"-style suspensions, develops the descending scalewise figure in preparation for the even longer, larger, higher descending scales of measures 17–18. There, the piano echoes the voice in *Terzensteigerung* as it had done before with the shorter figures of measures 6–7, keeping the constant eighth-note tactus going until the dramatic pause of a full measure (measure 20), a big intake of breath for the flamboyant tonic $^6_4$. The fermatas prolonging the high A in the vocal line of measure 22 and the eighth-note rest in the piano—the singer trumpeting abroad the final arithmetic tally unaccompanied—is a typically witty detail. But the funniest text-setting stroke of all is in the instrumental postlude, nine measures of tonic revelry in which one can hear both mockery of the protagonist and delighted collaboration with her excesses. The singer is so impressed with the inflation apparent in the final figure, "zehn in Castiglione," that the postlude repeats the phrase several times in different rhythmic guises before launching into the virtuosic conclusion in which the upper neighbor to each chord tone in the tonic triad, an extension of the $\hat{6}$–$\hat{5}$ upper neighbor in the final vocal phrase, ranges over several octaves. The triplet eighths in measure 30 and the ridiculously bombastic flatted sixths are the last of the multiple means of emphasis in this character portrait, a brilliant conclusion to the *Italienisches Liederbuch*.

COMIC SERENADES IN THE
ITALIENISCHES LIEDERBUCH

In Eichendorff's "Rückkehr" and "Das Ständchen" (Wolf's 1883 setting of the former seems like a preliminary study for the latter, one of Wolf's masterpieces), the poetic persona–singer listens to music played by a serenader or town musicians, represented in the piano part, and reacts to the sound.[100] Heyse culled a section of *Serenate* from his Italian sources, and Wolf once again gravitated to the serenades, both serious ("Mein Liebster singt am Haus im Mondenscheine," "Heut' Nacht erhob ich mich," "Nicht länger kann ich singen") and comic ("Schweig' einmal still" and "Ein Ständchen Euch zu bringen"). "Schweig' einmal still" in particular is a humorous commentary on perception: we hear the lover's serenade as the exasperated listener hears it. In Tigri's anthology of Tuscan verse, the rispetto appears as follows:

> Stattene zitta, brutta cicalina:
> I tuoi rispetti m'hanno stomacato.
> Se tu durassi fino a domattina,
> Non cantaresti un rispetto garbato.
>
> Stattene zitta, e vattene alla paglia:
> Canta meglio di te un asin che raglia.[101]

In Heyse's German translation, this becomes:

> Schweig' einmal still, du garst'ger Schwätzer dort!
> Zum Ekel ist mir dein verwünschtes Singen.
> Und triebst du es bis morgen früh so fort,
> Doch würde dir kein schmuckes Lied gelingen.
> Schweig' einmal still und lege dich aufs Ohr!
> Das Ständchen eines Esels zög' ich vor.[102]

(Do shut up, you wretched babbler; I am sick of your cursed singing. Even if you kept on until tomorrow morning, you would not achieve one good song. Do be quiet and go to bed! I'd rather be serenaded by a donkey.)

The sense is not changed, but sarcasm is often idiomatic to the point of defying translation. One can—and Heyse does—locate corresponding terms of nonendearment in the second language, but the tone will be different: a "garst'ger Schwätzer" (nasty or foul babbler, chatterer) is not quite the same as a "brutta cicalina." "I tuoi rispetti" is a reference to a particular Italian poetic form, which Heyse paraphrases as the more general "verwünschtes Singen," adding the unflattering adjective.

Wolf twice parodied inept musicians in the *Italienisches Liederbuch*, in "Schweig' einmal still" and "Wie lange schon war immer mein Verlangen."[103] The labored affectations of the violinist in "Wie lange schon" are confined to the postlude, however, while the serenader who torments the singer of "Schweig' einmal still" is omnipresent, a study in dogged and ungifted effort.[104] His persistence and lack of imagination are evident in the unceasing eighth-note chords in the left hand, unlyrical and obtrusive. Wolf's chord voicing for the initial harmonies is indicative of the serenader's hard work, since the chord tones are distributed over the span of a tenth or a ninth, forcing those pianists with smaller hands to work as hard as the would-be lover. The composer's pedantic precision about the performance of the trill figures in measures 2 and 3 is delightful, as the trills are too long for a brief emphasis and too short for the prolonged ornaments of a skilled performer. Wolf's sense of comic timing would do Chaplin proud: each time the serenader is poised to begin again, in measures 6 and 15, the singer cannot bear the realization and sings "Schweig' einmal still," the imperative "Schweig'" prolonged across the barline, just as the instrumentalist is off and running, an unstoppable force.

From the introduction in measures 1–6, the serenader is so ungifted as to be virtually antimusical; everything about the prelude is wrong in a caricature that required considerable artistry to create. The tonality is A minor, ironically the archetypal Schubertian and Wolfian tonality for love-laments by forsaken women, a key now turned on its ear to become both a serenade and the lament of someone who would welcome abandonment by this suitor. The progressions are bungled, and the harmonic rhythm is laughably awkward. The melodic leap downward from the raised fourth degree D♯ to the tonic pitch A in measure 1 is melodic near-nonsense; the raised fourth is not used as a means of intensifying the approach to the dominant degree or in any other traditional way. In its awkwardness, it is one of the principal hallmarks of the serenade, since the suitor insists on repeating the gesture over and over, right to the end of the piano postlude. The grace-noted figures in measures 4–6 that outline the descending scalar motive E–D–C, with the conspicuous cross relation of D and D♯, cut across the bar line—nothing so consciously planned as syncopation—and culminate in a descending diminished fourth. The wildly gesticulating character of these figures seems to anticipate his later characterization as an ass before the analogy is actually stated, as do the insistent leaps in the right-hand part at measures 2 and 4. The tactus is certainly steady and boring, but the meter is, comically, a jumble by the time the serenade reaches the grace-noted figures in measures 5–6. The trill figure at measure 2, beat

4 displaces the $\frac{4}{4}$ meter by creating a $\frac{3}{4}$ measure across the bar line. He then seems to rectify the confusion with the chord change at measure 3, beat 3, but once again, a trill figure on the next beat creates yet another $\frac{3}{4}$ measure across the bar line. Perhaps most telling of all, the serenader is so intent on his suit, so insistent, and yet so musically insensitive that the right-hand melody never "breathes." Antecedent-consequent phrasing with rests or pauses in between is a mystery into which he has not been initiated.

The singer's vocal line is both adapted by necessity to the lunatic instrumental music so irritatingly within earshot, and a mockery of it. The descending chromatic inflection in measure 13, "doch würde dir kein [schmuckes Lied gelingen]", with the serenader trilling away both above and below her words, is both parodistic lamentation and a mocking use of his D♯/D♮ wavering. As she castigates his inability to concoct a pleasing song, the serenader blunders about in his most inept manner until, finally, in measure 15, he gives up, taking refuge in three noisy dominant-seventh chords of tonic A minor—a preparation that sounds suspiciously like "Für Elise." Here for once, the raised fourth degree is used properly to intensify the fifth scale degree. When the singer repeats her previously ineffectual order—"Schweig' einmal still!"—Wolf indicates her heightened anger by means of melodic *Terzensteigerung* at the end of the phrase and by the dramatic ascending major seventh F–E in the vocal line, the octave displacement of the $\hat{6}$–$\hat{5}$ resolution at the words "und lege dich *aufs Ohr*"—her up-and-down intervallic leaps emphasize her exasperated "cease and desist" orders throughout the song.

It is near the end of the serenade that the piano part seems most obviously transmitted through the singer's outraged sensibilities. In measures 17–20, the "braying" motive first heard in measure 2 reappears to a progression that is too sophisticated, in part because correct, for the serenader, a progression culminating in the Neapolitan sixth. The outright donkey's bray that follows is surely her invention, not his. In the postlude, the figure he invents in measure 1 alternates with the braying *she* hears. If he is a caricature in his own right, her mockery magnifies his asinine qualities and his ineptitude—ineptitude become art in Wolf's hands. When caught up in the exhilaration of composing, Wolf customarily referred to each successive work as the best thing he had ever done, so one is not surprised to find him writing to Melanie Köchert on 23 April 1896 to tell her that his two newest songs, the serenades "Nicht länger kann ich singen" and "Schweig' einmal still," are "museum pieces, fit for display."[105] One can only agree.

The other comic serenade is sung by a man and *to* a man: the sweetheart's father. The original Italian text comes from Tommaseo's *Canti Popolari* of 1841:

> Io son venuto a farvi serenata,
> Padron di casa, se contento siete.

So che ci avete una giovin garbata:
Dentro le vostre mura la tenete.
E se per sorte fosse addormentata,
Questo da parte mia voi le direte:
Che ci è passato un suo caro servente,
Che giorno e notte la tiene in la mente.
Tra giorno e notte son ventiquattr'ore
E venticinque la tengo nel core.[106]

Heyse translates the rispetto as follows:

Ein Ständchen Euch zu bringen kam ich her,
Wenn es dem Herrn vom Haus nicht ungelegen.
Ihr habt ein schönes Töchterlein.
Es wär' wohl gut, sie nicht zu streng im Haus zu hegen.
Und liegt sie schon im Bett, so bitt' ich sehr,
Tut es zu wissen ihr von meinetwegen,
Dass ihr Getreuer hier vorbeigekommen,
Der Tag und Nacht sie in den Sinn genommen,
Und dass am Tag, der vierundzwanzig zählt,
Sie fünfundzwanzig Stunden lang mir fehlt.[107]

(I have come here to sing a serenade, if the master of the house approves. You have a beautiful daughter. It would be very good not to keep her indoors too strictly. And if she is already in bed, I beg you to let her know, for my sake, that her true love has passed this way, who thinks of her night and day, and misses her twenty-five hours out of every twenty-four.)

The German serenader is comically concerned with the courtesies, with making a good impression on his sweetheart's father. At the same time, he is an ardent wooer and cannot hide the fact. He even ventures a little advice to the father, a charming bit of temerity that the more plain-spoken Italian lover does not say: "It would be very good," he suggests politely, not to keep his daughter so secluded at home.

In Wolf's reading of the poem, the serenader has arrived with the expectation of a conventional serenade to his beloved, unobserved by parental watchguards. "I have come to sing *you* a serenade," he announces in insouciant $\frac{3}{8}$ dance rhythms and recitational repeated pitches at the beginning, with the bass line anchored on C for a serenader who stands fixed in place. The visual humor of the single measure of full rest at the beginning as the serenader readies his guitar and assumes his wooing posture is one index of a miniature scena pictorially conceived. The shock when the serenader sees not the beloved but her father is registered in the sudden tritone leap in the bass (measure 13, including the silence in measure 1 in the bar-count) en route to C♯ major by phrase's end. If one hears C major as a key emblematic of sunny conventionality, a key "for directness of character or expression,"[108] the tonal humor is all the greater. The tonal distance between the two keys is a hilarious analogue to the distance between expectation and reality, especially as the serenader preserves enough sangfroid to keep going, to maintain uninterrupted the swaggering "guitar" chords of his accompaniment. He even uses the previous comic elision of the phrase ending in the voice with its cheerfully, bumptiously accented repetition in the piano (measures 9–11) to new advantage now that the situation has changed, thereby emphasizing his hope that his serenade will not be unwelcome ("nicht ungelegen") to the master of the house. "Nicht" is prolonged across the bar line, both as humorous prosodic stress and as rhythmic impetus at the last half of the phrase where the recitational chanting gives way to intervallic movement—Wolf's melodic pattern for much of the song. And yet, despite the distance between the tonalities in the first section of this serenade, Wolf foreshadows the multitude of sharps to come when he introduces a G♯ passing tone and a tonic augmented triad in measure 6 and foreshadows the F♯ major of measures 36–44 in measures 13–15. The G♯ of measure 6 seems in retrospect a sly warning to the listener since it underlies the word "Euch," and the person to whom the serenader thinks he is singing will shortly turn out to be someone quite other.

The hapless wooer from here on addresses the father directly. Regaining his composure in measures 24–25, the serenader reestablishes the C♮s in the vocal line from measures 5–6 and moves by chromatic sideslipping to A minor, the relative minor of the key in which he began his serenade and a new function in a different register for the G♯ from earlier. One notes with amusement the pianissimo dynamics of the words "You have a beautiful daughter"; for all his swagger, the singer is at first a trifle tentative about wooing the daughter in these less-than-desirable circumstances, about displeasing the master of the house with so direct a reference to the sweetheart's beauty. When he suggests to the father that it would be good not to keep her so strictly immured within the house, the tonicized F♯ passage—F♯ clearly the tonal region denotative of enclosure and the father's hegemony—is comically as far away as possible from the plein-air openness of C major, the serenader's realm, while the mild dissonance and diminished-seventh harmony on the raised fourth degree in measure 35 are indeed "nicht streng." The close relationship, the pitches reordered on recurrence, between the phrase "wenn es dem Herrn vom Haus nicht ungelegen" and "sie nicht zu streng im Haus zu hegen" confirms the amusing inside/outside and father/lover disparity from the lover's point of view—C major is the "natural" key, F♯ the more unusual tonality. So strongly does the serenader feel about his suggestion to the father that he repeats measures 34–38 in the accented instrumental echo, in effect saying once more that "you should not keep her so closely confined in the house."

When the serenader begins to relay his lover's message of adoration, ardor can no longer be held in check, and the bass line begins to move. At first, the lover is relatively restrained, acknowledging the father's F♯ sphere and repeating the same G–F♯ voice-leading progression both in measures 45–50 and in its repetition just after in measures 51–58. However, one notices the *Terzensteigerung* at the phrase ending, G–D–C♯ rather than G–B–A♯, as an index of intensification "meinetwegen." Thereafter, the same progression is repeated as a rising sequence marked by overlapping seventh chords, with the bass and soprano alike tracing the ascent from G to A to B (the ardent prolongation of the word "sie" in the phrase "der Tag und Nacht *sie* in den Sinn genommen" across the bar line recalls the similar rhythmic disposition and fervor of "nicht" in measures 15–16) and, finally, to C. There, C in measure 71 becomes the point of departure for the most unsettled chromaticism of the song, the vocal line and the soprano voice climbing up to high G at the climax in measure 80, the bass tracing two descending chromatic lines (measures 71–75, 76–82) in which significant harmonic events are recalled from earlier. A day with the usual twenty-four-hour span—"der vierundzwanzig zählt"; measures 74–77—elicits the C♯ harmonies associated with the father's prosaic clock-time, while the twenty-five hours of the lover's experience of time painfully prolonged by absence from the sweetheart inspires the reinterpretation of G♯ as the A♭ neighbor to 5̂ of C, the return to the lover's C-major sphere, and the operatic sweep of the vocal line in measures 80–83, its intensity of expression new to the vocal line. The restraint imposed by the father's presence is cast to the four winds, and fortissimo ardor, no longer to be denied, blazes forth. So intensely does the lover miss his beloved that he misses tonic closure as well, the B♭ to which he falls downward a semitone rather than resolving upward prolonged for more than four bars—"so lang" indeed.

The newly unleashed exuberance surpasses words and requires one of Wolf's lengthier piano postludes before the serenader comes full circle, back to the initial guitar-strumming measures of the introduction. The C pedal point of the first line of text here ranges up and down a two-octave span from the low C of measure 2 to the middle C of measure 87, yet another tonal analogue to the rising passion traced throughout the lied. The refusal to "settle down" in the right hand is evident in the fact that Wolf continues to circle around the flatted seventh degree and chord while sinking back down to the initial register; in fact, the entire postlude is an implicit and charmingly stubborn refusal to go away, father or no father. After the dominant seventh of measure 86, at the end of the texted body of the song, Wolf does not bring that cadential harmony back in the postlude, which is simultaneously a prolongation of tonic in the left hand and a refusal to affirm the tonic resolution in the right hand. It is a delightful conceit, one necessitated in musical terms by the abrupt deflection from C major near the beginning of the lied and therefore the need to establish C in no uncertain terms so that the true serenade can start in some future tense beyond the point where this one "ends." It is also humor of an uncommonly sympathetic nature. If the joke has its tendentious side—that is, laughter at the discomfiture of a suitor suddenly confronted with the beloved's father—the humor born of aggressive impulses quickly modulates from criticism to empathic identification. With Wolf, we become allies of a lover so sweet, ardent, and merry as this one.

CONCLUSION

Nineteenth-century composers did not generally associate comedy with the most advanced music. Light music—operettas, comic opera, waltz songs—in Vienna and elsewhere was written in more conservative harmonic and tonal styles than those of serious music. For avowed Wagnerites, humor was of a special category that Wolf described as "world-redeeming comedy,"[109] in which levity lives side by side with Wagner's ever-present theme of tragic renunciation. Wolf wanted neither one and instead devised his own comic style. An anecdote told by Wolf's friend Friedrich Eckstein reveals Wolf's feelings about composers of musical comedy, all the more indicative because the tale begins with Wolf's turmoil over Nietzsche's *Der Fall Wagner* (The case of Wagner), Nietzsche's diatribe against the composer he had earlier idolized. When Wolf first heard music by Peter Gast, the composer Nietzsche touted in his post-Wagner days, he was both appalled and amused. "The devil! who wrote this? Is this by Millöcker? It couldn't be! Impossible! Millöcker is incomparably more interesting!"[110] Karl Millöcker (1842–99) was then among the most popular of the Viennese operetta composers. Wolf's invective is notable for its dual message: someone who can write light music well is more deserving of respect than someone who writes serious music badly, but Millöcker was no Wagner. The choice of a Viennese operetta composer as the standard of comparison underscored Wolf's contempt for Gast's opera, *Der Loewe von Venedig* (The lion of Venice).

Carl Schorske has proposed that in fin-de-siècle culture, rational man gives way to psychological man, whose treacherous instincts are scientifically examined, paraded on stage, painted by the artists of the Secession, and embodied in poetry and prose. Wolf, who looked for "truth to the point of terror" in art, was most attracted by comedy with a psychological slant, whether in the fantastic vein of Mörike or the village voices, entirely and endearingly human, that one hears laughing, scolding, cajoling, wooing, and mocking in the *Italienisches Liederbuch*. The latter in particular were created by a composer who wanted more than anything in the world to write opera situated in a real world of emotional experience. Accordingly, every gesture, every shift of feeling, every nuance is imparted to songs that depict wonderfully vital personas—comedy of any kind asserts that "in the midst of death, we are in life," and the voices we hear in Wolf's comic songs are emphatically, assertively alive. If the characters he found most appealing in his favorite poets often have a strong strain of malice in their makeup, they are more human for it. To bring them to life, Wolf uses an arsenal of late-Romantic tonal devices; no less than in the serious songs and sometimes more so, the comic personas are endowed with the refinements of nuance available to a late-nineteenth-century composer. Wolf may not have invented humor in music, but he did reinvent it for the world after Bayreuth.

CHAPTER 3

Influence without Anxiety: Wolf and the Ballad Tradition

IN A REVIEW of 10 April 1887 for the *Wiener Salonblatt*, Wolf wrote, "But on one account we must take Herr [Paul] Bulss emphatically to task, namely, that on this occasion he sang no Loewe ballads, a sin of omission admitting of no pardon."[1] This is not the only evidence of Wolf's advocacy of Carl Loewe, or, to give him his full roll call of names, Johann Carl Gottfried Loewe (1796–1869), the great ballad master of the nineteenth century. His friends Gustav Schur and Edmund Hellmer, the sculptor of Wolf's grave monument in Vienna's Central Cemetery, both state that the composer liked Loewe's setting of "Erlkönig" (The elf-king) better than Schubert's,[2] and Heinrich Werner writes of Wolf's enthusiasm for Loewe's op. 128 setting of Theodor Fontane's Scottish ballad "Archibald Douglas."[3] Nor was the liking for Loewe solely a phenomenon of Wolf's youth. In 1894, he recommended the *Legende* (ballad-style narrations of incidents from the lives of saints) "Der grosse Christoph" (The great Christopher), op. 34 of 1834, to his friend Hugo Faisst and volunteered to coach him in the ballad. "It is made for you," he promised.[4] Commenting on the inordinate length of the work, he quotes Schumann on Schubert's Ninth Symphony, "But this is a heavenly length." Whether Freudian slip or conscious and comic warning, Wolf retitles the *Legende* "Der *lange* Christoph" (The long Christopher). None of his own ballads approach the gigantic dimensions of Loewe's larger specimens of the genre.

Wolf's championing of Loewe, who died when Wolf was nine years old, is part of a singular episode in German cultural history. The musical tradition Loewe had so single-mindedly sustained from the publication of his first ballads in 1824 until his death was already the object of revivals in Wolf's lifetime, including as the most important manifestation Max Runze's edition of the songs, ballads, *Legenden*, and selections from the five operas of Loewe.[5] Loewe's swift rise to acclaim and decline in popularity during his own lifetime attracted the notice of Philipp Spitta, whose essay "Die Ballade" (The ballad) was published in 1894.[6] Spitta believed that Loewe's works deserved greater attention and lauded the foundation of a Loewe society in Berlin in 1882 for the purpose of resurrecting a composer and a genre undeserving of extinction. In explaining Loewe's decline, Spitta does not merely point to the rise and fall of fashion, of movements and trends that suddenly enthrone artists and as suddenly dethrone them, but emphasizes the role of Schumann and his imitators in the fin-de-siècle decline of balladry. The Schumann lied, characterized by refined details, by "ominous presentiments, the overwhelming intimacy of emotional expression, the symphonic interweaving of the voice and piano,"[7] found such favor with the public by midcentury as to supplant Loewe's ballads.[8] The lied, he continues, had by that time passed more and more to women's voices, while the ballad belongs by rights to male singers. Furthermore, the public no longer had the patience, taste, or sufficient contextual knowledge for the long stories[9] or the dramatic mien the singer must assume. The ballads themselves, he adds, have their deficiencies and difficulties as obstructions to revival: the challenging piano parts (Loewe's "Harald," op. 45, no. 1, to a text by Ludwig Uhland, is one example among many of pianistic virtuosity), the wide vocal compass demanded of the singer, and, in his opinion, insufficient musical variety. But despite these flaws, this is music "sung from deep within the German heart," Teutonic to the core.[10] Spitta's call for regeneration culminates in recognition of the ballad as a nationalistic phenomenon, a German genre that celebrates German history and culture. Wolf's enthusiasm for Loewe can be understood both as the expression of his own tastes, his regard for earlier nineteenth-century tradition, and as part of a contemporary process of revival.

Wolf may have also known that Loewe was claimed by the Wagnerites as a predecessor.[11] According to the reminiscences of two Wagnerian singers, Eugen Gura and Lilli Lehmann (Wolf had harsh words for the latter's Viennese performances as Isolde), Wagner knew and liked Loewe's works, and his reported regret that Loewe's compositions were no longer performed as frequently as they once were reinforces Spitta's observations.[12] Gura wrote of visiting Bayreuth in the summer of 1875 and singing "Edward," "Herr Oluf," and "Erlkönig" for Wagner, who admonished him for omitting some of the repeated "Oh" exclamations in "Edward," praised Loewe's "Walpurgisnacht," and ended by saying in summation, "Yes, he is indeed one of the truly German masters."[13] However, the observation that ballads are to opera as pencil sketches are to completed oil paintings has also been attributed to Wagner,[14] who wrote no ballads independent of opera—Senta's story-within-a-story, the ballad "Johohoé! Traft ihr das Schiff" in *Der fliegende Holländer*, belongs within a larger dramatic context. The notion of a musical relationship between the two composers based on supposed similarities of leitmotivic development is tenuous at best, but was enthusiastically argued by those wishing to claim as proto-Wagnerian anything they considered praiseworthy. The imprint of nationalism—that is, a similar attraction to ancient Germanic themes—was a further link between ballads and Wagnerian opera, although the ballad is epic and narrative in nature rather than dramatic.

The efforts by a partisan few to resurrect Loewe were briefly successful. Even Eduard Hanslick, the champion of absolute music and therefore disinclined to like the pictorial ballad, paid it heed. In a review from 1887, Hanslick points out the solfeggiando flourishes and the recurrent "flea-jump" fig-

ures for the piano in Loewe's setting of Friedrich Rückert's "Des Glocken-
thurmers Töchterlein" (The bell-ringer's daughter), op. 112, as elements inimical to modern composers (or so Hanslick wished) but always "naive and
natural" in Loewe.[15] But after the First World War, Loewe once again disappeared from the recital stages and concert halls. If he has never vanished
altogether, he has tended to be honored more in the breach than in the observance. In a parodic Proustian recital for the Edinburgh Festival in 1963, the
soprano Cathy Berberian spoofed the formerly obligatory inclusion of Loewe
ballads on turn-of-the-century recital programs and took broadside aim at their
dated style. Her target, "Thomas der Reimer" (Thomas the poet), op. 135, to
a text by Theodor Fontane, is "one of Herr Loewe's less tedious ballads," a
tongue-in-cheek Paul Griffiths writes in the program notes. "Thomas der
Reimer," which takes place "am Kieselbach bei Huntley Schloß" (at the peb-
bly brook by Huntley Castle), is a Scottish-Teutonic hybrid of the sort popular
in the nineteenth century; Fontane wrote dozens. Unusually for Loewe, this
work begins with a fourteen-bar preamble in which the basic chords of the key
are repeated until the restive contemporary audience begins to laugh. Their
amusement is subsequently fueled by the grace-noted silver bells on the mane
of a white horse ridden by a mysterious blonde woman and by a plethora of
other illustrative details in the accompaniment.[16]

What modern listeners found comic was the ballad aesthetic itself, the sub-
ordination of lyricism to a special brand of musical narrative. One of those
most concerned in the 1880s and 1890s with the resuscitation of balladry, the
composer Martin Plüddemann (1854–97), said in praise of Loewe, "Telling
tales, he sings; singing, he tells tales" ("Erzählend singt er, singend erzählt
er"),[17] but telling tales in song was no longer a dominant mode of musical
discourse, and it never regained its former footing. And yet, there was much
in his predecessor's music that appealed to Wolf's own tastes. Furthermore,
because his harmonic language and compositional techniques go far beyond
Loewe's idiom, he could safely pay the older composer homage without the
intense Oedipal anxiety created by Schubert and Wagner in the two genres he
considered his own: lied and opera. Wolf's lamentations about living in Wagner's wake are well documented,[18] and friends later reported his half-angry,
half-reverential response to the inevitable comparisons with Schubert ("They
fairly threaten me with Schubert, but I cannot keep my mouth shut because a
man of genius lived before me and wrote splendid songs"[19]), but there is no
such reaction to Loewe. Possibly Wolf's loyalty to Loewe stemmed in part
from the perception that both of them lived in Schubert's shadow, although
this is only speculation. Wolf's admiration for Loewe resembles Loewe's own
assessment of *his* predecessor, Johann Rudolf Zumsteeg (1760–1802). In his
autobiography, Loewe wrote of his esteem for Zumsteeg's ballads, with the
single criticism that his master's motives were too aphoristic, insufficiently
developed, and therefore his ballads were not as dramatic as they might be.[20]

Loewe could therefore find satisfaction in improving his predecessor's legacy on the basis of an altered conception of balladry. Wolf, although he said nothing of the kind, did likewise with Loewe's legacy, shunning the classic ballad texts by Gottfried August Bürger, Ludwig Uhland, and Schiller for poems in which events are experienced rather than recounted, and embellishing his ballads with the artifice of a later tonal language. He even implicitly criticized Loewe by setting two of Goethe's ballads previously claimed by Loewe:[21] the Harper's ballad "Der Sänger" (The minstrel) from *Wilhelm Meisters Lehrjahre* and "Gutmann und Gutweib" (Good man and good wife), a humorous tale of Scottish parsimony, stolen pudding, and marital conflict, the latter possibly all the more attractive to him because Schubert had not found it "komponabel." Wolf might have rightly assessed Loewe's setting as not among the composer's best—added incentive to devise his own versions for the *Gedichte von Goethe* of 1890.

In his youth, Wolf was drawn repeatedly to Romantic ballads, but most of his efforts were either left unfinished or subsequently lost. One of his earliest extant compositions is an unfinished ballad, "Der Raubschütz" (The robber marksman) to a text by Nikolaus Lenau, on which the fifteen-year-old autodidact labored for much of 1875, to little avail. Walker cites an amusing anecdote from Wolf's diary of a failed attempt to induce composition by seeking the proper natural surroundings in the Vienna woods, a failure Wolf blamed on the deep snow.[22] Pencil sketches and an incomplete ink revision for the Romantic horror-ballad about the ghost of a murdered gamekeeper ("It was here he shot me like a sow!" the spectral Kurd dramatically proclaims) are currently in the collection of the Vienna City Library, and a brief quotation from the ink sketch can serve to show why the young composer abandoned the project as hopeless in 1876.[23] The subtitle could be "Teenage composer encounters diminished-seventh chord and goes wild." However, Wolf evidently understood ballad conventions, even if he could not yet manipulate them (Example 15). The spooky unisono introduction is a standard formula of the genre, and diminished-seventh chords run rife in horror ballads; by the time he set Lenau's "Nächtliche Wanderung" (Nocturnal wandering) in 1878, Wolf had completely mastered such haunted musical atmospheres and, from his close study of Wagner's operas, knew how to deepen and darken the eeriness by means of Wagnerian chromaticism. But in 1876, he and Lenau were ill-matched. Lenau, who became famous early and thereafter published nearly everything he wrote, should have revised "Der Raubschütz" out of existence before it could fall into the hands of an adolescent musician as yet lacking his later refined literary sensibilities. The poem ends with a nugget of existential philosophizing, the nihilism characteristic of Lenau's thought but so inappropriately grafted onto the ballad as to be unintentionally comic. The miller to whom the apparition appears asks what the afterlife is like, and the specter replies, "Es ist halt nichts!" Wolf, fortunately, never got that far.

Example 15. Hugo Wolf, unfinished sketch of "Der Raubschütz" (1875)

Example 15, continued

The completed ballads from the apprenticeship years[24] include the *Drei Balladen von Friedrich Hebbel*, once again from 1878, and Wolf's first two Mörike settings, "Suschens Vogel" (Susie's bird; composed 24 December 1880) and "Die Tochter der Heide" (The daughter of the fields; composed 11 July 1884). Of the three ballads by Hebbel,[25] "Schön Hedwig" (Beautiful Hedwig) is lost,[26] but the other two, unpublished in Wolf's lifetime, remain. "Das Kind am Brunnen" (The child at the well; composed 16–27 April 1878) and "Knabentod" (Death of a youth; composed 3–6 May 1878) foreshadow Wolf's later predilection for ballads in which events happen in the present rather than the past. The narrator in "Das Kind am Brunnen" is a bystander who observes a nursemaid asleep while her wakeful, exploring child comes closer and closer to a well and finally falls in. The disaster happens as the poem unfolds, with the narrator—a commentator set apart from participation in the events he recounts—unable to do more than observe and express his horror at the tragedy, like the radio announcer at the crash of the Hindenburg; he cannot awaken the sleeping guardian or prevent the child from tumbling headlong into the depths. (Was Wolf consciously, or unconsciously, invoking the child's repeated cries of "Mein Vater, mein Vater!" in Schubert's "Erlkönig" when he transposed the narrator's warnings, "Frau Amme, Frau

Amme," a semitone higher with each repetition?) The same is true of the small ballad "Knabentod," in which the narrator watches a young man drown in a wild stream. Both poems are miniature poetic dramas of tragic destiny in which human will to act is powerless against the inexorable mechanisms of fate and death. The Mörike poems exemplify that poet's sophisticated reworking of folk-song models, imitation folk ballads with a twist. "Die Tochter der Heide," for example, begins with its female narrator ordering her sisters to adorn themselves for the wedding of faithless Robin to proud Ruth. The sisters go uninvited, in best Grimm Brothers fashion, to confront the groom, to sing shrill and evil songs to him, to burn down the wedding hall. The last verse is the twist: the narrator tells her actual sisters to be merry, that what she has just sung is only a nursery tale. Yet, there really is a "false Rob" who exists outside of the vengeful ballad she has just told. "I forgot him a long time ago," she insists; she has another sweetheart, and false Rob would be astonished to see them dancing. This is a ballad within a ballad, a demonstration that the archetypal themes of folk narratives have their counterparts in "actual" experience, both "fiction" and "reality" Mörike's invention in this poem.

Wolf's settings of these texts show that he knew the requirements of the ballad after Loewe's model. In contrast to lied, with its greater emphasis on a unitary structure, ballads are episodic and sectional, the composer seeking the musical analogue to each situation in the narrative as it occurs. The distinction is crucial. Spitta writes that the debate about which setting of "Erlkönig" is better, Schubert's or Loewe's, is the wrong question. The true question should be: "Is Schubert's 'Erlkönig' really a ballad?" In Spitta's opinion, it is more lied than ballad because of its unity of mood and melodic lyricism and because the differentiation between different characters, another requirement of ballad narration, is subordinated to the unifying impulse.[27] His strictures concerning lyricism are at the heart of another essential element of art ballad composition—the proper nature of narrative in both the vocal line and the instrumental part. Liedlike lyrical melody is only appropriate at occasional points of repose in the narrative. Should it trespass beyond proper bounds, its emotional expressivity would distract the listener from the conveyance of plot, usually mediated through a narrator who recounts events from the distant past. Operatic recitative either secco or dramatic was not the solution because it belonged to the world of drama, and Loewe therefore devised a rapprochement between lyrical melody and sung narration in his ballads. This "narrative melody" often resembles folk song in its square-cut phrases, simplicity, syllabic text setting, and peculiar objective neutrality. Throughout, the pictorial details belong largely to the piano, above which the singer tells his tale with a minimum of effusive sentiment from the realm of lied or opera, with one notable exception. Loewe occasionally includes vocal melismas in his ballads, such as the roulades exemplifying the musical powers of "Der Nöck" (The water-sprite), one of Loewe's best-known ballads to a text by August Kopisch. Like Monteverdi's Orpheus in the infernal halls, Loewe represents supernatural musical beauty and watery cascades by putting both the singer and the pianist to the test.

Most of Wolf's youthful ballads are hybrids, a compound of ballad and lieder elements in which ballad conventions are compressed into a small space. Wolf begins both "Knabentod" and "Suschens Vogel" without a piano introduction and with simple, syllabic melodies after Loewe's model for the initial narration in a ballad. However, the appoggiatural stress on the word "kaum" ("Er kann sich *kaum* noch tragen") in measure 7 of "Knabentod," the accented word followed by a rest to create still more emphasis, already hints at Wolf's taste for multiple dramatic details, for prosodic nuances surpassing Loewe's wont. "Knabentod" is an unusual ballad—Wolf typically chose atypical ballads—because it is so compressed; Hebbel progresses very swiftly from the matter-of-fact narration of something commonplace to catastrophe and death. The seriated form of the classic ballad is squeezed into dimensions no bigger than a small lied. There is not time and room enough to allow for firmly established modulations to other key areas, but the accompaniment figuration depictive of the roaring flood changes every few bars, and Wolf revels in off-beat accents and two-against-three patterns, pairing rhythmic tumult with Nature on a rampage. "Suschens Vogel" two-and-a-half years later gave him somewhat more room to demonstrate his mastery of the hybrid of ballad conventions and song form that Loewe used on occasion and christened the *Ballade in Lied-Form*.[28] Here, Wolf sets Mörike's poem as a three-part song form in which the framing sections are written in the square-cut manner of Loewe's narrative melody, while the middle section in the dominant is a showcase for the pianist-cum-bird. The hybrid is particularly appropriate here because the text is a combination of ballad narrative and lyric poem in which the narrator is the faithless woman herself. "Die Tochter der Heide," the last of Wolf's early ballads, is in varied strophic form, the same motive in the piano sounding almost constantly. This work is an exciting premonition of "Der Rattenfänger" from the Goethe volume, with its similar hypnotically rhythmical $\frac{6}{8}$ vocal phrases, recurrent virtuosic piano refrain, and savage energy. Loewe had earlier resorted to transposed and varied reiteration of a single instrumental motive throughout in such famous short ballads as "Walpurgisnacht," so Wolf had ample precedent for his own works similarly conceived.

Of Wolf's mature compositions from 1888 on, the Mörike and Goethe collections include the following ballads: "Storchenbotschaft" (The storks' message), "Nixe Binsefuss" (Fairy reed-foot), "Der Jäger" (The hunter), "Die Geister am Mummelsee" (The spirits at Mummel Lake), "Zur Warnung" (A warning), "Abschied" (Farewell), and "Der Feuerreiter" (The Fire-rider) from the *Gedichte von Eduard Mörike* and "Gutmann und Gutweib," "Ritter Kurts Brautfahrt" (Knight Kurt's bridal journey), "Der Sänger," and "Der Rattenfänger" from the *Gedichte von Goethe*. With Wolf's turn southward for his song texts after 1890, the ballad vanishes from his works, both the lengthier episodic ballads and the *Balladen in Lied-Form*; the Italian and Spanish songbooks and the Michelangelo songs include nothing definable as a ballad. Edward Kravitt observes that Wolf is not known as a ballad composer in part because he never called attention to the fact by composing entire sets or collections of ballads and because he never set the classic texts by Uhland, Schiller, and Bürger that would have identified him immediately as a ballad composer.[29] Nevertheless, of the composers who took up Loewe's banner at century's end, Wolf is among the most significant, in both magnitude and quality. Wolf found in Loewe's massive repertoire a tradition he could adapt to his own ends, adding his stylistic stamp to the enterprise. Too, he could confirm in Loewe's respected achievements his own detestation of absolute music as a fin-de-siècle ideal.

Revivals usually impel a renewed critical assessment of whatever is being revived, and the attempts to restore the ballad were no exception. Wolf, who sought a balance between his own style and the traditions to which he claimed allegiance, was uninterested in perpetuating tradition per se, but Wolf's contemporary, the ballad-master Martin Plüddeman, was. His polemics for "correct" ballad composition and his late-Romantic modernizations of Loewe's model form an interesting backdrop to Wolf's version of balladry, especially since Eduard Hanslick paired Wolf and Plüddemann together as similarly prone to illustrative excesses and contaminated by Wagnerism to boot. Hanslick's dismissive judgment aside, the two composers are indeed an interesting pair, as much for their dissimilarities as for their resemblances.

MARTIN PLÜDDEMANN AND THE BALLAD REVIVAL

Plüddemann was a man on a mission. After he lost his voice at age twenty-six in 1880 and could no longer pursue a career as a singer, Plüddemann devoted his life to the cause of reviving the ballad. In 1886, he founded a ballad school in Berlin, followed by another in Graz in 1890, and in 1893, he tried to establish a journal entitled *Blätter für Balladenwesen* (Journal on the nature of balladry), although he was unable to find sufficient financial support for any of his ballad enterprises.[30] For a public that, in his opinion, no longer understood the nature of balladry, Plüddemann attempted to define its essential components in the the explanatory notes to each of his eight ballad collections (1891–99) and in his articles on the subject in various publications. In his purist efforts to preserve a threatened species, he clearly defined the genre from the historical vantage point of almost a century's span.[31]

According to Plüddemann, the ballad was originally the product of medieval folk sensibilities, having little in common with the modern mentality or even less with daylight rationalism. Its purpose is "to tell tales of earlier

Figure 4. The ballad-composer Martin Plüddemann
(1854–1897)

times," and that purpose precludes subjective expressivity and the depiction
of an emotional inner life. Instead, the poet feigns the removed stance of an
anonymous folk narrator many generations distant from the events recounted.
Because of this stricture, true ballads have something "harsh, raw, yet coldly
chaste," essential to their nature, uncontaminated by subjective emotion and
therefore unlike either lied or opera.[32] The temperature of balladry is cooler;
even the sorrowful scenes so prominent in many ballads should be merely
suggested rather than passionately enacted in full emotional force.[33] In accord
with his call for "cooler temperatures" and a curb on lyricism, the purist
Plüddemann, who was a devout Wagnerite and treasured the memory of his
visit to Wahnfried, nonetheless rejects late Romantic-harmony in its farthest
reaches as too heated for his purposes. He considered the story-telling func-

tion of balladry inimical to tonal experimentation and inveighed against the modern practice of "beginning, continuing, and ending a composition with unrelieved dissonance."[34] Nor was Wagnerian "endless melody," in his opinion, compatible with the correct declamation necessary for narrative art. Schubert's longer songs, such as "An Schwager Kronos" (To Coachman Chronos), D. 369, and "Gruppe aus dem Tartarus" (Group from Hades), D. 583, and Schumann's ballads were better compositional models.[35] He even speculated that the ballad might come full circle back to its origins, back to the repetitive incantations of the ancient bards.[36]

And yet there is, as so often, a gap between theory and practice—the latter less regressive than the composer's prose might suggest. Plüddemann's need to present himself as more a conservator of earlier practices, which he undoubtedly was, than an innovator is especially remarkable when one examines the works themselves. In ballads such as his giant (thirty-five pages) setting of Bürger's "Der wilde Jäger" (The wild hunter) in volume 3, one finds numerous indices of his debt to Wagner and his firm location in the fin-de-siècle. The rapidity of tonal change, at times necessitating a new key signature every measure or two; his frequent evasion of cadential resolution; the late-Romantic chromaticism of several of the principal motives; and their extensive development along Wagnerian lines all mark him as a contemporary of Wolf, albeit a less tonally radical contemporary. Like other Wagner disciples who took their cue from Ernst von Wolzogen and his leitmotif-naming exercises (Wolf in his opera *Der Corregidor* would do so as well), Plüddemann assigns names and verbal meanings to the musical figures of this ballad, including the Warning motive, the motive of Compassion (unalloyed shades of Wagner), the "springing" figure for the chase after a herd of deer, and finally, the riot of chromaticism for the Wild Hunt of the dead. There is ample precedent in Loewe for the notion that each episode of the tale should prompt music illustrative of its principal images, but Plüddemann describes the genesis of his work in terms influenced by Wagner[37] and then composes his ballads in a tonal language that is more up-to-date than he would admit in words. Sensitive to the charge that ballads were often somewhat ramshackle in construction, especially when compared to the rounded forms of lied composition, he frequently points out in his explanatory notes the existence of unifying head-motives (*Hauptthemen*) or bass figures and the unifying musical relationships between the themes in different sections. A passage in which Plüddemann establishes and then develops what he calls the Warning motive can serve as a sample of his compositional methods and characteristic style (Example 16).

Even beyond Loewe's wont, the piano part of "Der wilde Jäger" is orchestrally conceived, Plüddemann's propensity for massive piano textures especially evident in the climactic Wild Hunt. Plüddemann considered orchestrating his ballads but decided against it because the singer-narrator would be constrained by a conductor necessarily concerned with holding together more

Example 16. Martin Plüddemann, "Der wilde Jäger," measures 287–314

than two musicians in an ensemble. This, he felt, would be inimical to the nature of balladry, but he compensates by filling his ballads with orchestral effects—in particular, lengthy passages of tremolando figuration.[38] The virtuosic nature of the writing for piano has precedent in tradition. In his essay on the ballad, Spitta discusses the special nature of the piano accompaniment in ballads, weightier than in lyrical song. The piano part must not only sustain the melody and fortify it, must not only provide a deeper resonance to the changing affects of the story, but is also responsible for the narrative content,

Example 16, continued

for the scene painting and the progression from one event to the next.[39] Those events are often highly charged, as when Schiller's doomed young man plunges into an oceanic maelstrom in "Der Taucher" (The diver), even more wild and furious than the seething waters one hears in Schubert's setting (D. 77; 1813–15)—surely an unadmitted spur to Plüddemann's later endeavors. The accompaniments to such acts of derring-do and disaster are frequently a test of pianistic technique.

Example 16, continued

Few composers wrote ballads in perfect conformity with Plüddemann's ideal. Only Loewe and Plüddemann himself are given credit for utmost fidelity to the genre. Zumsteeg was merely a path-breaker for Loewe, he declared (Zumsteeg, and Schubert after him, use recitative liberally in their ballads, and Plüddemann did not consider recitative a proper constituent of a true ballad), and most of those who came after Loewe were song composers at heart.[40] Lied, a companion-genre to balladry for many years, had become its

Example 16, continued

victorious rival. In the contentious afterword to the first volume of ballads, Plüddemann complains that the public now prefers lighter fare, that is, the "strongly erotic-colored lied," and explains that there are only three pure vocal genres: the song, the ballad, and music drama, with the ballad located midway along a crescendo of greater amplitude.[41] In a phrase influenced by the writings of his favorite philosopher Schopenhauer (a very Wagnerian choice), Plüddemann characterized the genre as standing alongside the great works of music like a dream next to actual life and therefore requiring the salutary exercise of imagination on the listener's part.[42] Unlike lieder, which wear their hearts on their sleeves, ballads rely doubly on fantasy, as neither the text nor the music tells all.

No imagination is required, however, to discern most of the ballad traditions to which Plüddemann, in his fervor, adheres. This is, with few exceptions, a male genre—one, furthermore, in which maleness is equated with vocal heft and strength. In his directives to performers, Plüddemann calls for a specific type of voice as the only sound suitable for a particular text; only a true basso profundo, he says, should sing "Das Grab im Busento" (The grave in the Busento River). His favorite vocal type is a heroic baritone with an extended upper register; even *Heldentenors*, for all their carrying power, lacked access to the darker lower registers he demands so often. Lyric tenors were too light and unheroic, too much the denizens of lied and and opera for the stern stuff of which ballads are made, and women's voices are only heard through the scrim of a male narrator, poet, and composer.[43]

The kinds of tales this Teutonic blood-brotherhood tell are also a matter of tradition. Plüddemann was evidently concerned to prove his mettle in most of the different subspecies of balladry to be found in Loewe, although the later composer complains in the foreword to volume 5 that Loewe's fondness for the *Legende* had left him with few suitable poems to set to music. He located several nonetheless, including one by Goethe ("Die Legende vom Hufeisen," or "The legend of the horseshoes") that Loewe—an omnivorous Goethe composer—unaccountably missed. Nor did Plüddemann attempt the so-called great ballads with choruses and multiple dramatis personae, a hop, skip, and jump away from outright secular oratorio, such as Loewe's settings of Goethe's "Gesang der Geister über den Wassern" (Song of the spirits over the waters), op. 88, and "Die Braut von Corinth" (The Corinthian bride), op. 29;[44] given the later composer's historicist insistence on purity of genre, one would not logically expect him thus to confuse categories. Plüddemann's eight volumes *do* include history ballads, comic tales, animal fables, knightly tales (*Ritterballaden*), ghost and horror stories (*Geister-* and *Schauerballaden*), Scottish and English pseudo–folk ballads by Theodor Fontane, ballads to classic texts by Heine ("Frau Mette," or "Dame Mette"), Goethe, Uhland ("Siegfrieds Schwert," or "Siegfried's sword"), Schiller ("Toggenburg" and "Der Taucher"), and Bürger (the mammoth comic ballad "Der Kaiser und der Abt," or "The king and the abbot"), and an entire volume each of texts by Fontane and Ludwig Giesebrecht (1792–1873), who had earlier been a favorite of Loewe's. The first volume, significantly, begins with a setting of Schiller's "Die deutsche Muse" (The German muse), brief but in true ballad manner and representative of the nationalistic fervor that informs so much of

German balladry.[45] In his notes, Plüddemann is careful to define each category where the reader might be in doubt or be ignorant of the correct classification, especially where differentiation from the lied is concerned. "Graf Eberhard's Weißdorn" (Count Eberhard's white thorn tree) and "Einkehr" (The inn), both to texts by Uhland, are more "nature idylls" than true ballads, he tells us, because there is too little action, too little plot; and "Venetianisches Gondel-lied" (Venetian gondola song) is virtually a lied, "in which I find little worth." He published it anyway.[46]

By lingering for a moment on a representative ballad from Plüddemann's second volume, we can better understand both what he considered to be a proper ballad art and some of the reasons for the genre's demise. Loewe and Plüddemann were both practitioners of the historical ballad, settings of texts that require either hefty footnotes or a thorough command of ancient and modern Teutonic history in order to understand the context fully. Loewe in particular marches through the history of the Germanic tribes and kings from Carolingian times onward, from the time of Heinrich I (Henry the fowler) and his son Otto the Great in the tenth century to the Prussian monarchs he himself served. The op. 99 cycle of four ballads about Charles V (1844) and the op. 124 cycle of three ballads collectively entitled "Der letzte Ritter" (The last knight) on the sixteenth-century Austrian ruler Maximilian I were, according to Loewe's testimony, particular favorites of the Prussian king Friedrich Wilhelm IV. No wonder: this eccentric Hohenzollern monarch, who fused Prussian and nationalist German affairs inextricably and later died mad, was deeply affected by Romantic veneration of an idealized national past. Fascination with medieval lore of all kinds was endemic throughout Europe, but historical ballads such as these had a barely veiled political raison d'être in Loewe's day, born of German history in the wake of the Napoleonic Wars. Germany was carved into an ineffective confederation of over thirty autonomous states after the Congress of Vienna in 1815, with Prussia and Austria the only two forces with any real power in the German-speaking realms of Europe. The confederation was an empty failure from the beginning, and Friedrich Wilhelm's dream of unification found models and inspiration in the Hohenstaufen empire, the Carolingian and Ottonian kings, in the glories of the Holy Roman Empire and the Reformation. This was what the Christian-Teutonic land had been in the past and what it could be once again, celebrated in song and story. A composer who shared a monarch's Romantic ideals encapsulated those ideals in music, and those same ideals were in turn perpetuated by Plüddemann in his self-appointed role as "son of Loewe"—a regressive exercise, however reverential, by 1890. Wolf had nothing to do with the historical ballad, not even in his youth.

Plüddemann's 1883 setting of Count August von Platen-Hallermünde's "Das Grab im Busento"[47] can serve to exemplify the problem for listeners of insufficient context in historical ballads. Platen's poem has to do with a dramatic chapter in the dissolution of the Roman Empire, under attack by waves of Huns, Visigoths, Ostrogoths, Franks, and Vandals. Shortly after the Roman Emperor Theodosius the Great died at Milan in A.D. 395, the Visigoths elected a king named Alaric, who revolted from Roman rule and began to cut a spectacular swath of destruction across the crumbling Empire. His opponent was Stilicho, a Vandal-born but loyal general in Theodosius's service who became a power because he was a skilled military tactician and because the emperor's two sons were nullities. When Stilicho's execution was ordered in 408 after the Romanized army rose against the half-barbarian general whose ambition they feared, Alaric stormed Italy and headed straight for Rome itself, which he devastated in 410. "The human race is included in the ruins," wrote St. Jerome, and even St. Augustine ceased his imprecations against the pagan gods and goddesses to admit that the whole world groaned at the fall of Rome. Alaric had planned to storm Africa next, but was shipwrecked in a storm near Sicily and turned back. Scarcely had he done so before he died at Cosenza in 410 and was buried, or so goes the legend, in the bed of the river Busento, the grave site concealed by the massacre of the slaves who first diverted and then restored the stream. "He had been a great destroyer," concludes C. W. Previté-Orton in his classic work on medieval history.[48]

Platen, however, tells his reader almost none of this. All that interested him was the end of this Gothic Rambo's life. In "Das Grab im Busento," Alaric becomes a prototypical Teutonic blond hero slain tragically young and buried by a worshipful horde of warriors in a suitably singular manner; the archetype has been fatally contaminated by its twentieth-century associations with the politics and aesthetics of the Third Reich. The conquest of Rome is not mentioned at all. Only the reference at the end to this watery burial as eternal protection from "Rome's wicked envy" hints to the historically uninformed that this eerie tale has something to do with that city at all.

> Nächtlich am Busento lispeln, bei Cosenza, dumpfe Lieder,
> Aus den Wassern schallt es Antwort, und in Wirbeln klingt es wider!

> Und den Fluß hinauf, hinunter, ziehn die Schatten tapfrer Goten,
> Die den Alarich beweinen, ihres Volkes besten Toten.

> Allzufrüh und fern der Heimat mußten hier sie ihn begraben,
> Während noch die Jugendlocken seine Schulter blond umgaben.

> Und am Ufer des Busento reihten sie sich um die Wette,
> Um die Strömung abzuleiten, gruben sie ein frisches Bette.

> In der wogenleeren Höhlung wühlten sie empor die Erde,
> Senkten tief hinein den Leichnam, mit der Rüstung, auf dem Pferde.

Deckten dann mit Erde wieder ihn und seine stolze Habe,
Daß die hohen Stromgewächse wüchsen aus dem Heldengrabe.

Abgelenkt zum zweiten Male, ward der Fluß herbeigezogen:
Mächtig in ihr altes Bette schäumten die Busentowogen.

Und es sang ein Chor von Männern: "Schlaf in deinen Heldenehren!
Keines Römers schnöde Habsucht soll dir je dein Grab versehren!"

Sangen's, und die Lobgesänge tönten fort im Gotenheere;
Wälze sie, Busentowelle, wälze sie von Meer zu Meere!

(Muffled songs murmur softly by night on the Busento, near Cosenza.
An answer resounds from the waters and echoes in the eddies! And along
the river, upstream and down, are the shadows of the valiant Goths who
weep for Alaric, the best of all their dead. They must bury him here, far
from home, so young, with the blond locks of youth yet falling on his
shoulders. And on the banks of the Busento, they lined up, dared to
divert the river's flow, and dug a fresh bed. In the cavity, empty of the
river's waves, they excavated the earth and lowered the corpse, in his
armor and on horseback, deep within. They covered him and his proud
possessions with earth once more, so that the high river reeds might grow
from the hero's grave. Diverted a second time, the river drew near; in
their old bed, the Busento's waves foamed mightily. And a chorus of
men sang: "Sleep in your heroic glory! No Roman in his evil envy shall
deface your grave! So they sang, and the songs of praise resounded
loudly from the Gothic troops. Roll on, Busento, roll on from sea to sea!)

Plüddemann, in his notes to the performers, does not explain the events that
lead to the legendary burial, nor does any ballad composer.[49] Here, as in the
newly important genre of history paintings, the ballad tells the tale of a single
moment, of one episode purposely devoid of context. Ideally, that instant
should express the meaning of the entire historical event, significance that the
viewer or listener should be able to grasp without specialized knowledge.
Historicist trends that encouraged the search for what is specific, time-bound,
and unique, or the wish to show things as they actually are, clash throughout
the century with the longing for idealized former ages, fictively re-created in
ballads, novels, paintings by the Nazarenes, and opera. Neither Platen's text
nor Plüddemann's music were written to impart information about Alaric,
king of the Visigoths, but rather to make an isolated moment from the past
mythic in microcosm. The poem is simultaneously a lament and a celebration
of the long centuries of militaristic Teutonic confraternity—in the preface to
volume 2, Plüddemann calls Platen's work a "beautiful, sorrow-laden poem,
wonderfully illustrative of German brotherhood"—to which the composer

adds his homage to a more recent musical hero. Because the poem tells of awe at a great man's death, someone who could inspire superhuman deeds and universal songs of praise, I wonder whether Wagner's death in Venice that same year might not have had something to do with Plüddemann's choice of this particular text, in which a conqueror of a different sort dies in Italy.

Plüddemann recommended his shorter works, such as "Das Grab im Busento," to a public that might not have the necessary stamina for his setting of Schiller's gigantic "Der Taucher" (twenty-seven six-line stanzas) but nonetheless wanted to experience what he calls "a true ballad in the strict sense of the word"—that is, a tale told in through-composed episodic structure rather than *Ballade in Lied-form*. Plüddemann alternates between composing lengthy piano introductions for his ballads, such as the expanse of horn-call figures at the start of "Der wilde Jäger," and launching into his story with scant instrumental preamble, as he does here. A mere two measures of tremolandos from deep in the bass—the muffled reverberations from the depths of the river—precede the narrator's entrance (Plüddemann is fond of the nethermost reaches of the piano) and continue throughout the initial section in the Mozartian-Schubertian "tragic" key of D minor. The declamation on repeated notes in the first vocal phrase and the proclamatory octave leaps in the subsequent sequential phrases exemplify not only Plüddemann's attention to prosody but the narrative melody and epic tone he considered proper to ballad composition (Example 17). The pathos of Alaric's youth and early death far from his native land evokes a turn to D major and music reminiscent of *Tannhäuser*, ending with a turn to B♭ major by means of a linear chromatic descent and by deceptive motion. For the Goths' labors of diverting the river and digging the grave, Plüddemann gives the piano a neighbor-note figure divisible into two components, one higher and one lower, the uppermost swing of the spade alternating between the lowered and natural forms of the sixth scale degree. If it has a certain "Yo heave ho" quality about it, that is only appropriate to the subject matter. Plüddemann brings the spade-diggers' figure back in a suitably eerie chromatic variant when the Goths return the river to its course. Despite the atmospheric effectiveness of his music, Plüddemann was not always successful in avoiding outworn formulas. The macabre standing occupant of the riverbed-tomb is lowered into his final resting place to the cliché of slow, solemn descending chromatic harmonies and too many diminished-seventh chords. Plüddemann was proud of the Goths' funereal strains, the D-major apotheosis (the lowered sixth scale degree is, however, in evidence right to the end) derived from the tremolando harmonies in the first section and the arpeggiated bass figuration originally heard in measures 23–26. This is indeed "a true ballad in the strict sense of the word," but Plüddemann nonetheless carefully rounds off the form by building musical bridges between the beginning and ending in a composition short enough for such relationships to be readily perceived in performance.

Example 17. Martin Plüddemann, "Das Grab im Busento," measures 1–21

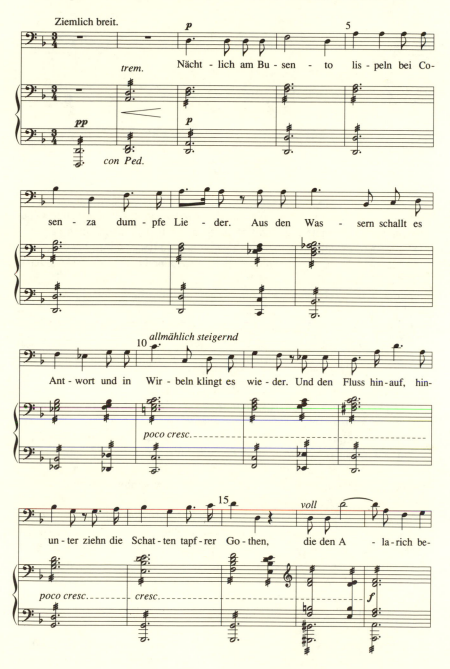

Example 17, continued

wei - nen,   ih - res Vol - kes be - sten Tod - ten!

As with any historic genre, one must know and accept its conventions before one can appreciate Plüddemann's "special effects." Then, such passages
as the ancient Friedrich Barbarossa's speech from deep within his centuries-
old enchanted sleep, accompanied only by a sustained octave deep in the bass,
in Friedrich Rückert's "Der alte Barbarossa" (The old Barbarossa); the muffled sounds of the church bells submerged beneath the water ("barely audible," Plüddemann directs) in Wilhelm Müller's "Vineta;" the riot of arpeggiated harp chords in Uhland's "Des Sängers Fluch" (The minstrel's curse);
and the entire massive spread of "Der Taucher," which Plüddemann considered his masterpiece, can be heard in context and with proper appreciation of
his historical enterprise, however ill-fated.[50] When he includes unaccompanied vocal passages marked *erzählend* ("narrating") in "Vevros und sein
Pferd" (Vevros and his steed), akin to Loewe's directive "in bequem er-
zählendem Zeitmasse" (at a tempo suitable for narration) for his "Treu-
röschen," op. 2, no. 1, Plüddemann points out yet again the special nature of
ballads. "Dreams next to real life," he called the genre: he chose to continue
dreaming of the past and laboring for its restitution in the present, but Wolf
looked elsewhere in the ballad tradition for the more sophisticated fantasy and
psychological realism he preferred.

   In fact, Wolf found Plüddemann's historicist mission and his regressive
attitude downright contemptible. Loewe's earlier nineteenth-century grave-
yards and phantoms were one thing; Plüddemann's attempts to become Loewe
redivivus, another. In a letter written from Graz to Melanie Köchert on 27
November 1893, Wolf, with his characteristic devastating wit, describes the
self-proclaimed balladeer as a creature out of one of his own ghoulish creations: "Dined with Potpeschnigg and Purgleitner at the Thonethof [a café] and
had the pleasure of seeing the 'famous' balladeer Plüddemann there, who was
feeding at the nearby table. Looks quite disreputable and seedy, exactly like
a ballad-ghost in Plüddemannic garb."[51] Wolf's perception of Plüddemann's

ghostlike lack of substance—without the wherewithal to create something new, Plüddemann cobbled together a counterfeit identity from Loewe and Wagner—is implicit in the capsule caricature. In his description of his fellow-composer as shabby and without refinement ("feeding" like an animal), one also hears Wolf's rejection of Plüddemann's *music* as shabby and disreputable.

WOLF AND LOEWE

Plüddemann criticized most ballad singers for overacting, for a love of "bright lights and strong color,"[52] but for Wolf, cool temperatures had little to do with ballad singing. In his music criticism for the *Wiener Salonblatt*, "the wild Wolf" castigates the German baritone Theodor Reichmann (1849–1903) not once but three times for his insufficiently dramatic renditions of Loewe.

> Some lieder sung by Herr Reichmann were well received, although the utterly undramatic rendition of Loewe's ballad, "Edward," left the audience cold. How is it possible to sing a song that places us immediately in the center of a dramatic situation [Wolf's own preference for ballad texts] with the amiability of a night-watchman? Why this ambling tempo? Why this passion in a high collar? From so splendid a dramatic singer as Herr Reichmann one is entitled to expect better.

> In the following ballad, "Heinrich der Vogler" [Henry the fowler], Herr Reichmann demonstrated once again that he lacks the slightest understanding of this genre. A ballad by Loewe needs to be interpreted as well as sung. Herr Reichmann, however, appears to be of the opinion that all one has to do is sing, and everything will come out all right. Such was not the case, and I can assure him that he sang pretty badly, that he made a mess of the ballad, and that he was most ably assisted in so doing by his accompanist.

> Once again he sang the ballad, "Heinrich der Vogler," and once again with the same indifference toward the now epic, now dramatic character of the poem. Whether it is the narrator or the hero who speaks, it's all the same to him. With Herr Reichmann one dares not expect to hear the various groupings plastically illustrated by modulation of voice and mode of delivery. All that he has to offer are lovely, sweet, mellow sounds. Simply to hear him is an aural delight. Whoever expects from art, however, no more than the satisfaction of sensuous titillation will recognize in Herr Reichmann the ideal artist. Our man he is not.[53]

The reviews are typically lively. Wolf's likes and dislikes were seldom in doubt, and Loewe was entrenched among the composers to be admired, defended, and emulated. Figures from Loewe's ballads even resurface in Wolf's own music, probably as the result of unconscious recollection—the fanfare figures from Loewe's "Der Edelfalk" (The falcon), op. 68, no. 2 seem the precursor for similar figures in Wolf's "O wär' dein Haus durchsichtig wie ein Glas" (If only your house were transparent like glass) from the *Italienisches Liederbuch* (Examples 18a and 18b). Both poetic texts are proclamations of love, although of a different kind and in a different tone. Ferdinand Freili-

Example 18a. Carl Loewe, "Der Edelfalk," Op. 68, no. 2, measures 19–22

Example 18b. Hugo Wolf, "O wär' dein Haus durchsichtig wie ein Glas,"
measures 1–3

grath's ballad tells of the love of an anthropomorphized talking falcon for a beautiful princess, while in Heyse's translation of an Italian folk poem, the lover wishes that her beloved's house were made of glass so that she could see him when she goes by, could send him more heartfelt glances than the number of water droplets in a March flood or a rain shower. The hunting-horn fanfares that echo the falcon's proclamation of love are transformed in Wolf to become crystalline emblems of raindrops and love's sweetness, the modal vacillation between major and minor an index of the mixed emotions of love.

Of the gamut of ballad species in Loewe's oeuvre, Wolf would later confine himself to humorous ballads, ballads of the supernatural, or a merger of those two categories. Although he admired "Archibald Douglas" and "Der große Christoph," he was not thereby inspired to search through Fontane's ballads or poetic accounts of saints' lives for texts he could claim as his own. (Significantly, "Der grosse Christoph," the only *Legende* mentioned in his letters, contains both comic episodes—the pagan Oferus, before his conversion and renaming, is a genial giant—and encounters with a Moorish Satan, the humor and the infernal scenes to Wolf's taste). But the humor is of a different order in the two men's works, Loewe's gentler brand of comedy distinct from Wolf's preference for contentious jokes in verse. In his autobiography, Loewe recounts a meeting in 1837 with one Alexander Baumann, a zither-player–cum–poet who praised the composer's talent for musical humor and volunteered to write a comic libretto on Don Quixote for him—the project came to nought.[54] He *did* write humorous ballads, however, and his lighter side was noted with approval by the critics; the reviewer for the *Neue Zeitschrift für Musik* preferred the settings of comic animal fables, such as the four ballads of op. 64 ("Der verliebte Maikäfer," or "The cockchafer in love"; "Der Kukuk," or "The cuckoo"; "Die Katzenkönigin," or "The queen of the cats"; and "Wer ist Bär?" or "Who is the bear?"), to the graveyard tales of the supernatural for which Loewe was best known.[55]

In such works, Loewe keeps the joke light, the texture clear and uncomplicated, the harmonic idiom conservative. Many of the passages in Loewe's op. 64 sound uncannily like Gilbert and Sullivan, with their tick-tock chordal pulsations, melodic lines whose comic edge comes from large intervallic leaps treated sequentially, ornamented instrumental echoes of the vocal cadences, declamation on repeated pitches for the beginnings of vocal lines, square-cut phrases repeated literally, and common-tone mediant modulations from one scene or speech to another. The diatonicism of these works and Loewe's use of sectional repetition, however, would not later be to Wolf's taste for his own music. Given his more specific mapping of the text, he preferred variation to literal repetition and formal structures that end, like the poetic plot, in a different tonal place than that in which they began. A closer precursor of Wolf's later accomplishments in musical humor can be found in Loewe's longer comic tales such as "Die Heinzelmännchen" (The brownies), op. 83, composed in 1841 to a poem by August Kopisch (1799–1853). One stanza of its eight will suffice as a sample of Kopisch's style.

> Wie war zu Köln es doch vordem
> Mit Heinzelmännchen so bequem!
> Denn war man faul, . . . man legte sich
> Hin auf die Bank und pflegte sich:
>> Da kamen bei Nacht,
>> Ehe man's gedacht,
>> Die Männlein und schwärmten
>> Und klappten und lärmten
>>> Und rupften
>>> Und zupften
>> Und hüpften und trabten
>> Und putzten und schabten . . .
> Und eh ein Faulpelz noch erwacht . . .
> War all sein Tagewerk . . . bereits gemacht!⁵⁶

(How convenient things were a long time ago in Cologne with the little men! Then one could be lazy—one could lie down on a bench and take it easy. At night, the little men came and swarmed about and rattled and roared and plucked and picked and jumped and trotted and scoured and rubbed—and before a lazybones even awoke, his day's work was already done!)

The author of a volume of *Gedichte* published in 1836 and the *Allerlei Geister* (All manner of spooks) of 1848, Kopisch cultivated the comic-fantastic ballad as a specialty, including "Der Nöck" (Loewe's op. 129, no. 2) and "Die Heinzelmännchen." His version of a Lower Rhenish fairy tale tells of secretive gnomelike creatures, the *Heinzelmännchen*, who formerly did all the work for lazy humanity; while the humans ostensibly responsible for various tasks snore in their beds, the gnomes do the baking, building, tailoring, and wine and sausage making. The tale is actually a comic version of the Fall, complete with a curious woman who pries into matters beyond her ken and therefore causes the loss of a secular Garden of Eden, compounded of indolence and ready-made goods.

Wolf says nothing of this ballad in the extant letters or in his friends' anecdotes, but Loewe's liberal use of accents, grace notes, and onomatopoeic figuration in "Die Heinzelmännchenn" seem an obvious ancestor to Wolf's own preferred means of comic emphasis. From the beginning, Loewe matches Kopisch's verbal extravagance with a swarm of measured trills, grace notes on weak beats, sequential Scotch-snap figures, and scalar passages, a translation into music of beelike, frenetic industry (Examples 19a and 19b). The comic energy of the Heinzelmännchen's incessant hustle-and-bustle activity

Example 19a. Carl Loewe, "Die Heinzelmännchen," Op. 83, measures 21–49

Example 19a, continued

is rendered in a succession of changing *moto perpetuo* figures whose registral contrasts and repeated-note ostinatos Wolf would later press into service. In particular, the use of grace notes and harmonic seconds would seem to foreshadow Wolf, as when the snipping of the gnome-tailors' scissors is accompanied by onomatopoeic grace-note figures in the high treble register—the kind of clustered grace-note figures Wolf would later use in such songs as "Rat einer Alten" (An old woman's advice), "Ich hab' in Penna," "Schweig' einmal still," and others. When the tailor's wife, curious to know who has completed the official robe for the mayor, spies on the gnomes, the little men flee, tumbling down the ladders and stairs with grace-noted wailing and shrieking, and then disappear—"husch, husch, husch, husch, husch!" The sawing and hammering, plastering and chopping of the carpenter gnomes inspires the repeated harmonic major seconds that one later finds in Wolf's "Mein Liebster ist so klein," "Ich hab' in Penna," and "Storchenbotschaft" to convey littleness, sharpness, emphasis, or acerbic criticism. Finally, Loewe arranges the episodes of his lengthy ballad as a chain of third relationships—not the more complex chains of thirds that Wolf would later use, but an interesting design nonetheless. If Loewe's use of chromaticism hardly equals Schubert's bolder tonal designs, he could and did use chromatic sequences to pointed effect in "Die Heinzelmännchen," in which neither the gnomes nor the harmonic progressions within an episode/tonal region are allowed to rest.

Example 19b. Hugo Wolf, "Die Heinzelmännchen," measures 227–34

The influence of works such as "Die Heinzelmännchen" is apparent in Wolf's setting of Eduard Mörike's comic ballad "Storchenbotschaft" (The storks' message), composed on 27 March 1888. In this poem, Mörike creates a world in which human beings and supernatural creatures coexist in a humorous but uneasy alliance. The demons of Romantic fantasy are semidomesticated as grotesques, the fearsome-elemental constrained in the guise of ludicrous beings whose capacities for malice are nonetheless still apparent.[57] By 1888, Wolf had left behind his youthful taste for Romantic subjectivity but without renouncing his love of fantasy. No wonder Mörike appealed to him so deeply: in this poet he found the classic artificer, the Rabelaisian lover of deformity, and the inventor of droll and fantastic scenarios combined in one Protean imagination. Here, a poetic vision of human psychology, even the abnormal psychology that so fascinated Mörike,[58] did not entail the autointoxication that suffuses Heine's works.[59]

> Des Schäfers sein Haus und das steht auf zwei Rad,
> Steht hoch auf der Heiden, so frühe, wie spat;
> Und wenn nur ein Mancher so'n Nachtquartier hätt'!
> Ein Schäfer tauscht nicht mit dem König sein Bett.
>
> Und kam ihm zur Nacht auch was Seltsames vor,
> Er betet sein Sprüchel und legt sich auf's Ohr;
> Ein Geistlein, ein Hexlein, so lüftige Wicht',
> Sie klopfen ihm wohl, doch er antwortet nicht.
> Einmal doch, da ward es ihm wirklich zu bunt:
> Es knopert am Laden, es winselt der Hund;
> Nun ziehet mein Schäfer den Riegel—ei schau!
> Da stehen zwei Störche, der Mann und die Frau.
>
> Das Pärchen, es machet ein schön Compliment,
> Es möchte gern reden, ach, wenn es nur könnt'!
> Was will mir das Ziefer?—ist so was erhört?
> Doch ist mir wohl fröhliche Botschaft beschert.
>
> Ihr seid wohl dahinten zu Hause am Rhein?
> Ihr habt wohl mein Mädel gebissen in's Bein?
> Nun weinet das Kind und die Mutter noch mehr,
> Sie wünschet den Herzallerliebsten sich her?
>
> Und wünschet daneben die Taufe bestellt:
> Ein Lämmlein, ein Würstlein, ein Beutelein Geld?
> So sagt nur, ich kam' in zwei Tag oder drei,
> Und grüßt mir mein Bubel und rührt ihm den Brei!
>
> Doch halt! Warum stellt ihr zu Zweien euch ein?
> Es werden doch, hoff' ich, nicht Zwillinge sein?—
> Da klappern die Störche im lustigsten Ton,
> Sie nikken und knixen und fliegen davon.[60]

(The shepherd's house stands on two wheels, stands high on the heath both night and day. Many a person would like to have such fine sleeping quarters! A shepherd wouldn't change beds with the king. And even if something unusual should happen to him at night, he just says a little prayer and goes back to sleep. A little ghost, a little witch, airy beings like that, they may knock at his door, but he doesn't answer. But one time things were really too much; there was a scraping at the shutter, and the dog whined. My shepherd drew the bolt, and look! there stood two storks, a male and his wife. The couple made a polite curtsy and would gladly have spoken, ah, if they only knew how! "What does this poultry want from me? Have you ever heard of anything like this? But perhaps there is a happy message in store for me. You probably live back there on the Rhine? You've perhaps bitten my girlfriend in the leg? Now I suppose the baby is crying, and its mother even more, and she wishes her sweetheart were with her. And also wishes to have the baptism arranged: a little lamb, a little sausage and a little bag of money? Tell her I'll be there in two or three days, say hello to my little boy for me and stir his porridge! But wait! Why are there two of you? I hope it isn't twins!" Then the storks clapped their beaks in the merriest music. They nodded and curtseyed and flew away.)

As in Kopisch's tale, human beings and supernatural creatures inhabit the same world and yet are separate from one another. The spirit creatures infringe on the human sphere, but the nonhuman beings are only mildly threatening at most. Mörike's shepherd, who lives in a fairy-tale version of a mobile home on the heath, knows that it requires no more than a miniature charm to banish the "airy creatures" that want entrance at night. The diminutives ("Geistlein," "Hexlein") belittle the menace of the nocturnal visitations. The intrusions of the otherworldly have to be notably persistent before the shepherd responds—one notices that his dog merely whines rather than barking in more active alarm. When he trustingly unbars the door without knowing what stands outside, he finds a wordless and *galant* pair of "poultry" with their traditional message.

Despite the assumed syntactical naiveté of the first verse and the colloquialisms ("Rad" rather than "Räder," "spat" instead of "spät," the elision of "so ein" as "so'n"), the Puckish humor is the product of a sophisticated poet. The poem is filled with rustic word-music (the "klappern" sounds of the storks' "nikken und knixen") and idiomatic expressions: the shepherd does not merely sleep but "legt sich auf's Ohr," and the pain of childbirth becomes the stork biting the mother's leg, with the alliterative *b*, *s*, and short *i* sounds underscoring the comic euphemism ("Ihr habt wohl mein Mädel *gebissen in's Bein?*"). But beneath the rustic surface is profundity at the level of symbolic reading. The genial visitants are inhuman and cannot speak, although Mörike slyly accords them the desire to do so. What they have to "say" must be interpreted by the one receiving their news. As the shepherd leaps past the expected equation of storks and birth to expatiate on the requirements for the christening, they wait patiently for him to grasp the meaning of their appearance as a couple. When he finally reads the news aright, they are delighted and fly away—and the poem ends. Since much of Mörike's poetry is also *about* poetry, whether overtly or covertly so, it is tempting to find in the ballad an extended metaphor for the poet visited by Muses (of sorts), an inspiration to imaginative invention, who solicitously wait until their charge "has got it right." When he does, when he realizes what they have brought him and himself "gives birth" to the correct message, the poem is over, the poetic process concluded. The shepherd-poet fantasizes, his imaginative powers running full tilt, until the truth strikes him, when he comes to an abrupt halt with an embarrassment of riches as his reward. On one level, "Storchenbotschaft" seems a fable of poetic creation.

There are multiple reminiscences of Loewe in Wolf's setting of this ballad. Its dimensions parallel Loewe's shorter ballads, which include some of his most compelling compositions,[61] and the minimal introduction (not a separate, discrete instrumental introduction—the singer joins in very shortly after the tale gets underway in the piano) is patterned after such ballads as "Der gefangene Admiral," op. 115, to a text by Moritz Graf von Strachwitz.[62] The "Gemächlich" (easygoing) tempo for "Storchenbotschaft" is a narrative indication,[63] a moderate pace that allows syllabic declamation in eighth-notes to be understood. The syllabic declamation and motivic or intervallic repetition within vocal phrases are modeled after one variety of Loewe's narrative melody; one notes in particular the repeated intervals of a third, like a child's chanting game, at the words "und wenn nur ein Manchers s'on [Nachtquartier hätt'!]." The "two wheels" were evidently the inspiration for the "turning" motive with its perfect fourths and fifths and the neighboring semitones at the uppermost compass, elided between the right and left hands. The asperity of the G♯ against G♮ in the paired accompanimental voices—the wheels that spin to set the song in motion—and the rasp of D♭, D♮, and E♭ ("*so frühe, wie spat*") against one another in measure 3 announce from the outset that Wolf's musical humor, like Mörike's, has a bite to it. The variation techniques Wolf uses in stanza 2 in order to depict the otherworldly are straight from Loewe's arsenal, with the measured trill intensifying the semitone neighbor-motive, the descending chromatic filler in the bass, and the grace-noted knocking figures (in the treble, appropriate to the "airy creatures") that are not answered, the refusal emphasized by the cadential Neapolitan sixth. Those grace-noted knocking figures seem a comic metamorphosis of the figuration throughout Loewe's setting of Platen's "Der Pilgrim vor St. Just" (The Pilgrim at the door of St. Just), op. 99, no. 3, with the abdicated Emperor Charles V hammering wearily on the doors of the monastery in Estremadura where he ended his life; this eerie nocturnal scene, which forms part of the *Kaiser Karl V* ballad cycle, is justly one of Loewe's best-known works (Examples 20a and 20b).

Example 20a. Hugo Wolf, "Storchenbotschaft," measures 13–15

It is with the third stanza that the action of "Storchenbotschaft" begins, and Wolf leaves the opening tonality of G minor to venture farther afield as events unfold. The interlude for the piano does not, as before, continue sequentially with the addition of the voice, but is expanded to lead to D minor in measure 13 and a more thoroughgoing variation of the supernaturalism of stanza 2. This time, it is "really too much": the knocking motives from measure 10 reappear intensified and refuse to go away. For the hushed statement, "Da stehen zwei Störche, der Mann und die Frau," Wolf evokes the supernatural by means of registral extremes and the contrast of widely spaced and closely voiced chords, a slow harmonic trill with parallel fifths in the bass and its chords spread over a four-octave span—the same device he would shortly thereafter use in the "Cophtisches Lied II" from the *Goethe-Lieder*. Loewe had earlier exploited contrasting high and low planes in his piano accompaniments to a greater degree than is ordinarily permissible within a song: for the sounds of pagan battle at the end of Ferdinand Freiligrath's "Der Mohrenfürst" (The Moorish prince), op. 97, no. 1, Loewe sends the right hand shooting upward to a protracted trill high above the repeated chords below, the postlude then sinking five octaves below the tumult. Wolf's seesawing motion on the interval of a seventh in both the vocal line and the piano when the storks arrive (measures 16–17) is also a gesture with precedents in Loewe,

Example 20b. Carl Loewe, "Der Pilgrim vor St. Just," Op. 99, no. 3,
measures 1–6

a latter-day descendant of the refrain in Loewe's "Die Katzenkönigen," op.
64, no. 3, to a text by Adalbert von Chamisso.

If G minor belongs to the haunted world of the shepherd on the heath, then
B♭ major is identified with the storks and does not appear until they do in
measure 18. An entire little tonal drama is played out in the process of getting
from B♭, the key of the storks' arrival, to—that same B♭, the key of final
resolution. The shepherd does not understand the full import of their arrival

and misses the point several times. As soon as he begins speaking for them, he goes back to his earlier G-minor tonality and then, in frank bewilderment ("What do the poultry want from me?"), throws the whole question open with a diminished seventh on G (measure 20) before approaching B♭ again. In the interlude between stanzas 4 and 5 (measures 22–23), Wolf alternates between further statements of the previous motive on the dominant sevenths of B♭ and G minor; just when a resolution to B♭ seems inevitable, the shepherd begins to sing another variation of the first stanza, starting on D and G. The rising sequences from before are extended through two consecutive stanzas of questions, Wolf brilliantly eliding the end of each one with an unharmonized octave figure in the piano, as if the storks were flapping their wings in assent. The questions trace a rise in pitch from D through E♭, E, and finally F, the dominant of B♭. Even so, when B♭ returns in measure 31 ("So sagt nur, ich käm' in zwei Tag oder drei"), it is not yet secured, and the shepherd has not realized the extent of his good news. Wolf yet again alternates between reminiscences of G minor and B♭ until measure 34. When the significance of the paired creatures suddenly strikes the shepherd ("Doch halt!"), he plunges downward a minor ninth, the deceptive motion dramatizing the shock of the moment. The halting prosody and avoidance of tonic closure for the shepherd's last question are delightful touches. The beleaguered new father of multiple progeny can hardly bring himself to put the question into words, his stammering a comic contrast with the volubility that precedes it. The delay between the stork's arrival on B♭ and their vociferous delight, again in B♭, when the singer finally realizes his double indemnity is such that an extended diatonic conclusion is required, the relaxation of tension in boisterous basic chords a feature familiar from "Abschied."

For all his reliance on Loewe's model, Wolf does not merely copy what came before. In particular, it is in the alliance between text interpretation and tonality that Wolf most extends Loewe's legacy, transforming what is "naive and natural" in Loewe into a display of late-Romantic ingenuity. The conceit by which the shepherd gropes about for the tonality that should have been obvious to him from the storks' first appearance makes of the joke a matter of mordant musical wit. Wolf also renews the often routine instrumental figuration on which his predecessor relies and incorporates the scalar passages, repeated chords, and the like within a more colorful chromatic milieu. The outbursts of simple laughter, the diatonic guffaws at the end of "Storchenbotschaft" and "Abschied," are all the more enjoyable by contrast with the subtleties that precede them. Even where Loewe's various tonal regions follow one another at a rapid pace, as in "Die Heinzelmännchen" and "Walpurgisnacht," the harmonic vacillations, substitutions, and extensions responsible for much of the comic effect of "Storchenbotschaft" outstrip even Loewe's boldest inventions.

MOTIVIC UNITY IN BALLADS OF
THE SUPERNATURAL

Horror ballads[64] were Loewe's mainstay and a principal source of his renown in the first half of the century. The necromantic imaginings of Romanticism often produced little more than exercises to make the flesh creep, a dated diabolism whose visual and verbal symbols for evil seem powerless or even comic today. Poets of the *unheimlich* (that which is uncanny, strange, beyond human apprehension)[65] often relied on sensationalist effects that teeter on the brink of the ridiculous; anyone who has felt an impulse to laugh during the Wolf's Glen Scene of Weber's *Der Freischütz* knows the phenomenon. However, the exceptions—Goya's demons and witches, for example—constitute an exploration of night zones of the unconscious and the cosmos that retain their full measure of horrific force. Loewe had a lifelong predilection for sound worlds of the supernatural, beginning with his first published ballads, the 1824 op. 1 settings of "Edward" and "Erlkönig" and continuing with such wonderfully evocative compositions as "Harald," op. 45, no. 1, to a text by Uhland, and "Odins Meeresritt" (Odins' sea ride), op. 118, to a text by Aloys Schreiber. According to Runze, Loewe in later life used to tell a tale of looking out the window as a child at an old ruined churchyard with its crumbling gravestones and ancient linden tree, of beseeching his mother to play the violin for him, of the unforgettable impression made by her melodies in the moonlight: the perfect formative impression (even if apocryphal) for the later composer of such secularized apocalypses as "Walpurgisnacht" and "Die nächtliche Heerschau" (Schubert refused to set the latter text).[66]

A less beneficent version of a mother-child scenario was among Loewe's earliest horror ballads, fashioned along lines that Wolf would later emulate in his own way. Willibald Alexis was the pseudonym for Georg Wilhelm Heinrich Häring (1798–1871), whose *Balladen* of 1836 include "Der späte Gast" (The late guest), "Friedericus Rex," and "Die Hexe" (The witch) or "Walpurgisnacht," all of which Loewe set to music. The latter, written "on a stormy first of May," or so Häring tells us, was Loewe's op. 2, no. 3, first published in 1824 as an example for an essay "Über Balladenpoesie" (On ballad poetry) in *Hermes* for that year and later included in Loewe's *Balladen* of 1835. Lilli Lehmann rightly considered the "Walpurgisnacht" difficult to sing because of its crescendo-accelerando to the final *Feroce* section, with its acknowledged borrowing from Ludwig Spohr's *Faust*, act 2.[67] Loewe increasingly shortens the pauses between the daughter's questions and the mother's responses until there is no rest at all, the breathless *stringendo* at the end culminating in a sustained high B♮. The text achieves much of its undoubted power from the lack of narration in this dialogue poem between a daughter and her witch-mother, who finally reveals the truth of her nocturnal whereabouts to the shrinking and frightened girl.

> Liebe Mutter, heut' Nacht heulte Regen und Wind.—
> "Ist heute der erste Mai, liebes Kind."—
> Liebe Mutter, es donnerte auf dem Brocken droben.—
> "Liebes Kind, es waren die Hexen oben."—
> Liebe Mutter, ich möcht' keine Hexen sehn.—
> "Liebes Kind, es ist wohl schon oft geschehn."—
>
> . . . .
>
> Liebe Mutter, dein Bett war leer in der Nacht.—
> "Deine Mutter hat oben auf dem Blocksberg gewacht."

("Dear Mother, the rain and wind howl tonight." "It is the first of May, dear child." "Dear Mother, it is thundering up above on the Brocken." "Dear child, there are witches up there." "Dear Mother, I don't want to see any witches." "Dear child, that has already happened quite often." [. . .] "Dear mother, your bed was empty at night." "Your mother held watch up above on the Blocksberg.")

Loewe unifies this relatively short, swift ballad by means of a single motivic figure in the piano, a figure transposed to different tonalities and registers but otherwise little altered—not the more thoroughgoing variation technique of Wagner or Wolf (Examples 21a and 21b). Spitta might have questioned whether this work, as well as Schubert's "Erlkönig," was a true ballad because Loewe repeats one *Geh-figur*, or motive indicative of motion, throughout the composition. The contrasting musical episodes typical of larger, longer ballads are not to be found here—the ballad is a monomaniacal crescendo leading to the revelation at the end, a revelation the daughter suspects and we can hear from the beginning of the wild ride in the accompaniment. Loewe does not label "Walpurgisnacht" a ballad in song form as he does with other ballads similarly unified, but that is what it is. Questions of categorization aside, it is an electrifying showpiece. Loewe relies on rapid motion through different keys and contrasting modes to generate tension and forward impetus rather than contrasting motivic material. The speakers' close relationship is underscored at first by the simple device of setting the daughter's agitated observations in minor and the mother's replies in brighter, "reassuring" parallel major (B minor/major, A minor/major, E minor/major), but as the tension mounts, the tonal relationship changes, first to contrasting relative modes (B minor/D major, A minor/C major) and finally to a chromatic sequential ascent through C minor/C♯-major, D minor/D♯-major harmonies rising to the conclusion in the opening tonality. The closer the daughter comes to the moment of revelation, the more rapidly Loewe changes tonal place and the quicker the harmonic rhythm—the better to raise the listener's blood pressure.[68]

Example 21a. Carl Loewe, "Walpurgisnacht," Op. 2, no. 3, measures 1–6

Example 21b. Carl Loewe, "Walpurgisnacht," Op. 2, no. 3, measures 11–13

Wolf composed a ballad in song form that is remarkably close to the "Walpurgisnacht" model: his setting of Goethe's "Der Rattenfänger" (The rat-catcher). As in Loewe's ballad, demonic powers—demonic in Wolf's reading of the poem—are given expression in music that is swift and forceful, limited in motivic variety, and tonally restless, traveling through various keys and unstable harmonic progressions before returning to the point of origin. Goethe's poem[69] does not invite the episodic structure of a true ballad—there is no narrator reporting bygone events, no plot of any kind, but rather the boasting of a legendary creature proud of his powers of superhuman compulsion, one of the troupe of poet-singers in folk tales who can compel mere mortals to do their bidding through the spell cast by music. "Der Rattenfänger" is a role poem that one reads against the backdrop of a familiar folk legend warning children against strangers lest evil befall them. In Goethe's poem, that tale is significantly abbreviated. The Pied Piper himself proclaims his mission as benevolent, the vermin he drives out of the towns through which he passes perhaps symbolic of the scurrilous elements in human nature that music expels by its superior might. Such is his power of compulsion over weaker mortals that he can overcome the worst truculence in children and any unwillingness in women; he is one of a kind with the poetic persona of "Der Musensohn," to whose beat everyone and everything keeps time. He is, he proclaims, "good-humored," a charmer of children and women, a singer of fairy tales and love songs. But in the words "Kinderfänger" ("child captor") and the adjectives "blöde," "spröde," "stutzig," "trutzig" (stupid, coy, obstinate, recalcitrant) by which the Piper contemptuously characterizes the women and children he seduces are strong hints of his true intent, his darker reputation as a kidnapper. No wonder the tale is truncated: he cannot go any further without revealing the threat openly. Readers who know the legend, as so many do, realize that the story actually ends beyond the ending of the poem, beyond the point where the Piper will not disclose what follows.

> Ich bin der wohlbekannte Sänger,
> Der vielgereiste Rattenfänger,
> Den diese altberühmte Stadt
> Gewiss besonders nötig hat.
> Und wären's Ratten noch so viele,
> Und wären Wiesel mit im Spiele:
> Von allen säub'r ich diesen Ort,
> Sie müßen miteinander fort.
>
> Dann ist der gutgelaunte Sänger
> Mitunter auch ein Kinderfänger,
> Der selbst die wildesten bezwingt,
> Wenn er die goldnen Märchen singt.
> Und wären Knaben noch so trutzig,
> Und wären Mädchen noch so stutzig,
> In meine Saiten greif' ich ein,
> Sie müßen alle hinterdrein.
>
> Dann ist der vielgewandte Sänger
> Gelegentlich ein Mädchenfänger;
> In keinem Städtchen langt er an,
> Wo er's nicht mancher angetan.

Und wären Mädchen noch so blöde,
Und wären Weiber noch so spröde:
Doch allen wird so liebebang
Bei Zaubersaiten und Gesang.

(I'm the famous bard, the much-traveled rat-catcher, which this old and famous town undoubtedly needs more than most. And if there were innumerable rats, with weasels thrown in as well, I'd cleanse the place of them all—they would all have to be off. Moreover the cheerful singer is also at times a friend to children, who can tame even the wildest of them when he sings his beautiful fairy tales. However stubborn the boys may be, however recalcitrant the girls, when I strike my strings, they must all follow me. Then the versatile singer sometimes beguiles maidens; there's hardly a town he's visited where he's not done for many. However stupid the girls may be, however prudish the women, they all become lovesick when he plays the fiddle and sings.)

The young Schubert missed the whiff of sulphur and brimstone altogether. Despite the midmeasure forzando accents at the end that bespeak bravado and power, his strophic setting of this poem, D. 255, composed 19 August 1815 during his "Goethe year," is far lighter stuff. *His* rat-catcher is a merry folk character whose diatonic music in G major might well charm children but has nothing of demonry in it at all; he is closer kin to Papageno than to Beelzebub, the song exemplary of the young Schubert's debt to Mozart (Example 22). But in Wolf's reading, the poetic persona's presentation of himself as a beneficent force is a lie, a promotional ploy to gain access to those he would overpower. The Pied Piper is unable to disguise his contempt for humanity; the menace breaks through the hypocritical surface, just as the demon musician with Paganini-like powers means it to do—he is, he reminds us, "well known." Wolf's piper shows his true diabolic colors in the whip-cracking strains of the lengthy piano introduction, interludes, and postlude, without words to mask his malice or hide the use of music as an agent of force. Perhaps most revealing of all, Wolf repeats the first stanza of the poem at the end, a procedure contrary to his usual practice and his principles of text setting by 1889. In so doing, he ends the body of the song with the words—"Sie müßen miteinander fort"—most charged with menace, followed by an instrumental postlude in which "all must leave," rather than allowing the Piper to conclude his self-advertisement with the merrier image of the wives and maidens made lovesick by his magic music. There is no denying that Wolf's compositional decision warps the poem, but one can argue that he takes his cue from Goethe, magnifying the self-revelation already contained in the poetry.

"Der Rattenfänger" is thus a poem about the diabolical powers of music— music as a force not to be denied. Wolf makes the demonic force of the rat-

Example 22. Franz Schubert, "Der Rattenfänger," D. 255, measures 1–9

catcher's strains evident in every aspect of his setting. Ballad texts are often strongly rhythmical, and here, the regular rhythms are a primary agent of compulsion. The listener is meant to be swept up in the accented rhythmic pulse of the repeated $\frac{6}{8}$ quarter-note–eighth-note patterns. Loewe was perhaps *too* fond of jog-trot $\frac{6}{8}$ rhythms, but Wolf only uses them when a dancelike gaiety is called for ("Nixe Binsefuss") or in the service of relentless motion, as in "Der Rattenfänger." The sense of compulsion is further heightened by the way in which one vocal phrase follows right on the heels of another. There is, for example, no indicated rest or break in the vocal part from measure 9, when the singer first enters, to measure 17; the performer must catch a breath as best he can and press onward. The repeated whip-cracking figures, as if the rat-catcher were lashing his listeners, are reserved for the virtuosic introduction, interludes, and postlude, as are the pounding diminished-seventh chords and the "Devil's Trill" figures that animate the cadences and the overt threat musically represented by the unfinished cadences, "endings" that stop just short of the final tonic A-minor chord—displays of dynamism distinct from the chordal strumming that accompanies the text. Wolf even galvanizes that cliché of guitar minstrelsy with an extra rhythmic charge, the sixteenth-note impulses on the weak beats, and invokes elemental, mythic folk magic by means of a succession of root-position triads atop parallel fifths in the bass.

The relentless forward drive of the rat-catcher's music infects the tonal design; not surprisingly, the harmonic progressions are *vielgereiste*, well-traveled and restless. Wolf's rat-catcher refuses to stay fixed in place for more than an instant, although he continually circles back to the A minor of the beginning. Because of the B's so heavily stressed in the topmost voice of the whip-cracking figures above the D-minor triads (measures 1–2, 29–30, 59–60, 90–91, 118–19), we hear the harmony as nontonic, as a goad to a progression that only culminates in root-position tonic at the end of the introduction. At the end of the first verse (measures 28–29), the singer completes the cadence to A in the vocal line ("sie müßen miteinander *fort*"), but the piano does not do likewise. Rather, the whip-cracking figures are brought back in the higher treble register; when the A-minor resolution does occur in measure 36, it is not in the same register as the resolution denied in measure 29. The second verse then begins on G major, not A minor, and travels rapidly to tonal references—touched on but never established securely—as distant from the tonic as E♭ major and G♯ major. The voice exchange in measure 3 prefigures other instances of the same device, as in the inner voices of measures 25–26 while the singer sustains the flatted fifth degree at the verb "müßen." The tension of forces compelling all to follow is evinced by the pull in opposite directions. The same is true of measure 23 at the words "[von] allen säub'r ich," especially as the ascending line is doubled in octaves. For the lovesick women and girls of the third stanza, Wolf writes a chromatic variant of the same scales in contrary motion that he had first introduced in measure 23. The same motion-filled magic creates both inner and outer turmoil, scourging vermin and inducing lovesickness by similar means. And the virtuosic postlude, among the most brilliant of Wolf's many "dying away" postludes, is a latter-day manifestation of the descending chromatic lines that are a cliché of musical *diablerie*.

TRADITION AND WOLF'S BALLAD MASTERPIECES

In traditional fashion, we save the best for last. Two of Wolf's Mörike ballads must be counted among his most brilliant homages to Loewe's art: "Die Geister am Mummelsee" and "Der Feuerreiter." Wolf was so proud of the latter that he arranged it for chorus and orchestra; when it was performed by the Gesellschaft der Musikfreunde on 2 December 1894, even Brahms applauded at some length and Hanslick accorded it a few grudging words of praise, although within the context of pointed gibes about Wagner, descriptive music, and Wolf's approach to song composition. At least, he was forced to sit up and take notice.[70]

The Mummelsee is a lake in the Black Forest long reputed to be haunted and therefore the locale for numerous ghost stories and ballads, tales that belong within the realm of German *Wasser-Mythos*, or water magic. The bonds for good or ill between Nature's magic forces and humankind and the associations of watery realms with supernatural female powers of eroticism and death are favorite topoi of German folk literature and nineteenth-century German art, poetry, and prose: the Lorelei, Undine, Melusine, Heine's siren Ilse, Klimt's water-sirens, and Böcklin's nymphs are but a few. Mörike's Nixie Reed-foot is a benevolent water-sprite, although powerful and capable of malice, but in most water-magic tales, water and death are closely allied. In these watery kingdoms, beauty conceals fatal force. Too, water is both a mirror that reflects back one's own magically altered countenance and a mask concealing—what? The name "Mummelsee" is etymologically related to the word "die Mumme," a disguise, a mask or masquerader; the name itself suggests that the surface of the lake is a mask beneath which hides something unknown and fearsome.

As with "Der Rattenfänger," Wolf had a precursor for his Mummelsee ballad, although not a setting of the same poem, on which he could improve: Loewe's "Der Mummelsee," op. 116, no. 3 is not one of the ballad-master's better compositions. Loewe's text comes from the "Zehn Romanzen vom Mummelsee" (Ten tales of the Mummelsee) in the *Badische Sagenbuch* of 1846 by August Schnezler (1809–53), where it is entitled "Die Lilien" (The lilies). Schnezler was not a particularly good poet; despite the accumulation of sensationalist effects near the end, this rather pallid work is more unintentionally comic than it is horrific. When night falls and the moon is shining, beautiful young lily-women appear on the banks and, woven together as if in a garland, dance to the music of the wind and reeds. Then storm winds blow, the pine forest rustles, clouds cover the moon, the waves swell, and a giant arm with its fist clenched rises from the lake, followed by a reed-crowned and bearded head. A thunderous voice orders the lily-maidens back to their abode, and the frightened maidens flee beneath the depths of the Mummelsee. Masculine tyranny and multiple submissive women from the realm of male fantasy and nineteenth-century reality masquerade as a "Nature-magic" ballad but without the crucial sense of something uncanny; there are no human observers on the scene to be affected by the strange spectacle they see. Reading the poem, one understands why Schnezler's ballads did not survive beyond their own day and why Heine was already making fun of the fad for ballads in *The Romantic School*.[71] Loewe did not find the matter sufficiently compelling for musical inspiration at his highest level. Despite the unflagging ingenuity that produces a different instrumental pattern for each textual exigency and each episode of Schnezler's tale, much of the musical material is conventional to a fault: routine scalar passages, broken-chordal triplet figures, tremolandos and unison texture for the thunderous voice of the lake tyrant, and menace expressed in clichés of linear chromaticism, none of it deployed in a particularly unusual or colorful way.

Wolf could and did improve on such humdrum goings-on. He began with incomparably better poetry (Loewe seems either not to have encountered Mörike's verse or not to have found it to his liking) from a poet capable of wringing a new *frisson* out of the ingredients of nature-magic balladry.

> Vom Berge was kommt dort um Mitternacht spät
> Mit Fackeln so prächtig herunter?
> Ob das wohl zum Tanze, zum Feste noch geht?
> Mir klingen die Lieder so munter.
>   O nein!
> So sage, was mag es wohl sein?
>
> Das, was du da siehest, ist Totengeleit,
> Und was du da hörest, sind Klagen.
> Dem König, dem Zauberer, gilt es zu Leid,
> Sie bringen ihn wieder getragen.
>   O weh!
> So sind es die Geister vom See!
>
> Sie schweben herunter ins Mummelseetal—
> Sie haben den See schon betreten—
> Sie rühren und netzen den Fuß nicht einmal—
> Sie schwirren in leisen Gebeten—
>   O schau,
> Am Sarge die glänzende Frau!

Jetzt öffnet der See das grünspiegelnde Tor:
Gib acht, nun tauchen sie nieder!
Es schwankt eine lebende Treppe hervor,
Und—drunten schon summen die Lieder.
　Hörst du?
Sie singen ihn unten zur Ruh'.

Die Wasser, wie lieblich sie brennen und glühn!
Sie spielen in grünendem Feuer;
Es geisten die Nebel am Ufer dahin
Zum Meere verzieht sich der Weiher—
　Nur still!
Ob dort sich nichts rühren will?

Es zuckt der Mitten—o Himmel! ach hilf!
Nun kommen sie wieder, sie kommen!
Es orgelt im Rohr und es klirret im Schilf;
Nur hurtig, die Flucht nur genommen!
　Davon
Sie wittern, sie haschen mich schon! [72]

(Who are those coming down there from the mountain in such splendor, with torches, at the late midnight hour? Are they going to a dance or a feast at this time of night? Their songs sound so cheerful! Oh, no! Then tell me, who can they be? That which you see is a funeral procession, and that which you hear is lamentation. They are mourning for their king, the enchanter, and they are bearing his pall again. Oh, woe, it is the spirits of the lake! They are floating down into the Mummelsee valley—they have already stepped onto the waters of the lake—they aren't even moving or wetting their feet. They are murmuring quiet prayers like a buzz. Oh, look at the shining woman by the coffin! Now the lake is opening its green-mirrored gate. Watch out, now they are submerging! A living staircase comes swaying forth, and the hum of their songs is already coming from down below. Do you hear? Down there they are singing him to rest. How beautifully the waters burn and glow! Greenish fire plays over them. The mists spook along the shore; the pond is silently condensing into a seal! Is anything going to move over there? There's a twitching motion in the middle. Oh, heaven, help! Now they are coming again! There is an organ roar in the reeds and a clanking in the sedges. Look lively, now is the time to run! Let's get away from here! They have scented me—they're grabbing for me already!)

Wolf knew the original context of this poem. His devoted friend Heinrich Werner listed the contents of the composer's library, since destroyed in World

War II, in his account of the Vienna Wagner Society; the modest collection included a copy of Mörike's first novel *Maler Nolten* (Nolten the artist; first published in 1832) in which many of the poems Wolf set to music are interpolated after the manner of Goethe's *Wilhelm Meister*. This lengthy and complex novel contains an inset play, "Der letzte König von Orplid: Ein Phantasmagorisches Zwischenspiel" (The last king of Orplid: A fantastical interlude) about the mythological island realm of Orplid that Mörike and his friends—chiefly Mörike—invented during their university days in Tübingen. Orplid is peopled with humans and gods; rustics (Shakespeare was one source of inspiration); a king named Ulmon who is bound by a curse to prolonged life and cannot die until the gods release him from life; a fairy princess named Thereile who loves the king; the grotesque Wispel; the fairy Silpelit; and a supporting cast of fairy children with names like Talpe, Windigal, Mawy, and Morry.[73] Two of the fairy children speak to one another at the beginning of the ninth scene, the surroundings described as follows:

> Night.   Moonlight.
> A wooded valley. The Mummelsee. In the background, coming down the mountain and toward the lake comes a funeral procession of misty figures. In the foreground, the king, looking fixedly at the procession. On the other side, crouched down low, not noticing the king, two fairy children, talking to one another.

Their "conversation" was published separately six years later in the first edition of Mörike's collected poems (1838) as "Die Geister am Mummelsee."

Although the ballad is a self-sufficient poem and Wolf sets it as such, events in the inset play continue beyond the end of the poem. When the frightened children run away, the cortege again ascends the mountain. As it vanishes, King Ulmon calls out desperately for the mourners to stop; they have sunk an empty coffin into the lake, he tells them, a coffin that should be his. In desolation, he wonders whether the "shining woman," his Queen Almissa, has been true to him in the long years of waiting. Gentle music tells him that the nocturnal spectacle is the prelude to his long-awaited death, that the goddess Weyla has heard his plea and prepares the way for him. In the fourteenth and final scene, the premonitory phantom events of scene 9 find their completion. Here, the fairy Silpelitt arises from the middle of the lake and holds up a mirror to the king, who sees his image as a boy and then as a crown prince. At the sight, he falls powerless from the rock and vanishes beneath the lake. The funeral scene of "Die Geister am Mummelsee" is itself a ghost, the spectral premonition of death to come. Freud, in his essay on "Das Unheimliche" (The uncanny), describes a sense of return as the principal source of the uncanny, that is, when repressed or hidden aspects of the personality come back to haunt the consciousness.[74] "Die Geister am Mummelsee" is thus part of Mörike's unique variation on both the *Doppelgänger* theme of German Romanticism—unexpected confrontations with one's own earlier self, a sudden surge of buried experience into conscious awareness—and water myths.

Unlike many of the classic ballad texts, events happen as they are narrated, the feint of immediacy to Wolf's liking. The dialogue form of "Die Geister am Mummelsee" is traditional, however; by contrasting the agitated imaginings of someone who does not understand what he sees and hears with the somber voice of knowledge, especially in the first two stanzas, Mörike could heighten the sense of Otherness that separates the children, who have an adult poet's gift for the most vivid description, from the ghostly beings on the lake. That sense of Otherness is established and underscored in every detail of the imagery and the language. For example, the inhuman provenance of the spirits' music is all the more evident when the excitable, questioning speaker at first mistakes the music of the funeral cortege for merry dance music. The eeriness of the ghostly obsequies is registered as well in Mörike's choice of the verbs "summen" and "schwirren" for their songs and prayers and in the verbal doubling for emphasis: "um Mitternacht spät" rather than merely "Mitternacht" or "spät"; "zum Tanze, zum Feste"; "rühren und netzten"; "brennen und glühn." Furthermore, Mörike has the second speaker explain the purpose of the procession in archaizing parallelisms that match the cortege in rhythmic solemnity: "Das, was du da siehest, ist Totengeleit, / Und was du da hörest, sind Klagen." By Mörike's day, there might have seemed few other variations possible on spectral apparitions and the language in which to evoke and embody them (Heine thought so), but Mörike finds them. The pond condensing into a sea, with multiple z and v-w consonants ("zum Meere verzieht sich der Weiher"); the ominous concatenation of dark vowels in the injunction to flee ("Nur hurtig, die Flucht nur genommen!"); the image of the living, swaying staircase descending into the lake; music as a death-incantation in the line "sie singen ihn unten zur Ruh'," with its progressive darkening of the vowels; the green-mirrored door of the lake and the greenish fires; the ghosts who glide without walking or wetting their feet; the unnamed "shining woman" whose privileged place by the coffin is not explained; the waters that "spook," "geisten" as a verb; the reference to bearing the pall "again"; and the impersonal "Es" construction (not always so impersonal as it seems), a traditional means in German poetry of conveying a sense of the uncanny, powerfully used in the line "Es orgelt im Rohr, und es klirret im Schilf"—all of this is both in accord with the ballad tradition and a replenishment of it.

For his setting, Wolf borrows a compendium of devices from Loewe and replenishes them as well. The $\frac{8}{4}$ meter is unusual, both an accommodation to the changeable iambic-anapestic tetrameters and trimeters of the poetry and an archaism that underscores, in the length of each bar, the solemnity of the spectacle, its otherworldly rarity. The open fifths sounding over a span of three octaves in the bass announce the work as *schauerhaft* before the singer enters with funereal chanting on the tonic pitch in a key Wolf associated with somber themes. Loewe was fond of "tolling bell" effects in his ballads, such as "Die Glocken zum Speier," and Plüddemann would later use similar tolling perfect fifths and octaves at the beginning of his "Vineta," to a text by Wilhelm Müller. In "Die Geister am Mummelsee," the green-mirrored door of the lake opens to admit its inhuman visitants with a sequential triadic progression that turns on a mediant relationship; as in "Der Rattenfänger," sequences of root-position triads are emblematic of the elemental-supernatural. Wolf, like Mörike, pushes the genre to its limits, evident in the "special effects" one hears in the first verse (measures 1–12): the accented fanfare figures in the right-hand part that act as rhythmic goads near the end of virtually every measure/line of verse, the brightness of dominant and V/V for the brilliant torches; the vaulting leap upward of an octave-plus-tritone in the vocal line over a diminished-seventh harmony for the horrified exclamation "O nein!" and the even more dramatic plunges from one vocal register to another in measures 11–12; the fourths and fifths in the initial vocal phrases to underscore the elemental power of the scene; the vocal lines that individually ascend in terror; the sepulchral use of neighbor harmonies at the midpoint and end of this first section (measures 7 and 12), the vocal phrase and its half-cadence aftermath recurring in measure 17 at the words "am Sarge die glänzende Frau." One lists it all and wonders how Wolf avoids overkill—and he does.

Wolf had already used the keys of F♯ major/minor and Chopinesque figuration in his early Heine song, "Mein Liebchen, wir sassen beisammen," as indices of a watery, paradisaical spirit world of love, music, death, and ghosts, and he does so again here in a more developed manner. One recalls as well the water figuration of Loewe's "Der Nöck," a diatonically tame foreshadowing of Wolf's stanza 5. In stanza 3 ("Sie schweben herunter in's Mummelseetal"), where the meter changes to $\frac{4}{4}$ and the key to F♯ major, the arpeggiated vocal lines are not the superficial vocalise acrobatics of Loewe's lily maidens but outgrowths of the initial stanza instead. The augmented extension of the rising-third motive in measure 18, when the lake opens to interlocking third-related harmonies; the variation of the same motives as a "living staircase"; and the harmonic trill of diminished and dominant sevenths in the lower register (measure 21), the analogue to the strange humming of the ghostly obsequies, are more inventive than Loewe's often stereotypical figuration. And where Wolf borrows such familiar clichés as the measured-trill figures in the inner voice as part of repeated chordal patterns (measure 31), diminished-seventh chords at the climax, and the unharmonized descending semitone figures as the narrators flee in terror, it is with an exploitation of range and a boldness that surpasses the earlier nineteenth-century model.

Wolf's most famous ballad and one of his best works is "Der Feurerreiter," composed in a single day on 10 October 1888. Wolf, justly proud of its brilliance, performed it on those occasions when he hoped to win new converts to his cause. The core of inexplicability and the violence of the ballad came as a surprise to those unfamiliar with Mörike, except as a Biedermeier artificer of classical idylls. Joseph Schalk, whose article "Neue Lieder, neues Leben" (New songs, new life) for the *Münchener Allgemeine Zeitung* of 22 January 1890 was the first lengthy and favorable public notice of Wolf's songs, exclaimed "What audacity!" and extolled the boldness both poetic and musical. Three of the Mörike songs in particular were, Schalk felt, most indicative of the future of the lied: "Erstes Liebeslied eines Mädchens," "Das Lied vom Winde" (The song of the wind), and "Der Feuerreiter."[75]

Even the title of the ballad evades translation by suggesting several meanings at once: "The Fiery Horseman," "The Rider to Fires," "The Fire-rider." Like "Die Geister am Mummelsee," the poem begins with the narrator uneasily pointing out that something unusual is impending, and addressing his observation to—an unseen, unnamed, unknown companion, or to us, the readers of the poem? Once again, events are narrated as they occur, with the exception of the epilogue in the final stanza. The red-hatted creature who paces up and down behind the window, then bursts forth in furious action, has been interpreted in various ways, including the early identification of this figure with the great poet Friedrich Hölderlin, lapsed into insanity by the time Mörike went to Tübingen to study theology at the university. According to a letter by Mörike's childhood friend Rudolf Lohbauer to his bride, it was upon seeing the mad Friedrich Hölderlin wearing a red cap and roaming restlessly up and down his attic room in Tübingen that the image of the "Fire-rider" first occurred to Mörike, although recent commentators reject the identification.[76] Mörike's friend Wilhelm Waiblinger had become obsessed with the insane Hölderlin, befriended him, and wrote a sensitive, if occasionally inaccurate, study of the poet before his own early death. Through Waiblinger, Mörike met Hölderlin and even came to own some of Hölderlin's manuscripts, but his attitude to the older poet (whom most at the time ignored) was equivocal at best: he felt that Hölderlin's works early showed signs of incipient insanity. Few could understand psychological extremity as well as Mörike or were more interested in psychopathology, but the composition of poetry, he knew, required all one's faculties of rational, disciplined endeavor.

The central figure of "Der Feuerreiter" was probably borrowed from folk sources and adapted to Mörike's own purposes. A fire-fighter who calls on God's aid to quell flames is the protagonist of "Der Feuerbesprecher" (The fire-conjurer) from *Des Knaben Wunderhorn*, but there, the stilling of the fire through invocation of the Virgin is beneficial, not demonic.[77] Mörike later became a friend of the poet Justinus Kerner, who was, like Mörike, interested in the spirit world and who published a journal entitled *Magikon* on spiritualist phenomena of all kinds. In the *Magikon* for 1853, he wrote of "fire-seers," those capable of naming the location of fires they could not physically see.

Kerner's article on the subject appeared long after Mörike wrote "Der Feuerreiter," but it seems evident from the ballad that Mörike earlier knew of the same folk phenomenon.[78]

The poem, written in the summer of 1824, was first published as the "Romanze von dem wahnsinnigen Feuerreiter" (Romance of the mad fire-rider) in the 1832 edition of *Maler Nolten*, complete with a tame musical setting by Mörike's friend Ludwig Hetsch.[79] The second version of 1841, the one Wolf set, has an additional verse (stanza 3, given here) and is more explicit in its religious symbolism and in its references to blasphemy and confrontations with hell.

> Sehet ihr am Fensterlein
> Dort die rote Mütze wieder?
> Nicht geheuer muß es sein,
> Denn er geht schon auf und nieder.
> Und auf einmal welch Gewühle
> Bei der Brücke, nach dem Feld!
> Horch! das Feuerglöcklein gellt:
> > Hinter'm Berg,
> > Hinter'm Berg
> Brennt es in der Mühle!
>
> Schaut! da sprengt er wütend schier
> Durch das Tor, der Feuerreiter,
> Auf dem rippendürren Tier,
> Als auf einer Feuerleiter!
> Querfeldein! Durch Qualm und Schwüle
> Rennt er schon und ist am Ort!
> Drüben schallt es fort und fort:
> > Hinter'm Berg,
> > Hinter'm Berg
> Brennt es in der Mühle!
>
> Der so oft den roten Hahn
> Meilenweit von fern gerochen,
> Mit des heil'gen Kreuzes Span
> Freventlich die Glut besprochen—
> Weh! dir grinst vom Dachgestühle
> Dort der Feind im Höllenschein.
> Gnade Gott der Seele dein!
> > Hinter'm Berg,
> > Hinter'm Berg
> Rast er in der Mühle!

Keine Stunde hielt es an,
Bis die Mühle borst in Trümmer;
Doch den kecken Reitersmann
Sah man von der Stunde nimmer.
Volk und Wagen im Gewühle
Kehren heim von all dem Graus;
Auch das Glöcklein klinget aus:
   Hinter'm Berg,
   Hinter'm Berg
Brennt's!—

Nach der Zeit ein Müller fand
Ein Gerippe samt der Mützen
Aufrecht an der Kellerwand
Auf der beinern Mähre sitzen:
Feuerreiter, wie so kühle
Reitest du in deinem Grab!
Husch! da fällt's in Asche ab.
   Ruhe wohl,
   Ruhe wohl
Drunten in der Mühle![80]

(Do you see the red hat once more, there at the little window? It must be something out of the ordinary, because he's already walking up and down the room. And all at once what a crowd near the bridge, past the field! Listen! The fire bell is ringing shrilly: behind the hill, behind the hill, the mill is burning! Look, there he is, the fiery horseman, practically in a fury, dashing through the town gate, riding his skeleton-bony horse as if he were riding a fireman's ladder! Right across country, through the smoke and heat, he is already racing, and he's there! Over there, it keeps on ringing: behind the hill, behind the hill, the mill is burning! You who have so often smelled the red rooster from miles away, and with a splinter of the Holy Cross have sacrilegiously conjured away the flames, alas! the enemy in the glare of hell is grinning at you from the roof beams. May God have mercy on your soul! Behind the hill, behind the hill, he rages in the mill! It wasn't even an hour before the mill burst into ruins, but the bold horseman was never seen again from then on. People and wagons in a crowd return home from all that horror; even the bell dies away: behind the hill, behind the hill . . . fire! After some time, a miller found a skeleton, along with the hat, sitting upright against the cellar wall on the bony mare. Fiery horseman, how coolly you ride in your grave! Suddenly it all crumbles into ashes. Rest in peace, rest in peace, down there in the mill!)

The ballad is famously enigmatic. Winfried Freund's reading of the poem as a compensatory expression of the poet's abhorrence of contemporary politics[81] has much that is convincing about it, although she addresses only one of several levels of meaning in the poem. The antipolitical subtext seems especially convincing because Mörike's disinclination to political engagement and his mistrust of revolution, rebellion, and anarchy as instruments of history are well known and were established early in his life. His aversion to the brutality of history on the march was confirmed and deepened seven years after the composition of this ballad when his composer-brother Carl was imprisoned for his political activities in 1831, and he would later write a lengthy poem, "Nachtgesichte" (Night faces), in which history, led by the nocturnal specter of Napoleon, is a nightmare from which the poetic persona awakens in horror. According to the Mörike scholar Harry Maync, "Feuerreiter" was the name of a radical student society, fifteen men strong, formed by Mörike's fellow Tübingen theology student Wilhelm Hauff, probably in 1822. Hauff and his band of political activists even had their own song, the "Feuerreuter-Lied." Mörike could not have failed to notice the radical politicizing of student life, but the *Burschenschaften* were not to his taste, and he was no revolutionary. Not for him the red hats of the Jacobin-influenced political radicals—he praised King Wilhelm I's constitution of 1819 with the lines "Die alten Rechte gab er treu uns wieder, / Wie sie die Väter hatten, deutsch und bieder" (He faithfully gave us back once again the old laws our fathers had—staunch, German laws). No wonder he depicts the fire-rider as a being entirely alienated from humanity, as a Don Quixote–like creature on a skeletal Rosinante. Any such isolated stand against the power of the state is, in conservative opinion, as self-destructive and futile as a single-handed assault against fire or water or any other force of Nature, fire symbolic in this instance of the overwhelming reaction by the state to crush radical opposition.

The added third strophe, according to Freund, has to do with the addition of yet another element of student political radicalism in the years between 1824 and 1841: the "Nur ein Deutscher und ein Christ" (Only a German and a Christian) mentality that linked nationalism and Christianity. Mörike, the somewhat reluctant Protestant pastor, was no orthodox religious, but the complementarity of sin and sanctity is a crucial component of his poetic oeuvre, and he would have found the pairing of xenophobic nationalism and religion in the student *Burschenschaften* little short of blasphemous. Only in the third stanza does the poetic persona speak directly to the fire-rider, in an ambivalent mixture of accusation and horrified invocations of God's mercy. At the beginning of the ballad, the speaker pulls the reader into the psychology of mass panic, the crowd run amok, by asking, "Do you see . . . ?" and then recounts events as they happen, but in the later added stanza, he turns from narration to confrontation culminating in terrified pity for a creature damned before his very eyes.

In his ballad, Mörike can and does, as he could not in real life, rid the countryside of the "bold rider," who is never seen alive again after disappearing into a wall of flame at the mill. (The choice of the mill seems multiply determined: not only are mills and mill songs commonplaces of folk poetry, but mills are where the elements are harnessed to grind the flour that sustains mundane existence, a status quo in which anarchic extremity has no place.) Order is restored, and the country folk go home to their apolitical daily lives and domestic tranquility. The mill, the site of the conflict between absolute might and radical opposition, bursts into ruin and is no longer even named in the refrain of stanza 4. When the remains of horse and rider are found standing upright in the cellar wall (the *Opfertod* of blasphemers does not end in conventional burial), the red hat is still visible for a moment atop the skeletal rider before all crumbles to ashes. Nothing comes of the conflagration except the ruin of the mill and the fire-rider's death. At the close, in marked ambivalence, the poet twice invokes rest and peace ("Ruhe wohl, / Ruhe wohl / Drunten in der Mühle!") for the fire-rider he has blasted for sacrilege not two strophes earlier, a final and uneasy way to distance himself from the conflagration. A poem that began in an uproar, in the most frenzied activity, ends with the nervous, decidedly *un*peaceful invocation of peace, its underlying message fearful: "Remain ashes and do not rise again to trouble our peace." No wonder that Wolf sets that uneasy *requiescat in pace* as a rhythmically augmented variant of the refrain "Hinter'm Berg, hinter'm Berg brennt es in der Mühle!" and no wonder that he avoids tonic closure in the vocal line. The dread that fire may yet again break forth and burn out of control sounds covertly in the final measures.

The mad ride starts at the beginning, even before the crowd gathers and the red-capped creature bursts his bounds. Wolf tells us that something ominous and obsessive, not to be stopped, is already underway in measure 1 and then has the pianist charge on "ohne Rast und Ruh'" until the "long pause" in measure 104, the pause symbolic of the passage of time between the rider's grisly death and the ashen aftermath in the final stanza. In measures 1–14, Wolf presents two motives, one contained within the other. The first is a series of rising minor thirds, the G on the first beat of measure 1, B♭ [later A♯] on measure 3, D♭ at the beginning of measure 5, and E♮ in mid–measure 7, the progression then outlined even more explicitly in the bass and in the vocal line of measures 10–12. The initial section of "Der Feuerreiter" is thus essentially a dominant arpeggiation as a diminished-seventh chord whose associations with the musical-demonic are most famously developed in Weber's *Der Freischütz*. The same motive recurs outlined and reharmonized in measures 59–60 when the horrified narrator cries "Gnade Gott der Seele dein!" and *pppp* and prolonged throughout three bars (measures 118–20) of cadential approach to the final refrain, when the skeletons of horse and rider disintegrate. Nested within the outlined rising thirds is a rising chromatic line (C–C♯–D–E♭–E–F–

G♭–G), inversely related to the descending linear chromaticism of measure 1, beat 1, and repeated innumerable times thereafter. Certain of the chromatic fragments are emphasized in the vocal part; the C–C♯–D of the "rothe Mütze" inverts the descending motion of the accompanying D♭–C–B♭–A figure in the accompaniment (the diverging orthography of ascending and descending chromatic motion seems the graphic symbol of motion "auf und nieder"), while the leap of a minor ninth from E♭ to E♮ in measure 7 is indeed "nicht geheuer." Every component of the initial motive contributes to the sense of thrumming excitement, what Sams aptly calls a "gallimaufry": the chromatic descent from G to E; the repetitions of the figure preceded by an anacrusis pitch to accent the topmost note; the neighbor-note emphases on each pitch in the transition from one level to another; and even the refinements of prosody. The exactitude of the rest before the word "dort" in the first vocal phrase, "Sehet ihr am Fensterlein dort," and the placement of that word on the fourth and weakest beat of the measure would probably have offended Plüddemann in its simulated "immediacy"—it is as if the narrator-singer points upward to the window and, panic-stricken and breathless, cannot wait for the next measure but instead charges what is usually a weak beat with a verbal emphasis all the stronger because the single syllable begins and ends with plosive consonants, *d* and *t*.

The setting of the first stanza (measures 1–26) is both a sustained crescendo from the whispered pianissimo of the first bars to "wild" *fff* for the initial appearance of the refrain "Hinter'm Berg, hinter'm Berg brennt es in der Mühle!" and an initial development of the minor-third and chromatic-scale motives. The "Gewühle" in measures 15–22, with its newly added dotted rhythmic chords in the bass, is constructed from the same figures as before, the linear chromatic fragments and the horizontal and vertical forms of a different diminished-seventh G♯–B–D–F—we are led to expect resolution to tonic B minor in measure 15 and do in fact hear B and D in the outer voices, but within the context of deceptive motion to a diminished seventh. If one looks at the bass line, for example, B–C[–B–]E♭–E–G–F♯, the development of the earlier structural pitches is clear, especially as the leap upward of a minor ninth from E♭ to E♮ recalls the dramatic ascent in the vocal line of measure 7 at the words "nicht geheuer muss es [sein]." The scalewise outlined minor third figures in the right-hand part and the sequential repetitions of a rising and falling chromatic motive at the distance of a minor third (measures 16, 18) are by now familiar continuations into a higher register. Not only has the treble line risen relentlessly but the gulf between the right- and left-hand parts has widened. The crescendo culminates in the "wild" refrain, first stated in measures 23–26, with another of Wolf's evocations of the untamed elemental and supernatural by means of stark parallel fifths in the bass, the E-minor and B-minor triadic harmonies a capsule summary of the motion from the implied-incomplete E-minor harmony of the beginning to the tonic—a tonic that is not fully stated in the bass until measure 63. Not until the blasphemous fire-rider reaches the mill and rages about there does tonic arrive as well. The previous statements of the refrain in measures 23–26 and 43–46 do not state tonic so strongly; rather, the first two instances of the refrain end on the dominant and are then followed by deflection elsewhere. For example, in measure 27, as in measure 15, the B and D pitches of the tonic chord are retained, but the F♯ slips down chromatically to F♮, and the D in the bass then becomes the root of D minor in measure 31 and on to D major in measure 47. The resemblances between Wolf's refrain, a passage for the piano from Loewe's "Agnete," op. 134, and Loge's magic fire music from the end of *Die Walküre*. even to the structural pitches E and B, seem irresistible (Examples 23a and 23b). Mörike's ballad and the end of Wagner's opera are both fire-magic phenomena, and both musicians express the elemental-magical nature of flame in terms of nested minor-third figures (the bass line beneath Wotan's words "Loge hör'! lausche hieher! Wie zuerst ich dich fand, als feurige Gluth," etc.), similar trills and tremolandos, chromatic motivic figures, and the prominent voicing in perfect fifths in the bass.

The pause in measure 104 is of special significance because it marks the boundary between temporal worlds in the narrative. Until this point, we are led to assume a narrator simultaneously experiencing and reporting events that happen in the present, such that the distinction between "erzählte Zeit" (story time, or the time of the events recounted in the narrative) and "Erzählzeit" (narrative time, or the way in which the narrator presents the passage of story time) is narrowed. Mörike underscores the pretense by having the narrator point out, in the next-to-last stanza, that it took scarcely an hour for the mill to burn, after which he disperses the crowd in a single phrase. The cessation of sound in Wolf's setting at the end of that stanza, the tumult and "Graus" fading to an unharmonized dominant of B minor and then to silence, compresses into the brief span of a prolonged quarter-note all the unknown time that elapses between the fiery collapse of the mill and the miller's gruesome discovery. In the silence, we wait for the expected resolution, and the tension of the wait is such that we understand the "long pause" at that point in a cadential formula to be an apt symbol for the poet's phrase "Nach der Zeit" at the beginning of the final stanza. Any prolonged delay between dominant and tonic at what is clearly the end of a section and nearly the end of the ballad— the death of the fire-rider, the final instrumental measures of the refrain—is experienced as longer than it actually is.

The last two stanzas seem to register a shift from simultaneous narration— that is, the feint of on-the-spot reporting—to subsequent narration after the fact, the shift occurring where the narrator observes that the bold rider was never seen again from that hour on. The subsequent narrative, however, is given a psychological twist of just the sort that would appeal to Wolf: the miller, not the narrator of this first-person narration, finds the skeletal remains

Example 23a. Carl Loewe, Part 4 of "Agnete," Op. 134, measures 9–14

in the last stanza, and thereafter the narrator speaks as if he were an observer on the scene, as if the bones crumble to ashes then and there in front of his eyes ("da fällt's in Asche ab"). The result is a sophisticated intermingling of voices and presences, and yet the story is all of a piece, the narrator better able to convey his horror and revulsion at the fire-rider's fate by seeming to thrust his audience right into the conflagration as it happens; he does not pretend objectivity, a distanced stance from the tale he narrates. The musical story too is all of a piece; the final stanza is a variation of the same materials from before, the narrative thread/musical logic concluding with the revelation that the fire bells ultimately sound forth as funeral knells. As in Loewe's ballads, it is the piano that is responsible for the narrative mood, for the depictive

Example 23b. Richard Wagner, Loge's magic fire music at the end of
Die Walküre

(Hier bricht die lichte Flackerlohe aus.)
(Here flickering flames break forth.)

figures and their development that both underscore the plot and determine the affective reaction of the listener. In both composer's works, the instrumental part is crucial beyond the subordinate status implied in the word "accompaniment," yet neither composer wrote music of any significance for solo piano.

THE LOEWE revival of the 1880s had indeed succeeded in bringing Loewe out of the shadows, and Wolf was not alone in his enthusiasm for Loewe's ballads and his insistence that all male singers should know them and perform them with the proper panache. Beyond praise in words, Wolf demonstrated in his own music that Loewe's legacy was a generative force for composers who came after, especially in Wolf's settings of the Mörike ballads passed over by his predecessors and contemporaries.[82] Plüddemann would probably have disapproved of Wolf's ballads as impure, too dissonant, too contaminated with songlike lyricism, and yet it was Wolf and not the purists who paid tradition the greatest honor by enriching Loewe's heritage with all the resources of the late-Romantic tonal language. His homage to Loewe in the Mörike and Goethe ballads is no longer "naive and natural"—how could they be, these

products of revival several generations later?—but modernization is not repu-
diation, far from it. In this sphere, Wolf could demonstrate that he had learned
well the lessons of tradition, modernity, and reverence for German art in *Die
Meistersinger von Nürnberg*. If the resurgence of balladry did not survive
beyond World War I, there was still this last brilliant continuation of the tradition, these final flares lit by Wolf and those contemporaries who outlived
him—Richard Strauss, Hans Pfitzner, and others.

CHAPTER 4

A Spanish Tale: Wolf and the Lied
after 1850

MEASURING one's works against the obdurate backdrop of Wagner, Schubert, and Schumann meant looking back often and warily. Wolf's dialogue with the past was differently hostile from the dialogue with his contemporaries—both those composers whose works were part of the musical establishment in his youth and his peers, closer to him in age. We know of Wolf's inescapable anxieties with respect to his great predecessors, but what of the composers nearer his own time?

He had very little to say about their songs—with the exception of those of Brahms, his bête noir in Vienna—that has been recorded. Public lieder recitals were only beginning to come into vogue during his lifetime, and therefore Wolf expended virtually all his venomous wit, musical insight, and occasional approbation in the *Wiener Salonblatt* on opera, chamber music, and orchestral compositions. Of the composers who appear later in this chapter, he dismissed the great pianist Anton Rubinstein (1829–94) in one of his reviews as a composer prone to promising beginnings that come to nothing, and damned his opera *Nero* as one of "the sorriest phenomena since the creation of the world . . . this music could kill the Wandering Jew from sheer boredom." On the one occasion that he speaks of Adolf Jensen (1837–76), it is to say only that he left a concert before Jensen's unnamed orchestral work was performed.[1] He respected Peter Cornelius (1824–74) as both a poet and a composer, but only to a point, and he criticized Cornelius's "foolish" decision to compose a choral setting of Heine's "tasteless, trivial, and anodyne" poem "Der Tod, das ist die kühle Nacht" (Death is the cool night) as "a mistake."[2] By 1885, Wolf was almost cured of his youthful attraction to Heine's verse. Elsewhere in his reviews, the occasional novelties on Viennese concert programs bring out his considerable talent for vitriolic phrases—"petit bourgeois music," for example.

Two reviews from early 1887 about the new epidemic (Wolf's term) of lieder recitals are the only instances in which he inveighs in print and at length against the limited tastes of singers and the flood tide of trivial songs on the market.[3] He dubs one singer's lieder recital "a very mixed bag," and certainly the items he lists did not survive their own day. Evidently, he had to endure an entire program of lieder by the likes of Ignaz Brüll, Eduard Schütt, Carl Goldmark, Albert Amadei, Johannes Hager, Karl Schön, Rudolf Weinwurm, Hans von Zois, Richard Heuberger, and Adalbert von Goldschmidt, a program running the gamut from Brahms-imitators to songs in operetta style and from well-known, well-respected composers to rank amateurs.[4] Goldschmidt was a friend, and for that reason, Wolf lets him off lightly, characterizing his "Sommertag" (Summer's day) as "charming and fragrant." Looking at the undated autograph manuscript of Goldschmidt's setting of Heine's "Lehre," or "Der Brief, den du geschrieben" (The lesson, or The letter that you wrote) in the Austrian National Library,[5] one gives Wolf points for kindness or diplomacy and looks elsewhere in the review for critical acumen. His reasons for condemning the individual songs on the program reveal by negative deduction aspects of his own song aesthetic: he criticizes Carl Goldmark's "Die Quelle" (The fountains) for its resemblance to Schubert's "Gretchen am Spinnrade" (Gretchen at the spinning wheel), D. 118, another for being contrary to the sense of the poem, another for a melody like a street tune, one for its dullness, another for being one of "those perfumed things flirting coquettishly with the naive simplicity of folk music, and in a Brahmsian mask at that!"[6] Even the few songs he liked—somewhat—were unassuming miniatures, charming rather than profound, as when he condescendingly writes that Rubinstein's "Es blinkt der Tau" (The dew sparkles) has won "an enduring little spot" in the public's heart. The public is thereby damned with faint praise. Once freed from the bonds of music criticism, why bother commenting on such lesser lights?

And why should we bother with them? Large numbers of late-nineteenth-century songs are now entombed in libraries and seldom seen, much less performed, except by those scholars fond of the formulaic pronouncement "The works of Monsieur or Madame X are more significant than has yet been recognized." However, exhuming and examining the repertoire from below the Promethean level gives us valuable information about the heyday of Schumann's influence on lieder composition and about the poetry most in vogue for song composition in the latter half of the century. Even the effusions of such negligible composers as those whom Wolf tongue-lashes in his review of Rosa Papier's lieder recital demonstrate, if nothing else, what publishers considered to be commercially viable music. It may have been scant consolation for the unbanished ghosts of Schubert and Wagner that haunt his music, but Wolf could look about the musical landscape and know that his works were superior to most of what was trumpeted as praiseworthy. We know that he paid attention: his fury at the veneration accorded Brahms erupts periodically throughout his reviews for the *Salonblatt* and thereafter.

The lied repertoire of the last half of the century was composed against the backdrop of a sporadic debate about the future of song composition and doubts about the possibility for innovation in the genre. Hans von Bülow, for example, asked whether the lied "as a genre has reached its end point at the present time, and no new enrichments are possible," although he did so in preparation for his lavish praise of the Liszt epigone Eduard Lassen (1830--1904),[7] and Peter Cornelius called for a "healthier" choice of verse and a new music appropriate to it.[8] Not that lieder were on the decline in sheer num-bers—the lied was a mass commodity, although much of what was published was ephemera that has since disappeared. One provocation for Cornelius's call for renewal was the flood of new songs on the market, songs character-ized, in his opinion, by long-exhausted forms and formulaic patterns. The same *Three Songs* are advertised in the newspapers under different compos-ers' names, he points out; for his part, he declares he will not publish any lieder that cannot stand alongside those of Schubert, Schumann, and Franz.[9] The mingled anxiety and bravado are all the more moving in light of history's consignment of his songs to the same twilight zone as those of Robert Franz—the names known by cognoscenti, the songs occasionally performed, but never ranked with even the lesser lieder of Schubert and Schumann.

Not wanting to excavate songs at random, I have chosen to examine a chap-ter in both the German-speaking world's continuing fascination with Spain and the lied's reliance on folk poetry, thereby illuminating one aspect of Wolf's conservative literary tastes. He could very well have extended his as-sertion that certain poems had to await the development of a post-Wagnerian musical language for their fullest realization to include most of his own songs, since so many are settings of the poetic repertoire from Schubert's and Schu-mann's lifetimes. One of the most popular poetic sources for song composi-tion in the second half of the century was the *Spanisches Liederbuch* of 1852, translations of Spanish poetry by the poets Emanuel Geibel and Paul Heyse.[10] With his *Mörike-Lieder*, Wolf contributed to the critical reevaluation of Mörike's poetry at the century's end,[11] but he did not perform the same feat for Geibel and Heyse. The two men were prolific poets as well as translators, and both their original poems and their translations were set to music many times in the last half of the nineteenth century, almost on a par with the im-mense popularity of such works as Nikolaus Lenau's *Schilflieder* from earlier in the century. Although poems such as "Auf dem Wasser" (On the water), "Volkers Nachtgesang" (Volker's night song), "Wenn sich zwei Herzen scheiden" (When two lovers part), "Für Musik" (For music), "Ich sah den Wald sich färben" (I saw the forest blush), and "Gondoliera" (Gondola song) were favorites of lieder composers from the time of Fanny and Felix Men-delssohn, Robert Schumann, and Robert Franz on, Wolf spurned the original poetry by both men; when the publisher Schott sent Wolf a poem by Heyse, Wolf, who disliked working on commission, refused to set it.[12] But Geibel's and Heyse's accomplished translations both of folk poetry, purged of any folklike roughness of poetic technique and transformed into sophisticated German lyric verse, and of more learned Spanish verse were another matter—this he indeed found "komponabel."

Comparing different settings of the same poetic texts has an enduring fasci-nation. The fact that different composers set the same poetry in radically un-like rhythms, formal structures, melodic contours, and harmonic idioms makes evident the multiplicity of possible musical readings and a composer's freedom to impose his own imperatives on a literary work. But in the *Spanisches Liederbuch*, Wolf once again succeeded in locating a relatively uncolonized group of poems, the operative word being "relatively." Looking at Ernst Challier's *Grosser Lieder-Katalog*, one finds that certain poems from the *Spanisches Liederbuch* had been set by a number of minor composers before Wolf appropriated the anthology, but seldom by anyone we know nowadays or anyone that Wolf would have considered an impediment. Given his virulent "anti-Brahmimentum," he likely paid little heed to Brahms's early lied, "In dem Schatten meiner Locken" (In the shadow of my tresses)—in this instance, posterity has granted him the privilege of ousting his most hated rival among his contemporaries. And what, I wonder, did he think of Schumann's duet settings for his *Spanisches Liederspiel*? Despite the musical beauty of works such as "In der Nacht" (In the night), two-voice settings of a poetic persona who speaks in the singular are an obvious transgression of the kind of literary fidelity Wolf imposed at one level of his songs.

"IN DEM SCHATTEN MEINER LOCKEN"
(In the shadow of my tresses)
—Challier, 789

Johannes Brahms, op. 6, no. 1; Josef Giehrl, op. 2, no. 10; Friedrich Gustave Jansen (1831–1910), op. 34, no. 4; Adolf Jensen, op. 1, no. 4; Arno Kleffel (1840–1913), op. 17, no. 4; J. Schulze, op. 1, no. 5[13]

"DEREINST, DEREINST, GEDANKE MEIN"
(One day, one day, my thoughts)
—Challier, 161

Caspar Joseph Brambach (1833–1902), op. 15, no. 6; Leopold Damrosch (1832–85), op. 11, no. 4; Ferdinand Hiller (1811–85), op. 100, vol. 2, no. 3; Adolf Jensen, op. 4, no. 7; Adolf Bernhard Marx (d. 1866), op. 22, no. 12; A. Naubert, op. 4, no. 2; H. von Sahr, op. 5, no. 6; Hermann Wichmann (1824–1905), op. 31, no. 4; duet with the title "Liebesgram" (Love's sorrow) in Schumann's *Spanisches Liederspiel*, op. 74, no. 3

"KLINGE, KLINGE, MEIN PANDERO"
(Ring out, ring out, my timbrel)
—Challier, 474

Joseph Dessauer, op. 65, no. 1; Ferdinand Hiller, op. 100, vol. 2, no. 8; Aline Hundt, op. 10, no. 1; Adolf Jensen, op. 21, no. 1; Franz Paul Lachner (1803–90), op. 111, no. 9; Adolf Bernhard Marx, op. 22, no. 6; Heinrich Molbe, a pseudonym for Heinrich Freiherr von Bach (1835–

1915), op. 3, no. 5; A. Naubert, op. 4, no. 3; Anton Rubinstein, op. 76, no. 6; H. von Sahr, op. 5, no. 1; Hans Michael Schletterer (1824–93), op. 10, no. 6; Friedrich Hieronymus Truhn (1811–86), op. 61, vol. 2, no. 4; Hermann Wichmann, op. 29, no. 5

"BEDECKT MICH MIT BLUMEN"
(Cover me with flowers)
—Challier, 102

Leopold Damrosch, op. 11, no. 7; Ferdinand Hiller, op. 195, no. 2; Aline Hundt, op. 3, no. 3; Adolph Bernhard Marx, op. 22, no. 2; Heinrich Molbe, op. 3, no. 2; A. Naubert, op. 4, no. 8; Anton Rubinstein, op. 76, no. 5; S. Warteresiewicz, op. 2, no. 3; Robert Schumann, duet op. 138, no. 4

"ALLE GINGEN, HERZ, ZUR RUH'"
(All have gone to rest, O heart)
—Challier, 36

Caspar Joseph Brambach, op. 15, no. 3; Aline Hundt, op. 10, no. 4; Arno Kleffel, op. 17, no. 5; Adolph Bernhard Marx, op. 22, no. 1; A. Naubert, op. 4, no. 7; H. von Sahr, op. 5, no. 5; Bernhard Schädel, op. 29, vol. 4, no. 3; duet with the title "In der Nacht" in Robert Schumann, *Spanisches Liederspiel*, op. 74, no. 4

"WENN DU ZU DEN BLUMEN GEHST"
(When you go to the flowers)
—Challier, 945

Albert Hermann Dietrich, op. 7, no. 5; Adolf Jensen, op. 21, no. 5; Arno Kleffel, op. 14, no. 6; Wilhelm Karl Gottfried Taubert (1811–91), op. 149, no. 1

"UND SCHLÄFST DU, MEIN MÄDCHEN"
(And if you are sleeping, my dear)
—Challier, 854

J. Böie, op. 11, no. 5; Ferdinand Hiller, op. 100, vol. 2, no. 4; Adolf Jensen, op. 21, no. 3; Jacob Axel Josephson (1818–80), op. 6, no. 2; Arno Kleffel, op. 17, no. 3; Heinrich Molbe, op. 3, no. 1; A. Naubert, op. 4, no. 11; Bernhard Schädel, op. 29, vol. 4, no. 4; F. Siebmann, op. 62, no. 3; Hermann Wichmann, op. 29, no. 6; duet with the title "Intermezzo" in Robert Schumann, *Spanisches Liederspiel*, op. 74, no. 2

Most of these composers are now the inhabitants of footnotes, if they are known at all. Wilhelm Taubert was an immensely prolific song composer who published his *Sechs Lieder aus dem Spanischen*, op. 149 in 1868 and also tried his hand at an opera based on Shakespeare's *The Tempest*—Wolf would later consider writing a Tempest opera and would set some of the same *Spanisches Liederbuch* texts far more memorably. Some composers were better known in their day for their prose than for their music: Hans Michael Schletterer wrote biographies of Johann Friedrich Reichardt, based on fragments of that musician's autobiography, and of Ludwig Spohr; Adolf Bernhard Marx wrote theoretical and pedagogical treatises in wide use for fifty years; and Friedrich Gustave Jansen was a Schumann disciple who edited Schumann's letters, wrote a biography of the composer, and composed lieder in pallid imitation of his master's style. Thoughts of their compositions, if he even knew them, would not have disturbed Wolf at his writing desk.

As with his previous collections, Wolf found music where earlier composers and his contemporaries had not, setting poems such as "Ach, wie lang die Seele schlummert!" (Ah, how long the soul doth slumber!) and "Herr, was trägt der Boden hier" (Lord, what does the ground here bear) that had been passed over previously.[14] The publishing firm of Schott even told him that the poems he had chosen were "unsuitable for music," to the composer's ire.[15] It is typical of Wolf's conservative streak that he would make use of this anthology, a landmark on the musical landscape for almost forty years at the time he began composing the songs of his *Spanisches Liederbuch*. Wolf, according to his friends, read modern poetry assiduously in search of song texts but found nothing that suited his musical purposes and gravitated instead to repertoires from the eighteenth and earlier nineteenth centuries. Despite his wide reading and willingness to search anywhere for an opera text or song poetry, his deepest elective affinity was with the Biedermeier spirit. Confessional poetry, or any verse too redolent of its creator's subjective presence, displeased him. Wolf's mockery of bad contemporary verse, especially Richard Kralik von Meyrswalden's rhapsodizing à la Zarathustra, but without Nietzsche's superb command of the language, is a leitmotif of his music criticism.[16] Rather, Wolf took pride in finding the musical gestures appropriate to a variety of poetic personas and sought the poetry appropriate to his gifts. "Put me down as an objective lyricist who can pipe in all keys, who knows how to come to terms with the departed glutton's tune every bit as well as with the rainbow's or the nightingale's tune," he told Engelbert Humperdinck in a letter of 12 March 1891, eleven months after completing the *Spanisches Liederbuch*.[17] One notes the quotation from David's catalog of modes in act 1 of *Die Meistersinger von Nürnberg*: Wolf the mastersinger of song claims status with Wagner. Indeed, he considered his Spanish songbook as the prelude to opera. Near the end of his compositional labors, he told his friend Heinrich Rauchberg that he would shortly be finished with song writing and "Then I will only compose tetralogies."[18]

Figure 5. Emanuel Geibel (1815–1884), poet and translator of the
Spanisches Liederbuch

Before looking further at the Teutonized Spanish songs and their composers, a few words about the *Spanisches Liederbuch* and its creators are in order.
Paul Heyse (1830–1914), introduced in Chapter 2, was the son of a classical
philologist and related on his mother's side to the Mendelssohn-Bartholdy
family. Geibel (1815–84), fifteen years older than his handsome and gifted
collaborator, had already published the *Volkslieder und Romanzen der
Spanier im Versmaß des Originals verdeutscht* (Spanish folk songs and romances translated into German in the original poetic meters) in 1843, three
years before meeting Heyse for the first time in 1846 and nine years before the
Spanisches Liederbuch, and he would later collaborate with the poet Baron
Adolph Friedrich von Schack on the translation of *Romanzero der Spanier*

und Portugiesen (Romances of the Spanish and the Portuguese; published in Stuttgart, 1860). Geibel as a youth gained entrée into the Berlin poetic society "Der Tunnel über der Spree," where Adalbert von Chamisso helped to secure the publication of his first poems and Bettina von Arnim provided the means for the youthful classicist to visit Greece. He was ecstatic and wrote to a friend to say, "The South has captured me, as if in a magic net."[19] After his return, he began to learn Spanish and in 1841 was invited by a friend of his father, the Kammerherr von der Malsburg, to put his late brother's library in order. His brother was the Calderón translator Ernst Otto von der Malsburg, and the library was a rich repository of Spanish literature. His host's tales of Spain and his readings in the Schloß Escheberg collection confirmed Geibel's lifelong fascination with a romanticized fantasy-Spain of orange trees and cypress, monks, bandits, gypsies, glittering daggers, moonlit nights, and guitars—the stuff of such early poems as "Der Zigeunerbube im Norden" (The gypsy youth in northern lands) and "Der Hidalgo"[20] (The hidalgo). In the spring of 1842, he sought out a Professor Victor Aimé Huber, who had lived a long time in Spain and was known for his Spanish travel sketches, in order to acquire additional facility in the language, but Geibel himself never went to Spain, perhaps to protect the perfection of an exotic realm more literary than real. As Heine once observed to Théophile Gautier, "How will you speak about Spain when you've actually gone there?"[21]

The extant information about the genesis of the poetic collection comes from Geibel's and Heyse's published correspondence. On 22 January 1851, Heyse wrote Geibel a business letter entirely devoted to the collaboration on a volume of Spanish poetry. In this letter, he proposes the title *Spanisches Liederbuch. Eine Sammlung Volkslieder, nachgesungen von E. G. und P. H.* (Spanish songbook. A collection of folk songs, translated by E[manuel] G[eibel] and P[aul] H[eyse]) as a less recondite alternative to Geibel's suggestion *Der Pandero*; advises that the poems arranged in a "colorful succession according to mood" rather than according to genre, again with popularizing intent; and proposes publication in two volumes, the second to contain Heyse's translation of Provençal troubadour poetry as well as translations from the Spanish. The romances "Que por mayo era por mayo" ("Ach, im Maien war's," or "Ah, in May it was") and "Yo me levantara maire" should be included, he writes, among the songs, as they are very "komponabel"; Wolf would later agree that "Ach, im Maien war's" was suited for music. Heyse's naive desire that publication should begin in a week [!] was countered by the more experienced Geibel, who suggested that the anthology appear in time for the Christmas gift trade. By October, Geibel had sent a group of poems to Heyse, who wrote back to acknowledge receipt and to praise Geibel's translation of Lope de Vega's "Pues andais" ("Die ihr schwebet um diese Palmen," or "Ye who hover about these palm trees"). The single volume—the publisher was unwilling to bring out a second anthology—was not completed in time for Christmas 1851 but appeared the following spring.[22]

The division of labor in the *Spanisches Liederbuch* is clear. After the title in the table of contents, the initials "P. H." or "E. G." designate the translator, each man responsible for about half of the translations. Many of Geibel's contributions had appeared earlier in the *Volkslieder und Romanzen der Spanier* of 1843, including eleven of the poems later set by Wolf. Unlike Heyse in his *Italienisches Liederbuch* of 1860, the two collaborators did not write an introduction explaining their philosophy of translation or discussing their sources, perhaps because Geibel had already done so earlier in his *Volkslieder und Romanzen* of 1843. The two men were not field ethnographers, and they relied on printed sources from England, Austria, Germany, France, and Spain, in particular, Nicolas Böhl von Faber's *Floresta de rimas antiguas castellanas*, a three-volume set published in 1821–25.[23] From their sources, they chose thirteen "Geistliche Lieder" (Spiritual songs) for the initial section of their anthology and ninety-nine "Weltliche Lieder" (Secular songs) grouped thematically (woman's faith in love, flowers, paired poems about a sleeping lover, lovers' quarrels, lovers' farewells, and women's views on love), followed by fifty-five seguidillas[24] and thirty gypsy songs. Most of the poems in the *Spanisches Liederbuch* are anonymous products of popular lyrical art (fifty-two of the "Weltliche Lieder" and three of the religious poems), brief works in Castilian measures rather than lengthy narrative romances. The known authors include the following:

1. Alvaro Fernandez de Almeida: "Tango vos, el mi pandero"/ "Klinge, klinge, mein Pandero," no. 1 of the "Weltliche Lieder"

2. Juan Ruiz, archpriest of Hita, the fourteenth-century author of the famous *Libro de buen amor*, a poetic miscellany published in Salamanca in 1343 containing fabliaux, parodies, religious lyrics, accounts of the archpriest's hilariously scandalous love affairs, and an allegorical mock-epic "Battle Between the Lord of Flesh and Lady Lent": "Quiero seguir"/ "Nun bin ich dein, du aller Blumen Blume" (Now am I thine, thou flower of all flowers). This is the earliest poem in the anthology, a poem in which Ruiz adapts some of the conventions of courtly love poetry to religious verse.

3. Gil Vicente (ca. 1470–ca. 1536), a Portuguese dramatist who wrote some of his plays and lyric poetry in Castilian: "San está la nina"/ "Weh, wie zornig ist das Mädchen" (Alas, how angry the maiden is); "Si dormis, doncell"/"Und schläfst du, mein Mädchen" (And if you are sleeping, my dear); "Del rosal vengo, mi madra"/"Von dem Rosenbusch, o Mutter" (From the rosebush I come, Mother); "Muy graciosa es la doncella"/"O wie lieblich ist das Mädchen" (Oh, how gentle the maiden is)

4. Juan Lopez de Ubeda, a sixteenth-century poet whose *Cancoñero general de la doctrina cristiana* appeared in 1579: "Los ojos del niño son"/"Ach, des Knaben Augen" (Ah, the boy's eyes)

5. José de Valdivivielso (1560?–1636), a prolific religious poet of such works as *4 Romancero espiritual, en gracia de los esclavos del Santissimo Sacramento para cantar quando se muestra descubierto*: "Feridas teneis mi vida"/"Wunden trägst du, mein Geliebter" (My beloved, thou art wounded)

6. The Portuguese master Luis de Camoes (1524?–80), author of the epic *The Lusiad; or, The Discovery of India*: "De dentro tengo mi mal"/ "Tief im Herzen trag' ich Pein" (Deep in my heart, I bear pain)

7. Nicolas Nuñez: "O Virgen que á Dios pariste"/"Die du Gott gebarst" (Thou who didst bear God)

8. Lope de Vega Carpio (1562–1613), the great dramatist who also wrote several of the finest religious sonnets in the Spanish language: "No lloreis, ojuelos"/"Weint nicht, ihr Äuglein" (Eyes, weep not); "Pues andais en las palmas/Die ihr schwebet um diese Palmen; Madre, unos ojuelos vi"/"Mutter, ich hab' zwei Äugelein" (Mother, I have eyes)

9. Rodrigo de Cota, the fifteenth-century author of *Dialoga entre el amor y un caballero viejo* (Dialogue between love and an elderly knight): "Vista ciega, luz oscura"/"Blindes Schauen, dunkle Leuchte" (Blind gaze, dark light)

10. Cristóbal de Castillejo (1492?–1550), a court poet who incurred the displeasure of the Inquisition with his lengthy comic poems: "Alguna vez"/"Dereinst, dereinst, Gedanke mein" (One day, one day, my thoughts); "Aqui no hay"/"Hier hilft dir nichts" (Here nothing can help you)

11. A mysterious Comendador Escriva: "Ven muerte tan escondida"/ "Komm, o Tod, von Nacht umgeben" (Come, death, shrouded in night)

12. Miguel de Cervantes Saavedra (1547–1616): "Cabezita, cabezita"/"Köpfchen, Köpfchen, nicht gewimmert" (Little head, do not be so tearful)

13. Francisco de Ocaña, whose *Cancionero para cantar la noche de Navidad, y las fiestas de Pascua* was published in Alcalá in 1603: "Otro Villancico de camina Senora: Dize Ioseph a nuestra Señora," or "Caminad, esposa"/"Nun wandre, Maria" (Now journey on, Mary)

14. Don Luis el Chico: "La tu madre, o mis amores"/"Deine Mutter, süsses Kind" (Your mother, sweet child)

15. Don Manuel del Rio: "Vengo triste y lastimado"/"Mühvoll komm' ich und beladen" (Weary I come, and heavy laden); "En las aguas del Jordan"/"Auf des Jordans Wassern zieht ein glorreicher Schwann die Kreise" (A glorious swan moves in circles on the waters of the

Jordan); "Virgenes sabias"/"Ihr klugen Jungfrau'n" (You wise young women)

Don Manuel del Rio and Don Luis el Chico are pseudonyms for Geibel and Heyse, respectively—Geibel, who married a woman of Spanish origins, borrowed the name of an ancestor, Don Manuel del Rio, for his own exercise in pseudo–folk art.[25] The *Spanisches Liederbuch* also includes one poem by St. John of the Cross (1542–91) and the great Baroque poet Luis de Gongora (1561–1625), but I have listed only the authors of texts set by Wolf. The poem by St. John of the Cross, "En una noche oscura"/"In mitternächt'ger Stunde" (In the midnight hours), is one of only three of the thirteen "Geistliche Lieder" that Wolf did not set to music—perhaps because it was too long for lied dimensions, perhaps because its eroticized mysticism was not to his taste. The other two omitted poems are not so long as the work by St. John of the Cross, but they are lengthier than the first ten poems, and their subjects—the dying swan singing its last glorious song and the seven wise virgins—are not so personal as the ten chosen poems, including one by Geibel. "Mühvoll komm' ich und beladen" is among "Don Manuel's" folk-song imitations, its theme of anguished personal responsibility for Christ's suffering in accord with the psychological intensity Wolf sought both in the Geibel-Heyse anthology and elsewhere.

Geibel and Heyse were skilled translators whose philosophy of translation can be deduced from their collections. They were careful to duplicate the form of the original, but with its irregularities and imperfections corrected. The content is translated by and large literally but without fear of paraphrase or a change in tone resulting from idiomatic German expressions and a poet's attention to language. Where the Spanish poem has a commonplace word, for example, Geibel and Heyse will substitute a word that is more colorful, more allusive. It is probable that most of the anonymous folk poems were poesia per musica, and they become so once again in German but with considerable alteration in tone by a learned poet. If one compares passages from the Spanish sources with the Geibel-Heyse translations, the difference is apparent.

A la sombra de mis cabellos	In dem Schatten meiner Locken
mi querido se adurmió	Schlief mir mein Geliebter ein.
¿si le recordaré ó no?	Weck' ich ihn nun auf?—Ach nein![26]

(In the shadow of my tresses my love fell asleep. Shall I wake him now? Oh no!)

Qué producirá mi Dios	Herr, was trägt der Boden hier,
tierra que regais asi?	Den du tränkst so bitterlich?
"Las espinas para mí,	"Dornen, liebes Herz, für mich,
y las flores para vos."	Und für dich der Blumen Zier."[27]

(Lord, what does the ground here bear, that you water it so with your bitter tears? "Thorns, dear heart, for me, and for you a garland of flowers.")

Ven muerta tan escondida	Komm, o Tod, von Nacht umgeben
que no te sienta comigo,	Leise komm zu mir gegangen,
porque el gozo de contigo	Daß die Luft, dich zu umfangen
no me torne á dar la vida.	Nicht zurück mich ruf' ins Leben.[28]

(Come, O death, shrouded by night, softly come toward me, lest the desire to embrace thee recall me to life.)

Heyse reproduces the central thought, the rhyme scheme, and the octosyllabic lines of the Commendador Escriva's "Ven muerte tan escondida," although German is a metrical language and Spanish is not; octosyllabic lines are differently calculated and have a different function and effect in the two languages. Beyond those fidelities, however, Heyse embellishes the original, decking its austere frame with his own words and images. Escriva speaks of death as "hidden," ("escondida"), but Heyse invokes death more elaborately as cloaked or shrouded in night. He further adds the adjective "Leise" and makes more of the analogy between the air or breezes ("Luft") and the breath of life. The greater emphasis of Heyse's verb "rufen" in the phrase "mich ruf' ins Leben" compared to Escriva's "torne á dar la vida" is characteristic of the alterations evident in the other examples as well. The Spanish folk song "A la sombra de mis cabellos" ("In dem Schatten meiner Locken") does not answer the question "Si le recordaré ó no?"—but Heyse does, taking his cue from the teasing complaints throughout the poem. The added adverbial compound "so bitterlich" in "Herr, was trägst der Boden hier," the substitution of the alliterative verbs "trägst" and "tränkst" for the neutral Spanish words "producirá" and "regais," the endearment "liebes Herz," and the "Blumen Zier" rather than "las flores" are all elements of a conversion from folk poetry (or imitations of folk poetry) in one language to translations by a sophisticated poet in another language. The stages of transformation throughout the "translation chain" are clearly marked:[29] the simple Spanish folk-song sources become stylized German art poems and finally song settings of great chromatic intensity.

Wolf had no interest in folk music, folk poetry per se, or imitation–folk song except to cast scorn on the latter enterprise as a concern of Brahms and his ilk. His Spain was a musical colony of late-Romantic Germany, fashioned in Wolf's post-Wagnerian image, and its poetic personas speak in the language of extended tonality, with no pretensions to folklike simplicity. Wolf's predecessors and contemporaries found much less incendiary tonal material in the anthology than he did. Several of them were ardent Wagnerites and disciples of Liszt, but their songs only occasionally reflect the tonal derring-do of their elders and betters. Others precede the heyday of Wagnerian influence or were opposed to it. Whatever the stance for or against Wagner, it is a revealing exercise to discover what were the settings that Wolf's songs subsequently deposed, with the notable exception of Brahms's "Geistliches Wiegenlied" ("Die ihr schwebet um diese Palmen"), op. 91, no. 21; one can argue, as so many have, that Wolf's setting both pays closer attention to the poem and is an exquisite musical construction, but Brahms's song, originating in an entirely different approach to song composition, is a fixture on the world's concert stages. And yet, although it is possible to have more than one musically distinguished setting of a single poem (Schubert's and Wolf's Mignon song "Heiß mich nicht reden," or "Bid me not speak," is another example) coexisting in the recital repertoire, it is more often the case that one version crowds out and suppresses the others. Who, knowing Wolf's "In dem Schatten meiner Locken," could hear Jensen's setting, or even Brahms's, without remembering the more compelling strains and making invidious comparisons?

ADOLF JENSEN'S SPANISH SONGS

Browsing through the crumbling heaps of nineteenth-century lieder in the antiquarian section of Doblinger's music store in Vienna, one occasionally finds copies of Adolf Jensen's songs, the compositions for which he was most respected in his lifetime and for a brief season thereafter. Typically, the clerk shrugs and prices the volumes at a few shillings each; not many visitors to the store know his name or have any interest in his music. Jensen was never acclaimed with the Liszt or Brahms he revered, but he was once more fortunate than that.

Adolf Jensen, like Wolf a generation later, was at first a disciple of Schumann and later, unlike Wolf, a disciple of Liszt. Jensen, who was born 12 January 1837 in Königsberg, East Prussia, came from a family of musicians: his grandfather Wilhelm Martin Jensen was a pupil of Johann Adolf Hasse and Karl Heinrich Graun, his uncle Eduard was a singer, his father Julius a piano teacher and copyist, and his brother Gustav a respected violinist and composer. He was strongly influenced by Schumann in his youth and, like a proper disciple, composed a setting of Heine's "Lehn' deine Wang' an meine Wang'" (Lay your cheek against my cheek) as the first song of six in his op. 1 of 1856, a commercial and critical success at the start of the young composer's career. Jensen, who obviously did not know of the older man's mental illness, saved the money he earned at his first post in Grodno, Russia for a trip to the Rhine in hopes of being accepted by Schumann as a composition student, but the older composer died shortly after Jensen's arrival in Germany.[30] Jensen subsequently served as music director for theaters in Posen, Bromberg, and Copenhagen in the late 1850s, as director of the Music Academy in

Figure 6. Adolf Jensen (1837–1879)

Königsberg in 1861–62, and piano teacher at the Carl Tausig Institute in Berlin from 1866 to 1868. He had operatic ambitions, and his single completed opera, *Die Erbin von Montfort* of 1858–65, is fatally marred by its numerous dramaturgical incongruities. In 1868, he left Berlin for Dresden in order to devote himself entirely to composing and there became an ardent proponent of Wagner, to whom he had been introduced in 1861. As his lung and throat condition worsened, he took baths and cures at various spas and moved first to Graz in 1870, then to Baden-Baden in 1875 in search of alleviation—but to little avail. Toward the end of his life, he was befriended by Brahms, who, as he proudly told a correspondent, "recently even forced me to sing a whole string of songs to him."[31] His health was too poor to permit much work on composition in the last three or four years of his life, and he died 23 January

1879 in Baden-Baden after a lengthy bout with lung disease, probably tuber-culosis.

Jensen's 170-plus songs include forty to texts by Geibel and Heyse; thirty to poems by Joseph Viktor Scheffel, whose poetic anthologies *Der Trompeter von Säkkingen* (1854) and *Gaudeamus* were phenomena of late-Romantic me-dievalizing verse (Wolf jumped on that bandwagon with his setting of "Bite-rolf," published in 1888); ten to poems by Otto Roquette; the op. 11 settings from Georg Friedrich Daumer's *Liederblüten des Hafis* (Blossoms of song by Hafiz), or German paraphrases of the Persian poet Hafiz; and a sprinkling of poems by Goethe, Chamisso, Eichendorff, Heine, Rückert, Uhland, Hoffmann von Fallersleben, Robert Hamerling, Robert Burns, and Theodor Storm—a mélange of textual choices both from older poetic sources and from his own day.[32] In songs such as the Daumer-Hafiz setting "Als einst von deiner Schöne" (As once by your beauty), op. 11, no. 1 (1863), Jensen's declamatory vocal writing, the richness and independence of the piano ac-companiment, and the use of chromaticism to bring out nuances of meaning in the text do indeed foreshadow Wolf's approach to lieder composition, with-out attaining the refinement of nuance and the mastery of musical form evi-dent in the later master's work. Jensen's chromatic idiom placed him among the "moderns" in the 1860s and 1870s; in a letter written in 1870, the com-poser contrasted his uncharacteristic bellicose glee over the Franco-Prussian War with his characteristic musical manner, concluding, "H'm! how these languid chromaticists can thunder when put to it!"[33] Like Wolf a decade later, Jensen lamented the plight of composers in Wagner's wake and wrote in a letter of 11 January 1871 to his friend Paul Kuczynski, a Berlin banker and pupil of Hans von Bülow, of his wish to transfer Wagnerian concepts of beauty to smaller forms:

> Strange as it may seem, I have been subject here in Graz to curious fits of returning interest in the opera. If I had been able to make up my mind to accept the subject proposed by Rob[ert]. Hamerling, I should perhaps have even now the libretto of a grand (i.e., spectacular) opera. In this connection, subjects like Byron's "Sardanapalus," "The Veiled Prophet of Khorossan" by Thomas Moore, etc. have always hovered before my mental vision . . . you know my enthusiastic Wagner-veneration, but just because it is so unbounded I am afraid to follow in his footsteps— and tell me, your hand upon your heart, who of all mortals can? To transfer the application of Wagner's ideas of Beauty and Truth to smaller forms has been my aim in all my last compositions and, it seems to me, successfully achieved. But can I venture to follow him in larger things as well?[34]

This was Wolf's fear, too.

Jensen's star rose early and fell swiftly. In 1863, Hans von Bülow praised Jensen as the successor par excellence to the Schumann of the character pieces for piano and the 1840 lied outpouring; Bülow was particularly impressed by the richness of the piano accompaniment, which nonetheless never overwhelms the singer, and the chromatic idiom in the op. 4 Spanish songbook settings and the op. 11 Hafiz songs.[35] His approval was echoed by many, but the tide turned soon after the composer's death. In his 1881 article "Das deutsche Lied seit Robert Schumann" (The lied since Robert Schumann), Hermann Kretzschmar, who nonetheless considered Jensen a master of the lied, criticizes him for his "feminine" sentimentality. The "languid chromaticist" had a tendency to lapse into salon mannerisms, a habitual vein that another writer nicely describes as "luscious."[36] Jensen, sensitive to the criticism, attempted to remedy this defect in his later works by recourse to contrapuntal procedures inspired by his studies of Bach's music and by more orchestrally conceived writing for piano, but cloying moments still intrude. Kretzschmar observes that in his own day Jensen had great influence, but that now "in stronger times," it is principally only women and effeminate men who prize "the gentle artist." One notes the equation of enduring musical value, of compositional rigor, with masculine strength and winces. Whether Jensen's songs would survive further developments in musical taste was, he thought, doubtful.[37]

Jensen's *Sieben Gesänge aus dem spanische Liederbuche* (Seven songs from the Spanish songbook), op. 4 precede the composer's awareness of Liszt and Wagner, while the op. 21 settings are mature works, more Lisztian in style. The two sets include six songs to poems that Wolf would later choose for his anthology: "In dem Schatten meiner Locken," op. 1, no. 4; "Sie blasen zum Abmarsch" (The bugles are sounding for departure), op. 4, no. 4; "Dereinst, Gedanke mein, wirst ruhig sein," op. 4, no. 7; "Klinge, klinge, mein Pandero," op. 21, no. 1;[38] "Und schläfst du, mein Mädchen," op. 21, no. 3; and "Ob auch finst're Blicke glitten" (Even though dark glances flashed), op. 21, no. 7.[39] "In dem Schatten meiner Locken," op. 1, no. 4 reflects Schumann's influence in every measure, in such formal traits as its contrasting sections in A minor and C major, with a modulatory transition between for the question "Weck' ich ihn nun auf?" and the answer "Ach nein, ach nein!" The prominence of the piano accompaniment, the precisely indicated tempo fluctuations in measures 16–21 and measures 22 (nachsinnend–zurückgehalten–a Tempo–Die Viertel wie zu Anfang), even the cliché Spanish habañera rhythms that Schumann did not disdain using in his *Spanisches Liederspiel* duets, are other hallmarks of a song composed, like so many at the time, "under the sign of Schumann." Jensen, unlike Wolf, lacked the forcefulness of musical personality to break away from the influences that impinged on him, and therefore "In dem Schatten meiner Locken" is a well-crafted capitulation to his first master.

The text is a teasing, psychologically ambivalent, erotic poem, the eroticism and affection predominant over the complaints.

A la sombra de mis cabellos	In dem Schatten meiner Locken
mi querido se adurmió:	Schlief mir mein Geliebter ein.
¿si le recordaré ó no?	Weck' ich ihn nun auf?—Ach nein!
Peinaba yo mis cabellos	Sorglich strählt' ich meine krausen
con cuidado cada dia,	Locken täglich in der Frühe,
y el viento los esparcia	Doch umsonst ist meine Mühe,
revolviéndose con ellos,	Weil die Winde sie zersausen.
y á su suplo y sombra de	Lockenschatten, Windessausen
ellos	
mi querido se adurmió:	Schläferten den Liebsten ein.
¿si le recordaré ó no?	Weck' ich ihn nun auf?—Ach nein!
Diceme que le da pena	Hören muß ich, wie ihn gräme,
el ser en extremo ingrata,	Daß er schmachtet schon so lange,
que le da vida y le mata	Daß ihm Leben geb' und nehme
esta mi color morena,	Diese meine braune Wange.
y llamándome sirena	Und er nennt mich seine Schlange,
él junto á mí se adurmió:	Und doch schlief er bei mir ein.
¿si le recordaré ó no?	Weck' ich ihn nun auf?—Ach nein!

(In the shadow of my tresses my love fell asleep. Shall I wake him now? Oh no! I comb my curly tresses carefully, early every morning, but my labors are in vain, for the wind tousles them. The shade of my tresses, the rustling of the wind, lulled my beloved to sleep. Shall I wake him now? Oh no! I must hear how he grieves, how he has languished so long, how my brown cheeks give him life and take it away from him. And he calls me his serpent—and yet he fell asleep beside me. Shall I wake him now? Oh no!)

The woman within the poem sings this song with her lover asleep at her breast and shadowed by her long hair. As she looks at him and wonders whether to awaken him, she compares the daily task of combing her hair, only to have it disordered by the wind, to love making with someone who each time tells her of his longing, calls her his serpent, and then goes to sleep. The eroticism lies in knowing that the pair has made love (the wind has tousled her locks) a short time before and will do so again to the same script on his part. Therefore, she can enjoy the deferment of his awakening/arousal in the certainty of love's renewal. The hint of teasing ennui ("If it is always going to be like this, why should I wake him up?") adds to the eroticism the spice of ambiguity that so attracted the psychologically inclined Wolf—ambiguity he brings out in his setting far more than Jensen.

Jensen once told a friend that he hoped his songs would reveal more of the substance and emotional life of a text than mere reading of the "naked poem" could do.[40] Like Schumann, he wishes his songs to be "nach dem Sinn des Gedichts" but asserts musical setting as a better experience than pure poetry. Within his limits, he had a capacity for relatively bold compositional choices and refined prosodic-interpretive details. In the first section in A minor, for example, Jensen first places the durational and pitch emphasis on the word "Ge-*lieb*-ter" in the repeated phrase "schlief mir mein Geliebter ein," with a secondary emphasis on the proprietary adjective "meine" (placed on the first beat but as part of a continuing melodic scalar ascent through the bar line). The second time, however, the durational and harmonic (Neapolitan sixth) accentuation falls primarily on the verb "schlief," in mock-outraged emphasis, and he repeats the same nicety of varied interpretational stress when the verb tense changes: "schläferten den *Lieb*-sten ein, / *schlä*-ferten den Liebsten ein" in measures 31–32, 34–35 (Example 24).[41] It is possible that similar concerns for prosodic nuances led Jensen to set measures 22–25 in $\frac{5}{4}$, where the words "sorglich" and "täglich" are stressed, the latter all the more emphatic for the vault upward of a tenth. That same leap upward later serves to convey the lover's passion in the phrase "dass er *schmach*-tet schon so lange" when the C-major section returns. The unusual meter can also be interpreted as an aspect of characterization: precisely because the poetic persona's complaints are not tragic in the slightest, she revels in a touch of melodrama, the extra beat per measure an added means of emphasis. Jensen treats both episodes of mock-lamentation as nearly literal repetitions, unlike Wolf, who devises a more passionate variant for the words "Hören muss ich, wie ihn gräme." There is a slight resemblance between Jensen's setting of the words "Sorglich strählt ich meine krausen Locken" in measure 22 and Wolf's, but Jensen repeats the melodic phrase for measure 24 and the line "Doch umsonst ist meine Mühe," resulting in emphasis on the word "doch." This is a perfectly legitimate expressive choice, but Wolf's accentuation of "um-*sonst*" by means of the leap to a higher register and placement on the first beat is even more apt.

There are striking conceptual similarities between Wolf's and Jensen's settings, although the differences, especially in harmonic idiom, are as marked as one might expect: a generation separates the two songs. (And yet, Wolf and Jensen each use blatant parallel fifths in the bass to suggest a peasant or folk ambience without otherwise departing from the refinements of art song.) Both composers embody the not-so-serious polarity of love and complaint as contrasting tonal regions, although Jensen's sectionalization into closely related A minor/C major areas with the recurrent question-answer "Weck' ich ihn nun auf? Ach, nein!" as the pivot point, the transition from one to the other, is less complex than Wolf's chain-of-thirds relationships. Most revealing of all, both men apportion the final round of complaints as repetitions of one- or two-bar

Example 24. Adolf Jensen, "In dem Schatten meiner Locken," Op. 1, no. 4, measures 1–21

Example 24, continued

phrases, each one beginning with a passionate stress on a high pitch from which the remainder of the phrase descends. Could Wolf have heard or known Jensen's setting and then later, without conscious awareness of the source, have reworked one or two of its formal premises in his own way? Or did both composers, concerned as they were with tonal analogies to textual nuance, arrive independently at a similar means of emphasis for the woman's "lamentation"? In both settings, the "Frisch und frei" or "Leicht, zart" rhythmic *Schwung* of the piano part continues much as before, untouched by complaints that are all bark and little or no bite. In the same spirit of light self-dramatization, Jensen invests the repeated questions "Weck' ich ihn nun auf? Weck' ich ihn nun auf" with parodic suspense and feigned tension: the widely spaced chords, the contrary motion between the outer voices, the unharmonized drumbeat pitches in the accompaniment, the fermata-extended pause. The melodrama is laid on with a trowel and therefore not to be believed.

Like Schumann and his imitators, Jensen periodically wrote folklike lieder, such as his op. 21, no. 3 setting of "Und schläfst du, mein Mädchen," marked "Im Volkston" (In folk-song style) and the op. 4, no. 4 setting of Heyse's "Sie blasen zum Abmarsch" (The bugles are sounding for departure), with the indication "Volksliederartig vorzutragen" (To be performed after the manner of a folk song). "Sie blasen zum Abmarsch" lends itself to genre painting in music, with its distant military fanfares and a woman's lamentation for her departed soldier-sweetheart, and therefore to a conservative harmonic style and music *im Volkston*.

En campaña, madre   Sie blasen zum Abmarsch,
tocan á leva,   Lieb Mütterlein.
vanse mis amores   Mein Liebster muß scheiden
sola me dejan.   Und läßt mich allein!

Apenas del dia	Am Himmel die Sterne
se muestra el alva,	Sind kaum noch geflohn,
cuando hace salva	Da feuert von ferne
la infantería	Das Fußvolk schon.
y la gloria mia	Kaum hört er den Ton,
cuando el son siente	Sein Ränzelein schnürt er,
parte incontinente,	Von hinnen marschiert er,
porque es á leva:	Mein Herz hinterdrein.
vanse mis amores	Mein Liebster muß scheiden
sola me dejan.	Und läßt mich allein!
Quedo cual el dia	Mir ist wie dem Tag,
faltando el sol queda,	Dem die Sonne geschwunden.
sin que aliviar pueda	Mein Trauern nicht mag
la tristeza mia:	So balde gesunden.
no quiero alegría	Nach nichts ich frag',
si ausente le tengo,	Keine Lust mehr heg' ich,
y no me entretengo	Nur Zwiesprach pfleg' ich
sino con pena:	Mit meiner Pein—
vanse mis amores	Mein Liebster muß scheiden
sola me dejan.	Und läßt mich allein![42]

(The bugles are blowing for departure, dear mother; my beloved must depart and leave me alone! In the heavens the stars have scarcely vanished, and already the infantry is firing from afar. Scarcely had he heard the sound than he buckled on his knapsack and he marched away, taking my heart with him. My beloved must depart and leave me alone. It is as if the sun had vanished from the day. My griefs cannot be healed so quickly: I ask for nothing, take no more pleasure, converse only with my pain—my beloved must depart and leave me alone!)

Jensen makes ample use of fanfare fourths and fifths, including the traditional post-horn motive (measures 1, 11–14), and a beautifully expressive half-cadence for the plaintive repetitions "allein, allein, allein" at the beginning, midpoint, and end of the song. The change of accompanimental patterns and texture from the initial F-minor section to the arpeggiated figuration in measures 16–28 recalls Schumann's characteristic figurational contrasts between sections, and the way in which the piano "bugle calls" in measures 24 and 26 fill in the gaps between vocal phrases is also a device familiar from many of Schumann's songs. In fact, the entire setting is representative of what Schumann and his successors conceived as the amalgam of folk song and lied, although closer to the latter than the former. In addition to the folk-song delivery Jensen indicates, the passages in which the piano doubles the vocal line in thirds and vocal phrases in which a simple motive is repeated twice (measures

16–19, "Am Himmel die Sterne sind kaum noch gefloh'n'") are other indices of a lied that feigns folk song. As a result of the choice to simulate some, not all, of the naiveté and directness of folk song, the composer thereby abjures any search for up-to-date chromatic analogues for grief that says "Mir ist wie dem Tag, dem die Sonne geschwunden" (Example 25). The precedence of conventional melodic design over declamation and poetic syntax is indicative of an older model of lied composition. Jensen's adherence to square-cut phrasing, unlike Wolf's synthesis of traditional melodic symmetries and musical prose, is nowhere more evident than in the recurrent rhyming-repeated motives "Sein Ränzelein schnürt er, / von hinnen marschirt er," later repeated to the words "Keine Lust mehr heg' ich, / Nur Zwiesprach pfleg' ich." The ascending octave leaps in the vocal part, flanked by piano echoes on either side, are certainly dramatic, but the prosody is on occasion quite awkward as a result. Wolf creates instead melodic prose in which the poetic line "Nur Zwiesprach pfleg' ich" is joined to its continuation, "mit meiner Pein." The poetic persona's sense that a black hole has engulfed her entire world upon her lover's departure is given a more psychologically inflected musical portrait in Wolf—farther distant from folk song.

For all its niceties of detail, Jensen's lied is entirely outclassed by Wolf's setting.[43] In his imaginative conception, we hear the military fanfares through the filter of the lamenting woman's perceptions, the dissonances, off-beat accents, and chromatic darkening the musician's registers of her distress. The sevenths and ninths between the soprano and bass voices in the piano fanfares, dissonances Wolf maintains for lengthy stretches of the song, not only invest the music with the conflict appropriate to new and therefore raw grief but evoke the overtone series of distant cannons, bells, and trumpets. Wolf makes the delay in tonal arrival the concomitant to the young woman's emotional agony, the sharp grief of parting far from repose of any kind. The tonality of the lied is B♭ major but Wolf does not arrive at tonic until measure 16 at the words "Am Himmel die Sterne sind kaum noch geflohn," and then only to avoid it thereafter until the last word of the song, "allein." Wolf's compositional craftsmanship, the details of structural design beyond the capacities of a Jensen or a Rubinstein, are evident in the development of the initial soprano-bass pitches D–E♭, motivically and harmonically. Wolf approaches the dominant via the third relationships on either side, the harmonic motion beginning with D and progressing first to F, the identity of the key as either G minor or B♭ major in doubt for a moment. He implies throughout the song that the soldiers march to battle in the major mode, but the persona's grief wrenches or bends the tonality to the relative minor. The dominant of B♭ major is prolonged throughout the piano interlude (measures 9–15), in which the low bass first appears—the distant fanfares invoked at the beginning sound in the middle register and the treble. With measures 16–24, one hears, pianissimo as if from afar, the tramp of the infantry (the "Fussvolk") in a variant of the fanfare

Example 25. Adolf Jensen, "Sie blasen zum Abmarsch," Op. 4, no. 4, measures 1–14

figures. Dwelling on her recent loss, Wolf's grieving maiden brings back in measures 25–31 an extension of the Eb–D progression from the beginning of the song (measures 1–2), the singer's words "und lässt mich allein" echoed in the piano of measures 29–31.

The grief-stricken withdrawal into interiority (measures 32–42) begins with the respelling of F♯ as the Gb a ninth above and against the dominant F in the bass and the chromatic darkening of the tonal palette ("Mir ist wie dem *Tag, dem die Sonne geschwunden*") by means of telescoped circle-of-fifths motion.

At measure 36, the bugle fanfares in parallel thirds and the low drumrolls are succeeded by multiple motivic reorderings of the semitones and intervals of a third that are primal materials of the initial fanfares, the dissonant cross paths of the piano lines and the vocal part an acerbic realization of the singer's insistence on the word "nichts." The contrary motion and voice exchange in measures 36–39 seem the appropriate voice-leading gestures for a "conversation [Zwiesprach] with my pain," especially coupled with the descending motion throughout the phrase. After the extension of E♭ throughout measures 36–39, the piano part continues the descending motion to D. The whole passage is thus revealed as another larger-scale variant of the E♭–D pitches from the beginning, a variant that returns to the obsessive semitone figures, the harmonies of measures 1–2, and the refrain "Mein Liebster muß scheiden und läßt mich allein." This time, there is closure in tonic B♭, unlike the previous refrain-cadences on F and D, followed by one of Wolf's "dying-away" piano postludes—he was fond of these "allmählich verklingend" conclusions—in which distant military music finally fades from our hearing. In an especially evocative final touch of tone color, Wolf repeatedly invokes the lowered sixth degree G♭ in the last half of the postlude, recalling the earlier use of that pitch in this song, as a chromatic constituent in altered dominant ninth and subdominant seventh chords. The final *pppp* setting of the fanfare melodic figure is particularly haunting given Wolf's chord voicing in those last two bars. Jensen's setting is no match: his version of military music dying away in the distance and the half-cadence with which his postlude ends are effective enough, but his song cannot stand comparison with the formal mastery and intensity of text expression in Wolf's lied.

There is another setting of this poem contemporaneous with Jensen's, but representative of an earlier and more conservative musical style. Carl Gottfried Wilhelm Taubert (1811–91) was a Berlin composer who remained true to a Biedermeier mentality well after the midcentury mark and whose idiom is characterized by a pleasant but forgettable fake-folkishness. He was massively prolific: there are 184 opuses for solo voice and piano, including fifteen sets of lieder for children. He also composed at least that much piano music; three operas; incidental music for plays; four string quartets and four symphonies; overtures; and so on and on, all of it now lying forgotten in the archives. His *6 Lieder aus dem Spanischen von Paul Heyse*, op. 149 were published (1868?) by B. Schott in Mainz, later the publishers of Wolf's Spanish songbook, and are typical of this composer. Only the first song, "Wenn du zu den Blumen gehst," and the fourth, "Mein Liebster muß scheiden, und läßt mich allein!" (My lover must depart and leave me alone) are settings of texts that Wolf would later choose. The initial motive in the introduction to "Mein Liebster muß scheiden," a motive repeated as a bass figure in measures 5–6, recalls a bugle fanfare, but in a manner much less specific than either Jensen's or Wolf's setting. The song has its attractive details: the change of chord color

Example 26. Wilhelm Taubert, "Mein Liebster muss scheiden, und lässt mich allein!" measures 1–18

Example 26, continued

hört__ er den Ton, sein Ränz - lein schnürt er, von hin - nen mar-schirt er,

mein Herz hin - ter drein. Mein Lieb - ster muss schei - den, und

lässt mich al - lein.____

and function in the refrain (measures 19–27), from a descending arpeggiation of tonic G minor to ascending motion outlining V/IV and leading to a sustained high G in the vocal line. The unaccompanied final vocal phrase too is effective (Example 26). The harmonic palette is limited in conformity with an ideal of folk-music naiveté. The song typology represented by Taubert's setting is diametrically opposed to that of Wolf, closer to the folk-song arrangements of Brahms but without comparable ingenuity and craft.

Returning to Jensen, his op. 21 songs include three texts that Wolf would later choose for his Spanish songbook: "Klinge, klinge, mein Pandero," the folk song–like "Und schläfst du, mein Mädchen," and "Ob auch finst're

Blicke glitten" (Even though dark glances flashed). The first of those poems is an open invitation to musical setting because its gypsy protagonist laments her misfortunes in love while accompanying dancers on her stringed pandero; the juxtaposition of instrumental music for a merry external world and the musician's inner grief was a challenge to music's capacity to convey more than one poetic event, to evoke conflict by means of differentiation between the voice and piano. "Ob auch finst're Blicke glitten," however, is neither a genre picture of lovelorn gypsies nor a traditional theme from the folk-poetic canon but a glimpse, devoid of all background or context, into an interestingly complex state of mind. The brief poem tells of hopeless adoration, a passive and melancholy address to a beloved who is angry for unknown reasons. The poetic speaker tries to comfort himself with the fact that she at least looked at him, noticed him, even if the glances are not now in his favor. The poem is written as if the humble voice speaks directly to the beloved, perhaps hoping to convert her anger to forgiveness by such a self-abnegating display of devotion. In another reading, one can imagine an interior dialogue with an absent object to whom the lover dares not even speak.

Aunque con semblante airado	Ob auch finstre Blicke glitten,
me mirais, ojos serenos,	Schöner Augenstern, aus dir,
no me negareis al menos	Wird mir doch nicht abgestritten,
que me habeis mirado.	Daß du hast geblickt nach mir.
Por mas que querais mostraros	Wie sich auch der Strahl bemühte,
airados para ofenderme,	Zu verwunden meine Brust,
que ofensa podeis hacerme	Giebt's ein Leiden, das die Lust,
que iguale al bien de miraros?	Dich zu schaun, nicht reich vergüte?
que aunque de mortal cuidado	Und so tödtlich mein Gemüthe
dejeis mis sentidos llenos,	Unter deinem Zorn gelitten,
no me negareis al menos	Wird mir doch nicht abgestritten,
ojos, que me habeis mirado.	Daß du hast geblickt nach mir.

(Even though dark glances flashed from you, fair, starry eyes, it cannot be denied that you looked my way. Even though their rays sought to wound my breast, is there any sorrow for which the joy of seeing you is not rich compensation? However deathly my feelings, stricken under your anger, it cannot be denied that you looked my way.)

Heyse converts the "serene eyes" of the Spanish poem into "schöner Augenstern"—"Augenstern" meaning both the pupil of the eye and "darling" or "sweetheart." He also transmutes "semblante airado" into the more poetic "dark and lowering glances," the initial phrase notable for Heyse's favorite internal alliteration ("f*i*nst're Bl*i*cke gl*i*tten"). The beloved's ire is emphasized in the German by the direct reference to "your anger," reinforcing all the more the psychological complexities of the poem. The cause of displeasure is not explained in either the Spanish source or the German translation; instead, the speaker regresses to his original wonder that such an exalted being should notice him at all. "Wohl kenn' ich Euren Stand" in the *Italienisches Lieder-buch* shares something of the same mood of helpless, hopeless adoration and likewise elicited from Wolf a particularly beautiful song.

Wolf's and Jensen's settings are based upon entirely different readings of the poem. The sentimentality of Jensen's lied, the harmonic language in which the overt emotion is expressed, the massive right-hand chords spanning a ninth or a tenth in the central section, the multiple repetitions of the phrase "daß du hast geblickt nach mir" at the end, even the melodic lines demonstrate the influence of Liszt's songs (Example 27). Any suggestion of humbleness, uncertainty, wistfulness is gone from this reading. Jensen, who dispenses with a piano introduction, indicates that the song should be sung "with great gravity and depth of feeling" ("voll Ernst und Tiefe") and makes of both the beloved's anger and the protagonist's sense of being mortally stricken a more dramatic matter than does Wolf. Jensen's singer is lyrical and passionate, capable of tonal motion that presses forward, of a solemn marchlike tread throughout measures 1–10 and increasing rhythmic activity thereafter. Wolf's poetic persona is too uncertain and unsure of himself ever to sound like this. The dramatic tension evident in Jensen's prolongation of the same diminished-seventh harmony throughout measures 17–20, with its full-textured triplet chordal pulsations and dotted scalar figures in the bass, is utterly unlike Wolf's quieter enactment of the same words. And the saccharine descending arpeggiation with which Jensen's postlude ends represents a cliché of the sort Wolf would discard after the songs of his teenage years.

In Wolf's reading,[44] obsessive devotion of this sort is an emotional tape loop, circling back constantly to its point of origin, in both the larger structure and the smaller details of phrase construction. The two-and-a-half-bar introduction later becomes both the interlude and the postlude (a familiar type of organizing repetition in Wolf, but one singularly apropos in this instance), while the motive presented in that introduction is also circular. There are numerous indices of uncertainty and tenuousness before the singer enters to give them voice. Wolf avoids the first beat in the "bass," places the recurring piano introduction/interlude/postlude in the treble register, and creates voice leading that constantly shifts about. The bass in measures 1–2 states the defining pitches of the B-minor tonality, that is, the tonic, leading tone, and dominant, without the upper voices ever producing a tonic triad in conjunction with the bass. Rather, the introduction is reducible to VI–V, both the natural and

Example 27. Adolf Jensen, "Ob auch finst're Blicke glitten," Op. 21, no. 7, measures 1–10

raised-sixth upper neighbors to the dominant, the compositional choices analogous to the emotional paradox of the words. The poetic persona abases himself before the angry sweetheart, but at the same time he asserts his own identity, his right to be heard, as verified by her past action of "looking his way." The paradox of a curiously muted self-assertion and self-denial finds its musical match in the pairing of a bass line that asserts or identifies a tonality and shifting overlays of uncertainty above it. The confusion about whether the

Example 27, continued

introduction is in minor or major mode is first evident in the initial first-beat stress of measure 1, which states a chromatic pitch, the raised third scale degree D♯, and does so briefly without an accompanying harmonic context. The metrical ambiguities of measure 1 are also, like the uncertainty of modal identification, another realization in abstract musical terms of the poetic speaker's tenuousness, as is the half-cadence with which each interlude and the entire song end (Example 28).

The singer enters with a variation of the circular motive from the introduction, only this time it is not circular but descends by degrees over the span of more than an octave. Similarly, the second vocal phrase descends from its enharmonic/chromatic and rhythmic emphasis on the word "nicht" almost to the previous depth, only to turn upward at the words "hast geblickt nach mir." That cadence on the dominant is marked by the same minor third–major third mixture that one hears in the introduction—the modal shifting from bright to dark marks both ends of the tonic-dominant polarity and permeates the song. It is only at these points that the compass of the piano accompaniment is extended upward, above its rather cramped boundaries elsewhere in the song. One notices in measure 4 the Neapolitan sixth that so beautifully singles out the adjective "schöner," its relationship to tonic B delayed until measure 5. By that time, the B-major harmony (the D♯ the culmination of rising chromatic motion in the alto voice) sounds in a mediant relation with the intervening G and D harmonies, the mediant-related succession indicative of awe, of the near-miraculous. The setting of the words "doch nicht" as an E♯ sixth chord, the D♯ of the Picardy third preceding it reinterpreted enharmonically as the Neapolitan to III, is a particularly effective compositional choice if one considers both the tonal distance from B minor, perhaps emblematic of the distance between happy past and unhappy present, and the subsequent enharmonic transformation of B♭ back to A♯ in the half-cadence at measures 9–10.

Example 28. Hugo Wolf, "Ob auch finst're Blicke glitten," measures 1–6

In measure 18–21, the singer restates the circular motive rhythmically relocated and more richly textured at the words "gibt's ein Leiden, das die Lust, dich zu schaun, [nicht reich vergüte]?" The circularity of the emotional process is here identified explicitly with the circular figure of the introduction, the singer caught musically on a treadmill that returns him to the beginning. The transposition of the circular motive upward a half-step in measures 21–23 only leads back to a restatement of measure 3 onward, a tonal metaphor that epitomizes the poetic persona's failed attempt to find masochistic compensation in his beloved's anger. Indeed, when the initial phrases return, the singer cannot this time repeat the progression evocative of worship and wonder from measures 5–6 because he is too conscious of "your anger." This, sadly enough, is the only substantive change and Wolf marks it unerringly. The ending is less a closure than an admission of defeat, of inability to progress beyond the emotional dilemma and the musical material presented at the beginning. Jensen's lyrical expansiveness at the close, his poetic protagonist repeating the words "daß du hast geblickt nach mir" three times in succession, misses the point—misses it quite beautifully on occasion but misses it nevertheless. Wolf, however, could and did make of the song's structure, and not just of the nuances of word painting, a vehicle of poetic expression in a manner beyond Jensen's ken.

THE OP. 76 GEIBEL-HEYSE SETTINGS OF
ANTON RUBINSTEIN

Adolf Jensen was respected in his day, but he was not nearly so famous as the great Russian pianist and composer Anton Grigorievitch Rubinstein (1829–94), whose 1884 Vienna concerts Wolf reviewed for the *Wiener Salonblatt*. Rubinstein was a facile—too facile—composer, whose long list of works includes over 150 songs in Russian and German, five symphonies, two oratorios, five piano concerti, five trios and a quantity of other chamber forms and genres, and thirteen operas, including the popular *Der Dämon*, first performed in 1875. Unlike Jensen and decidedly unlike Wolf, Rubinstein was unmoved by Wagnerism, a prejudice established early. In 1854 when Rubinstein visited Liszt in Weimar, Liszt observed that his Russian visitor "expresses consistent prejudice against *Zukunftmusik*"; Rubinstein would continue to do so the rest of his life, blaming the failure of his opera *Feramors* (1863) on the hostility of the Vienna Wagnerites and the evils of the new music drama. For his opposition to Wagnerism, he became an example of renunciatory virtue for Eduard Hanslick to applaud, the matter worth a momentary digression. The influential critic considered Wolf gifted but misguided, "the Richard Wagner of song." Just as Wagner had transmogrified opera into a new and condemnable entity, so too, he insisted, had Bruckner and Wolf turned symphony and song into something they were never meant to be.[45]

The original Beckmesser has had a bad postmortem press for his indictments of Wagner and Bruckner. Reading his mordant, witty criticism, one realizes that he waged for decades a rearguard and losing campaign against Wagner's influence, against the plague of "Wagner influenza" infecting so many European composers. His recognition of Wagner's importance is apparent in his measurement of virtually all opera—almost all music—against the Wagnerian standard and in his own frank statements of Wagner's cultural significance; despite his love of Italian opera, he gave Verdi's *Otello* a largely unsympathetic review because the music seemed too Wagnerian to him. His review of *Feramors* is typical, both in Hanslick's championship of the un-Wagnerian Rubinstein and in his implicit acknowledgment of Wagner as the standard of measurement.

> In truth, *Feramors* could have been composed note for note without any indication that a Richard Wagner had ever lived. If you are looking for reminiscences of other composers, you can find traces of Meyerbeer, of Gounod, perhaps also of Schumann, but Rubinstein's opera lies separated from Wagner's "music drama" by an insurmountable chasm. I consider Rubinstein to be the greater musical talent, although as a dramatic composer Wagner is due a much greater cultural-historical significance.[46]

In a review of Rubinstein's opera *Die Makkabaer*, performed in Vienna in 1878, Hanslick wrote:

The new Wagnerian style is moreover such a highly personal one that his younger disciples, with their long hair and short melodies, are thereby brought to disgrace. Wagner's later works are quite interesting exceptional cases but not prototypes of a universally valid and natural law of art, a foundation for future advancements. Rubinstein shares with us the conviction that a gifted composer in the operatic style that prevailed until now, that is, without endless melodies in the orchestra and without an aversion to choruses and ensembles, can still create something new, beautiful, and impressive.[47]

Hanslick's praise for Rubinstein has not stood the test of time. Wolf disagreed vehemently with the critic's anti-Wagner stance, but he would in 1890 echo in his own way the wish Hanslick once expressed for un-Wagnerian comedy rather than prehistoric-mythic subjects, for a return to "simple, human drama in which gravity and gaiety are conjoined."[48]

Rubinstein wrote songs untouched by latter-day developments of the Romantic tonal language. His op. 76 songs *Aus dem Spanischen Liederbuch* include "Bedeckt mich mit Blumen" (Cover me with flowers—the fifth song in the opus) and "Klinge, klinge, mein Pandero," the two representative of Rubinstein's strengths and weaknesses as a song composer. The poetry of "Bedeckt mich mit Blumen," erotic consummation in medias res its subject, should bring out whatever capacity for chromatic languor a late-nineteenth-century composer possesses.

Cubridme de flores	Bedeckt mich mit Blumen,
que muero de amores!	Ich sterbe vor Liebe.
Porque de su aliento el aire	Daß die Luft mit leisem Wehen
no lleve el olor sublime,	nicht den süßen Duft entführe,
cubridme!	Bedeckt mich.
sea porque todo es uno,	Ist ja Alles doch dasselbe,
alientos de amor y olores	Liebesodem oder Düfte
de flores.	Von Blumen.
De azuzenas y jazmines	Von Jasmin und weissen Lilien
aqui la mortaja espero,	Sollt ihr hier mein Grab bereiten,
que muero!	Ich sterbe.
Si me preguntais de qué	Und befragt ihr mich woran?
respondo: en dulces rigores	Sag ich: unter süßen Qualen
de amores.	Vor Liebe!

(Cover me with flowers; I am dying of love. So that the breeze with its soft breath may not carry the sweet scent away from me, cover me! It is all the same, the breath of love or the scent of flowers. You shall prepare my grave of jasmine and white lilies here. And if you ask me why, I'll say: from the sweet pains of love.)

For all his skill as a translator, Heyse was not able to duplicate the Spanish rhyme scheme in which the abbreviated third line chimes in close proximity with the rhyming word at the end of the second line; fidelity to the literal content made this impossible. There is no difference, the poet says, between the scent of love and the perfume of flowers; lest the gentle breeze dispel the fragrance, the lover begs to be covered with flowers, the grave site of "la petite morte" suitably adorned with lilies and jasmine. The languor is of the moment: "Ich sterbe," the lover says in the present tense, and then adds "sollt ihr *hier* mein Grab bereiten."

Rubinstein was resistant to any *Tristan*-esque chromatics of desire, but he begins his setting of "Bedeckt mich mit Blumen" with several effective, if harmonically conservative, nuances of text interpretation. The fragmented, languid descent in the vocal line; the diminished seventh on A♯; the prolongation of "*ster*-be" across the bar line while passing-tone motion in the right hand produces the tension-filled sound of an augmented triad; the even greater prolongation of "*Lie*-be" in measures 5–6; the uncertainty of tonal identity until the culmination of the cadence at the word "Liebe"; the phrase structure in which the initial 1 + 1 falling intervallic figures are succeeded first by a two-bar extension, then three bars, the motivic-phrase prolongations creating the impression of increasing erotic languor throughout the first line of the poem—all of these details in measures 1–7 indicate the composer's concern for poetic interpretation (Example 29). Rubinstein, however, does not develop the initial material further and instead produces superficial word painting for the one image of motion in the poem, unlike Wolf, who makes of elided and delayed cadential resolutions the musical metaphor for erotic delight prolonged. Throughout his setting, Rubinstein repeats motivic figures evocative of the soft, swaying breath of the breezes in the right-hand part, figures that sound at first to a suitably languorous chromatic descent in the bass. The vocal line shows the composer's characteristic slipshod prosody, especially the recourse to $\frac{6}{8}$ quarter-note–eighth-note trochaic patterns. Wolf would not have allowed such mechanical patterns to obliterate the syntactical separation in the words "sag' ich: unter süssen Qualen vor Liebe," but Rubinstein does. Most serious of all, the lied is paradoxically both brief and diffuse, without a convincing formal design. The framework provided by the built-in ritardando at the end, a compressed variation of the initial section, is not enough to compensate for the unimaginative repetitions of routine figuration in between. Kretzschmar, who considered Rubinstein to be a "natural genius" given to lightning flashes of brilliance, nonetheless pointed out that Rubinstein the composer, like Rubinstein the virtuoso, was prone to missed notes—failures due to lack of inspiration.[49] Wolf once observed that Rubinstein's compositions often begin well and end disappointingly, the composer unable

Example 29. Anton Rubinstein, "Bedeckt mich mit Blumen" from the songs *Aus dem Spanishcen Liederbuch*, Op. 76, no. 5, measures 1–14

to fulfill the promise of the opening measures. He could have been referring to "Bedeckt mich mit Blumen."[50]

For Wolf, "to die of love" post-*Tristan* is to create layers of chromatically shifting motives and voice leading above an initial dominant pedal (measures 1–4) and then delay its resolution not once but many times.[51] Compared to Rubinstein's tamer idiom, the pungent Romantic simultaneity at the start of Wolf's setting (diminished seventh on the raised fourth degree over a V pedal, the major-seventh dissonance E♭–D emphasized by the chordal pulsation) signals another musical world, one in which Wagnerian elisions and substitutions are the paramount musical gestures of desire. Wolf twice states a chromatic approach to the dominant-seventh harmony in measures 1–2 and 3–4, the vocal line overlaid across and through the repetition in the piano. The repetition, either literal or transposed an octave to a different register, of one- and two-bar units is the principal means throughout this song by which Wolf slows down the forward harmonic motion to produce the appropriately languorous atmosphere. The intertwining melodic lines in the right-hand part and vocal melody could be the melodic paradigms of the lovers themselves, different but closely related linear entities that diverge only to come together, to double one another in thirds or octaves, and to separate briefly once again. The crisscrossing directions produce the most acute direct dissonance (E♭–D, the end of measure 2) at the juncture just before one might expect tonic resolution to follow, but the passing motion in the vocal line leads instead to a repetition of measures 1–2 in the piano and another vocal phrase overlaid ("bedecken") with it. Here, the dominant seventh of measure 4 resolves to A♭ in measure 5, but A♭ against the dissonant seventh G♭ in the bass, impelling further motion forward rather than momentary repose. The vocal line finally reaches A♭ in measure 6, but as a constituent in a nontonic harmony; the leap upward to the initial pitch F and the initial harmony of measure 1 is especially telling because it counterbalances the descending motion that precedes it and because the languorously shifting voices return us to the same point at which we began. Such affective leaps of a sixth to a nontonic pitch at the end of a climactic vocal phrase occur at moments of particular intensity in Wolf's songs, such as the close of "Peregrina II" in the *Mörike-Lieder* ("Und Hand in Hand verließen wir das Haus," or "And hand in hand, we leave the house"). That expressive gesture comes as the culmination of multiple elements to evoke heightened erotic rapture at the words "Ich sterbe vor Liebe": the hemiola in the vocal line of measure 5, underscoring the verb "sterbe," as well as the rise of the left hand into the treble register and the transposition and expansion of the right-hand motivic figure from measures 1–2. Like the refrain in "Ob auch finstre Blicke glitten," this motive too is circular but to very different effect.

Wolf approaches cadences only to evade resolution and begin another harmonic progression as a matter of course throughout "Bedeckt mich mit

Blumen." The dominant-seventh chord in measure 8 once again does not resolve to tonic but is instead followed by the mediant C major, foreshadowed
enharmonically by the F♭s from measure 2 recurring in measure 8. The extension of the mediant chord for the "breeze with its soft swaying" begins the
further variation of all of the previous musical figures and processes—the
vocal phrases overlapping the piano phrases, the evasion of tonic resolution,
the scalewise descending and ascending fragments, the right-hand motive
from measures 1–2. Wolf emphasizes the words "süssen Duft" in measure 11
by means of the hemiola-prolongation of the noun "Duft" and by the B♭ seventh above the bass. Everything drifts back into sight and sound in this song:
with the words "oder Düfte von Blumen" of measures 19–21, a variant of the
E♭ pedal in measures 1–4 returns and leads to the varied return of the mediant
passage from measures 9–15. Measures 30–41 constitute one of the lengthiest
dominant prolongations in Wolf's lieder ("Und befragt ihr mich: Woran?"),
delaying tonic resolution throughout the "sweet pains of love." The rhetorical
question "Why [do you die?]" and its answer are set almost entirely over a low
E♭ pedal, beginning with a transposition of the previous C-major motive. The
vocal line reaches a sensuously weak tonic closure on A♭ (the weak fifth beat
of measure 38), dovetailed with the varied recurrence of measures 1–2 in the
piano. Only gradually does the piano come to rest on A♭ after a final prolongation of the dominant in measures 41–42 and a chromatic plagal decoration of
tonic in the inner voices of measure 42, a last reminiscence of the D♭s and D♮s
of measures 1–2.

In none of the other settings of this text by Rubinstein, Damrosch, Hiller,
Adolph Bernhard Marx, even Schumann, does one find such an accumulation
of text-derived compositional choices in so controlled a form. The $\frac{6}{4}$ meter,
which permits a gently erotic swaying motion and the languorous dwelling on
certain key words, the richness of the chord doublings, the registral shifts
from low bass to treble, the prosodic refinements, the "heartbeat" chordal
pulsations—all contribute to the heavily perfumed (but not cloying) atmosphere. But most of all, the experience encapsulated in the poem is equated
with the working-out of a delayed tonic consummation.

THE PRECIOSA SONGS OF PETER CORNELIUS
AND WOLF

"Köpfchen, Köpfchen, nicht gewimmert" could well have been among the
poetic texts that Wolf's publisher Schott considered unsuitable for music.
Only Wolf and Peter Cornelius (1824–74) set this poem to music; Cornelius,
like Wolf, searched for poems that had not been set to music by all and sundry. Although Wolf may not have known the Cornelius setting, which was
composed in Weimar during the winter of 1854–55 and published posthu-

mously in 1888, when he composed his own version, he came to know it later: he asked Melanie Köchert to send him a copy in 1893.[52] Two years earlier, he told her that he liked Cornelius's poetry better than his music:

> Once more: you should send for the poetry of Peter Cornelius. I cannot read enough of him. He is one of the truest poets that the Germans have—and fail to appreciate. I have to confess that his music, of which Grohe owns a fair selection, pleases me considerably less; his intentions are good, but not the execution. What he would like to do outstrips his ability to do it. I wish that 1/100th of Cornelius's poetic talent had been granted to me and then operas would issue forth into the world one after another from nothing. There is nothing more beautiful than to be both poet and composer; that is truly the complete man and artist.[53]

Despite Wolf's enthusiastic words, he never set any of Cornelius's poetry to music. The next year, he wrote to Grohe concerning a production in Karlsruhe of Cornelius's *Der Cid*:

> The acclaim for Cornelius's "Cid" in Karlsruhe does not count for much, in my opinion. It's merely a local thunderstorm, and if there's lightning in Karlsruhe, the thunder doesn't reach other, more distant cultural centers. A little sulfurous stench in the neighboring environs, that's all. There isn't much to get excited about, believe me, in the "Cid." I know the work with its at times highly poetic scenes and atmospheric depictions which, when detached from the whole, might well pass muster as purely lyrical outpourings, but are not worth much on the stage. Cornelius is, like Berlioz, one of those all-too-ingenious and gifted people who speak to the common people in a folklike manner and wish to write opera more than any other genre. But Cornelius, with his cleverly poetic Donquixotery, is caviar for the common folk; he speaks to them like Don Quixote to Dulcinea. The result . . . is that neither understands the other. . . . And Berlioz is altogether another sort of man than his pale copy, as the composer of the *Barber of Bagdad* appears to me.[54]

Wolf's judgment of *Der Cid* is apt.

Cornelius was a singular creative personality. His parents were actors and music-lovers, and his dual preoccupation with poetry and composition was determined early. In his "Autobiographische Skizze" (Autobiographical sketch) of 1874, he reproaches his parents for his incomplete musical training, something he felt was a hindrance throughout his life.[55] He spent the years from 1844 to 1852 in Berlin, where he lived with his uncle (the artist Peter Cornelius, 1783–1867) and became part of a circle that included Bettina von Arnim, Joseph von Eichendorff, and Paul Heyse. Cornelius moved to Weimar in 1852 in order to study with Liszt and while there came to know Hans von Bülow, Joseph Joachim, and Leopold Damrosch. During the early years in

Weimar, Cornelius concentrated on song composition (more than half of his nearly one hundred songs and duets were composed in the space of four years between 1853 and 1856), including the setting of "Preziosens Sprüchlein gegen Kopfweh" (Preciosa's charm against headache) in 1854–55. Five of his earliest extant lieder are settings of original poetry by Heyse, a close friend at the time; subsequent lieder include settings of sonnets by Gottfried August Bürger of "Lenore" ballad fame and poems by Platen, Eichendorff, Hebbel, Annette von Droste-Hülshoff, Heine, even Friedrich Hölderlin ("Sonnenuntergang," or "Sunset"; 1862). His best-known songs, however, such as the cycles *Trauer und Trost* (Mourning and solace), op. 3, and the *Weihnachtslieder* (Christmas songs), op. 8, are settings of his own poetry. The comic opera *Der Barbier von Bagdad* (The barber of Bagdad; 1855–58) was Cornelius's first operatic venture, a fiasco at first and the occasion of Liszt's departure from Weimar, later a popular and critical success. From 1858 to 1865, Cornelius lived in Vienna and there composed both the words and music for his second opera *Der Cid* (1860–62), his last completed sizable composition. When Wagner came to Vienna in 1861 to supervise the production of *Lohengrin*, Cornelius became part of the Wagner circle but struggled to establish a style of his own, "completely free of all Liszterei and Wagnerei!"[56] Wagner demanded discipleship and Cornelius was too independent to accede to a master he characterized as tyrannical, but he nevertheless found Wagner's musical influence difficult to expunge from his serious operas, *Der Cid* and the uncompleted *Gunlöd*.

Cornelius's lieder are often more classicizing in style than those of Liszt or Wagner, although Kretzschmar rightly points out that "Ein Ton" (One sound) and "An den Traum" (To dreams) from the *Trauer und Trost* cycle could have been composed by Liszt himself.[57] Cornelius was not a composer who felt at home with musical prose, and his early songs in particular reflect a lied aesthetic that he defined according to Schiller's polarity between the naive and the sentimental poets. In a review published in 1868, Cornelius compares the songs of two composers of the New German school, Eduard Lassen and Leopold Damrosch, with the prize going to Lassen for his "naive" and unaffected art. Damrosch's lieder were too artificial, his melodies not sufficiently free of affected contours and learned devices;[58] an ideal of naturalness and directness is at the heart of Cornelius's critique and influenced his quest for a "healthier" vein of poetry (he proposed Goethe and Bürger as models) and the music suitable to it. Elsewhere, Cornelius rejected the aesthetic formalism in Hanslick's treatise *Vom Musikalisch-Schönen* (On the beautiful in music) in favor of an expressive art of emotion, "music as a poetic, cultivated speech."[59] The conflict between the elements of word and tone should fuse, he felt, to be the bearer of both musical content and expression.

The text of "Köpfchen, Köpfchen, nicht gewimmert" comes from a poem in the folk manner sung by the central character in Miguel de Cervantes's "La gitanilla" (The gypsy girl) from the *Novelas ejemplares* of 1613. Since the arrival of the gypsies in Spain in the fifteenth century, public sentiment was aligned against these itinerants, and Spanish literature generally echoed official disapproval. Cervantes in "La gitanilla," however, creates a beautiful gypsy girl Preciosa as the heroine of the three love stories in this short novel. The poem "Cabecita, cabecita" appears near the end of the second love story, in which the fifteen-year-old Preciosa demonstrates that she "already knows, without being taught, how to instill fright, jealousy, and shock to subdue her lovers," in this instance, the young aristocrat Don Juan de Cárcamo. The poem is ostensibly a charm with "special grace to preserve and sustain the heartbroken and the lightheaded," although Cervantes tells us shortly that the quick-witted gypsy has made the words up on the spot.

> Cabecita, cabecita,
> tente en ti, no te resbales,
> y apareja dos puntales
> de la paciencia bendita.
> Solicita
> la bonita
> confiancita;
> no te inclines
> a pensamientos ruines;
> verás cosas
> que toquen en milagrosas,
> Dios delante
> y San Cristobal gigante.[60]

(Dear little head, dear head, get a grip on yourself, don't slip away, and join together two supports for blessed patience. Ask for the beautiful reassurance; do not incline yourself to base thoughts. You will see things that approach miracles, God and the giant St. Christopher leading the way.)

In Heyse's translation, the naiveté becomes Teutonic, miracles turned into *Märchen* and hair standing on end to the tune of a German idiom.

> Köpfchen, Köpfchen, nicht gewimmert,
> Halt dich wacker, halt dich munter,
> Stütz' zwei gute Säulchen unter,
> Heilsam aus Geduld gezimmert!
> Hoffnung schimmert,
> Wie sich's auch verschlimmert
> Und dich kümmert.

Mußt mit Grämen
Dir nur nichts zu Herzen nehmen,
Ja kein Märchen,
Daß zu Berg dir stehn die Härchen;
Da sei Gott davor
Und der Riese Christopher![61]

(Little head, little head, don't moan, be courageous, be cheerful, sup-
ported by two good stout pillars; patience is the best healer. Hope glim-
mers where once it deceived you and caused you grief. You must take
nothing painful to heart, no little tale to make your hair stand on end; may
God go before you and the giant St. Christopher!)

The sleight of hand by which the idiomatic expression "Solicita / la bonita /
confiancita"—"confiancita" a very personal and intimate confidence—becomes the Germanic invocation of hope is characteristic of Heyse's and
Geibel's willingness to engage in paraphrase where an idiom was, they felt,
untranslatable.

The text, a curative folk charm calling on God and St. Christopher, was
perfectly suited to a musical style Kretzschmar described as "sincere, childlike, yet earnest and deeply felt."[62] Cornelius, less pictorially imaginative
than Wolf, does nothing that suggests the pain, the hammer blows, or the
persistence of a headache, but instead uses literal or near-literal motivic and
phrase repetition for an effect of folkishness. The seeming naiveté, however,
is juxtaposed with such artful details as the initial declamatory motives
"Köpfchen, Köpfchen," echoed in the piano in altered rhythmic disposition,
and the turn to G-major (flatted III) harmonies for the injunction "Do not
moan, be brave, be cheerful" in measures 5–10, with its varied motivic repetition and its columnar ("Säulchen") chords in the accompaniment. Almost
forty years later, Wolf too would musically mark the first mention of promised
health and cessation of pain at the words "Heilsam aus Geduld gezimmert!"
with a lessening of the dissonance prevalent before that point; Cornelius hails
those words with proclamatory dotted rhythms in the vocal line of measure 11
and a cadence on B minor, the dominant minor—the minor mode seems indicative of pain still present, the cure not yet effective (Example 30). Cornelius
again resorts to charmlike incantation/phrase repetition at the words "Ja kein
Märchen, daß zu Berg dir stehn die Härchen" in measures 39–42 and the
multiple invocations of "der Riese Christopher" in measures 46–47 and 53–
54. Cornelius's classicizing tendencies in lied, his style on occasion closer to
Mendelssohn than to Wagner, are evident in the symmetrical phrase structure
and lyrical melodic design—nothing resembling arioso or declamatory style
here, also in the thinly textured broken chordal figuration and other such stan-
dardized accompanimental patterns.

Example 30. Peter Cornelius, "Preziosas Sprüchlein gegen Kopfweh," measures 1–13

There was not much opportunity in the *Spanisches Liederbuch* for Wolf to indulge his gift for humor in music, or even lightheartedness, since Geibel and Heyse clearly preferred the fabled Spain of turbulent amorous passions and anguished religiosity. "Köpfchen, Köpfchen, nicht gewimmert" is one of the few lighter moments in the anthology and in Wolf's songbook, a lied reminiscent of the earlier Mörike song "Mausfallen-Sprüchlein" in its sophisticated play on naiveté.[63] What is so enchanting about both these magic charms is the pairing of delicacy and dissonance, the pinpricks of childish malice or pain translated into conflict-laden intervals played pianissimo in the treble register. The pain of the headache is immediately apparent in the clash of the "bass" G♭ (the entire accompaniment is in the treble throughout) and the pedal point F in the topmost voice, its nonlegato groupings a stylized rendering of a pounding or hammering headache. Wolf continues to pit the flatted sixth degree (the ninth of the V^9 in this dominant prolongation) against the fifth F on the offbeats throughout measures 1–6. As so often in Wolf's best songs, every aspect of the structure mirrors the text in much greater detail than one finds elsewhere. When the singer enters in measure 3, joining the F of the pounding headache, it is with a descending *lamentoso* chromatic fragment, a miniature whimper that the singer then tells herself must cease, to be replaced with courage and cheer. There are no indicated rests between the vocal phrases in measures 3–11, surely because she adapts her words to the rhythmic pounding of her headache and perhaps as well because the words/vocal line are her weapon against the pain. If she falls silent, the headache and its ostinato would resume primacy and she cannot allow that if the charm is to work. Wolf plays on the traditional association of major mode with brightness and minor mode with grief, lamentation, and so on, in which the prominence of pitches from the parallel minor mode reflects the pain of the headache while the major mode might indicate that the charm's efficacy is taken for granted. With charming pseudonaiveté, Wolf enforces both the syntactical parallelism of the words "Halt' dich wacker, halt' dich munter" and the mixed mode by repeating the one-bar segment in the vocal line but with the D♭ of measure 5 becoming D♮, reflecting the word "munter," in measure 6. The ascending contour of those vocal figures also seem a corollary to the injunction "Be brave, be cheerful."

The most telling instance of a correspondence between musical structure and text, however, is surely the fact that tonic is delayed until near the end of the texted body of the song, its firm establishment only confirmed in the postlude. Not until the charm has worked is surety and tonic repose possible. The first delay begins in measure 7, appropriately at the point where the singer takes action ("stütz' zwei gute Säulchen unter") and the music deflects to the submediant. The tonal change and the lessening of tension are the musical analogues to the promise of surcease, the tonic substitution a foreshadowing of future health ("heilsam aus Geduld gezimmert!"). It is furthermore with those words in measure 9 that Wolf introduces the fuller texture and octave doubling of the ostinato, replacing the thinner, weaker sounds and preponderant dissonances with musical metaphors for increased strength. Next, he takes his cue from the words "Hoffnung schimmert"—hope is apparent but not yet fulfilled—and extends the tonic substitution throughout measures 12–18, repeating the same ascending scalewise figure without quite arriving at tonic. The motivic relationship between the streams of rising scalar parallel thirds in the left-hand part throughout the middle section (measures 12–22) and the piano accompaniment of "Nun wandre, Maria," with its similar theme of traveling through travail toward hope, seems too striking to be merely coincidental. Those streams of thirds culminate in measures 13, 15, and 19 with the F♮, the ostinato pitch of the first section of the song—the headache has not yet gone away. When Wolf returns to a variant of the beginning in measures 23–26, the familiar neighboring pitches G♭ and F are given their most dramatic configuration in the vocal line at the words "Ja kein Märchen, daß zu Berg dir stehn die Härchen), filled with leaps of a seventh, ninth, and octave, to heighten comically the reference to hair standing on end in terror.

With the invocations of God and St. Christopher, the tonal magic begins to work. Wolf first announces the incipient success of Preciosa's charm by breaking the hold of the nonlegato eighth-notes in measure 27 and arriving, at long last, at a tonic first-inversion chord on the first beat of the measure. The singer chants "Da sei Gott davor" on a repeated D♮, multiply doubled in the piano, to announce the advent of major mode, and the "naive" parallel fifths that appear at this point are familiar Wolfian indices of folklike or popular reference. The repetition of these last two lines of text—"Da sei Gott davor / und der Riese Christophor!"—is atypical for Wolf but apropos for a charm, a litanylike reinforcement of the final words to assure the efficacy of homespun enchantment. Also apropos for the prayer at poem's end is the emphasis on the subdominant in measures 30–31, the fermata in measure 30 yet another delay of tonic resolution. When the invocation of God and St. Christopher is repeated in measures 31–34, Wolf recasts the initial vocal phrase within the context of a B♭ cadential passage, establishing G♮ as the upper neighbor to F, leaping to F from B♭ in the vocal line at the beginning of measure 31 and thus reversing the descending fifth intervals from earlier. The end of the texted body of the song fills in that same perfect fifth with scalewise motion, a transposition and variation of the surcease promised in measures 9–11 ("heilsam aus Geduld gezimmert"). With the postlude, all is diatonic peace and resolution, the doubled thirds of measures 12–22 now in descending motion and the horn-call figures of measure 35 a charming Teutonic filip to the tonic closure. Here, the tapping of the nonlegato F♮s reappears but without the grating dissonances—the charm has worked more quickly than any ordinary panacea, the miraculous healing agent transmuted into music.

THE SPANISH SONGBOOK SETTINGS OF
LEOPOLD DAMROSCH

One of the members of the Weimar circle in the late 1850s, like Cornelius an associate of Liszt and Wagner (if not so close), was Leopold Damrosch (1832–85), whose works include eleven songs to texts from the *Spanisches Liederbuch*. Damrosch, whose grandson Walter was a force in the American labor movement, was born in Posen and trained, at his father's insistence, as a physician. Against his family's wishes, he became a professional musician and in 1855 procured through Liszt the position of solo violinist in the Grand Ducal Orchestra at Weimar. From there, he moved to Breslau in 1858–59 to conduct the Breslau Philharmonic concerts, organize an orchestral society, conduct the Breslau opera orchestra, and organize tours with Hans von Bülow and Carl Tausig. In 1871, he accepted the position of conductor of the Arion Society in New York City; his interest in the modern German school had aroused opposition in Breslau, and he was eager to find a better context for his organizational capacities. In New York, he founded the Symphony Society and the Oratorio Society, conducted the New York Philharmonic during the season of 1876–77, and became in 1884 the director of German opera at the Metropolitan. He died after a brief illness in 1885.

The fifty-eight lieder by Leopold Damrosch[64] mirror the poetic tastes of many song composers in the third quarter of the nineteenth century; Wolf as a young man was to echo those tastes. They are all early works (opp. 5–8, 10, 11, 13, 14, 16, 17, and three without opus number) belonging to the Weimar and Breslau years and include seven Lenau songs, two to texts by Rückert, the five Goethe songs of op. 17, twelve Heine songs, two Uhland texts, and a scattering of one or two texts apiece by other poets (Klaus Groth, Hermann Lingg, Peter Cornelius, Robert Reinick). Like many of the song composers identified with the New German school and with Wagner's influence, Damrosch received his share of outraged barbs in the press, one critic accusing him of "high-flying intentions, consumptive sentimentality, behind which lurk only ineptitude and abnormality, barbaric treatment of the voice and a love for absurd harmonies."[65] Others thought more highly of his abilities: Kretzschmar in 1881 praises him as having a particular gift for seductive, merry, and roguish themes in poetry and for his distinctive musical compound of grace and refinement.[66]

After Heine's *Buch der Lieder*, the *Spanisches Liederbuch* was Damrosch's second most favored choice of poetry for lieder. The ten songs of op. 11 are a miniature compendium of the most popular texts from the Geibel-Heyse anthology, including two different settings of "Bedeckt mich mit Blumen," "Dereinst, dereinst, o Gedanken mein," "Nelken wind' ich und Jasmin," "Wann erscheint der Morgen?" ("When will morning come?" set by Schumann as the dramatic lied "Melancholie," or "Melancholy"), "Unter den Bäumen" (Beneath the Trees), "Am Manzanares" (At the Manzanares River), "Unter dem Schatten" (Under the shadows), and "Von dem Rosenbusch, o Mutter." Another of the Geibel-Heyse Spanish poems, "Wer da lebt in Liebesqual" (Whoever lives in love's torment) was published in op. 14 as one of the *Three Songs "im Volkston" by Various Authors*. The single text in Damrosch's op. 11 not selected by other composers was "Geh', Geliebter, geh' jetzt!" (Go, beloved, go now!), which Wolf would later choose to be the final work, the culmination of his *Spanisches Liederbuch*.

The text is a folk variant of a theme from troubadour verse, the *alba*, in which an adulterous lover bids the beloved depart at dawn. Concern for reputation and the beloved's safety is at war with reluctance to allow the object of such passionate love out of sight, and the singer makes of the repeated injunctions to go repeated declarations of love that actually impede departure. The passion of the poetic rhetoric, with its imagery of morning raising its white wings and the pearls of dew and tears, its paradox of dawn light creating darkness and anguish for the poetic speaker, makes this perhaps the most dramatic expression of tormented love in the anthology. Both Damrosch and Wolf excised the third stanza, with its coarse image of the beloved "striking roots in the lover's breast," its brand of physicality a diminishment of the reader's or listener's sensibilities. Wolf, who strove for "truth to the point of terror" as an aesthetic imperative and who with Melanie Köchert lived the drama of "Geh', Geliebter" (Eric Sams suggests that Wolf would have responded to this poem with the empathic involvement born of experience[67]), would not have found explicitness per se offensive, but he knew bad taste when he saw it and must have recognized that the passion set forth in this poem was actually interrupted by the semantic photography of the third stanza.

> Geh', Geliebter, geh' jetzt!
> Sieh, der Morgen dämmert.
>
> Leute gehn schon durch die Gasse,
> Und der Markt wird so belebt,
> Daß der Morgen wohl, der blasse,
> Schon die weißen Flügel hebt.
> Und vor unsern Nachbarn bin ich
> Bange, daß du Anstoß giebst;
> Denn sie wissen nicht, wie innig
> Ich dich lieb' und du mich liebst.
>
> Drum, Geliebter, geh' jetzt!
> Sieh, der Morgen dämmert.

Wenn die Sonn' am Himmel scheinend
Scheucht vom Feld die Perlen klar,
Muß auch ich die Perle weinend
Lassen, die mein Reichthum war.
Was als Tag den Andern funkelt,
Meinen Augen dünkt es Nacht,
Da die Trennung bang mir dunkelt,
Wenn das Morgenroth erwacht.

Geh', Geliebter, geh' jetzt!
Sieh, der Morgen dämmert.

. . . .[68]

Fliehe denn aus meinen Armen!
Denn versäumest du die Zeit,
Möchten für ein kurz Erwarmen
Wir ertauschen langes Leid.
Ist in Fegefeuersqualen
Doch ein Tag schon auszustehn,
Wenn die Hoffnung fern in Strahlen
Läßt des Himmels Glorie sehn.

D'rum, Geliebter, geh' jetzt!
Sieh, der Morgen dämmert.[69]

(Go, beloved, go now! See, the day is dawning. Already people are going through the streets, and the market is becoming so lively that the pale daylight is already spreading its white wings. And I am afraid that you will scandalize our neighbors, for they do not know how deeply I love you and you love me. Therefore, beloved, go now; see, the day is dawning. When the sun shining in the sky chases the pearls of dew from the fields, I must also leave the pearls of tears which were my riches. What shines as day to others, my eyes consider night, for parting darkens my being with sorrow, when the red of morning awakes. Go, beloved, go now! See, the day is dawning. . . . Fly then from my arms! For if you are heedless of the time, we may exchange an eon of sorrow for a brief warmth. In the torments of purgatory, the day will yet arise when from afar, hope will let heaven's glory be seen in radiance. Therefore, beloved, go now! See, the day is dawning.)

As usual, Geibel takes pains to preserve the syllable count and rhyme, although his translation is more regularized and symmetrical than the original, and converts the Spanish idioms into German locutions. Where the unknown Spanish poet says simply "y pues passa tanta gente" in the first stanza, with no reference to a marketplace, Geibel writes the more vivid "Und der Markt wird so belebt." Leaving out the prosaic expression "sin duda" (without a doubt) from the third and fourth lines of that same stanza ("sin duda que la mañana / ya sus alas blancas tiende"), Geibel uses poeticizing inverted syntax to emphasize the white light, the pallor, of the dawn sky (that truly morning, the pale one, already raises her white wings). In the Spanish source, the first four lines of the last stanza are part of the same "sentence," the lover saying, "Flee my sweet embraces, for if you remain clasped in my arms, the [resulting] sorrow could last longer than this brief happiness" ("Dexa los dulces abraços, / que si entre ellos te entretienes, / vn mal nos podra dar largo / aqueste contento breue"). Geibel makes of the first line an exclamation in the imperative and then paraphrases the subsequent three lines such that the "kurz Erwarmen" is linked to the "Fegefeuersqualen" two lines later, and the reference to "die Zeit" in the second line foreshadows the end of the stanza—the future tense and afterlife of the passion expressed so emphatically in the present. It is unclear whether the invocation of purgatory and heaven at the end refers to the Christian afterlife, signifies a hoped-for metamorphosis of illicit passion into licit love, or both.

Either Damrosch or his editors changed the text of the ending in order to expunge the references to purgatory and heaven. By removing the cosmic backdrop altogether and reducing the lovers' torment to the smaller matter of enduring a day's wait before their next rendezvous, Damrosch diminishes the temperature and tone of this adulterous passion considerably.

> Eh' den hellen Sonnenstrahlen
> wir vertrauen unbedacht,
> lass der Trennung Sehnsuchtsqualen
> uns erdulden bis zur Nacht.

(Before we trust the sun's bright rays thoughtlessly, let us endure our parting and the pains of longing until nightfall.)

The music is cooler by far than Wolf's. Damrosch set the text as a strict strophic form in a style palely reminiscent of Brahms. The horn-call figure in the piano at the end of the refrain (measure 8), the first cadence to tonic completed in the piano after the voice fails to do so, is one such Brahmsian touch, attractively deployed here. It is left to the piano to extend sequentially the dotted descending motive in the voice and complete the cadence—the singer does not want the night of passion to end, does not want to admit that now that dawn is visible, its completion in day cannot be far behind. In a similar nuance of text interpretation near the end of the song, Damrosch prolongs the adjective "*kurz* Erwarmen" in what would be a contradiction of the words were it not for the singer's desire to prolong the rendezvous (Example 31). The lied is also Brahmsian in its prosody, bent to the abstract melodic design and the

Example 31. Leopold Damrosch, "Geh', Geliebter, geh' jetzt!" Op. 11, no. 6,
measures 1–17

strophic form. Damrosch is somewhat scrupulous about prosodic details in the
refrain, prolonging the second syllable of "Ge-*lieb*-ter" after the first-beat emphasis on the imperative "Geh'" and setting the weaker concluding syllable of
"däm-*mert*" on the second beat. But thereafter, despite such details as the
individual accents on each note of the triplet melisma for the normally unac-
cented connective "und" ("wie innig ich dich lieb' *und* du mich liebst") in

Example 31, continued

Markt   wird so be - lebt,   dass der Mor   -   gen wohl, der
Feld   die Per - len klar,   muss auch ich   die Per - le

15

blas - se   schon die wei - ssen Flü - gel hebt.
wei - nend   las - sen, die mein Reich - thum war.

measure 26, a bit of heavy-handed text interpretation, the prosody takes a
back seat to purely musical aspects of design.

Much else recalls Brahms as well. In Damrosch's musical reading of this
poem, a mood of melancholy yearning takes precedence over passion, with
the exception of one outburst at the peak of each strophe. That fortissimo and
con fuoco outburst (measures 23–28, at the words "denn sie wissen nicht, wie
innig ich dich lieb' und du mich liebst" in the first stanza) is set in the major
mode with incongruously Hispanic fandango chords in the bass, the chord
doublings at their fullest and most Brahmsian. There is no other attempt to
evoke a Spanish atmosphere, and the thinner textures, minor mode, and
poignant sadness of the refrain are soon reasserted. But Damrosch was not an
unskilled composer, and the song has its attractive features, even if there is no
impression of an original style. The rhythmic fluctuations of the unharmonized line in the bass at the beginning of the song, with its pitches accented
on the second and third beats of the measures in $\frac{3}{4}$, and the symmetrical construction of the introduction are notable. The emphasis on the semitone motive formed by the upper neighbor to the dominant pitch at the start, A–G♯,
and then succeeded by the prolongation of the lower neighbor, F✗–G♯, the
transpositions and rhythmic variations of the intervallic third motive both in

the vocal line and the accompaniment do not constitute any challenge to Wolf's setting, but are not unpleasing in their pallid melancholy. The strophes were clearly composed with the first stanza of text in mind, and the first stirrings of morning activity in the marketplace find their unfevered musical analogues in mild chromaticism—Damrosch never actually leaves C♯ minor—and the avoidance of first-beat stresses in the Brahmsian broken-chordal figuration in the piano. At the end, Damrosch has the singer accede to necessity and bid the beloved leave without further passionate continuation and delay, only an instrumental cadence marked by the Brahmsian hypermeasure as a built-in ritardando at the end. In the fermatas that prolong the closing tonic chord and the singer's silence, the beloved can presumably take his reluctant leave at last.

Wolf's setting is another matter altogether, its passion hotter and more complex.[70] The confused critic who in 1889 designated Hugo Wolf and Leopold Damrosch as the sole adherents of the "Wagnerian School"[71] in order to deny the existence of any such school was pairing a lion with a lamb, so dissimilar are the two composers. It is easy to sympathize with Wolf's feeling that, having composed such songs as "Geh', Geliebter," he was destined to compose opera—although the breadth of even the longest song is differently constituted from the command of lengthy stretches in opera. This masterpiece, composed 1 April 1890, is a fitting culmination to the *Spanisches Liederbuch* and must be counted among Wolf's best creations. Even the choice of a relatively rare and rich tonality (F♯ major) can be heard as analogous to a privileged realm of passion, especially since the major mode is permeated by the frequent lowered third, sixth, and second scale degrees of the parallel minor mode. In retrospect and in knowledge of the words that follow, the piano introduction in measures 1–3 seems virtually pictorial. The pull of the repeated rising semitone figure in the right-hand part against the ascending chromatic line in the inner voice and the dominant pedal in measures 1–2 suggests someone attempting to pull away but not getting very far, not wanting to go any farther away. The off-beat placement of the semitone figure elided with the typically Wolfian way of weakening downbeats in the left hand comes close to a musical reenactment of reluctant, unsuccessful parting. The low F♯ pedal throughout five measures of the refrain (measures 3–7) countermands the plea "Geh' jetzt" by remaining fixed in place, as do the lovers, while the vocal line and the right hand melody converge, diverge, intertwine around one another in a contrapuntal mimicry of lovers' meeting. The double sense in which "Geh'" means both "go" and "do not leave me" is evident at the beginning, before the singer further binds the lover to her with multiple reasons for leaving. Every detail of the refrain reflects the emotional mélange of anxiety, passion, fear, and love in the text, for example, the unsettled manner of the singer's initial entrance in measure 4, the singer leaping into the midpoint of a two-bar phrase already in progress in the piano—yet another example of Wolf's frequent distinction between the voice and the piano as two musical personas. The lowered sixth degree in the voice against the prolongation of the dominant pitch in the piano and the avoidance of the tonic pitch in the vocal line throughout the refrain speak volumes about the poetic persona's lack of repose. The upward inflection of the words "geh' jetzt!" in measure 5 is varied in measures 6–7, the same figure widened and its pitches shifted about to produce the expressive plunge downward of a minor ninth, then a rise upward in alarm at the verb "dämmert." Damrosch, his declamation less refined than Wolf's, does not separate the verbs in the imperative, "Geh'" and "Sieh'," from the remainder of the phrase by an eighth-rest evocative of breathless urgency, of gasping (one notices as well that the initial and more important verb, "go," occurs on the strong first beat, the weaker imperative "Sieh'" on the third beat in $\frac{9}{8}$), but Wolf does. Notably, the first two occurrences of Wolf's refrain are self-contained and end with a colorful cadence in the piano; the deeper notes of alarm dissipate, the tessitura rises upward, and the dissonances become bell-like raised fourths against the open fifth F♯–C♯ in the treble. Only with the third statement of the refrain are both passion and panic so heated as to deny the "dying-away" closure and meld the refrain to the subsequent strophe; only at the end of the entire song does the expanded refrain achieve closure in the low bass register of measure 3 and with tonic in the soprano voice. Until then, the injunctions to leave die away in the piano, the words belied and left behind.

Between each invocation of the refrain, Wolf varies its motifs. (A contemporaneous music critic named Richard Batka would defend Wolf soon thereafter against the anti-Wagnerite charge that his songs represented the so-called symphonic principle, according to which almost everything of interest happens in the instrumental part. "Geh', Geliebter" might well have been one of the lieder thus designated because of the development of a small cluster of figures throughout an almost incessant piano part of near-orchestral richness.[72]) The F♯ pedal in measures 12–14 is rhythmically activated, no longer a sustained tone, and leads in measure 16 to an unstable E major at the words "Morgen, der blasse" in anticipation of that same tonality much more strongly stated and developed in the second strophe. In the last half of the first strophe (measures 20–27), Wolf develops the dominant pedal of the piano introduction, stating it outright in measures 20–21 to the words "Und vor unsern Nachbarn bin ich bange"—explanation in retrospect of the unspoken thought underlying measures 1–2 that has led the singer to the exclamation "Go, beloved, go now!" In the second strophe, the reality of impending day, already tentatively identified as an E tonal realm other than the F♯-major dawn milieu, is the main preoccupation ("Wenn die Sonn' . . . Was als Tag"), the same obsessive scalar patterns and motifs that circle within the span of a third developed anew. The strophe is structured at the beginning as a dominant pedal of E (measures 37–40), followed by a deflection in measures 41–44 to V/relative minor, or C♯ minor, the minor mode and the larger-scale sighing figure A–G♯ in the bass illustrative of the weeping at that point in the text ("muß' auch ich die Perle weinend lassen"). The sudden shift at the word "Nacht"—the Tristanesque Night of Day without the beloved—in measure 48 ushers in a rapid and progressive tonal darkening to B♭ minor, the enharmonic mediant of tonic F♯ major; the same progression from an E-major sixth chord to B♭ minor, and thence back to tonic F♯ major, that one first hears in measures 45–53 recurs in the third strophe at measures 71–79, emblematic of a distant hope for the rays of heaven. (In measure 65, Wolf, like Damrosch, prolongs "*kurz* Erwarmen" in seeming contradiction of the phrase, the singer holding on to the "brief warmth" as long as she can.) With this transmutation of "Trennung bang" into "Hoffnung fern in Strahlen," the lover can at last bear to relinquish the beloved in another of Wolf's "verklingend" postludes, one in which the D♮s of measures 1–2 appear for the last time within the context of an extended tonic harmony. It is typical of Wolf's vivid imagination that the scene continues after the sound stops, in a protracted measure of silence: one imagines the singer listening intently for any last traces of the beloved's footsteps.

BRAHMS, WOLF, AND LOPE DE VEGA

Wolf's only great contemporary who also set texts from the *Spanisches Liederbuch* was Brahms, who came to know Geibel's poetry early. As a young man, he kept a notebook called "Young Kreisler's Thesaurus" in which he wrote down quotations from literary works he had read and particularly enjoyed, including a quatrain from an original poem by Geibel.[73] Brahms must have discovered the Geibel-Heyse anthology either immediately upon its publication or very shortly thereafter, as his setting of "In dem Schatten meiner Locken," op. 6, no. 1 was published in 1853. It would seem to be the only one from a larger mass of early Geibel songs that Brahms at the time judged worthy of publication.[74] Wolf's antipathy to the older master was such as must originate in admiration turned sour, and did; before an unpleasant encounter with Brahms in early 1879, Wolf showed considerable independence of thought for an avowed Wagnerite in his respect for both Wagner and Brahms. When the nineteen-year-old Wolf brought his manuscripts to Brahms for evaluation, the older composer was not impressed, telling Wolf, "You must first learn something, and then we shall see whether you have talent." He recommended that Wolf study counterpoint with the pedantic and tyrannical Gustav Nottebohm; it was probably fortunate that Wolf could not afford the lessons. Brahms's biographer Max Kalbeck bruited about a version of the incident biased by his animosity toward Wolf, although he later apologized after Wolf's death.[75] It was an episode with a long and acrimonious afterlife, exacerbated by Wolf himself, who seldom missed a chance to condemn Brahms's works as consummate exercises in boredom. And yet he praised the Quintet in F, op. 88 ("a delightful, open, sunny meadow") and even one of Brahms's lieder, "Von ewiger Liebe"[76] (On eternal love), after the unpleasant episode in 1879. His "anti-Brahmimentum," the cause of occasional sharp disagreements with friends and supporters,[77] could crack at times, but only rarely.

Brahms and Wolf represent two opposing attitudes toward song composition, for all that both men retain the traditional boundaries, the forms, even some of the literary repertoire of Schubert's lieder and all the anxiety of influence that was Schubert's legacy to later song composers.[78] (Brahms and his adherents apparently accused Wolf of a lack of respect for tradition, however. In his Brahms reminiscences, the Viennese critic and minor composer Richard Heuberger tells of an occasion in 1890 when he, Brahms, and Richter discussed the Wagnerites' claim that Wolf was the founder of the "symphonic lied" while Schubert, Schumann, and Brahms had only composed songs with "guitar accompaniments."[79]) Neither composer ever wrote down anything systematic on the subject, but their different approaches are evident in various disconnected comments over their lifetimes, especially from Brahms—since he was the more successful composer, there was more interest taken in his aesthetic stance, and in the songs themselves. The two men had differing tastes in literature as well as in music, and it is not often that Wolf set texts also composed by the older master; Mörike's "Agnes," Gottfried Keller's "Singt mein Schatz wie ein Fink" and "Du milchjunger Knabe," Goethe's "Phänomen," and "In dem Schatten meiner Locken," and "Die ihr schwebet um diese Palmen" (Ye who hover around these palm trees) from the *Spanisches Liederbuch* are the only instances of duplication between their lieder repertoires. We know in Wolf's own words what he most disliked in Brahms's songs from a technical stance, aside from the personal grudge whose flames Wolf so persistently fanned. In 1890, Wolf once played two of Brahms's Keller songs for a friend in order to deride the older composer's song style. When he recounted the incident in a letter to Melanie Köchert, he described Brahms as a "master of the bagpipes and concertina," yodeling along "in his well-known noble folk manner,"[80] and singles out Brahms's declamation for particular scorn. Wolf does not, to my knowledge, mention Brahms's "Geistliches Wiegenlied" (Sacred lullaby), op. 91, no. 2 for contralto, viola, and piano in the extant correspondence or reminiscences by his friends, but it seems probable that he would have known the work, as the two men were edgily aware of each other's activities.

To the pianist Louise Japha (one of the dedicatees of the six songs of op. 6), Brahms reportedly said, "When I read a poem, I read it once through very slowly and clearly, and then I usually already have the melody in mind."[81] Poetry thus becomes an occasion for melodic inspiration, to be followed by what was for him the more important task of musical elaboration.[82] Even where Brahms seems most concerned with overt correspondence of some sort between the poetry and the music, as in the beautiful Goethe lied "Dämmrung senkte sich von oben" (Twilight descends from above) or "Feldeinsamkeit" (Meadow loneliness), the prosody is often mangled in the service of rhythmic-melodic developments owing nothing to speech pattern—text as manipulable sound-material.[83] Brahms at times seems especially engaged by one or two striking details of the text, for which he finds a precise musical gesture: he sets the deluded maiden's assertion "Unsere Liebe ist *fester* noch mehr" (Our love is even stronger) to a notably weak chromatic harmony in "Von ewiger Liebe" (this is the only Brahms song that Wolf singles out for praise). But a clustering of many such nuances in company with refined declamation is not his wont. Brahms was aware of criticisms regarding his prosody and, in old age, waxed sarcastic in his own defense, notably when Richard Heuberger brought up the subject of Wolf's lieder. "When one doesn't trouble oneself about the music, then it is very easy to declaim the poem properly."[84] Brahms could occasionally bite back at his articulate and dogged foe, although in general he avoided ad hominem ripostes. He had evidently debated the properties of lied and the relationship of text to music with his friend Theodor Billroth, who wrote the composer a letter in 1882 with the following observation:

> Every musical work which deserves to have the name or be regarded as a work of art must have a certain form, so that one could almost translate it into the terms of architecture. This is as much so of music which is composed to suit words as it is for a free composition. One should not compose for poetry, which if poured into the form of a musical mold is destroyed. The words and thoughts in poetry should only in a general way influence the musical form. This last always remains the main thing.[85]

No wonder Brahms and Wolf irritated one another so much. Wolf recognized that music imposes a foreign (nonverbal) structure on texts, that poetic form is destroyed in music, but if ever anyone "composed for poetry," he did.

"Die ihr schwebet" is one of the most artful poems in the Geibel-Heyse anthology, an interpolated song-lullaby from the pastoral novel *Los pastores de Belén* (The shepherds of Bethlehem; 1612) by the great playwright Lope Félix de Vega Carpio (1562–1635).

Pues andais en las palmas,	Die ihr schwebet
Angeles santos,	Um diese Palmen
que se duerme mi niño,	In Nacht und Wind,
tened los ramos.	Ihr heil'gen Engel,
	Stillet die Wipfel!
	Es schlummert mein Kind.
Palmas de Belen,	Ihr Palmen von Bethlehem
que mueven airados	Im Windesbrausen,

los furiosos vientos	Wie mögt ihr heute
que suenan tanto,	So zornig sausen!
no le hagais ruido,	O rauscht nicht also
corred mas paso:	Schweiget, neiget
que se duerme mi niño,	Euch leis' und lind;
tened los ramos.	Stillet die Wipfel!
	Es schlummert mein Kind.
El niño divino	Der Himmelsknabe
que está cansado	Duldet Beschwerde,
de llorar en la tierra,	Ach, wie so müd' er ward
por su descanco	Vom Leid der Erde.
sosegar quiere un poco	Ach nun im Schlaf ihm
del tierno llanto:	Leise gesänftigt
que se duerme mi niño,	Die Qual zerrinnt,
tened los ramos.	Stillet die Wipfel!
	Es schlummert mein Kind.
Rigurosos hielos	Grimmige Kälte
le estan cercando,	Sauset hernieder,
ya veis que no tengo	Womit nur deck' ich
con que guardarlo:	Des Kindleins Glieder!
Angeles divinos	O all ihr Engel,
que vais volando,	Die ihr geflügelt
que se duerme mi niño,	Wandelt im Wind,
tened los ramos.[86]	Stillet die Wipfel!
	Es schlummert mein Kind.

(Ye who hover around these palm trees in the night and wind, you holy angels, silence the treetops! My child is sleeping. You palms of Bethlehem rustling in the wind, why must you bluster so angrily today? O do not rustle so loudly! Be quiet, bow your heads softly and gently; silence the treetops! My child is sleeping. The heavenly boy suffers heavy burdens: ah, how tired he is from the sorrow of the world! Ah, now he is softly soothed in sleep, his torment vanished . . . silence the treetops! My child is sleeping. Cruel cold winds blow down: with what can I cover his infant limbs? O all you angels who travel winged in the wind, silence the treetops! My child is sleeping.)

The translation abounds in Geibel's characteristic refinements, including the addition of the line "In Nacht und Wind" (In the night and wind) to the initial refrain-stanza—in Lope de Vega's poem, the reader is not told of the nocturnal tempest until the second verse. The translation of "Angeles divinos / que vais volando" as "O all ihr Engel / die ihr geflügelt / Wandelt im Wind" is typical of this translator in the alliteration, the doubled *v*'s of the Spanish "vais volando" becoming the German "wandelt im wind," and the added emphasis of "*all ihr* Engel." Rather than his customary metrical consistency, Geibel allows fluctuations from the basic five-syllable line, changing poetic meters that reflect at a structural level the swaying of the palm branches in the wind. The contrast in the refrain between the dactyl-and-trochee of the command "Stillet die Wipfel!" and the iamb-anapest pair of "Es schlummert mein Kind" is only one such example, nicely illustrative of the way in which poetic rhythm and meaning fuse. The imperative "Stillet" receives first-beat stresses, heightened even more by the "*s[ch]t*" consonant compound at the beginning of the line, followed by the gentler pairing of an iamb and a lilting anapest. And Geibel is, as usual, more emphatic than the original; Lope de Vega's "corred mas paso," for example, becomes the alliterative "Schweiget, neiget / Euch leis' und lind."

Brahms first set what later became the "Geistliches Wiegenlied," op. 91, no. 2 in 1863 as a gift for the recently married Joseph Joachim and his wife, the contralto Amalie Schneeweiss; Brahms stood as godfather later that same year to the couple's firstborn son, named Joseph. "In due course I shall send you a wonderful old Catholic song for singing at home; you will never discover a more beautiful lullaby," Brahms wrote his friend on 13 April 1863.[87] The "beautiful lullaby" was indeed old, going back at least to the sixteenth century and possibly earlier: "Joseph, lieber Joseph mein" is included in Johann Walther's *Wittembergisch Deudsch Geistlich Gesangbüchlein* of 1545 as a setting for the Christmas poem "Resonet in laudibus" and appears in many hymnals and motet collections thereafter.[88] Eric Sams points out that the melody would have been especially appropriate as a gift for the son of Joseph, baptized through Johannes, born to a mother whose name ("snow-white") evoked purity and who sang beautifully,[89] but Brahms was dissatisfied with his musical gift and withdrew it. Over twenty years later in 1885, he composed the second version for contralto, piano, and viola obbligato when Joachim and his wife were about to dissolve their marriage in the vain hope that music written for the two to perform together would be a means of reconciliation. His musical mission as marriage counselor came to nought, but the music itself, fortunately, remains.

Geibel's translation inspired Brahms to remember a preexistent lullaby melody and to compose polyphonic elaborations on the old tune, a conception entirely foreign to Wolf's compositional processes. Brahms recasts the melody in $\frac{6}{8}$ meter and devises contrapuntal variations on and around it. The onomatopoeic elements of the Geibel translation, such as the tempestuous motion of the branches and the cold night winds, are mitigated, gentled to little more than the diminished-seventh and half-diminished-seventh chords at the words "in Nacht und Wind" in measures 19–20 and the A-minor variations of the F-major lullaby at the words "Ihr Palmen von Bethlehem in Windesbrausen" and again at "Grimmige Kälte." Brahms translates the rocking of the cradle—

a more generalized image because it is pure motion rather than depictive in visual or auditory terms—into a bass line filled with constant rocking figures in two- and one-bar slurred phrases. Where the cold winds blow and the palm trees rustle in the A-minor episodes, the more active motion is transferred to the right-hand part and the viola. The triadic outlines of the old tune, the neighbor-note relationship of the fifth and sixth scale degrees, and the lengthening of a scalewise descending third until it spans a ninth in the refrain are among the basic elements derived from the antique lullaby. In Brahms's form, successive variations in F major and A minor–F major flank a brief central section in parallel minor mode at the words "Der Himmelsknabe duldet Beschwerde," the point of greatest rhythmic, motivic, and chromatic intensity in the song.

Wolf's setting is very different indeed, but first a word or two about the seeming discrepancy of a Nietzschean anticleric composing religious songs is in order. His mother was devout, and he was brought up to attend mass and observe Catholic practices, but he had lost his faith by the early 1880s and possibly sooner. It might appear odd that the Mörike-Lieder include songs on religious subjects and that he would begin the *Spanisches Liederbuch* with settings of ten religious poems, but lack of a professed creed does not preclude participation in the common human longing for the spiritual dimension of existence. Wolf did not hide from his mother his dissatisfaction with formalized Christianity and the hypocrisy of some of its adherents, despite her conventional religious beliefs. In a revealing letter written 29 April 1892 on the occasion of her name day, Wolf characterizes himself as an "unbeliever" (the words "believers," "unbeliever," and "name day" are placed in inverted quotation marks throughout the letter) and questions whether the institution of a name day has any validity amid the general irreligiosity of modern Christian civilization. "Who still thinks nowadays of saints? Who believes in them?" So-called pious folk gabble their Our Fathers and rosaries meaninglessly, like the ABCs recited by the smallest schoolchildren, he tells her, and twice states his own Nietzschean belief in godliness as the highest manifestation of pure humanity. "As a tree sinks its roots deep into the earth, the more strongly to reach into the heights, so too must the living word, the presentiment of godliness at the innermost core of human being, take root. Thus is the biblical proverb, 'By their fruits ye shall know them,' verified."[90] The intensity of Wolf's feelings in the matter are apparent in his adoption of Biblical imagery and rhetoric for the credo he sets forth in this letter. If he was not a "believer" in the prescriptions and proscriptions of Austrian Catholicism, he was spiritual in a nonformalistic sense—witness his settings of Mörike's religious poems. Mörike, although a Protestant pastor, was hardly a dogmatic believer himself, and the composer's awareness of a spirituality that strikes deeper than surface observance might have influenced his musical response to such works as "Schlafendes Jesuskind" (Sleeping Christ-child) and "Auf ein altes Bild"[91] (On an old painting). Great artists can and do empathize with conditions not their own, but between the lapsed Catholic composer and the Spanish sinners of the Geibel-Heyse anthology runs a common spiritual current beyond the realm of rituals and dogma.

Wolf was not a musical antiquarian and lacked Brahms's interest in German folk melodies and music in stile antico, nor would Wolf have made Geibel's poetry conform to a melodic design not inspired by those words. Where Brahms banishes the nocturnal winds and rustling branches by means of a lullaby, with only the single intrusion of a muted *minore* storm episode, Wolf read the poem with more attention to the mise-en-scène.[92] In this portrayal of maternal solicitude, the Virgin must repeat her pleas to the angels overhead, to the palm trees themselves, because the winds and the rustling noises continue unchecked throughout the song. The onomatopoeic sixteenth-note figuration in the right hand and the repetitions, transpositions, and extensions of the recurring melodic motive in the left hand never cease until the end of the piano postlude. Not until then is the Virgin's pleading finally answered and the instrumental sounds of Nature stilled. In the body of the song, the storm winds and rustling branches become gentler with the invocations of the refrain "Es schlummert mein Kind," the left-hand figure lifted into the treble register, but the constant accompanimental figuration still continues. The singer is therefore forced, in Wolf's invention, to accord much of her plea with the nocturnal winds depicted in the accompaniment, with the rising motion of the left hand-figure. Where the singer's melody is insistently dissonant with the bass, as in the repeated major seventh G–F♯ between the outer voices in measures 14–15, the pitch conflict is a register both of inclement Nature and of the imperative mode, the singer calling out to the palm trees with raised voice.

The sloughing, sighing figure in the piano is repeated largely unchanged but for the numerous transpositions. The motive is essentially a prolongation of a single harmony but with passing tones and neighboring note motion—translating the verb "to sway" into harmonic terms—that emphasize the flatted sixth and raised fourth degrees. Wolf states the one-bar figure twice (hovering?) and then extends the figure to the leading tone as indicated in the key signature, but not for the purpose of bringing D♯ within the E-major fold; rather, D♯ becomes the fifth of the mediant G♯ major, the beginning of a chain of third-related transpositions throughout much of the song. The initial chain of thirds I–III–flatted VI moves upward by intervals of a major third/diminished fourth E–G♯–C and then moves downward a semitone to dominant minor, thereafter to rise by intervals of a minor third B–D–F♯ major. In measure 25, Wolf uses the second measure of the extended two-bar motive to effect another D♯/E♭ change at the words "neiget euch leis' und lind": the A♭ spelling of the earlier G♯ major, this the only flat key area in the entire song, is the tonal analogue to "bowing softly and gently."

At measure 34 and the words "Der Himmelsknabe duldet Beschwerde," Wolf begins a varied repetition from the beginning, one in which the vocal line above the literal recurrence of measures 2–11 in the piano is altered for declamatory and interpretive reasons. In Wolf's reading, the Virgin, realizing that her pleas have not had the desired effect, begins over again but this time to more powerful words telling of her child's need for undisturbed slumber. The phrase lengths are different in measures 34–39, necessitated by the differing syntax of the later stanza; the rest after the words "Die ihr schwebet" in measure 2 is no longer applicable anywhere within the poetic phrase "Der Himmelsknabe duldet Beschwerde" (Brahms, less scrupulous about musical prose, sets that same line with a break between "Der Himmelsknabe" and "duldet Beschwerde"). The verb "duldet" is given a pleading emphasis as the apex of the phrase, and the words "müd' er ward" are chanted on the same D♯—emphasis of another kind. Because the text is longer than the initial strophe, Wolf extends the previous repetitions of the motive on C by means of the dominant of C, the G harmonies then becoming the common-tone vehicle for the motion to B minor and the source for the vocal phrase in measures 50–52 G F♯ B. Instead of the previous chain of thirds upward, from B to D to F♯, Wolf reverses direction in a chain of thirds descending to tonic (B–G♯–E). The turn to tonic E major only happens with the last statement of the words "es schlummert mein Kind," and it requires the piano to reestablish tonic firmly in the postlude. The instrumental acquiescence to the singer's wishes is indicated in the increasingly softer dynamics and in the transpositions downward by thirds to the register of the beginning and the ultimate cessation of motion. Wolf thus divides the text into almost exactly symmetrical halves, the second a variation of the first and the entire song shot through with transpositions of a single motive, onomatopoeia for rising (and motivically unchanged, a force of Nature not subject to alteration) gusts of wind.

WHEN Wolf completed the composition of "Nun wandre, Maria" (Now journey on, Mary) on 5 November 1889, he wrote to his friend and fellow composer Friedrich Eckstein, saying, "If you wish to experience this event [the flight into Egypt], then you must hear my music,"[93] and he told his brother-in-law Josef Strasser five months later that what he now wrote was for posterity. "These are masterworks," he told his relative.[94] Wolf was always given to hyperbolic exuberance when he was in full compositional flood tide, but songs such as "Nun wandre, Maria," "Herr, was trägt der Boden hier" (Lord, what does the ground bear here), and "Geh', Geliebter, geh' jetzt" bear him out. *His* Spanish songs have endured, while those by his lesser contemporaries have largely vanished. The works themselves are sufficient testimony, but the proud measure of worth evident in his letters and statements to friends is borne out all the more strongly when one compares his settings to those of Taubert, Damrosch, Rubinstein, and Jensen, to those composers unable to establish a stance independent of their various masters, and even to Brahms.

Others by century's end recognized the singularity of his achievement as well. In his assessment "The German Lied Since the Death of Wagner," Hermann Kretzschmar reserves the last and most enthusiastic words for Wolf, whom he calls a "talent without end," possessed of "boundless imagination," a composer whose significance for the late nineteenth century would no doubt be comparable with that of Schubert earlier in the century—again, the inescapable comparison. The composers Kretzschmar deems worthy of inclusion in his survey of fin-de-siècle lieder run the gamut from Brahms, Richard Strauss, and Wolf to such forgotten names as Hermann Behn, Hans Hermann, Eugen d'Albert, and Philipp Graf zu Eulenburg. Even more than Brahms, whom Kretzschmar considered a dangerous influence on contemporary song composers, Wolf wins the palm for his craftsmanship and for his mastery of many different impersonations and mood. "He is an irresistible humorist," a "lively storyteller," a composer who can depict "an Alberich as aptly as a Philine and without the sentimentality that mars so many songs of the day." "This Wolf is a genius," he writes in conclusion; "in the days to come, the rays from his glory will illuminate the entire song composition of our times."[95] The date was 1898, and the elegaic cast of Kretzschmar's words comes from his awareness that Wolf's creative life was over, the pity of it all still fresh—but pity alone did not instigate words of such acute and accurate praise.

CHAPTER 5

Wolf and the Dream of Opera

OF ALL THE ghosts of great composers haunting Wolf, Wagner was the most powerful and the most oppressive, the "Obergott" or Lord above all. When he discovered Wagner at an impressionable age, Wolf, newly confirmed in his composer's vocation, feared that the weight of the Wagnerian opus might crush him before he could gather sufficient strength to resist. The encounter with the Klingsor of Bayreuth redoubled his determination to compose opera and yet made it impossible for him to do so for many years, until his brief creative life was almost over. With such a powerful gravitational field emanating from Wagner's operas, how could one break away from it? What could a composer possibly write for the stage, or indeed for any other musical arena, that would not bring Valkyries and Flower Maidens instantly to mind?

On 18 January 1895, Wolf wrote to Oskar Grohe with news his friend might well have given up hope of ever hearing: "A miracle, a miracle, an unbelievable miracle has happened—the long-sought opera text has finally been found. It lies ready in front of me and I am burning with desire to start with the musical composition."[1] The miracle was actually a rediscovery of a libretto he had rejected, and quite contemptuously, five years earlier. Even before that time, when he was composing the Mörike lieder, he had written to his brother-in-law Josef Strasser about his intention of using Pedro Antonio de Alarcón's short novel *El Sombrero de Tres Picos* (The three-cornered hat) as the source for an operatic text.[2] Friends, unbeknownst to Wolf, had approached the writer Rosa Obermayer-Mayreder in 1890 about an adaptation after the composer abandoned the attempt to write his own, and had sent it to him anonymously. At that time, he rejected her libretto as too banal, but after five years of an increasingly desperate search for a text and long periods of compositional drought, his reaction was entirely different. The first week of January 1895, Wolf was given another libretto based on *Der Dreispitz* (the title of the 1886 German translation by Hulda Meister[3]) by the chairman of the Vienna Wagner Society, an imperial court judge named Franz Schaumann. Wolf's friend Gustav Schur had proposed Schaumann as a collaborator because the judge had a gift for comic verse and had already written several opera texts, including an operetta for Richard Heuberger and drama entitled *Die Bürgerreuth* intended for Anton Bruckner.[4] Of the friends who read the Schaumann libretto, only Joseph Schalk liked it. Wolf did not, and that was decisive. Wolf then reread Mayreder's work and pronounced it "not at all bad . . . I can't imagine what I was thinking before."[5] After much rejoicing and discussion of a suitable title (Wolf at first rejected the title *Der Corregidor*[6]), he began composition on the evening of 12 March 1895, the night before his birthday, with the Night Watchman's song "Ave Maria purissima" at the start of Act IV. The Miller's drinking song in praise of Spanish wine in Act II, scene ii followed; Wolf thus began his compositional labors with two encapsulated lyrical moments from the interior of the opera, a fact significant to those who find the opera too replete with songlike moments and lacking in dramatic breadth. By April, Wolf was entirely immersed in the great endeavor of his only completed opera.[7]

It is hard to imagine anyone wanting anything as much as Hugo Wolf wanted to become an opera composer. His earliest projects include the unfinished heroic opera *König Alboin*; twenty years later, he was working on another opera, the tragedy *Manuel Venegas*, in 1897 when his reason left him. His letters are filled with exuberant plans for operatic adaptations from the realms of poetry, prose, and drama; imprecations against librettists and librettos; fears that he might remain forever confined to song composition; criticisms of operas by his contemporaries; and always, the quest for the elusive Grail—a text.[8] To be a descendant of Schubert was to inherit as well, sixty years later, the fear that song composers were somehow second-class citizens until they could successfully apply their word-tone craftsmanship to the larger arena of opera.

> I am beginning to think of an opera text as a fata morgana, as something truly impossible. "Wahn! Wahn! Überall Wahn!" ["Madness! Madness! Everywhere madness!"—a quotation from Hans Sachs's monologue in act 3 of Wagner's *Die Meistersinger von Nürnberg*] I won't hear any more of it. I should almost like to believe that I am come to the end of my life. I cannot possibly continue for thirty years more to write songs or music to Ibsen's plays.[9] And yet the eagerly desired opera will never come. I am just about at an end.[10]

> The opera and always the opera! Truly I shudder at my songs. The flattering acknowledgment of me as a "song composer" distresses me to my innermost soul. What else can it mean but a reproach that I continue to compose only songs, that I only rule over a miniature genre and even that not completely, since there is in the songs only the predisposition for dramatic works. I am not even an ordinary song composer. God help me![11]

Tone and tune alike are typical. Only when he was most panic-stricken and downcast about Polyhymnia's absence could he settle for mere songwriting.

> You ask me about an opera! I would be content if I could only write the smallest little song—much less an opera! I believe it is all over with me—entirely over.[12]

When the flow of song began once more on 25 September, with the first songs of the *Italienisches Liederbuch*, Wolf quickly reverted to the great idée fixe of his life: "die Oper und immer wieder die Oper!"

Through the years, as the search wore on, his frustration deepened, and he periodically delivered tirades about librettists in general or librettos in particular. In June of 1891, he wrote to Emma Kauffmann about a libretto by a "master thief" whose scribbles set him off on another round of imprecations. Should she and her husband wish to know about this work, he could assure them that the "poem," in scornful inverted quotation marks, was the "most tasteless, talentless, crackbrained, dullest, in short, the most horrendous make-work creation in the world."[13] By January of 1892, Wolf told Grohe that he had a collection of bad librettos of all kinds and types.

> I already own a small library of the most atrocious, bestial, bloody, idiotic, hair-pullingest, murderously shameful opera texts imaginable— tragic, comic, tragicomic, comitragic—in short, what you will, but not what *I* want. I can't see postal packages and rolls without shuddering, expecting the worst. This is the inevitability to which my desire for an opera has doomed me.[14]

Elsewhere, he characterized librettists as robbers[15] and German opera composers as amphibious beings, neither fish nor fowl nor good red meat.[16] Nevertheless, he longed to find "der Rechte! der Echte!" (the right one! the true one!), comparing his state, deprived of a dramatic poet, to that of a maiden with no suitors. He envied those who, like Wagner and Peter Cornelius, wrote their own librettos, and tried on a few occasions to do likewise, but was forced each time to admit his limitations as a poet. He could not, he declared, be both father and mother to an opera; a collaborator had to be found somehow and somewhere.

One anecdote from 1890 can serve to underscore the intensity of Wolf's desire to conquer the operatic realm. When Grohe sent three of his songs to Wolf that year for comment, Wolf responded with a commendable mixture of tact, honesty, and humor, with more delicacy than he sometimes displayed in similar situations. Grohe's songs, he told his friend, were better than most of those currently flooding the market and displayed an honorable striving for truth and natural expression—but this was not enough. Grohe, he continued, did not know the trials of an artist's existence and did not realize that art is a vampire who consumes the vitals of those who serve her. "What else is my desire and quest for an opera text but a fearful, chronic hangover?"[17] Wolf was, of course, exaggerating in order to make a point; midway through the letter, he mock-tragically laments, "Oh, if only I were a district judge!" (Grohe's occupation) and then proceeds to relate his latest musical news, but it is notable that the search for a libretto was the most cogent example Wolf could cull from his own experience to epitomize the desperation inherent in dedication to art. No wonder it seemed a miracle to him when he could finally begin to compose the long-desired opera.

Der Corregidor has prompted mixed reviews from the beginning. Even the most ardent Wolf adherents have found fault with the libretto, the dramatic design, and the musical conception, although the problems identified vary from critic to critic. Walker, who looked askance at Wolf's comedic propensities, felt that Repela's part was a "disturbing influence" that would have been better eliminated, that the fourth act "degenerates with Repela's burlesque,"[18] contrary to Wolf's own assessment. He was delighted with his characterization of the Corregidor's sarcastic servant and told his librettist Rosa Mayreder that the fourth act was his "best-beloved child," filled with such rarities as would "make an epicure's mouth water." He even quotes Heine's ironic self-congratulatory couplet, "What a shame that I can't kiss him, / As I myself am that outstanding fellow."[19] (The opera's appeal to *Feinschmecker*, epicures and connoisseurs, is forecast in this passage.) The libretto has been the most frequent target of criticism, but in one notorious instance, Gustav Mahler, who directed an abbreviated version of the work at the Vienna State Opera in 1905,[20] dismissed the *music* as worthless to Wolf's friend Grohe. The occasion was social, and Mahler did not know of Grohe's association with Wolf; when Grohe expressed his regret that the text was not particularly effective on stage,[21] Mahler responded, "The text is perfect, but the music is not worth anything . . . Wolf did not have enough ideas. One cannot make an opera nowadays with a few motives loosely joined together. So I at least want the audience to enjoy the text and I shall allow the work to be performed in the lighted auditorium."[22] Grohe was dumbstruck. In 1897, when Mahler became director of the Royal Imperial Court Theater, Wolf had approached him about performing *Der Corregidor*, and Mahler had agreed to coach and direct the work the following January or February. According to accounts by friends, when Wolf consulted Mahler about the performance, he found that his former classmate at the Vienna Conservatory had doubts about the project and was considering Rubinstein's *Der Dämon* in its place.[23] Wolf, who respected Mahler as a conductor and director but did not think much of his music, felt betrayed by Mahler's lack of championship of his opera. The sense of betrayal ran so deep that his insanity was first evident in his delusion that he had replaced Mahler as director of the State Opera.

The most frequently cited objections to *Der Corregidor* include complaints that the libretto is structurally weak; that there are no dramatic crescendos, that is, cumulative developments leading to strategic dramatic goals; that Wolf was averse to composing massed ensembles to overwhelming effect, that he shunned spectacle; and that the opera consists of a series of lyrical moments—another song anthology—and lacks dramatic breadth. Attempts to explain the opera's lack of success by placing the blame entirely on Mayreder's libretto, as Grohe did, constitute an implicit statement about the rela-

tive importance of text and music in opera. Despite Grohe's valiant partisan-
ship, Wolf cannot be wholly absolved from responsibility for problematic
aspects of his first opera in that way. Wolf told Mayreder, when she reacted
to criticism of her text for *Manuel Venegas*, that "the best criterion for a good
text is good music,"[24] but, despite the obvious truth of the statement, composers not blessed with an innate or acquired sense of dramaturgy have come to
grief on bad librettos before. Sadly, Wolf understood very well what was
required for a good dramatic text—his knowledge of operatic architecture is
apparent from comments in his letters and from his music criticism—but his
desperation to compose an opera rode roughshod over tempered judgment.
The truth would seem to lie somewhere between Mahler's and Grohe's extreme opinions. The singularities of this opera, its faults and virtues alike,
stem from Wolf's desire to compose psychological opera in which the emotional life of the characters is traced in great detail and with great refinement
throughout and from discrepancies between time in the dramatic narrative and
spans of musical time. *Der Corregidor* is also a first opera, with everything
that implies of experiment and inexperience. No matter that Wolf was thirty-
five and nearing the end of his creative life—actually composing an opera is
a different enterprise from reviewing librettos and required a difficult shift of
perspective from the requirements of lieder to those of music drama.

But first a bit of pre-history to set the stage for the Corregidor and his crew:
Wolf discovered both his attraction to comic opera and his psychologizing
bent early in the long quest for an operatic text. In the summer of 1882, he had
briefly considered writing his own libretto based on the ballad "Die Prinzessin
Ilse" (the princess Ilse was a water-nixie who entrapped heroes in her under-
water realm) from Heinrich Heine's *Harzreise* (Journey in the Harz Mountains). The legend is in accord with the Wagnerian advocacy of myth, although one notes that Wolf's source is a lyric poem. Realizing that he needed
more information in order to expand Heine's ballad into a libretto, Wolf wrote
three lively letters to a folklore scholar named Gustav Winter[25] and was unhappy with what he learned. The causes of his displeasure are significant for
the quest to come and for the nature of *Der Corregidor*: he was dissatisfied
with what he felt was insufficient and unrealistic motivation for the nixie Ilse's
actions. In Winter's recapitulation, she seemed to Wolf to be "leichtsinnig"
(frivolous) rather than "frohsinnig" (of a happy disposition), a two-dimen-
sional creation lacking psychological credibility. The water-siren should, he
felt, be reinterpreted to represent an underlying principle of disorder and disturbance in men's lives, and therefore he proposed a dual scenario, a play-
within-in-a-play in which a human comedy would be juxtaposed with the Ilse
saga.[26] There is nothing comic either in the sources for the legend or in
Heine's ballad, so the comedic elements are speculatively of Wolf's devising,
foreshadowing his later resolution to compose comic opera. The insistence on
veracity and detail in human characterization already bespeaks the psycholog-

ical depiction on which Wolf would insist. When Emil Kauffmann, who knew that Wolf had recently completed his *Gedichte von Eichendorff*, suggested in 1890 that Eichendorff's novella *Das Schloß Durände* (The Dürande castle) might be a possible source, Wolf reread the work and then wrote to Kauffmann, explaining why the tale was not suitable for conversion into opera.

> Beyond the costumes and a little color, there is nothing individual to note in Eichendorff's figures. Of delineation and psychological development not a trace, only vague, shadowy outlines, without physiognomies, without personality. Like ghosts in dreams, they suddenly appear, from where, one does not know, then vanish again, where, one does not know. They seem like clouds in the sky . . . like still dreams overhead, taking now this, now that form and shape. The whole may be very beautiful and highly poetic, and the imagination agreeably occupied, but it is worthless on the stage.[27]

Wolf knew exactly what he wanted: the delineation of human characters and their individual desires and conflicts, not archetypes, symbols, or dream figures.

The decision to compose comic opera was what any psychologist would call over-determined. His liking for aggressive humor and detailed characterization was combined with a resolution to do something other than imitate Wagner, to compose un-Wagnerian subjects for purposes different from Wagner's messianism. In his early twenties, Wolf had undergone a severe crisis of confidence in which he questioned whether it was possible to be a composer at all in Wagner's wake. "Wagner's art has the pressure of a hundred atmospheres: stoop! what else can one do?" Nietzsche wrote, adding as well that "they [the best of Wagner's disciples] are simply right to admire Wagner . . . Wagner has given all of these artists a new conscience."[28] The young Wolf would probably have agreed with both statements. Determined not to stoop, Wolf became a song composer—not Wagner's genre—and began looking for operatic texts devoid of any hint of Wagnerian imitation. When the faithful Grohe in 1890 suggested as a possible source the Mannheim publisher Karl Heckel's drama on the life of Buddha, Wolf responded with a vehement rejection (he probably knew that Wagner had long contemplated an opera on that subject) and a veritable manifesto, a statement of what he felt was his own operatic mission in a post-Wagnerian age. Wagner's accomplishment, he told Heckel, was complete and left no room for successors to pursue the same approach. Ironically, Hanslick said much the same thing about the dangers of Wagnerian influence on his latter-day disciples.[29] Fidelity and redemption, mythology and love-death, were no longer viable operatic material. Rather, Wolf declared his desire for romantic comedy, for lightheartedness, guitars, moonlit nights, champagne carousals, and merry lovers. "*True* comedy," he hastily adds, without any pretensions to world redemption or serious philosophical foundations. Thus do great and antagonistic ghosts limit and determine the choices available to those who come after: Wolf at first felt himself banned from any sort of tragic or even serious opera because Wagner had left him nothing to do in that realm. He could not emend, extend, or improve Wagnerian tragic opera, as he could in the sphere of ballad and song. This justifiably famous operatic credo, written in Wolf's distinctive prose, is remarkable for its mingled resentment and adoration, exemplary of influence anxiety at its most acute.

So I must set Buddha to music, a sort of second edition of *Parsifal*, perhaps with variations on Wagner's motives? Really, I don't understand you. How little familiar you are with my artistic nature, that you expect me to solve such sublime problems. The world has as yet scarcely an inkling of the philosophical profundity which is expressed in the most extraordinary manner in the Master's last words, and already something else must come into existence to give people a new headache—*nota bene*, by already proven tricks—where everywhere the necessity for cosy enjoyment and friendlier images appears, where everybody in this doleful and brooding expression of our time longs for a hidden smile, a roguish trick. Shall we then in our time never be able to laugh heartily and be merry? Must we strew ashes on our heads, wear garments of repentance, cover our foreheads in thoughtful furrows and preach self-laceration? Let him redeem the world who feels in himself the redeemer's calling; that is not for me. I for my part will be merry, and if a hundred people can laugh with me, I am content. Nor do I strive for "world-redeeming" merriment. Anything rather than that. That we gladly leave to the great geniuses. Wagner has already achieved such a mighty work of redemption in and through his art that we can now at last rejoice that it is quite unnecessary for us to storm heaven, since it is already conquered for us, and that it is wisest to seek for ourselves in this fair heaven a really agreeable little nook. And this pleasant little nook I should much like to find, but on no account in the desert with water and locusts and wild honey, but in happy and original company, with strumming of guitars, sighs of love, moonlit nights, champagne carousals, etc.—in short, in a comic opera, and a quite ordinary comic opera to boot, without the sombre world-redeeming ghost of a Schopenhauerian philosophy in the background. For that I need only a poet, and truly for that one *must* be a poet and a devil of a poet too.[30]

Wolf compared Heckel's Buddha libretto to "an uninterrupted three weeks of rainy weather in the Salzkammergut,"[31] and the rejection of tragedy, especially messianic tragedy, is definitive.[32] His goal would, he felt, be that of a purveyor of comic relief, of laughter to lighten the Wagnerian gloom; he would bring humorous opera into the modern age as he had already done with comic ballads and lieder. It is intriguing to speculate that Wolf's attraction to the Spain of Alarcón's tale was the result in part of his determination *not* to compose a comedy of "die heil'ge deutsche Kunst" ("holy German art," the last words of *Die Meistersinger*), in addition to his already evident taste for Spanish themes.

Such was the plan, but Wolf discovered in the course of composition that "champagne and guitars" were incompatible with his avowed goal of psychological realism in music drama; the irreconcilable tension between the two aims is one source of the opera's unique and problematic nature. Pain is paradoxically a necessary ingredient in comedy of all kinds. Nor could Wolf banish the thought of *Die Meistersinger* as he wrote his own comic opera. Indeed, he no longer wanted to but rather invoked the Wagnerian comparison deliberately. Convinced that he had invented a new species of opera all his own, he could even declare himself grateful for having been born after Wagner—what an utter about-face from his earlier imprecations against the master of Bayreuth and his own fate as a latecomer. In a letter of 1 June 1895 to Rosa Mayreder, he wrote concerning her husband's efforts to learn something about opera:

> That I have such a good influence on your husband makes me very happy. He should not fail to concentrate especially on *Die Meistersinger*, even if there is a danger that in so doing he will figure out my own tricks, because without the *Meistersinger* the *Corregidor* would never have been composed. The "Old Magician" has bewitched us young ones and we should be pleased that we are allowed to follow his path.[33]

The magnitude of Wolf's relief that he would, after all, be granted time to create opera is measurable in this deluded assertion that it is actually desirable to follow after genius.

Every step of the way, Wolf measured his own creation against and with that of Wagner. On 8 June 1895, he wrote to tell Rosa Mayreder that he had suffered "three days of martyrdom" before finding the right musical expression for the words "Wenn es Gott gefallen hätte, mich durch schlimmen Schein zu prüfen?" in Lukas's third-act Jealousy monologue. When his difficulties were at their height, he wrote to a friend requesting a copy of the full score of *Die Meistersinger* as an aid in orchestrating act 1, his alternative to the compositional problems of act 3. The score duly arrived, but by that time, his creative dilemma was over, and he delayed the instrumentation a while longer to continue composition of acts 3 and 4.[34] Was there an unconscious motive for the request as well? Could he have wanted the score in order to confirm that he was not, in fact, echoing the mastersingers of Nuremberg, even as he proclaimed himself one of their company?

Despite Wolf's earlier call for "true comedy," *Der Corregidor* had become a comedy increasingly haunted by the awareness of tragedy, as *Die Meistersinger* is haunted by renunciation. Pathos and pain are never far away in either work. Hanslick, who accused Wagner of lacking a sense of humor in his "comic" opera, might well have leveled a similar accusation against *Der Corregidor*, had he bothered to pay attention to it.[35] Wolf eventually told his librettist that the designation "comic opera" was no longer appropriate,[36] and the work was performed and published with the noncommittal nomenclature "Oper." His psychologizing ideal is distinct from Wagner's philosophical-aesthetic foundation for *Die Meistersinger*, but the amplification of comedy through the expansion of lyrical expression is similar in conception, if not in practice. Wolf carefully explains the psychological characterization he desired and conveys his pleasure over its successful achievement in the letters to Rosa Mayreder, as when he points out the relationship between the Miller's leitmotif and the Neighbor's music in act 1, scene 1.

> Have you noticed how I treated "our" Neighbor with a truly apt musical expression of enmity? The Neighbor's motive is in quite perverse opposition to that of Tio Lukas, where the two figures cross one another. This is not just purely musical but deeply grounded in psychology. Lukas hates the neighbor, or rather, he scorns him. And then that I introduce the brave neighbor with a nasal voice!—that is a hallmark of this sort of person.[37]

Even discussion of such incidental details as typeface and dates for the premiere confirm that Wolf felt he had joined the elite company of the "Old Magician," that he had become a "Young Magician" and invited comparison with his predecessor. In November of 1895, he adds in a postscript to one of his letters to Mayreder that he hopes "it will be possible to have the print done in Gothic type—with the exception of the *Nibelung* and *Parsifal*, all of Wagner's texts are printed in Gothic."[38] One year after his joyous rediscovery of the Mayreder libretto, he tells her that the date of the first performance has been fixed for 22 May—Wagner's birthday—although that was not, as it turned out, the date of the actual premiere, which took place on 7 June 1896.

The source for Wolf's libretto was a venerable folk tale (there is a variant of the story in Boccaccio's *Decameron*) turned into social satire by a writer with a gift for ironic incongruities. Although he became a conservative in his later years, Alarcón (1833–91) was for much of his life an opponent of high society, and his aristocratic magistrate (the Corregidor) in *El sombrero de tres picos* of 1874 is a tin-pot king, a stand-in for more exalted representatives of the Bourbon regime. The novel's principal themes—the punishment of official power misused for personal pleasure and the celebration of domestic love—surely appealed to a composer who resented officialdom in all its guises and who idealized the married love he could not have. The parodically high-flown, exaggerated language would also have agreed with his tastes in comedy, all the more as there was nothing Wagnerian about either the subject matter or the style. The short novel, Alarcón's best work in most critics' estimation, was quickly translated into seven languages and was so successful that Alarcón became convinced it must be worthless. Finally, he consoled himself with the profits: "El asunto era de oro" (The stuff was a gold mine).

The woman Wolf's friends chose to convert Alarcón's prose into poetry for opera was a formidable person, a friend of Wolf's "lieber Eck," or Friedrich Eckstein, and a close friend as well of Marie Lang, also a longtime member of Wolf's inner circle. Rosa Mayreder has been given short shrift in accounts of Wolf's life and works because of the undeniable flaws in the librettos she wrote for him, but those ventures must be understood as peripheral to her true calling. Rosa Mayreder, born Rosa Adolfine Katharina Obermayer (1858–1938), was one of the foremost social philosophers and pioneering feminists in fin-de-siècle Vienna, as well as a poet, novelist, playwright, and amateur artist.[39] Her career as a writer began with fictional works, with the three novellas collectively entitled *Aus meiner Jugend* (From my youth; 1896); another collection of novellas, *Übergänge* (Passages; 1897); and the novels *Idole, Geschichte einer Liebe* (Idol: The story of a love affair; 1899) and *Pipin. Ein Sommererlebnis* (Pipin. A summer experience; 1903). Even after the publication of her first work of feminist social philosophy, *Zur Kritik der Weiblichkeit* (Concerning a critique of feminine nature) of 1905, she continued on occasion to write fictional works, including a collection of sonnets entitled *Zwischen Himmel und Erde* (Between heaven and earth; 1908), the *Fabeleien über göttliche und menschliche Dinge* (Fables on things divine and human; 1921), the novella *Sonderlinge* (Odd persons; 1921), and the mystery play *Anda Renata* of 1934. Her second large-scale feminist critique of society, *Geschlecht und Kultur* (Sex and culture) of 1923, is an examination of contemporary culture, of the relationship between evolving sexual codes and civilization, the crisis of patriarchal standards, the female-erotic, the stages of marriage, and the falsities of romantic love. In other essays for a variety of journals and for the Union of Austrian Women's Societies, she engaged Darwin's theories, the psychoanalytic theories of Wilhelm Fliess and Freud, and much else. She even wrote two literary fantasies on Richard Wagner.[40] She knew little about music, but she recognized Wolf's worth and strove to the best of her ability to help him realize his lifelong dream of opera. In 1896, she sketched an original libretto for a three-act opera to be entitled *Eldas Untergang* (Elda's downfall) that she submitted to Wolf, who did not like it. Looking through the thirty-two pages now in the collection of the Vienna City Library, one can see why Wolf rejected it. Social realism was not to his taste: in one of his letters to Emil Kaufmann, he wrote a blistering diatribe against "this damned social-missionary writing nowadays" as evinced in Dostoyevsky's *The Brothers Karamazov*. "I must now search for my librettist in the madhouse or the penitentiary," he fumed, envisioning an operatic duet for policeman and socialist reformer.[41] No contaminating trace of naturalism appears in Mayreder's text for the Alarcón novel.

Arthur Groos writes that literary critics and musicologists isolate two different relationships in discussing nineteenth-century librettos: that between the
literary source and the libretto, and that between the libretto and its music.[42]
Since much of the criticism of *Der Corregidor* has been directed against Rosa
Mayreder for relying too closely on Alarcón's prose tale, for a reluctance to
rearrange and invent anew, we begin with the relationship between the literary
source and the libretto, the first stage in the genesis of many operas. Although
Mayreder preserves almost all of the plot in Alarcón-Hulda Meister's order of
events, she had to eliminate Alarcón's omnipresent narrative voice and replace his prose narration with verse dialogue and monologues, disposed in
acts—no small task. Furthermore, she alters the nature of several major characters, especially the miller Lukas and his wife Frasquita. Alarcón devotes the
first chapters of the novel to a description of the mise-en-scène ("Concerning
the Date of the Occurrence," "How People Lived in Those Days," and "Give
and Take"[43]) and to a depiction of each of the three principal characters, chapters of course omitted from the libretto. In the fourth chapter, "A Woman
Viewed from Without," Alarcón begins by describing Frasquita's charm and
beauty, which have captivated all the members of the social group or *tertulia*
at the mill,[44] especially the Corregidor.

> Señá Frasquita was probably nearing her thirties. She was almost six feet
> tall and stout in proportion—or perhaps a little heavier than was proper
> for her proud height. Although she had never had any children, she was
> like a colossal Niobe: she resembled a (female) Hercules: she looked like
> a Roman matron of the type that is found in Trastevere . . . But the most
> notable thing about her was the mobility, the nimbleness, the animation,
> the grace of her imposing stature. She lacked the monumental repose
> essential in a statue such as the academician insisted she was. She
> could bend like a reed, whirl like a weather-vane, and dance like a
> top.[45]

With a further description of her five dimples, her fashionable dress, graceful
head and neck, and melodious voice, the chapter ends. For the Miller's introduction in "A Man Viewed from Without and from Within," Alarcón begins
by describing the Miller's homely exterior appearance ("Tío Lucas was uglier
than sin")—he is short, stoop-shouldered, with a scanty beard and a large nose
and ears—and then enumerates his attractive external features, in particular,
his well-shaped mouth and perfect teeth; his vibrant voice and persuasive
speech; and finally, his nobility of character, his courage, loyalty, and
honor.[46] Contemporary feminists might wince at depicting only the external
appearance of female characters and introducing the male protagonists as possessed of body, mind, and personality conjoined, but Frasquita shortly after
displays an impressive capacity for strong-minded action, while the disparity
between Lucas's homeliness of body and beauty of soul is a principal plot
mechanism.

Both figures are literary creations, Rabelaisian exaggerations, rather than realistic or naturalistic stage personas. Frasquita in particular is a comically incongruous amalgam of gigantism and seductive charm. Mayreder omits almost all traces of physical grotesquerie from the Miller and his wife, retaining only the passing mention of Lukas's hunchback. Frasquita is no longer a colossus-whirligig, and Lukas does not repeatedly dwell on his ugliness in the opera as he does in the book. Walker points out that Wolf, who longed for a happy marriage and could never achieve it, lavishes on these two idealized characters all of the warmth and tenderness of matrimonial wish-fulfillment. He is quite right, but Rosa Mayreder paved the way for Wolf by eliminating the references to giant classical statues and Roman matrons and by writing impassioned love speeches for the couple.[47] The depiction in act 1 of the couple's great love for one another originates with Alarcón's seventh chapter, "The Foundation of Felicity," and additionally serves to explain the Jealousy monologue in act 3.

> Yes, the Miller and his wife were quite mad about each other, and, in spite of his being so ugly and she so pretty, one might even have fancied that she loved him more than he loved her. I say this because Señá Frasquita used to get jealous and ask Tío Lucas for an account of himself when he was very late in returning from the city, or from the villages where he had gone for grain; while Tío Lucas beheld even with pleasure the attention of which Señá Frasquita was the object on the part of the gentlemen who frequented the mill; he was very proud and happy that she charmed others as much as she did him: and, although in the bottom of his heart he realized that some of them envied him; that they coveted her as mere mortals, and would have given anything had she been a less virtuous woman; he would leave her alone for days at a time without the slightest worry, never asking her what she had done or who had been there during his absence . . .
>
> However, this did not arise from the fact that Tío Lucas's love was less intense than Señá Frasquita's. It arose from the fact that he had more confidence in her virtue than she had in his; it meant that he had the advantage of her in intellect, and knew to what extent he was loved, and how much his wife respected herself; it meant chiefly that Tío Lucas was a man through and through: a man like him of Shakespearean fame, of few and indivisible feelings, incapable of doubt, who believed or died, who loved or killed, who would admit of no gradations or transitions between supreme felicity and the extermination of his happiness.
>
> He was, in short, a Murcian Othello in hemp sandals and peasant's cap—in the first act of a potential tragedy.[48]

Alarcón is at some pains to establish the marriage both as a domestic bulwark, seemingly impervious to threat, and yet subject to disaster from within because of male insistence on "all or nothing" in love's kingdom.

The title figure of the Corregidor, Don Eugenio de Zúñiga y Ponce de León, is remarkable chiefly for the gulf between the office and the person. Alarcón describes the Corregidor's showy dress—the scarlet cape, dove-colored waistcoat festooned with green sprigs, black silk breeches, white stockings, black shoes with gold buckles, sword with a steel guard, a walking stick with tassels, straw-colored chamois gloves, and a gigantic three-cornered hat, the symbol of his office—and the "peculiar and grotesque" figure who wears such vivid garb. Carl Dahlhaus's description of Sixtus Beckmesser as someone who "seems to be bewitched, forever falling into absurd plights where he only looks grotesque"[49] could apply as well to the Corregidor, the embodiment of ineptitude and comic incapacity.

> As to the grotesque bearing of the Señor Corregidor, it was caused (so they say) by the fact that he was round-shouldered—still more so than Tío Lucas—in fact, he was hunchbacked, if you will have it; of less than medium height; weakly; in ill health; bow-legged, and with a manner of walking sui generis (swaying from one side to the other and from front to rear), which can only be described by the absurd statement that he seemed to be lame in both legs. On the other hand (tradition adds), his face was not bad, although rather wrinkled from the utter lack of teeth. His complexion was greenish and dark, like that of nearly all of the sons of the two Castiles. His eyes were large and black, and gleamed with anger, despotism, and sensuality. He had delicate and dissolute features which expressed no personal valour, but rather a sly malice capable of anything; and a certain air of self-complacency, half aristocratic, half libertine, which revealed the fact that in spite of his legs and his hump, the man must have been in his remote youth, very agreeable and acceptable to women.[50]

He is a parodic Don Juan in old age, his libido undiminished but his capacities on the decline, a marionette figure and a perfect vehicle for ballet, as Manuel de Falla would later recognize. Whatever his ineptitude and the frailties of age, he is the representative of official power and does not hesitate to threaten its use when affairs are not going his way. For Wolf, whose relationships with authority figures—his father, his schoolmasters, his teachers at the Vienna Conservatory, Brahms and Brahms's partisan adherents, Richter and the musicians of the Philharmonic—were troubled at best and antagonistic at worst, the opportunity to depict an authority figure as possessed of genuine power, which he wields for ignoble purposes; grotesque and cowardly; and defeated in the end must have appealed to him enormously.

Although the Corregidora, Doña Mercedes Carrillo de Albornoz y Espinosa de los Monteros, is an important character, she does not appear until the thirtieth chapter of the novel/fourth act of the opera and then somewhat in the nature of a *dea ex machina*. Alarcón describes her as

. . . a very high-born woman, still rather young, and of a placid and severe beauty that was more suitable to the Christian brush than to the pagan chisel. She was dressed with as much dignity and seriousness as the taste of that period allowed. Her dress, with its narrow skirt and full, short sleeves was of black bombazine: a yellowish-white lace kerchief veiled her admirable shoulders, and extremely long mitts of black tulle covered the greater part of her alabaster arms. . . This beautiful woman was something of a queen, and a good deal of an abbess; and therefore instilled veneration and fear into whomsoever looked upon her.[51]

Both Alarcón and Mayreder introduce mention of Mercedes early in the action when the Corregidor is attempting to seduce Frasquita in the grape arbor, an episode Alarcón names "The Bombardment of Pamplona." Alarcón gives his would-be seducer an exaggeratedly belle-lettristic mode of address; the stuffy, pseudoliterary tone in which he tells Frasquita, "Suffice it for you to know that now, for example, when I chuck my wife under the chin, it has the same effect upon me as if I were chucking myself under the chin"[52] heightens the absurdity of the situation. Mayreder eschews the circumlocution and has the old roué utter, in comically hushed tones, that stand-by of married seducers, "Sie ist eine kalte Frau" (She is frigid).

As in many operas, the plot hinges upon the complementarity-polarity of couples, one happy (Lucas and Frasquita) and one unhappy (the Corregidor and Corregidora). Underlying the polarity is a conception of conjugal love as possession, the sort of love Nietzsche defined by opposition in praising Bizet's *Carmen* for its quite different vision.[53] Merely by mimicking in jest, in patent insincerity, the flirtatiousness of a sexually available woman makes Frasquita eligible for Lucas's rage, rooted in his insecurities about age and the claims of Frasquita's family, and her own self-condemnation. The only member of the quartet who does not subscribe to the doctrine of conjugal love as possession is, ironically, the only one with temporal power. And the Corregidor too argues the standard of marriage as male ownership in his attempt to wrest control of the situation at the end. His philandering, in his opinion, is no excuse for the Corregidora, a tragically isolated and dispossessed figure, to enact similar mores. (As with the Countess/Rosina in *Le Nozze di Figaro*, the Corregidor's wife is referred to both by her title and by her name, depending upon the context.) Her station removes her from the hoi polloi, and her husband's philandering removes her from any associations that might bring her comfort. When Mayreder's Corregidor describes his wife to Frasquita as "a frigid wife," he is, in part and for the wrong reasons, telling the truth: because she lives in limbo as a married woman with no hold on her husband, she has wrapped herself in a glacial mantle of reserve. And yet, she emerges from her isolation and seizes the reins of command at the end in order to foil her husband's schemes and reunite the Miller and his wife. Her own marriage is beyond repair. At the close of the novel, she turns to her husband when they are alone and, "in accents that a Czarina of all the Russias might have employed when thundering at a fallen minister the order of perpetual exile to Siberia," banishes him from her bedroom. The Corregidor merely mutters, "Well, I didn't expect to get out of it so easily!—Garduña will find another woman for me!"[54]

The secondary characters are little altered from the novel, but several of the minor changes are reminders that Rosa Mayreder was a pioneering feminist. The constable's name is changed from Alarcón's Garduña to Repela, a name taken from the author's preface (Alarcón claimed to have heard the legend of the Miller's wife for the first time from an old man named Repela who lived in his native town of Guadix). In the novel, Garduña is described as looking "exactly like his name," the bird known as the stone marten or beech marten:

> Thin, extremely agile, glancing ahead and behind, to the right and to the left as he marched along, with a long neck, a diminutive and repugnant face, and a pair of hands like two bundles of whips, he resembled at once a sleuth in search of criminals, the rope which was to bind them, and the instrument destined for their punishment . . . This black scarecrow seemed the shadow of his elegant master.[55]

Garduña/Repela is a misogynist (his comic Serenade in the fourth act tells us precisely what he thinks of love and its conventions), a cynically opportunistic servant who finds the Corregidor's antics both contemptible and amusing. In a scene reminiscent of Leporello snatching a bite of pheasant from Don Giovanni's banquet table, Garduña steals a pinch of snuff from the Corregidor's box, and Mayreder uses the incident as the basis for her snuff-taking scoundrel Repela. Juan López, the drunken mayor, is described as follows in Alarcón's tale:

> Señor Juan Lopez, both as a private citizen and as an alcalde, was tyranny, ferocity, and pride personified (when he dealt with his inferiors). However, at that hour of the night, after dispatching his official duties and his private agricultural business, and after giving his wife her daily beating, he condescended to drink a jar of wine in the company of his secretary and the sacristan—an operation that was more than half finished when the Miller appeared before his presence.[56]

The luckless wife never appears in either the novel or the opera, but Mayreder gives her a means of retaliation—she has locked the wine cellar and taken the key off to bed with her—and therefore provides an additional bit of comic byplay in the drunkards' scene, a mechanism for sending the alcalde out of the room. The maid Manuela is also a feistier creature than in the novel; she talks back to an employer she finds contemptible, and her resolve to leave his employ and ask for work at the mill leads to her discovery that Lucas has escaped, unlike in the novel.

Anyone who adapts a longer prose work as a libretto has to omit characters and episodes, but two of Mayreder's omissions create unexplained loose ends in the drama. In the first instance, she eliminated the contents of Alarcón's Chapter 12 ("Tithes and First Fruits") in which the Corregidor, after the Miller "discovers" him, is forced to sit in the arbor and converse with the Bishop, a lawyer, two canons, and the Bishop's secretary and pages. She thereby created a dilemma. The first act ends with a blaze of fanfares to announce the Bishop's arrival, but the Bishop himself does not appear on stage and is never mentioned again. The orchestral pomp and circumstance is a lively way to end the first act—Wolf evidently knew the importance of a first-act finale that would entice the audience to return for the second act—but has no dramatic consequences. One thinks of the rousing march with which Figaro's "Non più andrai, farfallone amorose" and act 1 of *The Marriage of Figaro* ends and realizes the difference; "Non più andrai" is intrinsic to the drama, the Bishop's music extrinsic. Both Gustav Mahler and Bruno Walter, who conducted the opera in Munich in 1920, eliminated the passage altogether.[57] In the second instance, Mayreder and Wolf offer no adequate explanation for Frasquita remaining at home when Lukas is arrested (act II, sc. ii in the summary below). Alarcón has Toñuelo refuse to allow her to come along: "My position and neck depend on it. That is what Señor Juan López told me." The couple then confers in whispers, Frasquita asking Lucas whether she should go into the city and tell the Corregidor what has happened. Lucas says, "No! Not that!"

"Then what do you want me to do?" said his wife vehemently.

"Look at me," replied the old soldier.

Husband and wife looked at each other in silence and were both so satisfied with the tranquility, the resolution, and the energy that their souls communicated to each other that they ended by shrugging their shoulders and laughing.[58]

Several of Mayreder's alterations of the Alarcón source were more felicitous, however, and demonstrate her awareness (tutored by Wolf?) of operatic conventions such as drinking songs for a soloist and chorus. There is no encomium to Spanish wine in the novel, and Lucas does not trick the mayor and his crew into alcoholic stupefaction. Alarcón's shorter and less vivid episode has Lucas say merely that he is tired and wants to go to bed, while the mayor and his cohorts, relieved that they need not interrupt their drinking, acquiesce. Further, it is not the maidservant Manuela who discovers that the Miller is missing but rather Toñuelo, when Frasquita arrives at the Mayor's house to announce that the half-drowned Corregidor is at her house. But in general, Mayreder does in fact preserve the plot, the characters, even some of the dialogue wholesale from the source. Whether one considers that a fault or a virtue depends upon whether one finds the Alarcón tale itself "komponabel" for the operatic stage.

Plot summaries of librettos do not make the best reading, as they are summaries of an incomplete entity, devoid of that which gives them their full meaning and eloquence: music. Furthermore, summaries are interpretations and faithfully reflect the writer's biases, whether acknowledged or not. Until Leo Spitzer's edition of *Der Corregidor* for the *Sämtliche Werke* is available, however, both a plot summary and a judicious sprinkling of musical examples are necessary aids for those unfamiliar with the work. The 1896 Mannheim editions and the 1904 orchestral edition have long been out of print and are comparative rarities in this country.

A SUMMARY OF MAYREDER'S AND WOLF'S SCENARIO
ACT 1: TIO LUKAS'S HOUSE
SCENE 1

A jealous neighbor envies the Miller, Tio Lukas, his good fortune. The Miller's grapes ripen earlier than anyone else's, and he will this very day entertain the Bishop in his grape arbor. When the Neighbor, for whom the grapes are decidedly sour, asks what such entertainments have cost Lukas over the years, the Miller merely laughs and says that he leaves arithmetic to such as the Neighbor. The Neighbor, who exists only to underscore Lukas's happiness in life, disappears from the opera after pointing out that the guests must come primarily to admire the Miller's "wonderfully beautiful wife," Frasquita.

SCENE 2

Frasquita enters, singing a small song of welcome for all and sundry guests. She and Lukas tease each other about her charms, about their love for and fidelity to each other. When they see the basso buffo Repela, Lukas says that he will hide in the arbor and listen to the conversation between his wife and the Corregidor.

SCENE 3

Repela enters sneezing from a pinch of snuff taken as he comes into view. When Frasquita asks him, "Now where's your master, Repela?" we hear the Corregidor's leitmotif played unaccompanied by the traditional solo horn of operatic cuckoldry. Repela and Frasquita banter with one another ("Schreckliche Müllerin, schweige!"—"Terrible Miller's wife, be silent!"—are his first words to her), ending with Frasquita's surprise announcement that the Corregidor is welcome to visit. Repela insinuates that Lukas will doubtless sleep the slumber of a trusting husband, and then leaves to the sound of more sneezing in the distance. Frasquita dances and sings a fandango.

SCENE 4

The Corregidor, who has entered during Frasquita's dance, calls out, "Heavenly, entrancing, wonderful!" Frasquita greets him, but the nervous Corregidor begs her not to be so talkative lest Lukas awake. Frasquita sings "In dem Schatten meiner Locken" from the *Spanisches Liederbuch*, one of two songs from the earlier collection included in the opera. Frasquita hints that she will perhaps give the Corregidor what he wants if he names her nephew to a secretarial post in Estella. When he waxes amorous, she asks about his beautiful wife and is told that "marriage is an evil sacrament" and that his wife is frigid. While attempting to embrace Frasquita, he falls off the chair into the grape arbor and sees Lukas. Realizing that he has been duped by the pair of them, he vows to pay Frasquita back.

SCENE 5

The infuriated Corregidor gives Repela a message to take to the mayor Juan Lopez and then bids him tell the Corregidora that he will be detained on business. Repela, referring to the Aesop fable of the fox and the grapes, asks if he would not be better to leave the grapes of virtue hanging high up, lest they prove green and sour. The Corregidor snaps at him, and the first act ends with the ceremonial march music that heralds the arrival of the Bishop, whom we never see. In the Alarcón novel, it is the Bishop who angers the Corregidor with a quip based on the Aesop fable.

ACT 2: LATER THAT EVENING
SCENE 1

This is a love scene for Lukas and Frasquita, culminating in the duet "In solchen Abendfeierstunden, / wie fühl' ich innig unser Glück!" The scene ends with the Corregidor's perpetually drunken deputy Tonuelo knocking on the door.

SCENE 2

Tonuelo tells Lukas that he must go immediately to the Mayor's house. When Lukas says he will go in the morning, the inebriated deputy insists they leave right away and without Frasquita, who suspects trouble in the sudden order.

SCENE 3

Alone in the house, Frasquita starts a fire (faint echoes of the end of *Die Walküre*) and sings two songs to reassure herself. A voice outside calls for help: the Corregidor, incompetent schemer that he is, has fallen into the brook. Frasquita, thinking Lukas has returned, runs to the door and opens it.

SCENE 4

Frasquita is furious on seeing the drenched Corregidor. He resorts to lies, telling Frasquita that he has come to free Lukas, wrongly detained by the Mayor, but she will hear none of it. He shows her the commission for her nephew; she threatens to go to the Bishop and the Corregidora. The verbal duel becomes a show of firearms: he takes out his pistol, she retaliates with a blunderbuss, and the cowardly Corregidor backs away. When he sinks as if fainting from his misadventure in the brook, she throws water in his face, calls for Repela, and worries about what Lukas and others will think, should the Corregidor die.

SCENE 5

Frasquita bids Repela help his master while she goes for a doctor. In a brief trio, Frasquita frantically asserts her wish to leave, the Corregidor begs for a bed and warm clothes, and Repela comments wryly on the spectacle of the Corregidor in Frasquita's bed.

SCENE 6

Frasquita having gone, Repela tells the Corregidor that she has gone in search of a doctor. The Corregidor, frantic lest she seek out his wife, sends Repela out to find Frasquita and stop her. Left alone, he sings the second of the two inset-songs from the *Spanisches Liederbuch*, "Herz, verzage nicht geschwind," a caustic commentary on women in which each verse ends with the refrain "Weil die Weiber Weiber sind" (For women will be women).

An orchestral interlude during a change of scene from Lukas's house to the mayor's house.

SCENE 7

At the mayor's house, the mayor Juan Lopez and his secretary Pedro are drinking wine, which the maid Manuela disgustedly tells us is their frequent pastime. Lukas and Tonuelo come in, and Lukas devises a fitting stratagem to outsmart a crew of drunkards: he calls for more wine and tells the trio that each time he sings the words "spanischer Wein," they must drain their glasses. Every other line is "O du guter, edler spanischer Wein," or "Oh, thou good, noble Spanish wine," to a canonic trio about the hero Don Rodrigo (El Cid) going to sleep; the would-be jailers do likewise.

Scene 9

Lukas escapes, after wondering aloud about the Corregidor's schemes for Frasquita.

Scene 10

Manuela, unhappy with her present employment, whispers to Lukas through the door that she would like to work for him at the mill. When she receives no answer, she finds him escaped.

Scene 11

Manuela arouses the drunken Mayor's crew and all go stumbling out into the dark to search for Lukas.

Act 3: Outside, two paths—one in the foreground, one in the background
Scene 1

Frasquita, alone on the dark path, wonders at the strange night-sounds and begs the moon to veil itself and conceal her from sight.

Scene 2

She bumps into Repela and the two conduct a lengthy dialogue, culminating in a lively duet, "Muss es denn sein / Sage nicht nein" (Must it be / Don't say no) and in Frasquita's renewed resolve to find Lukas.

Scene 3

Lukas comes back to his house, finds the door open, peers through the bedroom keyhole, and finds the Corregidor asleep in his bed and the commission for Frasquita's nephew. Thinking the worst, he resolves to take a like revenge on the Corregidor, exchanges his clothes with the Corregidor's and departs, laughing bitterly.

Scene 4

The Corregidor, in his nightgown and sleeping cap, opens the door and wonders if a spook with Lukas's voice has been about. When he looks for his garments, he can find only "vagabond's clothes."

SCENE 5

Before the Corregidor can leave, a party consisting of Repela, Frasquita, Juan Lopez, and Tonuelo arrive. At first, they think that the Corregidor is Lukas. Frasquita and Repela, more quick-witted than their companions, figure out what Lukas is doing and why. The scene and the act end with a quintet in which Tonuelo and the Mayor vow to catch Lukas, Frasquita is beset with anxiety, the Corregidor swears revenge on Frasquita, and all set out immediately for town.

ACT 4: LATE NIGHT, THEN DAWN—THE STREET
IN FRONT OF THE CORREGIDOR'S HOUSE
SCENE 1

The night watchman's song, "Ave Maria purissima! halb fünf ist die Stunde."

SCENE 2

The Corregidor tells Repela to knock. Repela takes out a guitar and sings a perversely mistuned antiserenade to the duenna, "Blim blam! Blim blam! Mach' auf!" The duenna duly appears and demands to know who is outside; when the Corregidor announces himself, she does not believe him. The Corregidor, she tells him, came home an hour ago and went to bed.

SCENE 3

General consternation, augmented by a troop of bailiffs/male chorus.

SCENE 4

The Corregidora Mercedes, who Alarcón tells us has married the dissolute Corregidor because of family coercion, appears for the first time and asks, "What is all the noise about?" She addresses her husband as "Tio Lukas" and asks if some misfortune at the mill has brought him out at this hour. The Corregidor blusters and demands to know the state of his honor. She will only say that her husband is in bed where he ought to be. When Frasquita steps forward, Mercedes speaks warmly to her, says that they share the same grief, and promises comfort and resolution soon.

SCENE 5

Lukas appears in the Corregidor's clothes and asks Frasquita if she has already sent her nephew's commission to him. The Corregidora assures Lukas that his wife is guiltless, and Lukas demands that Frasquita explain her actions. Frasquita says, "No, I will not speak first when the truth is that you . . . ," and the two couples exchange rapid-fire accusatory phrases: "Und du? Nun und du? hast nicht auch du—Aber du? Nein, du!" Repela, the Corregidor, and Frasquita all explain to Lukas that the Corregidor was in bed alone, and the Miller and Miller's wife are reconciled.

(The following portion of the concluding scene was omitted from the 1904 orchestral score published by Lauterbach and Kuhn: The two men go inside to change back into their rightful clothes, and Frasquita asks for a full explanation of the night's events. The mixed chorus embarks on a lengthy narration, augmented by the duenna and Mercedes.)

The Corregidor demands an explanation from his wife, who tells him bitterly that if he lives to be a thousand years old, he will never know the truth of what happened. She then turns to the others on stage and wishes them good morning, and they sing a concluding chorus of greeting to her.

LEITMOTIFS AND MUSICAL CHARACTERIZATION IN *DER CORREGIDOR*

Non-Wagnerian subject matter was one thing, non-Wagnerian musical composition another. "Must everything be Wagnerized?" ("Muss denn immer gewagnert sein?") an unhappy colleague of Hanslick's once asked,[59] and Wolf in 1895 would have answered with a qualified yes—qualified because he accepted certain Wagnerian practices wholeheartedly and rejected others. When he told Rosa Mayreder that by studying *Die Meistersinger* she would thereby learn his tricks, he must have been referring to certain late-Romantic aspects of the score, aspects so evident that even a novice could detect them: his use of number-opera conventions, although with continuous orchestral music carrying the narrative and the listener from one scene or number to the next, and the recurring musical figures—the ones Mahler so disliked—that appear in many guises and contexts. "Leitmotif" is a term under attack nowadays, and rightly so, since the obsession with nonmusical signification has tended to obscure purely musical processes, and yet it is a historical designation whose heyday was Wolf's lifetime. Wolf himself thought in terms not only of leitmotifs but of thematic relationships as reflecting the drama, in particular, the relationships between characters. In the same letter of 8 June 1895 in which he tells Rosa Mayreder of his struggles with Lukas's Jealousy monologue in act 3, he also explains the relationship between Lukas's leitmotif and the Corregidor's in that scene, the most extended and complex solo in the opera. "Clothes make the man," he tells her, quoting the old proverb in appreciation of its rightness for this context, and therefore Lukas's theme appears in the rhythmic garb (*Verkleidung*) of the Corregidor's figure, to which it is related by inversion, each beginning with a perfect fifth upward or downward. Lukas, he tells her, as a "blunt, rough countryman" has a melodic line that strives upward, while the Corregidor, a decadent member of the nobility, has a theme that sinks downward (Examples 32 and 33). The Corregidor's leitmotif, with its sustained first beats, dramatic dotted rhythmic pattern, and descending sequence to tremolando augmented triads, is expressive of the "decadent nobleman's" menacing power, rather than any aspect of personality (the office, not the man), and is aptly suited for service as a bass line in various counterpoints. Several of the themes, this one among them, seem to have been invented with contrapuntal artifice in mind. Wolf was quite delighted with the symbolism, although he only noticed it when he combined the two themes.[60] "Isn't that noteworthy?" he asks, impressed with the unconscious workings that produced such a coincidence.

Actually, the dramatic function of Wolf's themes is not so much depiction or characterization, but differentiation between those grouped on either side of the conflict: the Corregidor's circle, or what Margarethe Saary calls the "Machtbereich" (the domain of power), and the Miller-Frasquita alliance. This would seem in accord with Wolf's creation of psychologizing opera—that is, music whose development registers the changing nuances of the dramatic relationships. For example, the melodies and motives associated with the miller couple are closely related. Lukas's theme is a conglomerate of three separate figures, the first having the character of a bass line and usually found there, the second and third being sixteenth-note figures closely related to one another by the anticipation tones moving either downward or upward. When Wolf conceives Frasquita's leitmotif as a rising sequential structure filled with appoggiaturas and anticipations, he underscores the close relationship between husband and wife by means of similar compositional hallmarks (Example 34). Lukas's and Frasquita's themes are also related in the sixteenth-note figures that delineate a scalar third on the last beat of the $\frac{3}{4}$ measure. The fact

Example 32. Hugo Wolf, the Corregidor's theme from the prelude,
measures 1–4

Example 33. Lukas's theme from Act, 1, scene 1

that Frasquita's theme is a rising sequence in constant motion while Lukas's theme is more stably anchored in place—the first three bars are repetitions of the same figures—can perhaps be interpreted as extensions of the drama. Frasquita is a quicksilver, lively, flirtatious creature,[61] even the music of her undisturbed domestic happiness in constant motion, and Lukas is, or seems to be, stolid and secure. The Love theme is notable for a further development of the third figure in both the topmost and inner voices, for the first-beat descending appoggiaturas in the topmost voice related to Frasquita's theme, and for still more anticipation-tone patterns. The bass of the love theme is closely related to the first half of the Miller's theme, the association an obvious one.

Example 34. Hugo Wolf, Frasquita's theme from Act 1, scene 2

Notably, Wolf does not use any of these themes for the act 2, scene 1 duet "In solchen Abendfeierstunden," one of the most beautiful points of repose in the opera. Instead, he sets this moment of idealized marital concord, calm and tender rather than passionate, apart from the couple's music elsewhere in the opera, from their erotic embraces in act 1, their teasing banter, or their conflict to come. The duet is, one notices, cast in a broad $\frac{12}{8}$ meter, thereby reducing the number of strong first-beat emphases and enhancing the tranquility of the fireside idyll (Example 35). Saary finds a relationship, if only in the repeated chords and doubling in thirds, between this brief number in E major and Mozart's trio "Seid uns zum zweiten Mal wilkommen" in the second act of *Die Zauberflöte*, an opera in which marriage is the microcosm and building block of a harmonious society.[62] Subsequently, Richard Strauss would also use parallel thirds, quasi-chanted declamation on repeated pitches, rhythmic unanimity, and the limitation of dissonance for the duet "Und ich will dein Gebieter sein" (And I will be thy master), a vision of future matrimonial happiness, in the same key of E major for Mandryka and Arabella in act 2 of *Arabella*. Even Strauss's overlapping echoes between the two lovers will re-

Example 35. Hugo Wolf, "In solcher Abendfeierstunden" from Act 2, scene 1

mind those who know Wolf's opera of Frasquita's and Lukas's similarly overlapping phrase "Der erste Blick an jedem Morgen" (The first glance each
morning) in the earlier duet, both composers thus suggesting the characters'
individuality (different points of entry) and perfect concord (the lovers sing
the same phrase).

Adulterous passion is a matter not of farce but of serious, and very Wagnerian, music in this opera. When Wolf changed the designation of his work
from "comic opera" to "opera," it was in part because the title character's
attempted lovemaking is far less comedic than his model in Alarcón's novel.
Whether Wolf's long-standing situation as the lover of a married woman had
any influence on his characterization of the Corregidor or not, he gives the
Corregidor-as-Seducer music of Tristanesque ardor in act 1, scene 4, with no
ironic commentary from the orchestra to contradict what is stated in the vocal
line. Neither the rising chromatic sequences nor the Corregidor's words are in
any way comic; his worshipful phrase "Süße Zauberin Frasquita" (Sweet sor-
ceress Frasquita), with its widely spaced C-minor chordal harmonies, is the
expression of reverential awe at Frasquita's beauty and is untouched by any
hint of farce. His ardor—in Wolf's conception, a genuine emotion, not a
cynical ploy—is evident in the chromatic and contrapuntal richness of his love
music (Example 36). Nor is it only in the character of his lovemaking that the
Corregidor escapes caricature. Where he is concerned, the comedy throughout is largely situational and has to do with his marked cowardly streak (the
nether side of authoritarian bluster), for example, the chattering sixteenth-
note declamation of his words "What you want is utterly impossible!"—the
flurried seducer leaping in to deny the request even before Frasquita finishes
her demand. Throughout the Corregidor's would-be wooing, Wolf develops
two linked themes, one associated with the Corregidor's wish to grant
Frasquita anything she desires and the other first stated in conjunction with her
nephew's secretarial appointment. The first is marked by the same rhythmic
pattern and motive of a rising or falling scalewise third that one finds in Bach's
B♭-minor prelude from *The Well-Tempered Clavier*, Book 1 (Examples 37a
and 37b). This motive is then incorporated into the theme of the Nephew's
appointment as the interior cell, with a prefix and suffix added (Example 38).
The series of variations Wolf devises on these themes, the fresh counterpoints
in the inner voices, are remarkably ingenious, continuing until the point in the
scene at which the Corregidora is mentioned for the first time and her music
introduced.

The shifting tonal center of the Corregidora's leitmotif—a succession of
majestic block chords in a progression marked by mediant relationships—is
an apt expression of her pathos: not for her a stable sense of key, the diatonic
surety of love such as Lukas and Frasquita express in their act 2 duet. The
third-related chords spreading outward from the starting point remind one of
block-chordal invocations of the names of Christ and the Virgin Mary in Gio-

Example 36. Hugo Wolf, the Corregidor's love music, from the prelude to
Act 1, measures 5–8

Example 37a. Johann Sebastian Bach, Prelude no. 22 from *The Well-Tempered
Clavier*, Book 1, measures 1–2

Example 37b. Hugo Wolf, the Corregidor's wish theme, Act 1, scene 4

und doch wag' in   stil - lem Glüh'n kei - nen Wunsch ich zu ge - steh'n.

vanni Gabrieli's polychoral motets for St. Mark's, similarly evocative of solemnity and majesty. When her theme, used only sparingly for maximum
effect, first occurs, it interrupts the swifter tempo of the Corregidor's attempts
to seduce Frasquita, just as she intends (Example 39). The Corregidor is not
pleased when the subject of his wife, "the crown of all married women," is
introduced and hastily launches into imprecations against marriage. For his
self-serving lamentations, Wolf takes the descending chromatic scalar figure
at the beginning of the Corregidora's theme and simplifies it, renders it diatonic; employs the dotted rhythmic pattern associated with the Corregidor's

Example 38. Hugo Wolf, the nephew's theme, Act 1, scene 4

theme, and activates the inner bass voice with a series of thrumming repeated notes associated shortly thereafter with the Corregidor's anger. Frasquita, still bent on teasing him, persists in reminding the Corregidor of his wife, saying, "From others I hear that she disciplines you strictly, that she keeps an Argus-eyed watch on the man who married her" to a transposition of the Cor-regidora's theme a minor third higher. Both instances of Mercedes's theme in this scene are the vehicles by which Frasquita can divert the Corregidor from expressions of passion, tonally and literally unsettling the seducer and forcing him to press his suit still further, his goal postponed yet again.

Wolf merely reduced, but did not eliminate entirely, the comic elements from *Der Corregidor*. Comedy is confined to those secondary figures with whom Wolf did not personally identify, that is, the drunken mayor Juan Lopez, his secretary Pedro, the judge's messenger Tonuelo, and the maidser-

Example 39. Hugo Wolf, the Corregidora's theme, Act 1, scene 4

vant Manuela and Repela. The Corregidor's motive is rhythmically related to that of the mayor Juan Lopez, the latter figure beginning with an ascending statement of the same C–G pitches one hears at the start of the Corregidor's leitmotif. Amusingly, the Alkalde's dotted figures, first introduced by Tonuelo when he comes to fetch Lukas in act 2, scene 2, are more short-breathed, less powerful than the Corregidor's theme, while the rising C-major scalewise bass line underscores the mayor's comic self-importance.[63] Both the Corregidor's and the Alkalde's themes are harmonically simple and straightforward—the Corregidor brandishes the threat of his power with all the subtlety of a right upper-cut, and the drunken mayor is far from bright. The Alkalde's theme is like a proclamatory flourish; the fact that it lacks the tension-inducing harmonic element of the augmented triads signals his lack of capacity for any real menace (Example 40). The misogynistic Repela is given a leitmotif that suggests both his sneaking, sidling motion and the periodic

Example 40. Hugo Wolf, Juan Lopez's theme, from the interlude preceding
Act 2, scene 7

sneezing of a habitual snuff-taker. The theme is close kin to the principal
accompanimental figure throughout the "Spottlied" from *Wilhelm Meister* in
the *Goethe-Lieder*—Repela is likewise a mocker. When he is first introduced
in act 1, scene 3, the first of his and Frasquita's verbal jousts, he makes his
position plain: women are trinkets of little value, and yet for such inconsequential creatures, men will act like fools. Wolf sets Repela's backhanded
homage to Frasquita's beauty to extensions of the servant's motive, punctu-
ated by cadential outbursts of sneezing—comically unloverlike and antilyrical
(Examples 41a and 41b). Wolf wrote to Melanie Köchert on 18 April 1895 to
tell her that by early afternoon, he was finally pleased with the "wonderful
motive for friend Repela" and then paraphrases—what else?—*Die Meistersinger*: "Glück auf zum Meistersingen."[64]

Repela is in the comic tradition of basso buffo servants with more common
sense and ironic insight than their masters, but he is not a sympathetic character. In act 2, scene 2, Frasquita tells him to his face that no one can take him
seriously because he never misses an opportunity for a joke. His one solo is
the parody of a serenade in act 4, scene 2 ("Blim blam! Blim blam! Mach'
auf!"), Wolf's reply to Beckmesser's "Morgen ich leuchte in rosigem
Schein." Beckmesser, however, is a would-be lover who becomes the target
of humiliation, while Repela, even as he participates in the action, is psychi-
cally removed from the various lovers' intrigues and laughs at them. Here
Wolf parodies not the "radical new art" of Wagner's opera but his own use of
parallel fifths and guitar-mandolin figuration in such earlier serenade songs as
the Eichendorff lied "Das Ständchen." He must have remembered the wrong-
note technique, the jarring dissonances, the unromantic turns of phrase, the
goatlike intervallic leaps he gave Repela when he came to compose the comic
serenade "Schweig' einmal still!" in 1896. The conjunction of simple harmonies—expressive of Repela's opinion of the proceedings?—with such deliberately mis-tuned touches as the tritone intervals in the vocal part, the phrases
interspersed with grace-noted hammering in the orchestra, is indeed comic,
especially in contrast to the Night Watchman's song just before it. The prolongation of the verb "*muss* [ich im Schlummer dich stören]," Repela delivering

Example 41a. Hugo Wolf, Repela's theme in Act 1, scene 3

Example 41b. Hugo Wolf, "Spottlied aus Wilhelm Meister" from the *Goethe-Lieder*, measures 1–5

another verbal jab at his employer, is a typically comic inflection of Wolfian prosody, as is the melismatic flourish for the "Ständchensänger"—Wolf's jab at the vocal acrobatics he disliked so much in Italian opera (Example 42).

At their best, Wolf's ingenious combinations of these themes exemplify the ideals of musical refinement and psychological drama he hoped to create in this work, especially the many combinations of the Corregidor's and Lukas's themes. At the end of the first act, after the Corregidor falls over in mid-

Example 42. Hugo Wolf, Repela's serenade in Act 4, scene 2

Example 42, continued

wach - sam spä - hen - de Mäg - de schmä - hen - de Duen - na, mach auf!

embrace and Lukas emerges from his hiding place, the ensuing exchange of courtesies between the two men shows Lukas in the ascendant, with the Corregidor's theme, weaker and in the treble register, merging into the latter half of Lukas's theme. When the Corregidor in act 2 lies to Frasquita, telling her "Nur um deinen braven Mann, den der Bürgermeister fälschlich eingezogen, zu befrei'n, kam ich her" (I've come here only in order to free your good husband, wrongly imprisoned by the mayor), Wolf combines a variant of the mayor's theme in the upper orchestral parts with Lukas's bass figure. The sixteenth-note motive—the second cell in Juan Lopez's theme—is chromatically twisted, unlike the simplicity of the theme when the mayor himself first appears in the second act. Once more, the rapid-fire declamation is comical, the flustered Corregidor racing through the patent lie (Example 43). When the Corregidor asks in act 3, scene 5, "Liess ein Vagabund die Kleider hier zurück?" (Did a vagabond leave these clothes behind?), Lukas's bass figure clearly identifies whose garments these are; intertwined with Lukas's theme in the low register is a subtle variant of the Corregidor's figure, its first descending interval widened to an octave. For the "Feinschmecker" or epicures to whom Wolf addresses this opera, there are indeed delights aplenty.

PROBLEMS OF STRUCTURE AND DESIGN

And yet, even if one properly takes into account Wolf's new ideal of opera in which psychological depiction takes precedence over stage spectacle, there are still disquieting anomalies in the dramatic architecture of *Der Corregidor*, especially acts 2–4. With the invisible and extraneous Bishop heralded beyond his deserving at the end of act 1, flaws of proportion and design cluster thick and fast; to that point, the dramatic architecture is well planned and effective. In accord with the traditions of comic opera, the event that sets the plot into motion—Lukas's and Frasquita's practical joke on the Corregidor—

Example 43. Hugo Wolf, the Corregidor, "Liess ein Vagabund die Kleider hier
              zurück?" from Act 3, scene 5

unfolds throughout the first act, with the Corregidor already plotting his revenge when the curtain falls. The audience's curiosity to learn what happens
next should, according to pragmatic stage lore, tempt them back for the second act and beyond, but when they return, the events that follow on occasion
play havoc with one's sense of time, both narrative and musical.

The beginning of the opera already signals a departure from the conventions. Edgar Istel, who wrote a treatise on what he considered to be the proper
construction of an opera libretto, stresses the importance of the opening
scene,[65] its purpose fourfold: to present the milieu and era; to introduce at least
some of the principal characters; to begin establishing the conflict from which
the tale unfolds; and to give the audience only as much of the prehistory as is
necessary for comprehension of the narrative. Schaumann, the author of the
other Alarcón libretto given to Wolf, evidently understood the tradition of
delaying crucial information until the audience can assimilate the milieu, and

of beginning with a stage spectacle of some sort—in this case, a wine-harvest festival with choral singing and dancing. Mayreder, however, shuns the massed theatrical scenes for which Hanslick grudgingly praised Wagner and instead begins act 1 with a conversation between Lukas and an envious neighbor who thereafter disappears from the opera (his music recurs in thematic transformation when Lukas imagines others laughing at him as a cuckold). Wolf told Melanie Köchert in April 1895 that he had disliked this scene at first—he does not say why—and thought of striking it from the libretto, but now he considered it a grand idea.[66] Mayreder clearly wanted to establish such themes as Lukas's good fortune, Frasquita's beauty, and the open hospitality at the mill from the start, and she does so in a distinctive way, in accord with Wolf's psychologizing bent. The jealous Neighbor is entrusted with most of the revelations in scene 1; it is he who speaks of Lukas's prosperity and hints that the Miller's hospitality might threaten his marriage to the "wonderfully beautiful" Frasquita. The Miller fans the flames of jealousy with his statement that the Bishop, no less, will visit the mill this very day—an assertion Wolf sets as a melodic line marching straight up the octave. The ascending motion is a precise musical metaphor for rising status, for climbing up the ladder of success. When the malicious neighbor asks whether Lukas has realized the possible danger of so much company, Wolf changes key and meter (a third-related shift from A major to F major, from $\frac{3}{4}$ to $\frac{4}{4}$) and has the orchestra intersperse a variant of Lukas's bass leitmotif with rests, while the neighbor's theme—a descending chromatic figure in the topmost voice—evokes muted menace. After only eight bars, the neighbor has shifted to the darker, distant tonality of A♭ major. Lukas, unperturbed, returns to his original tonality and meter; he even sings the bass line of his leitmotif to the words "Nun dann ist's ein Glück, daß Euch das Geschick nicht an meinen Platz gesetzt" (Then it's a good thing that fate has not put you in my place) to enforce his identity with happiness and good fortune. The turning point back to V/A major begins with the neighbor's beautiful phrase "das Frasquita eine schöne, eine wunderschöne Frau," he and Lukas in agreement on the matter of Frasquita's beauty (Example 44). Of such microcosmic subtleties of response to the text is this opera made. From the beginning, the scale is miniature and the modus operandi refined.

The second scene between Lukas and Frasquita serves to develop facts implied or stated outright in the conversation with the neighbor. Lukas, believing himself secure in his love for Frasquita and hers for him, repudiates any suggestion of a possible threat to his marriage from the stream of visitors to the mill. The scene also introduces Frasquita and establishes both her individual character and the nature of the marriage, and introduces as well the key word "eifersüchtig" (jealous) in the context of a teasing conversation between the couple. The possibility of jealousy is mentioned only to be jokingly denied

Example 44. Hugo Wolf, the Neighbor's and Lukas's colloquy in Act 1, scene 1

Nachbar.

A - ber glaubt Ihr nicht, dass man - cher nicht al - lein der Trau - ben we - gen

Freund.

o - der an - drer Leck - er - bis - sen sei - ne Ge - gen - wart Euch schenkt?

Wä - re ich an Eu - rer Stel - le dann be - däch - te ich ge - nau,

Example 44, continued

das Fras - qui - ta ei - ne   schö - ne,   ei - ne wun - der - schö - ne Frau.

as impossible, but in the great third-act Jealousy monologue, one remembers the earlier dialogue and understands it as preparation. When Lukas denies in act 1, scene 2 that he is jealous of "the old man," he tells Frasquita, "In der Sünde liegt die Strafe! denn die Meine, denn Frasquita wird von allen Erdenmännern ewig nur den Einen lieben, ewig ihm nur angehören" (In the sin lies the punishment! Of all men on earth, Frasquita will love only one, only belong to him). When Frasquita teasingly asks what he would do if she showed him she could love a second man, he replies in the language of possession and its Janus-faced opposite, abandonment and rejection, "O dann wärst du nicht Frasquita, meine süße, holdeste Frasquita." (Then you would not be Frasquita, my sweet, most noble Frasquita). Her very identity would be negated should she love someone else. The two are playing with fire for the purpose of catching fire erotically, for incitement to a passionate embrace, but the dialogue also states the origins and the terms of later conflict.

In the best librettos, each episode, each twist and turn in the tale, conveys crucial information about the plot, the emotional life of the characters, and the relationships between the dramatis personae. Walker rather severely says that everything up to the *Verwandlung* in act 3 is extraneous and a distraction from the forward motion of the plot, beginning with Frasquita's song to the moon. This is Mayreder's and Wolf's invention: Alarcón has his stout-hearted female protagonist suffer only a minor attack of nerves on her way to the village at night:

> The only adventure that befell the Navarrese on her journey from the mill to the village was being a bit startled by noticing someone striking a light in the middle of a field.
>
> "Could that be one of the Corregidor's hirelings? Is he going to detain me?" thought the Miller's wife.

At this point she heard a bray from the same direction.

"Burros in the fields at this hour of the night!" said Señá Frasquita to herself. "Why, there isn't any orchard or farmhouse near here. Good gracious, the goblins are flying about as they please tonight! For it can't be my husband's burro. What would my Lucas be doing stopping in a field in the middle of the night?

"No indeed! It must be a spy!"

The donkey that Señá Frasquita was riding thought the moment opportune to bray herself.

"Hush, you demon!" said the Navarrese, sticking a farthing pin into its withers.[67]

The Frasquita we find at the beginning of act 3 is more sympathetic than the comically pragmatic creature who sticks pins into donkeys and uses deductive reasoning to counter twinges of fright. Wolf's atmospheric tone painting in the orchestra for the "Sonderbare Nachtgeräusche," the semitone D♯–E motive the impetus for the rising syncopated "heartbeat" figures at the words "Oder ist's mein eig'nes Blut, das mir in den Ohren saust?" (Or is it my own blood that roars in my ears?), strikes genuine fear in the composer's Frasquita and prompts one of the loveliest lyrical moments in *Der Corregidor*, her song "Neugier'ger Mond, du hast uns belauscht." (The first part of Lukas's leitmotif, or the bass figure, underlies the orchestral "night sounds." Lukas is on the path and passes by, unseen and unseeing.) It is surely no coincidence that this miniature song—twenty-five measures, including the six bars of orchestral postlude/transition to a renewed bout of sneezing from Repela—is set in E major, the tonality of the love duet "In solcher Abendfeierstunden" (Example 45). The span of a tenth in the first four notes of the vocal line, such wide-ranging lines a melodic hallmark of pathos in *Der Corregidor*, begins another of Frasquita's solitary lyrical musings. One notices in particular the rhythmic and motivic relationships to both Frasquita's theme and the Love theme, also the structural extension in the latter measures of the song—"So hilf mir nun treu, verrathe mich nicht; / Birg heute in Wolken dein strahlendes Licht!" (Help me now, do not betray me; cover your rays of light in clouds")—of the A♯–B pitches stated in the first seven measures.

"Neugier'ger Mond" is lovely but tiny, smaller than either of the interpolated songs from the *Spanisches Liederbuch* to which Walker took exception—"a sufficient measure of desperation," in his estimation.[68] He also considered both this scene and the dialogue with Repela that follows to be excess baggage, and he is, regrettably, right. Wolf missed an opportunity here, not for the first or the last time in this opera. A solo scene can be, indeed should be, an important revelation of a character's inmost desires and thoughts. Had Wolf requested Mayreder for an expansion of this text into a reflective mono-

Example 45. Hugo Wolf, Frasquita's song to the moon, "Neugier'ge Mond," in
Act 3, scene 1

Example 45, continued

logue, Frasquita perhaps musing on her love for Lukas and her fears about the
night's misadventures, the first scene of act 3 would have been of more import
than the beautiful but dramatically inconsequential moment we now have.
Istel and others who write about the proper construction of opera librettos are
right to warn against "the demon of tedium" induced by too much rhetoric on
the poet's part,[69] but a larger number of well-chosen words more intrinsic to
the drama than this "aside" to the moon would have aided both characterization and plot.

TIME AND OPERATIC NARRATIVE

Walker was among the first to point out that there are problems of temporal incongruity in *Der Corregidor*, a mismatch between the duration of narrative events and the duration of their musical setting.[70] Already complex considerations of narrative become even more complex in opera when one must take into account the relationship between story time and the duration of a musical section or number. Completely isochronous narratives in an unchanging speed, without accelerations and ritardandos and ellipses, do not exist except as a hypothetical mental construct; all narratives are by definition anisochronous and have a textual rhythm generated by the relationship between external divisions, such as acts, and internal narrative articulations. Those internal narrative articulations in opera include changes of focus from action to reflection or vice versa, the appearance of another character on stage, and the shift to another formal structure. By means of such articulations, actions and emotions alike are nearly always recounted either more slowly or more swiftly in opera than in actual experience; the license to dwell upon certain moments and abbreviate others is a given in opera, inherent in the genre from its beginnings. Librettist and composer, can, for example, devote considerable time and space to soliloquized thought processes such as the Jealousy monologue and then pass over or swiftly summarize a longer period of time. Problems arise where discrepancies between narrative time and musical duration are perceived as straining credibility within the opera's own frame of reference or where the audience's attentiveness is tried by prolongation that induces boredom or excessive rapidity, the listeners unable to assimilate actions, insights, or thoughts that whiz by too swiftly.

The first act of *Der Corregidor* is arranged in straightforward chronological order, but thereafter one finds anachronies insufficiently accounted for in the dramatic structure. There is, for example, an implied lapse of time from afternoon to evening of that same day between acts 1 and 2. The first six scenes of act 2, up until the orchestral interlude, are chronologically continuous once again, but the orchestral interlude leads not only to a change of location and a new cast of characters (the rest of the Corregidor's crew, embarked on their evening's carouse) but possibly to an implied change of time. The hands of the clock seem to move backward to an earlier point in the evening, although time in this act is so skewed that it is difficult to discern whether the chronologies overlap or whether time has been implausibly compressed. While Frasquita copes with a sopping-wet Corregidor in scenes 4–6 at the mill, Lukas arrives at the Alkalde's house by the seventh scene and engineers a lightning-fast escape by the end of the act. The same split between chronologies as well as locations is then repeated in the third act, which begins with Frasquita alone and en route to town; she encounters Repela, and the two set off together for the Alkalde's house. Here, between the second and third scenes, the orchestral change of scene from the open field to the Miller's house is performed, presumably allowing time both for the Frasquita-Repela duo to reach Juan Lopez's house and for Lukas, traveling a nearby road, to return home. After the Jealousy monologue, we once again rejoin Frasquita and Repela, who have arrived at the Alkalde's house, in the sixth scene. In other words, we shuttle back and forth between the town and the mill in a manner that might have been unexceptionable—transitions and scene changes are operatic commonplaces—had Wolf allowed more time for the transitions from one time and place to the next.

Even before the divide in act 2, one's sense of a reasonably accordionlike give and take between the duration of the music and events in the plot is disturbed in the third scene, a succession not of complete songs but of song fragments sung by Frasquita, alone and anxious but determined to be courageous as she waits for Lukas to return. This is the first time in the opera that one asks, "What? Over so soon?"—the first, but not the last. The scene begins with an unharmonized figure in the bass, an extension and variation of Lukas's bass line and a modulatory passage from the E♭ major of Lukas's and Tonuelo's departure to G minor. One can imagine uneasy and unspoken thoughts of Lukas's safety and whereabouts rising in unharmonized unison texture from the depths, then flowering into the "ruhig *ppp*" determination to keep a waking vigil, to light a fire, to work at her spinning, to sing. The visceral understanding that the bass figures are "bösen Gedanken" (bad thoughts, troubling thoughts) is confirmed shortly thereafter when their recurrence is identified: "Schleichen die bösen Gedanken / drohend dir um das Haus, / schliesse Fenster und Türen / blicke nicht spähend hinaus" (Should troubling thoughts creep menacingly about the house, close the windows and doors; do not look watchfully outside). It is all effective, including the miniature battle song "Auf Zamora geht der Feldzug" that she sings while spinning, but every section of this scene is compressed to song dimensions or less; many of the lyrical moments in *Der Corregidor* are not as long as a medium-length Mörike or Goethe song. The fire music is as quick to catch as a modern gas range, and the passage of time in which the "bösen Gedanken" occur, are fought back, recur, and are subdued once again is implausibly brief, as Walker points out, hardly enough time for Lukas and Tonuelo to reach the Alkalde's house.

The same disturbing discrepancy between narrative time and musical duration is evident in act 2, scene 8, a scene containing action crucial to the plot rather than the soliloquies and songs of Frasquita's solitary period of waiting. The seventh scene just preceding Lukas's and Tonuelo's arrival does not seem temporally disjunct, with its dialogue among the Alkalde, his tart-tongued maidservant Manuela, and the amorous secretary Pedro. Wolf alternates dialogue with song in this scene—Pedro mocks his employer's less-than-amicable marriage and signals that he is on the prowl for a sweetheart in the little strophic song "Ich und mein holdselig's Weibchen"—to apt effect, the small-scale dimensions suitable to Pedro's place as a minor character. Once again, happy and unhappy matrimony is everyone's preoccupation. But when Lukas appears, Wolf steps on the gas pedal and races through the subsequent activity at a pace well over the speed limit and the bounds of credibility. The Alkalde greets Lukas to a clever combination of his own and Lukas's theme, followed by a rapid-fire ensemble in which that same leitmotivic combination is stated a dozen more times, shading from duet (four bars) to trio (another four bars), and the preliminaries to Lukas's drinking song. In a mere three pages of vocal score, Lukas reduces a company of experienced inebriates to a state at which they are incapable of anything other than singing themselves to sleep with a nonsensical-delightful four-part canon about "Don Rodrigo" (El Cid) going to bed at seven o'clock. If the great hero of medieval Spain can retire early, so can they. The canon, clever as it is, lasts a mere nineteen measures; with its yawning figures for flute, its soft drumbeat ostinato, and the harmonic surprise at the word "[streckt sich aus und schnarcht im] *Nu*," one would like to hear more, but that desire is destined to be frustrated many times over. When one recalls that it was Wolf who encouraged Engelbert Humperdinck to expand a small domestic singspiel into the opera *Hansel und Gretel*, first performed in 1893, and that Wolf was understandably jealous of the opera's great success, one wishes that Humperdinck could in some way have returned the favor.[71] Had someone been able to prompt Wolf into revising the opera's temporal proportions, the work would be the better for it.

Wolf's compression of multiple musical subtleties within small-scale boundaries negates the possibility of grandiose Wagnerian stage effects, of crowd scenes that place Wagner's characters within the framework of a society. Wolf's characters are individualists largely divorced from any social context—a fact that is tempting to interpret in light of the composer's own personality. Wolf the purist, who generally refused to repeat words, phrases, and verses in his songs, inveighed against the text repetition common in operatic ensembles and choral-ensemble scenes, an operatic tradition he considered just as condemnable as coloratura in arias. Mayreder would have had to provide a massive amount of text in order for Wolf, excessively principled in the matter, to concoct extended conclusions for his third and fourth acts. In a letter to his collaborator of 13 June 1895, Wolf writes:

I have been considering a richly worked finale for the end of the third act. If I wanted to follow the old model of text repetition, especially in the choral pieces, a pair of verses would suffice to sound over and over, like the well-known Amen in church music that Hector Berlioz so delightfully parodies [Wolf was fond of *La Damnation de Faust*, especially the demonic glossalalia toward the end].[72]

Five weeks later, he tells her of his difficulties with the ending of the opera:

> The working-out of the final chorus, "Guten Morgen, edle Donna," has
> caused me unspeakable troubles. I despaired of completing a proper con-
> clusion and had the idea of letting the work end with Mercedes's last
> words, even at the danger of denying myself the most beautiful closing
> effects. But my artistic conscience rebelled forcefully against such
> faintheartedness; with the expenditure of my last energies, with what was
> truly the courage of despair, I made myself continue the difficult work
> and labored uninterrupted for a week—and behold—it succeeded and
> succeeded beautifully. The last chorus with the rising sun now ends as it
> should.[73]

Taking into account Wolf's usual hyperbolic tone, one wonders if the "un-
speakable troubles" were not occasioned in part by awareness that "the most
beautiful closing effects" required that he accede for once to Wagnerian dramaturgy, precisely what he resists with such tenacity throughout most of *Der
Corregidor*. The final ensemble for solo quartet (Frasquita, the Corregidor, the
Alkalde, and Lukas) and chorus *is* in fact rousing, effective—and over much
too soon. Wolf was not able to abjure text repetitions completely, either here
or in the other short choruses and solo ensembles, but he came as close as he
dared, to the detriment of operatic breadth. One remembers how many times
Verdi has his Windsor Forest revelers repeat "Tutto nel mondo è burla"
(Everything in the world is a jest) in the finale of *Falstaff* or, closer to home,
the verbiage and polyphonic tumult of the St. John's Eve riot at the end of act
2 of *Die Meistersinger*. Even in the shorter concluding chorus at the end of the
entire opera, Wagner does not shrink from repeating "uns bliebe die heil'ge
deutsche Kunst" quite a few times, culminating in the wonderfully theatrical
plagal cadence at "Heil! Sachs! Nürnberg's theurem Sachs!" (Hail! Nurem-
burg's dear Sachs!). Rosa Mayreder, whom Wolf in a fit of exasperation once
characterized as a stranger to Polyhymnia, might not have known that finales
require what Lorenzo da Ponte called "noise, noise, and more noise" and
therefore enough words from which to construct a gripping conclusion—and
Wolf, averse to text repetition, did not ask for more text from which to construct more imposing conclusions to the midpoint and concluding finales.
When Frasquita sings "Ich verstehe keine Sylbe, alle schreien sie zugleich" (I
don't understand a single syllable—they all shriek at once) after the chorus at
Mercedes's bidding has begun their explanation of the night's madcap events,
she could be the mouthpiece for Wolf's own objections to traditional finales
in which everyone "cries out at once."

When Mayreder worried lest the fourth act and therefore the opera itself be
too long, Wolf in irritation asked, "Who has put this giant flea in your ear
about length?" and asserted that operas require an epic element,[74] but he
balked at too much of the epic infiltrating the psychological subtleties of his

operatic vision. For example, at the confrontation in front of the Corregidor's house in act 4, scenes 3 and 4, Wolf has the chorus of Alguacils, or town guardsmen, burst through the door with muskets in hand, demanding to know where the Corregidor is. A mere nine measures later, they are done; two bars of orchestral uproar, and Donna Mercedes appears to ask, "Was soll diese Lärm bedeuten?" (What is the meaning of all this noise?). One thinks wistfully of the great choral-and-solo ensemble Wagner would have concocted from Frasquita's lamentations, Repela's assertions that Lukas is the Corregidor, the Corregidor and the Alkalde shouting in rage, and the soldiers milling about—but Wolf does nothing of the kind. As Wolf was composing *Der Corregidor*, he tellingly quoted Nietzsche's condemnation of theatrical folk to Rosa Mayreder.[75]

> No one brings along the finest senses of his art to the theater, least of all the artist who works for the theater—solitude is lacking; whatever is perfect suffers no witnesses. In the theater one becomes people, herd female, pharisee, voting cattle, patron, idiot—Wagnerian: even the most personal conscience is vanquished by the leveling magic of the great number; the neighbor reigns, one becomes a mere neighbor.[76]

Wolf wanted to be the exception, to "bring along the finest senses of his art to the theater," but he seems to have confused expansiveness with pandering to the box office, with cheap tricks to lure the buying public into the theater.

Comparing the finales of *Die Meistersinger* and *Der Corregidor*, one notices another crucial difference as well. *Die Meistersinger*, the product of "an untrustworthy sense of humor"[77] and shot through with violence, nevertheless ends with an apotheosis in which the malice that pervades so much of the opera is replaced by a celebration of art and artifice, but *Der Corregidor* ends otherwise, and not only because of proportional differences in length. The final chorus is Mayreder's addition; Alarcón has nothing of the kind. Words and music alike betray the composer's desire not merely for a rousing conclusion but for something approximating the redemptive ending of Wagner's opera. In comic operas such as *Le Nozze di Figaro, Falstaff*, and *Die Meistersinger*, the "tutti a festa e cena" (everyone to the banquet and rejoicing) gaiety at the end is purchased at the cost of the suffering that precedes it. At the radiant peak of high comedy, discord ends in harmony tempered by tolerance, in which the players, who understand both themselves and others better than they did at the start of the drama, banish pain with an explosion of ensemble and choral mirth. In *Die Meistersinger*, Wagner concludes with Sachs's response to a final flaring-up of rebellion on Walther's part; the comedic celebration of the multiple betrothals is mingled with summations of the opera's profounder themes. But when the cast at the end of *Der Corregidor* sings "Alle haben sich verständigt, und es hat das Abendteuer noch für Alle gut geendigt" (Everyone has come to an understanding, and the adventure has ended well for all), one hardly knows what to think or feel. To be sure, Lukas and Frasquita are reconciled, their reconciliation a matter of a single phrase (!) with an orchestral aftermath of ten bars, but their newly restored harmony is then followed by this bitter dialogue between the Corregidor and his wife.

CORREGIDOR: Now my lady, I await *your* explanation!

MERCEDES: If you live a thousand years, you will never know what took place tonight in my bed chamber. If you had been in it, you would have no need to ask anyone about it.

CORREGIDOR (incensed): Then I will, unheard by you, tell everyone about it, even the judge—

MERCEDES (scornfully): And I advise you, Caballero, to throw a thick veil over what has happened lest the evening's adventures come to the Bishop's attention.

She then turns to those assembled on stage and bids them good morning, the phrase "Guten Morgen, liebe Leut'" beautiful but tainted by the bitter after-taste of the words that immediately precede it. Her icy threat to tell the Bishop of her husband's misdeeds ends poised on a high G as the culmination of an ascending melodic sequential pattern and the fortissimo dominant seventh does not resolve immediately. Rather, after an ominous measure of silence in which her threat hangs in the air, the expected C-major harmony is the beginning of her words of greeting, the breadth of the brief vocal phrase and its mediant-related chords the familiar indices of her dignity and pathos. For the noblewoman who receives the greetings of the assembled cast at the close, not all has "ended well," and the psychological realism of her bitterness at the end, the ambivalence of the conclusion, is not mitigated by the final chorus. Were that chorus more expansive than it is, the wormwood-and-gall flavor of the close would still be present, but counterbalanced by a stronger opposing force—and therefore a contradiction of the psychological truth of the real ending with the Corregidora's threatening words to her errant husband. The "grand choral conclusion" Wolf wanted is both too clipped for genuine grandeur and too much at odds with the tale.

In a witty review of a comic opera since sunk into oblivion, Hanslick complained that each of the dramatis personae came on stage as if shot from a pistol, that the luckless operagoer was thereafter deprived of any opportunity to know their prehistories, desires, or character.[78] One final carping note about the end of *Der Corregidor* has to do with Mercedes's role, one that denies her full characterization. When the Nurembergers hail Hans Sachs at the end of *Die Meistersinger*, they hail someone we know well by then, but Wolf does not allow Mercedes the luxury of a solo monologue or even a lengthy passage of through-composed dialogue. There is no "Porgi amor" to tell us of her nature and her plight. When Frasquita introduces the Corregidora's leitmotif in act 1, as she is duping the Corregidor into believing his tryst successful, with the words "Doch Eure Frau Gemahlin! So hold, und engelgleich, der Ehefrauen Krone, an Güte überreich" (But your wife! So noble and angelic, the crown of married women, so very virtuous), she adopts the broadly arching vocal style identified with the Corregidora. The passage is majestic and far from cold in its chromatic inflections and enharmonic changes. One wishes for further development of her theme and for more music such as her words to Frasquita, "Ach, Frasquita! Nicht vertheidigt Euch vor mir! Alles was Euch widerfahren, fühle ich so tief wie Ihr" (Oh, Frasquita! Don't defend yourself to me! Everything that has happened to you, I feel as deeply as you do), or the beautiful combination of Lukas's leitmotif and the Corregidora's broad-spanning vocal lines at the words "Tio Lukas, trotz der Dinge, die Ihr mir als wahr erzählet, sag' ich: Eure Frau ist schuldlos" (Lucas, despite what you have told me as truth, I say to you: Your wife is innocent). But the intriguing hints of a complex, wronged and yet powerful woman—she is the *dea ex machina* of the drama—are never developed at a sufficient length to satisfy our curiosity about her.

Only once in *Der Corregidor* does Wolf abjure song dimensions and compose a number that is genuinely operatic: Lukas's act 3, scene 3 Jealousy monologue, by everyone's estimation the pièce de résistance of the opera. Monologues such as this are a particularly interesting genre of narration because the solitary character recounts his progressive discoveries, emotions, perceptions aloud, transforming what in real life would be an inner experience into outward expression for an audience. The dramatization of psychological life was in accord with Wolf's ideals, especially as the orchestral music beomes the bearer of those unspoken or only partially revealed emotions just beneath the surface of the words. When Lukas escapes from the Alkalde's and returns home, he notices that the door is not closed and wonders why she would have opened it—to whom, of her own free will, under duress? Struck by the silence, he wonders if Frasquita has gone away with the Corregidor, or if the Corregidor has forced Frasquita to leave, or if the guilty pair is behind the bedroom door at this moment. Better death than such terrible certainty, he tells himself, and then sees the Corregidor's clothes. Stunned, he first asserts that his eyes deceive him, but when he sees the document for the nephew's appointment lying on the table, the "Murcian Othello" considers it instant proof of Frasquita's guilt. He loads his blunderbuss and goes toward the bedroom, but pauses on the first step in doubt, wondering if perhaps God is testing him with a hallucinatory false image. He peers through the keyhole and sees the Corregidor's face; in agony, he imagines that everyone will laugh at him, a hunchback who had the temerity to marry a beautiful wife. Instead, he will laugh, he vows, when he has his revenge. The Corregidor's wife is also a beautiful woman, and Lukas, like the Corregidor, is hunchbacked—she will be his revenge. Laughing bitterly, he dons the Corregidor's clothes and leaves.

This is not song material, and Wolf does not treat it as such, but instead brings back and develops earlier material in his most advanced chromatic manner. This scene proves that operatic breadth was indeed within Wolf's ken. With the rising curtain, Wolf combines Lukas's bass figure with an orchestral quotation of the love duet "In solcher Abendfeierstunden," the sense of betrayal that follows so shortly after all the greater by contrast with the expectation of conjugal love and domesticity. The chanted declamation of the duet melody is subsequently transformed into an ominous tactus within a diminished-seventh chord on the way from A major to C minor and the unisono development of Lukas's bass figure (Example 46). Lukas's initial panic over his wife's whereabouts—"Aber wie? warum? wozu? auf Befehl? aus freier Wahl?" (But how? why? where? at someone's command? of her own free will?)—traces the rising contour of a diminished-seventh harmony in combination with the further chromatic development of the Lukas leitmotif. When Lukas observes, "Welches Todesschweigen!" (What deathly silence), the first pianissimo statements of the Corregidor's leitmotif sound in the bass between vocal phrases whose ascending scalar configurations are the latter-day descendants of accompanied recitative, the vocal gestures as descriptive as the orchestral music. The words "Jeder Schritt ein Schritt zum Tode" (Every step a step toward death), for example, lead downward step by slow step to low G, the spare orchestral accompaniment leading to an implied skeletal dominant. As Lukas wonders whether he will find his wife and the Corregidor together behind the bedroom door, an emphatic variation of the music first associated with Frasquita's statement in act 1 that she loves only Lukas appears, each sixteenth-note accented against the vocal figures in contrary motion, as if the two lines crossed and intertwined like the anguished fancies of his wife and the decadent magistrate; the B♭–E♭ tonal regions of the music for Frasquita's and Lukas's love in act 1 fail to resolve at the cadential point. The music instead moves first to C minor and then to C major, the key of "Grässliche Gewissheit" (Terrible certainty) and multiple invocations of the Corregidor's themes. Wolf alternates the powerful leitmotif of the Corregidor's office, the fortissimo statements in the first half of the measure followed by its echo in the second half, with the linear chromatic figure in rising sequence associated with the Corregidor's lovemaking—music Lukas himself has heard before and now recalls.

The sight of the document on the table ("Die Ernennung ihres Neffen!")—the rush of thirty-second–notes a prosodic mimicry of great agitation and distress—recalls the figures formerly associated with the nephew's appointment, beginning in the Corregidor's C major but moving from there by Wolf's favorite mediant progressions through E major and G major to B♭ as the Neapolitan of A minor. Wolf makes the changing harmonic progressions closely track the onward motion of Lukas's thoughts, such that the sardonic proclamation "Ich verstehe!" (I understand), still in C, is followed by the new "understanding"

Example 46. Hugo Wolf, Lukas's jealousy monologue, Act 3, scene 3

Example 46, continued

that Frasquita has always loved her family more than she loves him in an
unstably tonicized E on its way to G. The threat of "Antwort, meine Antwort"
(Answer, my answer) is heightened by the Neapolitan sixth, the B♭s carrying
through the A pedal point that accompanies Lukas's action of loading the
blunderbuss and creeping toward the door to the sound of his own bass leitmotif stated softly a single time—the Miller's sense of powerlessness is clearly
evident. Doubts overwhelm him, and a new development of the Corregidor's
Seducer figure travels away from the A minor–C major constellation into a
passage without a strongly articulated key center but rather a sequence of
diminished seventh chords in veiled outline, the tonal corollary of the
"tausend Möglichkeiten," the uncertainties, that beset the protagonist; this is
the passage that Wolf told Rosa Mayreder had cost him three days of martyrdom to compose.

The groping excursions lead back, however, to their starting point, to A♭ as
the upper neighbor to V/C major and a massive authentic cadence on C when
Lukas peers through the keyhole and sees the Corregidor's face, triggering
once more the alternation of the Corregidor's Might and the Corregidor-as-
Seducer themes. From the latter, Wolf develops the mirror-image rising and

falling semitones as the bass line beneath the crescendo to an even more imposing and lengthier orchestral statement of the Corregidor's Might, crushing
the bass reiterations of Lukas's figure underfoot. When the reiterations of the
Corregidor's figure die away, C minor and the chromatic permutations of
Lukas's figure return, the parallel-mode relationship between the magistrate's
office in major and the Miller's despair in minor symbolic sides of the same
coin—Saary points out the Baroque descending chromatic tetrachord to which
Lukas sings the words "Da steh' ich betrogen, da steh' ich entehrt" (Here I
stand deceived, here I stand dishonored).[79] The scene returns obsessively to C
major at the words "Lachen würden sie," where an elaborate variation of
music not heard since the beginning of act 1 recurs, laden with trills and
neighbor-note figures in mocking profusion: a transposition of the music for
the Neighbor's jealous insinuations about Frasquita's hospitality. Wolf often
makes a distinction between Self and Other, vocal line and instrumental part,
and here the orchestra becomes the musical embodiment of a world turned
into jealous neighbors whose mockery Lukas dreads. Just when it seems another glissando-decorated authentic cadence in C will lead to another repetition of the Corregidor's music, Lukas conceives his apposite revenge and
substitutes the Corregidora's music instead. When he announces "Das soll
meine Rache sein!" (This shall be my revenge) and begins to laugh wildly,
Wolf combines the triplet chordal repetitions formerly evocative of the *Corregidor's* anger at the end of act 1 with a new rhythmic and motivic variation
of Lukas's bass figure. At the words "Schöne Frau Corregidora, hätten Sie das
wohlgedacht?" his figure assumes the dotted rhythms associated with the Corregidor—the two men seem, but only seem, to have become kin to each other
in the exchange of clothes and their similar designs on each other's wives.
Wolf, however, alternates the Corregidor-tinged variant of Lukas's figure
with straightforward statements of the Corregidor's theme, both the similarities and the differences thereby dramatized. Lukas has not become the Corregidor, but merely borrowed his rhythmic assertions of power.

It is no wonder that comparisons have been made to Ford's Jealousy monologue "E sogno? o realtá?" (Is it a dream? Is it reality?) in act 2 of *Falstaff*.
Wolf was justly proud of this scene, telling his librettist that he had gloriously
overcome his difficulties, that the world had a great experience in store for it.
For all his customary manic hyperbole, he was entitled to say so.

A LITTLE-KNOWN and semifictional account of the premiere of *Der Corregidor* at the Nationaltheater in Mannheim that June evening in 1896 can be
our leave-taking from Wolf's only completed opera. Siegfried Ochs, the director of the Berlin Philharmonic Chorus and a good friend of Wolf's from
their meeting in 1892, had introduced the twenty-four-year-old singer, composer, and writer Ernst Otto Nodnagel to Wolf during the Wolf-Bruckner
concert in Berlin on 8 January 1894. Nodnagel had come to know Wolf's

music two years earlier through the auspices of the composer Arnold Men-
delssohn and was an ardent disciple of Wolf's, one whom Wolf treated toler-
antly to his face but without much respect for his "nefarious compositions."[80]
Nodnagel's efforts on Wolf's behalf, though, were noble. His lengthy essay,
"Hugo Wolf, der Begründer des neudeutschen Liedes" (Hugo Wolf, the founder of the new German lied), was published in 1897; he included a profile of
Wolf in his *Jenseits von Wagner und Liszt, Op. 35* (Beyond Wagner and
Liszt) of 1902;[81] and an account of the premiere of *Der Corregidor* appears in
his novel *Käthe Elsinger: Bericht über Leo Borgs Liebe und Tod* (Käthe Elsinger: A report on Leo Borg's love and death) of 1905. The fictional composer
Leo Borg's tragic fate is recounted by a narrator who is sent early in the story
to Mannheim to review the first performance of *Der Corregidor*. Nodnagel,
eager to proselytize for the cause of Wolf's music, does not alter the names of
the composer, the opera, or the theater.

> Our rapture over the golden humor of this masterpiece and our joy at the
> enthusiastic, sympathetic reception accorded the opera by an audience
> appreciative of art knew no bounds. A friend, Arnold Mendelssohn, to
> whom I give thanks for my first acquaintance twelve years ago with the
> creations of this unfortunate master, sat with us.
>
> After the performance, a cheerful gathering took place that nonethe-
> less lacked the right atmosphere. Wolf was, one could clearly see, in a
> state of happy agitation. I can still see his small form dressed in a light
> suit, his ghostly, dark-glowing, enigmatic eyes skimming the audience.
> But mostly he sat with his Viennese friends around him, closed to strang-
> ers. The young master did not enjoy the tumult and the business of being
> lionized; he did not want to acknowledge banalities and absurdities with
> approving nods, to receive "golden words" with aplomb, understood
> nothing of the farce of being the center of attention. The words of praise,
> the rapturous phrases that people, in well-meaning importunity, heaped
> on him were truly a painful experience for him; there was perhaps even
> something doubly shameful about it, an offense to his proud and self-
> assured diffidence; it was an insult to his modesty to have drawn applause
> both from a small, select group of those who understood his work and a
> herd of stupid blockheads. Thus I understood his mixed emotions; as I
> only knew him superficially from Berlin and Darmstadt, I limited myself
> to but a few fleeting words of joy at his success and delight in his crea-
> tions . . . This memorable evening was the last time that I saw Hugo
> Wolf.[82]

Nodnagel's loyalty is all-embracing, with no recognition of anything
problematic in *Der Corregidor*. Passages from the opera are indeed a connoisseur's delight, and Lukas's monologue proves that sustained dramatic development was within Wolf's capabilities. But there are too many elements at

cross purposes with one another in this opera, too many ill-mixed and incompatible ideals—Wolf at war with Wagner all too audibly. His attempt to compress *Die Meistersinger* to lied dimensions, to retain Wagnerian dramaturgy and yet alter its substance in his own ways, ultimately did not, and could not, work.

THE SEARCH CONTINUES: THE SECOND ALARCÓN OPERA

Wolf had not even completed the composition of *Der Corregidor* before he was once again on the prowl for another libretto. This time, he was willing to consider tragic subjects, although the first of the will-o'-the-wisps he pursued ends happily. In May of 1895, Rosa Mayreder sent Wolf a copy of Wilhelm Meinhold's novel *Maria Schweidler, die Bernsteinhexe* (Maria Schweidler, the amber witch), a pseudoarchival farrago about seventeenth-century Pomeranian witch trials, as a possible source for his next opera. A few weeks later, Wolf told Melanie Köchert that the book had "a ghastly subject" but was full of stirring scenes and shot through with "a wholly demonic passion."[83] He also, as was his custom, began devising a fragmentary scenario on the spot, one in which he proposed to omit the climactic trial scene (Wolf had a propensity for eliminating crucial source material from the initial scenarios he would propose to friends in his letters), but the project never went any further.

The following year, Wolf pursued another possibility more seriously than Meinhold's mediocre witchery. He had been following the meteoric rise to fame of the German playwright Gerhart Hauptmann, in the hope of finding operatic material in each new drama. On 20 April 1892, he told Grohe that he had already obtained a copy of "Hauptmann's play"—he does not say which one—and had read it with great interest, but was disappointed.[84] In 1893, still hot on Hauptmann's trail, Wolf anxiously inquired about a fairy-tale drama he had heard Hauptmann had just written. Not one month after the first stage performance of *Hanneles Himmelfahrt* (Hannele's journey to heaven), Wolf was afraid that some other opera composer might have claimed it![85]

In early 1897 at Rosa Mayreder's suggestion, he considered adapting Hauptmann's latest play, not a naturalist drama any longer but a Nietzschean fairy tale he considered to be perfect operatic material: *Das versunkene Glocke* (The sunken bell), first performed in December 1896. It is no wonder he liked it. The play has sonorous verse; a tormented artist, Heinrich the bellmaker, opposing worlds of Christian, mortal humanity and pagan, immortal nature spirits (a wood-sprite, a water-king, a nixie, a sorceress/wise woman); and a powerful, tragic ending. Wolf realized that the play, with its five lengthy acts, would have to be cut, preferably by the playwright himself, but he was told by friends and intermediaries that Hauptmann would surely refuse to allow operatic setting of his drama.[86] Wolf would not have had time to complete a Hauptmann opera before his mental collapse, any more than his second Alarcón opera, but one regrets the loss nonetheless. Wolf would surely have noticed the Nietzschean ramifications of the tale, that is, the artist as Creator-God who tries, and fails, to make of his art a perfect spiritual realm; the drama both affirms and criticizes Nietzsche's philosophy of art. The psychological investigation of an artist's psyche is combined in this play with symbolist-fantastic elements that would appeal to a composer who loved Mörike's grotesques and Shakespeare's sprites and monsters in *The Tempest*. One wonders what Wolf would have made of the final scene between the nixie Rautendelein and the dying artist, whose last tragically ambiguous words are "Die Nacht ist lang" (The night is long)—something different, assuredly, from Ottorino Respighi's *La campana sommersa* composed over twenty years later.

The Hauptmann drama, however, only appeared on the scene when Wolf was waiting for the reluctant Rosa Mayreder to produce an adaptation of Franz Rudolf Eyßenhardt's German translation of Alarcón's short novel *El Niño de la Bola* (The boy on the globe [the Christ child]).[87] The operetta librettist Richard Genée had shown the tale to Wolf when the composer visited Berlin in February–March 1892, and Wolf immediately saw its possibilities for conversion, telling Grohe that it was "a godsend for modern opera": "The action, depiction, characters, color, passion, mysticism—in short, typically Spanish and yet essentially human: a marvelous painting with deep purple undercurrents of mysticism, vital, popular, and realistic to the greatest degree. Read it and tell me what your impressions are."[88] For six months thereafter, Wolf tried to find someone to adapt the brief work[89]—a difficult task given the necessity to account for quite a bit of prehistory before the actual events of the story; the lack of an antagonist of equal stature to the central figure Manuel Venegas; the conversion from narrative strongly colored by irony to dialogue; the need to fill out the characterization of the principal dramatis personae; and a singularly passive, indeed almost absent, female protagonist. Gustav Schur was the first to attempt a libretto, one that Wolf rejected as "all right for other bank managers" but not to his liking. He objected principally to Schur's beginning with the lengthy prehistory, to Soledad's passivity, and to what he described as a general resemblance to *Cavalleria rusticana*—not a work he respected.[90] (Later, Moritz Hoernes, the author of the second libretto, would also recount past events near the beginning of the text as well, and Wolf would even require that the prehistory be lengthened in order to account adequately for the "present" events.) The principal female protagonist, Manuel Venegas's beloved Soledad, is indeed a problem, since Alarcón's plot turns in part around the fact that the tragic lovers do not, cannot speak to one another until the denouement.

Nothing more came of the project until December of 1896, when Wolf solicited Rosa Mayreder to convert the tale into a libretto. She was unhappy

with the project because its Catholicism offended her nonreligious sensibilities and made her feel alienated from the text,[91] but she began work nevertheless. Revisions to *Der Corregidor* interrupted her labors, and she did not
resume the new libretto until the end of February 1897, completing the first act
by Wolf's thirty-seventh birthday on March 13. He was at first delighted and
told Potpeschnigg and Grohe that it was perfect, its exposition, structure, and
speech wonderful "except for a few trivialities." The "trivialities" would
shortly become larger matters for disquiet.[92] When the entire libretto was delivered to him at the end of April and the beginning of May, he once more
reiterated his enthusiastic praise, but with the proviso that he would show the
text to a "few specialists" (Kauffmann, Grohe, Karl Heckel, Michael Haberlandt, the Munich historian Karl Mayr) to double-check its theatrical
qualities.

Five days after delivery of the complete text, Wolf was already calling for
wholesale revision. No longer was he so ravenously eager to compose an
opera that he would accept the structural premises of her libretto without alteration (he made numerous local revisions to the Corregidor text but took the
large-scale architecture as it was). In a letter of 13 May to Grohe, he contemplated expanding the opera from three acts to four in order to dramatize part
of the prehistory in act 1, rather than recount it in the context of later events,
and making more of Vitriolo as a rejected suitor in order to provide a better
counterbalance to Manuel Venegas.[93] Three days later, he once again wrote to
Grohe, saying that the entire text had to be completely rewritten; whether
Mayreder would agree to do so was in doubt.[94] When his trusted friend Michael Haberlandt, founder of the Hugo Wolf Society, turned thumbs down on
Mayreder's libretto,[95] its doom was sealed, and Haberlandt in short order
found him another collaborator, an archeologist at the University of Vienna
named Moritz Hoernes.

Once again, Wolf's poet was someone inexperienced in the special requirements of opera. It is fascinating to see that Wolf, taking pains to instruct
Hoernes about the proper motivation and emotional depiction he wanted for
his second opera, continued to emphasize psychological portraiture. He told
Hoernes, for example, that Manuel Venegas should not immediately explode
into rage upon first seeing Soledad, but that the sight of her should first inspire
"sweet, passionate, then sorrowful emotions, then gradually intensify by degrees into an outbreak of anger."[96] Although Wolf immediately began setting
Hoernes's text to music, he was not happy with it either. Even before receiving the completed second version on 8 July, Wolf vacillated disturbingly between telling friends that the new text rivaled Shakespeare and requesting
alterations, critiques, and information from Hoernes and the composer's
friends. For example, on 21 June he asked Mayr if he had ever attended a
religious processional in Spain, if the people sang Latin or Spanish, and
whether Mayr knew of any collections of church songs to be sung to the Christ

child. Mayr promptly sent him a volume of Spanish folk songs, including
processional songs (Wolf does not identify the anthology), but Wolf was not
satisfied with any of them. Instead, Hoernes selected "Führ mich, Kind, nach
Bethlehem" (Lead me, child, to Bethlehem) from Wolf's own *Spanisches
Liederbuch* for the purpose.[97] Before the onset of insanity, Wolf recruited
Michael Haberlandt to provide a new text for the dialogue between muleteer
Morisco and the retired captain Carlos in act 1, scene 2 and made substantial
revisions to Hoernes's libretto himself, striking out some 100 of 350 lines and
revising around 66 more. Tragically, they are truly betterments of the text.[98]
With the collapse of his reason, he rejected the Hoernes libretto altogether. He
had become, he told the asylum director Dr. Svetlin and Rosa Mayreder, a
poetic genius and would write his own texts, the *folie de grandeur* heart-
wrenching. What he could not find for himself when sane he would grant to
himself when insane. On 29 November 1897, he wrote Rosa Mayreder to say
that an idea had occurred to him the preceding month to write his own text and
to incorporate into it her first act and the beginning of the second act; he was
also planning to include no fewer than ten orchestrated songs from the *Spanisches Liederbuch* (in the asylum, he orchestrated "Wer sein holdes Lieb ver-
loren," or "For him whom his sweet love has forsaken," and "Wenn du zu den
Blumen gehst" in December 1897 for inclusion in *Manuel Venegas*).

Over thirty years later, Mayreder wrote that Wolf identified himself with
the Romantic figure of the protagonist Manuel Venegas in his larger-than-life
passion.[99] It is a matter for somber reflection to realize as well that Manuel
Venegas is denied by destiny the one thing he most wants, and that he is an
irrational creature whose passions smolder just this side of insanity for years
before flaring into destruction and death. In Alarcón's tale, Manuel manifests
striking instability early, refusing to talk for three years after his father's tragic
death and living alone in the wilderness. He only speaks to Soledad once, and
then she does not answer him—in Rosa Mayreder's libretto for the third act,
she has only one word. The two fall in love without knowing each other and
die horribly in the same condition. Hoernes's libretto omits the early signs of
Manuel's abnormal psychology, but it was of course Alarcón's story that had
inspired Wolf, not the later dramatization.

SUMMARY OF THE HOERNES-WOLF LIBRETTO

Antecedents: Manuel Venegas's father fought honorably in the War of
Liberation against Napoleon's armies, but lost his entire fortune and fell
into the clutches of the usurer Elias Perez (Elias López, alias Caifás, in
the Alarcón tale). His humiliation and financial ruin led to his death, and
the orphaned Manuel (tenor) was brought up by Don Trinidad (bass).
While a youth at school, Manuel met Soledad (soprano), Elias Perez's
daughter, and the pair fell in love. Perez forbade them to see each other,
but Manuel hoped to convince him otherwise by becoming rich and by

feats of heroism. At an annual auction-dance in honor of the child Jesus at which men could bid for a dance with one of the village women, the proceeds to benefit the church, Manuel staked all his hard-won money on a dance with Soledad but was outbid by Elias Perez and humiliated for his father's debts. Manuel leaves the village, vowing to return with an even greater fortune and make a bid for Soledad. He further vows to kill any man who dares seek her hand in marriage. Elias Perez, however, on his deathbed makes Soledad promise to marry Antonio Arregui (baritone). She does so, despite her love for Manuel, and bears Antonio a son.

Act 1: In the first scene, the villagers in chorus sing "Frühling, Herrscher im sonnigen Blau" (Spring, ruler in sunny blue skies) as they prepare for the procession of the infant Jesus into the church of Santa Maria de la Cabeza. The bass-baritone Carlos and the apothecary Vitriolo (tenor) discuss the rumor that Manuel will return for the fiesta and recount in summary form much of the background, including Vitriolo's unsuccessful suit for Soledad's hand. In the second scene, the muleteer Morisco appears, leading a train of heavily laden mules bearing Manuel's accumulated wealth and possessions. The chorus of youths and maidens returns with flowers and wreaths to ornament the village. Two porters run in with the news of Manuel's arrival, followed by Manuel himself, who sings the beautiful aria "Stadt meiner Väter" (City of my ancestors) in the fourth scene. (The chorus must freeze in place, silent onlookers whom Manuel ignores, for the duration of the aria.) Don Trinidad appears, embraces his foster son, and asks if Manuel is healed, recovered from the disastrous events of his leave taking. In their dialogue throughout the fifth scene, Manuel recounts the history of the earlier auction, only fleetingly sketched in the earlier scene with Vitriolo and Carlos—it is with this scene that Wolf's composition ends.

On learning that Perez is dead and Soledad married, he rushes off with the intention of killing Soledad and her husband. The procession, Soledad and her mother Donna Maria (contralto) among them, begins; Manuel catches sight of Soledad and wants to kill her, but is stopped by Carlos. (It was concerning this spot in the libretto that Wolf instructed Hoernes regarding Manuel's reactions on first seeing Soledad after his return.)

Act 2: That evening, Soledad goes to Vitriolo's apothecary and begs him for poison to end her life. She tells him of a dream in which Manuel smothered her to death with kisses. Vitriolo refuses to give her poison but agrees to take her ring to Manuel as a pledge of their betrothal. The scene changes to the sacristy of Santa Maria de la Cabeza later that night, near dawn. Manuel hands Don Trinidad his will and refuses to renounce his intent to kill Antonio Arregui, despite Don Trinidad's pleas. Alone, in front of the painting of the infant Jesus, Manuel undergoes a mystical conversion, offering up the dagger with which he planned to kill Antonio and the jewels for Soledad to the image of Christ and resolving to leave the town once again. The priest returns and is overjoyed at the change of heart. When Antonio Arregui appears unexpectedly, Don Trinidad pleads for a reconciliation between the two, but Manuel refuses.

Act 3: In the countryside, near the town gate, Vitriolo confronts Manuel. In revenge for Soledad's contemptuous rejection of his suit, he plans to make public the lovers' vows in order to destroy them. Vitriolo tells Manuel about Soledad's avowal of love, but then lies, saying that Antonio Arregui is boasting that he drove Manuel from town with his threats. Manuel resolves to return to town in order to avenge his honor and to seek out Soledad. The scene changes to the "fine open space outside the city" in which the auction-dance takes place. Manuel bids the immense sum of one hundred thousand reals for a dance with Soledad. Antonio is unable to outbid him and is forced to watch the dance. On its conclusion, Soledad throws herself into Manuel's arms. He strangles her in a frenzy of desire—whether intentionally or not is left unclear. Antonio rushes to the altar, grabs Manuel's dagger, and stabs him with it.

It may be futile to mourn what Fate has left unfinished, but useless or not, it is irresistible. Much of the piano-vocal score for the fragmentary act 1 of *Manuel Venegas* is beautiful, its spaciousness evidence of progression beyond the liedlike misproportions of *Der Corregidor*. The prolonged tonic pedal of the orchestral introduction to act 1, with its bell-like added-sixth and chromatic seventh chords above the foundation bass tone, is a beautifully atmospheric beginning. The SATT Spring chorus in A major ("not just a women's chorus," Wolf told Mayr) extends for forty-two bars of broad $\frac{12}{8}$ meter— hardly Wagnerian in length but more leisurely than the ensembles of Wolf's first opera. The audience is given, in traditional fashion, time to assimilate the milieu while listening to Wolf's "Good Friday music," as Walker calls it, a reminder of Wolf's ambition to enhance his reputation by means of choral composition.[100] The overlapping antiphonal echoes on sustained D-major and C-major harmonies, the swaying motion evocative of spring breezes ("kühl uns die Stirne mit sanftem Wehn," or "cool our brows with your gentle motion"), the accompanimental trill figures reminiscent of "Karwoche" (Holy week) from the *Mörike-Lieder*, the crescendo to a proclamatory choral conclusion and the instrumental decrescendo leading to Vitriolo's and Carlos's appearance are evidence of lessons well learned from the first operatic foray. Measures 17–24 of the initial chorus, with its words in praise of the Christ child ("Komm zu begrüßen das herrliche Kind," or "Come greet the lordly child"), return in scene 3 with the cadence altered, leading to the dramatic exchange between the two porters and the full chorus of "das Volk," the basses appearing for the first time. One thinks irresistibly of a latter-day secular incarnation of Bach's Passion music, with the chorus excitedly responding to the news with short, exclamatory questions: "Was gibt's? Wie, er kommt? Was wird geschehn? Weiß er alles schon?" (What's happening? He's coming? What will happen? Does he know it all already?").

When Vitriolo first refers to "a stranger from a distant land," Wolf introduces Manuel Venegas's theme, and it thereafter dominates the dialogue between Vitriolo and Carlos. Even the malicious Vitriolo admits that "Majestät liegt in seinem Namen schon" (Majesty still lies in his name), and the theme is accordingly majestic, austere, first stated in dark G♭-major, D♭-major, and B♭-minor harmonies—a measure of processional chords followed by a slow, ascending fanfare. It is the development of this theme in Manuel's homecoming aria "Stadt meiner Väter" that most provokes mourning for this unfinished work. Here, classicizing grandeur marks what is no longer classifiable as lied. Had the opera been completed, "Stadt meiner Väter" would have intensified by contrast the tragedy to come because it makes clear that Manuel returns home not for vengeance but for consolation and surcease from pain. Homesick and wrongly supposing his past passions stilled, he comes back to the site of his "greatest joys and deepest sorrow." In the lengthy fifth scene that follows the aria, Manuel relives the tragic auction of years past in retelling it; the audience both discovers what drove him from the town and realizes that Manuel is not healed of his pain, whatever his words to the contrary. The score breaks off at Manuel's cry of pain when he remembers Soledad's father calling him "his debtor." Those who read this score might well be similarly pained at such an end to Wolf's dream of opera.

THOMAS MANN, in *Die Entstehung des Doktor Faustus* (The genesis of *Doctor Faustus*), writes that Wolf's letters from the 1890s and the biography of Wolf by Ernest Newman influenced the creation of Adrian Leverkühn from the earliest stages of the novel. Mann, fascinated by the nexus of disease, insanity, and creativity, saw the shadow of impending mental collapse in "the lack of judgment, the nonsensical humor, the enthusiasm for his wretched opera texts, the stupidities about Dostoyevsky . . . sad illusions about the operas. Not a single sensible word" in Wolf's letters to Grohe.[101] When the devil in *Doktor Faustus* tells Adrian (shades of Dostoyevsky's hallucinatory encounters) how his madness will first be manifested, he cites a variant of Wolf's pathetic ravings to Michael Haberlandt about his compositional endeavors on *Manuel Venegas*; between the staves of music manuscript paper he used for a message summoning friends to a hearing of his work in progress, Wolf wrote, "Piping hot! Straight from the frying pan! Am beside myself! Sell me up! Blissful! Raving!" But Mann to the contrary, the music of Wolf's second opera does not reflect "lack of judgment" but rather considered remedies to *Der Corregidor*'s faults and considerable beauty of structure, characterization, and expression. It was not a "sad illusion" that Wolf was engaged in his first truly operatic work when the devil of disease came for his soul on 19 September 1897. Miscalculations the first time around are the rule rather than the exception in opera, all the more so as Wolf's desperation to compose clouded his judgment. This is not to say that the course of his syphilis had no effect on his creative work; the very choice of *Manuel Venegas* as a subject, as an operatic alter ego, was possibly dictated at some level by identification with the mentally unbalanced protagonist. But no one who studies this last score can deny that Wolf was creating something extraordinary when all further creativity was denied him forever.

Notes

Chapter 1

1. "Ce spectre rouge" was Ernest Chausson's term for Wagner.

2. When Wolf informed Hellmesberger, the director of the Conservatory, of his dissatisfaction with Krenn and with the entire institution, he was expelled. As a prank, a fellow student mailed Hellmesberger a threatening letter, saying that his days were numbered, and signed the letter "Hugo Wolf." See Frank Walker, *Hugo Wolf: A Biography*, 2d ed. (London: Dent, 1968), 43–45.

3. The manuscript, a single leaf (twenty-four staves in vertical orchestral format), thirty-one bars only, is in the collection of the Vienna City Library, Music Division M.H. 6770/c and is dated "Wien am (1 April) 4. Mai 878."

4. Wolf may also have kept these fragments from the past in order to revisit them on occasion and thereby enjoy the distance he had traveled musically. Walker, *Hugo Wolf*, 36, writes of the legend that Wolf destroyed vast quantities of his early music, a legend contradicted by the survival of opp. 1–17, fragments, sketches, and manuscripts with disparaging comments scrawled across them in Wolf's own hand.

5. See Wolf, *Sämtliche Werke*, vol. 7, part 3: *Nachgelassene Lieder*, ed. Hans Jancik (Vienna: Musikwissenschaftlicher Verlag, 1976) for the extant completed lieder composed between 1875 and 1878 not previously published by Lauterbach and Kuhn in 1903, by Tischer and Jagenberg of Cologne in 1927, or by the Vienna Musikwissenschaftlicher Verlag in 1936. The examples remaining for publication in this third volume include the Goethe settings of op. 3 (1875), perhaps the clearest glimpse of Wolf's song-writing immaturity and ambitions together.

6. See Michael Hamburger, "Heinrich Heine," in *Reason and Energy: Studies in German Literature* (London: Weidenfeld and Nicolson, 1970), 169. Hamburger is of the opinion that Heine's long courtship of the lied in the *Buch der Lieder* was "too inhibited by Voltairean esprit and Byronic self-consciousness ever to result in an altogether happy marriage" (ibid., 146), but the public nevertheless relished the tension between poem and poet as they have relished few other poetic styles.

7. Hermann Kretzschmar, "Das deutsche Lied seit dem Tode Richard Wagners," in *Gesammelte Aufsätze über Musik und Anderes aus den Grenzboten* (Leipzig: Breitkopf and Härtel, 1911), 286–91. Kretzschmar writes (286) that although Wagner's music dramas have indeed influenced the most recent song composers, they have not dominated them as Schumann's songs have.

8. Jeffrey L. Sammons, *Heinrich Heine, The Elusive Poet* (New Haven: Yale University Press, 1969), 26.

9. Carl Loewe's few settings of Heine include "Die Lotosblume," from the "Nachtgesänge" or *Gesammelte Lieder, Gesänge, Romanzen und Balladen*, op. 9, part 1. Part 7 of the same opus contains the *Sechs Gedichte von Heinrich Heine und August von Platen* (the juxtaposition has a certain irony, as Heine mercilessly pilloried Platen in his *Die Bäder von Lucca*.) Five of the six lieder are Heine settings: "Im Traum sah

ich die Geliebte" (In a dream I saw my beloved), "Erste Liebe" (First love), "Neuer Frühling" (New spring), "Du schönes Fischermädchen" (Beautiful fisher-maiden), "Ich hab' im Traume geweinet" (I wept in dreaming), and "Leise zieht durch mein Gemüt" (Gently it steals into my heart), the last published posthumously. The op. 9 settings were composed in 1832, only three years after the publication of Schubert's *Schwanengesang*, but Loewe did not know the Schubert-Heine songs at the time. Loewe also set the famous "Der Fichtenbaum steht einsam" (The fir tree stands lonely) as op. 19, no. 3, a group of six works for male quartet or quintet. After the early 1830s, however, Loewe did not return to Heine until the 1867 publication of "Der Asra," op. 13, an Orientalizing ballade, and he does not mention Heine once in his autobiography. It is possible that Loewe, who chose the ballad as his primary genre, found Heine too subjective for his tastes, as Wolf did later; ballad texts, whatever their blood-and-thunder elements, were characterized by a certain objectivity of narrative approach. Mahler, on the other hand, often emended his chosen texts and may have felt that it was not possible to do so with an icon such as Heine; also, two subjectivities as strong as Heine and Mahler would surely have been incompatible.

10. Heinrich Heine, *Briefe*, vol. 2, ed. Friedrich Hirth (Mainz: Florian Kupferberg, 1950–51), 183. The letter from 3 May 1837 is written to his publisher Julius Campe when Heine was correcting proofs for a new edition of the *Buch der Lieder*.

11. Cornelius goes on to praise Heine as the best that poetic genius had produced in the "slumbering years after the Wars of Liberation," but then calls for a "healthier" strain of poetry for present times. See Peter Cornelius, *Literarische Werke*, vol. 2: *Ausgewählte Briefe (nebst Tagebuchblättern und Gelegenheitsgedichten)*, ed. Carl Maria Cornelius (Leipzig: Breitkopf and Härtel, 1904), 646. Also cited in Magda Marx-Weber, "Cornelius' Kritik des Liedes," in *Peter Cornelius als Komponist, Dichter, Kritiker und Essayist*, ed. Hellmut Federhofer and Kurt Oehl (Regensburg: Gustav Bosse Verlag, 1977), 172–73.

Cornelius was a composer bound to attract Wolf's notice, as he was a friend and disciple of both Liszt and Wagner, a poet-composer with a gift for comic opera (*Der Barbier von Bagdad*) and for song. See chap. 4 for more about Cornelius's aesthetic, Wolf's opinion of his predecessor, and the Cornelius and Wolf settings of "Preciosas Sprüchlein gegen Kopfweh" (Preciosa's charm against headache).

12. Eduard Hanslick, "Vesque von Püttlingen (J. Hoven)," in *Musikalisches Skizzenbuch. Der "Modernen Oper*," vol. 4 (Berlin: Allgemeiner Verein für Deutsche Literatur, 1896), 196–203. Hanslick's remarks here are comparatively gentle: they form part of the critic's obituary in 1884 for a friend he respected.

I have not been to locate any reference to Vesque von Püttlingen's songs in Wolf's criticism, letters, or the reminiscences by his friends. It seems unlikely that such a large collection of songs, published in Vienna by the Staatsdruckerei in 1851, would have escaped Wolf's attention, but co-existence in the same city is no guarantee of contact. The matter is especially interesting because Vesque von Püttlingen was indeed attracted to those comic-sarcastic poems by Heine that other composers shunned—"Der deutsche Professor" (The German professor), for example.

13. Eduard Hanslick, *Aus meinem Leben*, ed. Peter Wapnewski (Kassel and Basel: Bärenreiter, 1987), 144–45.

14. J. Hoven [Johann Vesque von Püttlingen, pseud.], *Die Heimkehr. Achtundachtzig Gedichte aus H. Heine's Reisebildern* (Vienna: Aus der kaiserlich-könig-

lichen Hof- und Staatsdruckerie, 1851). To cite only those songs on poems Wolf also set, "Ich stand in dunkeln Träumen (Ihr Bild)" is on 75–76; "Du bist wie eine Blume" on 133–34; "Sie haben heut' Abend Gesellschaft" on 157–61; "Mädchen mit dem roten Mündchen" on 139–41; and "Es blasen die blauen Husaren" on 192–94. One discovers rapidly that Vesque von Püttlingen had a limited repertoire of musical devices; for example, he is fond of unsubtle mediant tonal relationships, especially C major (his favorite key) and the secondary key of A♭ major. See also Helmut Schultz, *Johann Vesque von Püttlingen 1803–1883* (Regensburg: Heinrich Schiele, n.d.).

15. Max Kalbeck, *Johannes Brahms I 1833–1856*, 3d ed. (Berlin: Deutsch Brahms-Gesellschaft, 1912), 132–33. In a letter to Kalbeck from 1885, Brahms remarked that it was sad to see youthful composers rush their immature compositions into print. Asked if he had any of his own early works, Brahms replied that he had burned them all and poked fun at himself for papering the walls and floors of his first abodes with music, with sonatas and quartets and songs. "There were quite pretty little songs among them," he says—"recht nette Liederchen" not a complimentary designation—and adds, "Did you know that I too once set 'Du bist wie eine Blume'?"

16. These three songs have been published in Hugo Wolf, *Sämtliche Werke*, vol. 7, part 2: *Nachgelassene Lieder*, ed. Hans Jancik (Vienna: Musikwissenschaftlicher Verlag, 1969): "Du bist wie eine Blume," 37; "Mädchen mit dem roten Mündchen," 35–36; "Wenn ich in deine Augen seh'," 38–39.

17. Wilhelm Waldmann, *Robert Franz: Gespräche aus zehn Jahren* (Leipzig: Breitkopf and Härtel, 1895), 109 and 153. Given the fact that Franz was highly esteemed in the 1880s and 1890s, at times placed on a par with Schubert and Schumann, Wolf would probably have enjoyed Oscar Bie's unkindest cut of all in characterizing Franz as a "bureaucratic song composer" and "the first journalist of songs." See Oscar Bie, *Das deutsche Lied* (Berlin: S. Fischer, 1926), 189 and 191.

18. Ernst Challier, *Grosser Lieder-Katalog: Ein alphabetisch geordnetes Verzeichniss sämmtlicher Einstimmiger Lieder* (Berlin: privately published, 1885). The settings of "Du bist wie eine Blume" are listed on 178–79, including Anton Rubinstein's op. 32, no. 5 and Franz Liszt's setting. Rubinstein maintains the same rhythmic figure in $\frac{2}{4}$ throughout the lied, in which he repeats the final two lines of text three times in succession without deciding conclusively whether to emphasize "Gott" or "erhalte" the more greatly. Settings of "Mädchen mit dem roten Mündchen" are listed on 547 and include a setting by the ubiquitous Robert Franz (op. 5, no. 5) and Emil Kauffmann (op. 13, no. 3), who would later be one of Wolf's best friends and most caring supporters. (On the same page, Challier lists twenty-nine different cycles or sets, ranging from two songs to ten, all entitled *Mädchenlieder*!)

19. Heinrich Heine, *Historisch-Kritische Gesamtausgabe der Werke*, ed. Manfred Windführ, vol. 1, part 1: *Buch der Lieder*, ed. Pierre Grappin (Hamburg: Hoffmann and Campe Verlag, 1975), 262–63.

20. Walker, *Hugo Wolf*, 43.

21. Siegbert Salomon Prawer, *Heine: Buch der Lieder* (London: Edward Arnold, 1960), 24. Prawer also points out perceptively (26) that "there is a subtle pleasure to be had from loving an unworthy and an even subtler from loving a cruel object."

22. Heine told one Adolf Stahr in 1850 that this poem was the sort of thing that would remain valid in his works. See Heinrich Hubert Houben, *Gespräche mit Heine* (Frankfurt am Main, 1926), 745. For the text, see Heine, *Buch der Lieder*, 260–62.

23. Edmund von Hellmer, *Hugo Wolf, Erlebtes und Erlauschtes* (Vienna and Leipzig: Wiener Literarischer Anstalt, 1921), 137.

24. Wolf would surely have known Liszt's setting of "Du bist wie eine Blume" in A major, marked "Lento con molto sentimento" (Slow, with great feeling). The surface is all Lisztian sensuousness at its most melting, precisely the compound of seductive lyricism and pseudoreligiosity the poetic persona wishes to convey to the woman, but with discernible indices of his underlying disbelief. For example, at measures 32–33 in the piano interlude following the words "auf's Haupt dir legen sollt'," the chromatic figure A–B–B♯–C♯ previously heard in the vocal line of measures 17–18 at the words "[Wehmut schleicht] mir ins Herz hinein" returns. Even more telling, Liszt has the piano accompaniment vanish altogether at the word "Gott" in measure 36, followed, not by the resolution of the preceding V/F♯ minor chord, but by deceptive motion to A-major harmonies.

25. Most likely in the fall of 1876, Wolf began work on a "Romantic Opera in four acts" entitled *König Alboin*, to a text by a Viennese friend named Paul Peitl. Only a sketch in two voices for the orchestral accompaniment to the duel between the sixth-century Lombard king Alboin and his enemy Lintram survives in a manuscript from the Musik-Sammlung, Austrian National Library. The sketch, dated "Windischgratz um 9.4.877" and bearing the indication "3. Aufg.," is fortissimo, "stark markiert" (strongly accented), and scored for "C11. ctb." in the lower voice, "3 posaun." in the upper.

26. The sketch is to be published in Hugo Wolf, *Sämtliche Werke*, vol. 19: *Unvollständige Kompositionen, Entwürfe, Skizzen*, ed. Hans Jancik (in press).

27. Ernst Decsey, *Hugo Wolf*, vol. 2: *Hugo Wolfs Schaffen 1888–1891* (Berlin and Leipzig: Schuster and Loeffler, 1904), 1–2, records the reminiscences of the Viennese writer Franz Zweybrück, who claimed to have been the first to direct Wolf's attention to the *Italienisches Liederbuch* and to Mörike. Wolf frequented the Café Griensteidl, a meeting place for artists and eccentrics popularly known as "Café Grossenwahn" (Megalomania) near the old Hofburgtheater. There, Zweybrück was approached by Wolf's friend Friedrich Eckstein, who asked him, "Sir, do you perhaps know of any beautiful poetry that has not yet been set to music? Wolf has looked and looked, but finds very little that suits him." Decsey placed the encounter in 1878, but it almost certainly occurred four years later, in 1882. Zweybrück recommended to Eckstein and Wolf the Spanish and Italian songbooks of Geibel and Heyse, also Mörike. "And then I asked them both if they knew Mörike and laid great weight on this marvelous poet." Wolf would surely have known the *Spanisches Liederbuch* already from Schumann's *Spanisches Liederspiel* and other settings, and Wolf's copy of Mörike with the date 1878 inscribed within indicates that the composer already knew of the poet's works.

28. Adalbert von Chamisso, *Chamissos Werke*, vol. 1, ed. Hermann Tardel (Leipzig and Vienna: Bibliographisches Institut, 1907), 62. "Was soll ich sagen?" is one of a group of four individual poems (not a cycle) dedicated to his new bride, Antonie Piaste, whom he married in 1819 when he was thirty-eight and she eighteen. The painful uncertainty expressed in "Was soll ich sagen?" is not found in the other poems; indeed, "Morgentau" begins "Wir wollten mit Kosen und Lieben / Geniessen der köstlichen Nacht; / Wo sind doch die Stunden geblieben? / Es ist ja der Hahn schon erwacht" (With caressing and loving, we wanted to enjoy the beautiful night. Where have the hours gone? The rooster has already awakened).

29. Walker, *Hugo Wolf*, 20. "Unable to progress in the harmony class [at the Conservatory] as fast as he wished, Wolf used to sit at the Vinzenzbergs' piano for hours on end, striking successions of chords, and when he discovered a novel way of resolving a discord, used to call out into the living-room: 'Anna, Anna, another resolution!' and play it over to her a dozen times in succession." 30. Challier, *Grosser Lieder-Katalog*, 763, lists three previous settings of "Sie hat [*sic*] heut' Abend Gesellschaft" by Geisler, Metzdorff, and Sigmund Thalberg; forty-nine settings of "Ich stand in dunklen Träumen," 408, including one by Edvard Grieg; ten settings of "Das ist ein Brausen und Heulen," 151, including Robert Franz's op. 8, no. 4; twenty-five settings of "Mir träumte von einem Königskind," 589; six settings of "Wo ich bin, mich rings umdunkelt," 994; and seven settings of "Es blasen die blauen Husaren," 232.

31. The songs of the Heine *Liederstrauß I* have been published in Hugo Wolf, *Sämtliche Werke*, vol. 7, part 1: *Nachgelassene Lieder*, ed. Hans Jancik: "Sie haben heut' Abend Gesellschaft," 3–6; "Ich stand in dunkeln Träumen," 7–10; "Das ist ein Brausen und Heulen," 11–12; "Wo ich bin, mich rings umdunkelt," 56–57; "Aus meinen grossen Schmerzen," 13–15; "Mir träumte von einem Königskind," 16–17; "Mein Liebchen, wir sassen beisammen," 18–21; and "Es blasen die blauen Husaren," 22–23.

32. *Hugo Wolf: Ein Persönlichkeit in Briefen. Familienbriefe*, ed. Edmund von Hellmer (Leipzig: Breitkopf and Härtel, 1912).

33. Walker, *Hugo Wolf*, 112.

34. The manuscripts include 1) City Library 6683, "Aus dem Liederstrauss v. H. Heine IV —'Das gelbe Laub erzittert'"; 2) Musik-Sammlung, Austrian National Library 0015, "'Neue Gedichte' / Aus dem Liederstrauss v. H. Heine VIII. —Es war ein alter König," clearly a fair copy on the front and back of a single leaf; 3) the Konvolut von Skizzen in the Vienna City M.H. 6773/c includes a title page (no. 8 in the Konvolut), "Acht Lieder / von / Heinrich Heine / für eine Singstimme mit Piano-Forte. / componirt von / Hugo Wolf / 1878"; 4) in no. 29 of the same folder is a title and a single three-staff system with a B-major or G♯-minor key signature in the topmost staff (vocal line) only, entitled "Aus dem Liederstrauss / von H. Heine / XIII"; 5) the Austrian National Library owns S.m. 0016 (the autograph of "Ich stand in dunklen Träumen"), S.m. 0014 ("Das ist ein Brausen und Heulen"), and 0013, with nos. V and IV in that order on a single leaf ("Wo ich bin" and "Aus meinen grossen Schmerzen"); 6) the nine-measure variant to "Mir träumte von einem Königskind" in the Vienna City Library 6680/c; 7) the autograph manuscript 399 in the Austrian National Library of the *Vier Gedichte von Heine, Shakespeare u. Lord Byron*, the setting of "Wo wird einst" dated "24. Januar 1888"; and 8) the photograph in the Vienna City Library MH 11388/c of the autograph of "Sie haben heut' Abend Gesellschaft." The fair copies of "Spätherbstnebel," "Mit schwarzen Segeln," "Sterne mit den goldnen Füsschen," and "Wie des Mondes Abbild zittert" were destroyed during World War II.

35. Heine, *Briefe*, vol. 1, 28, undated letter to Heinrich Straube, probably written between February and April 1821.

36. Heine, *Buch der Lieder*, 272–73.

37. Walker, *Hugo Wolf*, 137–38. "'Rückkehr' is tinged with sadness and regret by the singer's detachment from the happy scene he describes. This gives Wolf the opportunity for the employment of what afterwards became one of his favourite devices: the depiction, in voice and accompaniment, of two conflicting emotions."

38. The autograph manuscript is currently in the private collection of Kammersänger Anton Dermota in Vienna, but the Vienna City Library owns a photograph of the first page of the manuscript (MG 11388/c), entitled "Aus dem Lieder-Cyklus von H[einrich] Heine I. 'Sie haben heut' Abend Gesellschaft.'" The manuscript is marked only "Lustig" (the qualifying words "etwas breit" were added later); the dotted halfnotes in measures 9–10, 17–21, and 23–24 are not sustained throughout the measure, as later; and the sforzando indications in measures 7–8, the final two measures of the piano introduction, are not present.

39. Adalbert von Goldschmidt introduced Wolf to Viennese society and the ways of the world. His oratorio *Die sieben Todsünden* (The seven deadly sins), dedicated to Franz Liszt, is a setting of an unsubtle text by the poet Robert Hamerling, a rambling three-part melodrama whose dramatis personae include a "Prince of Darkness," a demon for each of the seven deadly sins, a vaguely Tristan and Isolde–like archetypal youth and maiden in love, and a chorus of Bacchantes and youths proclaiming, "Frei sei die Liebe!" (Let love be free!)—which might have added a spice of scandal to the work's ephemeral popularity. Hanslick dubbed the work a "Monstre-Oratorium" and characterized Goldschmidt's lieder as "so puny as to be almost indistinguishable from nothingness." See Hanslick, *Concerte, Componisten und Virtuosen*, 396–97.

40. Robert Franz, *12 Gesänge für eine Singstimme mit Begleitung des Pianoforte*, op. 5 (Leipzig: F. Whistling, n.d.), 3.

41. Hugo Wolf, *Briefe an Melanie Köchert*, ed. Franz Grasberger (Tutzing: Hans Schneider Verlag, 1964), letter of 23 June 1894, and the English translation of the same book, *Letters to Melanie Köchert*, trans. Louise McClelland Urban (New York: Schirmer Books, 1991), 114–15. "How I envy the dull Robert Franz, who was recommended to [Gottfried] Keller (nota bene by Wagner) as an 'important composer.' They weren't well matched at all."

42. Eduard Hanslick, *Fünf Jahre Musik (1891–1895). Der "Modernen Oper,"* vol. 7 (Berlin: Allgemeiner Verein für Deutsche Litteratur, 1896), from the 1892 article "Zur Erinnerung an Robert Franz" (In remembrance of Robert Franz), 355. Franz had journeyed through southern Germany and the Tyrol in September of 1862 and met Eduard Hanslick in Salzburg; the famous critic encouraged Franz to publish his [Franz's] *Offener Brief an Eduard Hanslick: Über Bearbeitungen älterer Tonwerke, namentlich Bach'scher und Händel'scher Vokalmusik* (Leipzig: F.E.C. Lueckart, 1871), or "Open letter to Eduard Hanslick: on the arrangements of earlier works of music, namely, Bach's and Handel's vocal music."

According to Joseph Boonin, *An Index to the Solo Songs of Robert Franz* (Hackensack, N.J.: Joseph Boonin, 1970), Franz published a total of sixty-seven solo lieder to texts by Heine, including four sets of six songs, opp. 25, 34, 38, and 39. He did not set "Sie haben heut' Abend Gesellschaft," "Es blasen die blauen Husaren," "Mir träumte von einem Königskind," "Spätherbstnebel," or "Ernst ist der Frühling," five of Wolf's text choices. Franz's observations about the poetry he considered suitable for lieder in general, particularly Heine, and about other lieder composers are included in Waldmann, *Franz: Gespräche aus zehn Jahren*, 68–69. Franz considered Heine's poetry especially suited for music because it suggests rather than describes; it does not "say it all." He goes on to criticize—one suspects jealousy in the matter—several of Schubert's Heine songs, including the dramatic ending of "Am Meere" (At the sea). Schumann was the first, he felt, to show the public how to set a text vis-à-vis music. See also William Kenneth Gaeddert, "Robert Franz: A Biographical and Critical Study" (Ph.D. dissertation, University of Iowa, 1976).

43. Waldmann, *Gespräche aus zehn Jahren*, 356. Franz defensively insists that his approach to composition has its basis in a more distant past and was only enriched, not called into being, by the music of Schubert and Schumann.

44. Heine, *Buch der Lieder*, 166–67.

45. The earliest extant manuscript of no. IV is dated "Wien am 5. Juni 878" and appears at the bottom of the same leaf containing no. V, "Wo ich bin, mich rings umdunkelt" (Musik-Sammlung, Austrian National Library 0013). The opening indication "zart" does not appear in the accompaniment, nor the reduction to "*pp* zart" in measure 9. Most telling, there are almost none of the crescendo-decrescendo markings that were added later, although the ones notated in the last half of measures 1 and 3 show that the conception of the changeable dynamics was already formed.

46. Sammons, *Heine*, 30.

47. Laura Hofrichter, in *Heinrich Heine*, trans. Barker Fairley (Oxford: Oxford University Press, 1963), 90–94, discusses Heine's obsession with the spirit world in many of his youthful poems, his attempts to rid himself of the fascination with the world of dreams. The phrase "absoluter Traumweltherrscher" comes from Heine's "Jehuda ben Halevy."

48. Heine, *Buch der Lieder*, 172–73.

49. Challier, *Grosser Lieder-Katalog*, 589.

50. The variant has been published in Hugo Wolf, *Sämtliche Werke*, vol. 7, part 1: *Nachgelassene Lieder*, 69.

51. Walker, *Hugo Wolf*, entitles his sixth chapter (118–47) "Years of Indecision," referring to 1881–83.

52. See Hugo Wolf, *Briefe an Henriette Lang, nebst den Briefen an deren Gatten, Prof. Joseph Freiherr von Schey*, ed. Heinrich Werner (Regensburg, 1922), 196. Henriette Lang was the sister of Melanie Köchert and one of Wolf's principal confidantes during the period from 1878 to 1883. In a letter written 19 October 1882, he tells of studying some of "the blessed one's favorite compositions," the "blessed one" Vally Franck and the "favorite compositions" clearly his: "'Die Elfenkönigin' of Loewe, Chopin's [songs] 'Zwei Leichen,' 'Polens Grabgesang'—oh! it was too much! By God, I have loved him and will love him even in his transfigured guise. He was good and noble, entirely a man and entirely—a child. May he rest in peace."

53. Heine, *Buch der Lieder*, 172–75.

54. Vesque von Püttlingen subtitles his setting "Humoristica: Militär-Einquartierung" (A humorous piece: military quartering) and links it, by both the common C-major tonality and the fanfares that herald the Hussars, to "Es blasen die blauen Husaren" immediately after. Especially in the first song of the pair, Vesque von Püttlingen attempted to do what Wolf would later do more successfully, that is, to make overt the anger couched in words of seeming acceptance and love. When the poetic persona of "An deine schneeweisse Schulter" tells his beloved at the end of the poem, "Und in deinen schönen Armen / Will ich doppelt selig sein" (And in your beautiful arms, I will be doubly blessed), Vesque von Püttlingen has him repeat the words over and over, to increasingly louder accented chords in the bass. It is a laudable compositional choice for this passage, if only the harmonic progression, melody, and voice leading were more compelling than they are.

55. Heine, *Buch der Lieder*, 288–89.

56. The fragment will be published in Hugo Wolf, *Sämtliche Werke*, vol. 19: *Unvollständige Kompositionen, Entwürfe, Skizzen*, ed. Hans Jancik (in press).

57. The manuscript of Rückert's "Frühling, Liebster" is in the collection of the Vienna City Library 6665/c. It is dated "Wien am 20. Juli 878," marked "Ziemlich rasch," and breaks off in a rather dramatic fashion after thirty-four measures, just before the resolution of a cadence to G (probably G minor, as that tonality is important earlier in the fragment). The Schumannesque sixteenth-note triplet figuration in the right hand is the focus of attention.

58. The first and fourth songs have been published in Hugo Wolf, *Sämtliche Werke*, vol. 7, part 1: *Nachgelassene Lieder*: "Es war ein alter König," 58–61, and "Ernst ist der Frühling," 62–64. The second and third songs appear in *Sämtliche Werke*, vol. 7, part 2: "Mit schwarzen Segeln," 44–45, and "Spätherbstnebel," 40–43.

59. Challier, *Grosser Lieder-Katalog*, 251–52, 1026, 1070, 1136, 1220, and 1314.

60. Ibid., "Mit schwarzen Segeln," 592; "Sterne mit den goldnen Füsschen," 802; and "Wie des Mondes Abbild zittert," 964.

61. Sammons, *Heine*, 188. Much of the poetry in the "Neuer Frühling" first section was written for the composer Albert Methfessel. Heine, in *Der Gesellschafter oder Blätter für Geist und Herz* for 3 November 1823, praises Methfessel warmly for his folklike songs in an era of "elephant-music."

62. Prawer, *Heine: Buch der Lieder*, 23. The reference is from Heine's "Der Tannhäuser" in the *Neue Gedichte*: "Der Teufel, den man Venus nennt, / Er ist der schlimmste von allen . . . " (The devil that one calls Venus is the worst of all).

63. Charles Baudelaire, "Lettre à Jules Janin" (1865), in *Oeuvres posthumes, juvenilia, reliquiae*, ed. Jacques Crépet and Claude Pichois (Paris: Louis Conard, 1939), 231.

64. Of the four completed Hoffmann von Fallersleben settings composed between 9 August 1878 and 1 September ("Liebesfrühling," or "Love's spring"; "Auf der Wanderung," or "On the journey"; "Ja, die Schönst! Ich sagt es offen," or "Yes, the most beautiful! I say it openly"; and "Nach dem Abschiede," or "After the farewell"), two in particular made overt display of Schubertian derivation. "Auf der Wanderung," extracted from Hoffmann von Fallersleben's poetic cycle "Des fahrenden Schülers Lieben und Leiden" (Of the itinerant scholar's loves and sorrows), is actually a Viennese dance for piano with an obbligato vocal line, the writing for piano developed as if in a Schubert piano sonata. The first quatrain of "Nach dem Abschiede" inevitably recalls Heine's "Der Doppelgänger" ("Dunkel sind nun alle Gassen, / und die Stadt ist öd und leer; / Denn mein Lieb hat mich verlassen, / Meine Sonne scheint nicht mehr," or "Now the streets are all dark, and the town is deserted and empty; my beloved has left me, my sun shines no more"), although without Heine's power and arresting imagery, and Wolf responds with a measured half-note chordal tread in the accompaniment (measures 1–13) and a vocal line reminiscent in places of Schubert's Heine songs. See Wolf, *Sämtliche Werke*, vol. 7, part 2: *Nachgelassene Lieder*, ed. Hans Jancik (Vienna: Musikwissenschaftlicher Verlag, 1969), 18–29.

65. Sammons, *Heine*, 19.

66. Heine, *Briefe*, vol. 1, 46, a letter to Ernst Christian August Keller on 1 September 1822. The passage continues: "Whether men praise or reproach me makes no differ-

ence to me—I go my own harsh way . . . some say it leads me into the mud and filth, others say it leads me to Parnassus, and still others say it leads me straight to hell. No matter, the path is new, and I am looking for adventure."

67. Hugo Wolf, *Briefe an Emil Kauffmann*, ed. Edmund von Hellmer (Berlin: S. Fischer, 1903), 13, letter of 5 June 1890. Wolf was attempting to dissuade Kauffmann from his newfound friend's liking for Brahms's music and to explain his own aesthetic in brief. "For me, the highest principle in art is harsh, inexorable truth, truth to the point of terror." Wolf then cites Kleist's *Penthesilea*, Wagner, and Mörike's "Erstes Liebeslied eines Mädchens" (A maiden's first love song) as examples of the artistic truth of which he speaks.

68. The poem is a single quatrain from the "Lyrisches Intermezzo": "Die Mitternacht war kalt und stumm; / Ich irrte klagend im Wald herum. / Ich habe die Baum aus dem Schlaf gerüttelt; / Sie haben mitleidig die Kopfe geschüttelt." See Heine, *Buch der Lieder*, 194–95.

69. *Hugo Wolf: Ein Persönlichkeit in Briefen*, letter 17, 10 April 1878. Quoted in Walker, *Hugo Wolf*, 60.

70. Walker, *Hugo Wolf*, 129.

71. This title page was owned, according to Walker, *Hugo Wolf*, 501, by the Köchert family. They also owned a title page for two projected volumes of *Lieder u[nd] Gesänge nach Lenau u[nd] Eichendorff*. An incomplete sketch of the vocal line for a setting of "Verschwiegene Liebe" unlike the setting of 1888 survives in the Vienna City Library *Konvolut von Skizzen* no. 29.

72. Wolf, *Briefe an Kauffmann*, 128.

73. Walker, *Hugo Wolf*, 137.

74. Egon Schwartz, *Joseph von Eichendorff* (New York: Twayne Publishers, 1974), 88. See also Oskar Seidlin, "Eichendorff's Symbolic Landscape" in *PMLA* 72 (1957): 93–103, and *Versuche über Eichendorff* (Göttingen: Vandenhoeck and Ruprecht, 1965); and Lawrence Radner, *Eichendorff: The Spiritual Geometer* (Lafayette, Ind.: Purdue University Press, 1970).

75. In a letter to Melanie Köchert written from Perchtoldsdorf on 21 July 1894, Wolf wrote, "Since the air has cleared once again here, a truly uncanny stillness surrounds me. Oh, how lovely it is! Nothing around me but blue sky, green leaves and glorious sunshine and above all, the wonderful stillness with its otherworldly magic, its unfathomable depths, its intimate shadowy paths, its labyrinths of dreams." See Hugo Wolf, *Briefe an Melanie Köchert*, 106, and *Letters to Melanie Köchert*, 121–22.

76. Wolf's setting on 12 April 1878 of Friedrich Hebbel's "Das Vöglein" (The little bird) prefigures "Mausfallen-Sprüchlein," both songs with accompaniments largely in the treble and characterized by a similar lighthearted delicacy. Wolf avoided Hebbel's philosophical poetry on such themes as "Humanity and History," "Our Times," etc., and chose miniature nature lyrics and ballad texts instead.

77. Justinus Kerner, *The Seeress of Prevorst: Revelations Concerning the Inner Life of Man*, trans. Mrs. Crowe (New York: Partridge and Brittan, 1856), 5–6.

78. Christopher Hatch, "Tradition and Creation: Hugo Wolf's 'Fussreise,'" in *College Music Symposium* 28 (1988): 70–84.

79. Joseph von Eichendorff, *Werke*, vol. 1, ed. Ansgar Hillach (Munich: Winkler-Verlag, 1970), 62–63, the fourth and fifth stanzas of "Wolken, wälderwärts gegangen."

Chapter 2

1. Hugo Wolf, *Briefe an Melanie Köchert*, ed. Franz Grasberger (Tutzing: Hans Schneider Verlag, 1964), 165, and *Letters to Melanie Köchert*, trans. Louise McClelland Urban (New York: Schirmer Books, 1991), 190.

2. Wolf met Melanie Köchert, *née* Melanie Lang (1858–1906), in 1879 and became close friends with her sister Henriette and brother Edmund, her husband Heinrich Köchert (1854–1908), and his brother Theodor. It was probably in the summer of 1884 that Wolf and Melanie recognized that they loved each other. Because of the impossibility of divorce, because Heinrich was one of Wolf's most generous patrons, and because of the Köcherts' three young daughters, the relationship had to be kept secret. They arranged meetings through the personal columns of the *Neue Freie Presse* until 1893, when Heinrich discovered the existence of the affair. It is a credit to his extraordinary nature that his generosity toward the composer continued beyond the discovery of his wife's love for Wolf. See Frank Walker, *Hugo Wolf: A Biography*, 2d ed. (London: Dent, 1968), 166–69 and 342–71.

3. The *Italienisches Liederbuch* had a difficult and protracted genesis. Between 25 September 1890 and 14 November of that year, Wolf set seven poems from the collection to music and then had to turn to the incidental music for Ibsen's "Das Fest auf Solhaug," Wolf's one commission in his lifetime. He was unable to compose again until the end of the following year; between 29 November 1891 and 23 December, he composed fifteen additional songs from the Heyse anthology. A much longer compositional drought followed, beginning in 1892 and only broken in 1895 with the work on *Der Corregidor*. When most of the work on the opera was completed, he wrote Melanie Köchert a brief note on 23 March 1896 to say that he had lost his copy of the *Italienisches Liederbuch*: "Please send me your copy." He began composition of part 2 only two days later, composing twenty-four songs between 25 March 1896 and 30 April. From Perchtoldsdorf, he kept Melanie informed of his progress; see letters 196–209 in *Briefe an Melanie Köchert*, 165–73, and *Letters to Melanie Köchert*, 190–201. The letters announcing new compositions are exuberant:

> I have written two museum pieces ["Nicht länger kann ich singen" and "Schweig einmal still"], which go beyond all those composed so far. (*Briefe an Melanie Köchert*, 172–73, and *Letters to Melanie Köchert*, 200)

> I know that you are especially fond of this poem ["Heut Nacht erhob' ich mich], so it pleases me all the more that it shall not be omitted from the songbook. (*Briefe an Melanie Köchert*, 173, and *Letters to Melanie Köchert*, 201)

> I put away an opulent breakfast at Faischtling's house [Hugo Faisst] and then played for him by heart "Ich hab in Penna einen Liebsten wohnen," which threw him into a cannibalistic ecstasy. He wanted to hear it over and over again. (*Briefe an Melanie Köchert*, 174, and *Letters to Melanie Köchert*, 202)

4. Margarete Saary, in *Persönlichkeit und musikdramatische Kreativität Hugo Wolfs* (Tutzing: Hans Schneider Verlag, 1984), analyses the Romantic topos of the composer as mentally aberrant genius and the realities of Wolf's personality, influences, and life. Wolf's life has inspired several novels and short stories in which the

topos of the demonic creator, or the presumed linking of insanity with creativity at a high level, is the central idea of the work, including Josef Marschall's *Der Dämon: Eine Erzählung aus dem Leben Hugo Wolfs* (Leipzig: L. Staackman 1930); Luise George Bachmann, "Der Feuerreiter," in *Musikantengeschichten: Kleine Geschichten aus sieben Jahrhunderten um unsere grossen deutschen Meister* (Paderborn: Schöningh, 1939); and Dolf Lindner, *Der Feuerreiter: Roman um das Leben Hugo Wolfs* (Biberach: Koehler, 1950). Lindner is also the author of a nonfictional survey of Wolf's "life, songs, and sorrows" in the alliterative *Hugo Wolf: Leben, Lied, Leiden* (Vienna: Bergland Verlag, 1960).

5. Walker, *Hugo Wolf*, 146–47, discusses Wolf's emotional and musical crisis in the early 1880s, a crisis of creativity brought on by dejection over Wagner's sublimity and fears that his own talents were circumscribed. See Karl Heckel, *Hugo Wolf in seinem Verhältnis zu Richard Wagner* (Munich and Leipzig: Georg Müller, 1905).

6. See Deborah J. Stein, *Hugo Wolf's Lieder and Extensions of Tonality*, Studies in Musicology no. 72, ed. George Buelow (Ann Arbor: UMI Research Press, 1985), 83–87 for a Schenkerian study of "Wie lange schon war immer mein Verlangen."

7. That same year, Wolf published the *Sechs Gedichte von Scheffel, Mörike, Goethe und Kerner*, and the difference between the two sets was surely calculated. The *Sechs Lieder für eine Frauenstimme* is altogether in a lighter vein, including "Morgentau," "Die Spinnerin," "Das Vöglein," and the two Reinick *Wiegenlieder*, as well as "Mausfallen-Sprüchlein," while the *Sechs Gedichte* contains his most tonally adventurous songs to date, including the beautiful setting of Justinus Kerner's "Zur Ruh', zur Ruh'."

8. Hugo Wolf, *Sämtliche Werke*, vol. 6: *Lieder nach verschiedenen Dichtern*, ed. Hans Jancik (Vienna: Musikwissenschaftlicher Verlag, 1981), 24–25.

9. Eduard Mörike, *Sämtliche Werke*, vol. 1, ed. Gerhart Baumann and Siegfried Grosse (Stuttgart: J. G. Cotta, 1961), 218.

10. The tonality and the open fifths in the treble register anticipate "Nixe Binsefuss" by six years. The water-sprite and the child share a delicate liveliness and a strain of malice in common, and both belong to a charmed world of whimsy.

11. See Raphael Metzger, "Hugo Wolf's Symphonic Poem, *Penthesilea*: A History and Analysis" (D.M.A. dissertation, Peabody Conservatory of Music, 1979). The trial reading of *Penthesilea* in 1886 by the Vienna Philharmonic under Richter's direction was a fiasco. Hans Richter and Karl Grunsky exchanged open letters on the subject, beginning with Richter's "Offener Brief an den Herausgeber der *Musik*," in *Die Musik* 6, no. 1 (November 1906): 166–67, and continuing with Karl Grunsky's "Offener Antwort an Hans Richter," in ibid., 369–71. The final salvo was Richter's "Schlusswort," in ibid., 372.

12. Sigmund Freud, *Jokes and Their Relationship to the Unconscious*, vol. 8 of *The Standard Edition of the Complete Psychological Works of Sigmund Freud*, trans. James Strachey, Anna Freud, Alix Strachey, and Alan Tyson (London: Hogarth Press, 1960). *Der Witz und seine Beziehung zum Unbewussten* was first published in Leipzig and Vienna in 1905 by Deuticke. According to the editor's preface, Freud had long been interested in jokes; when Wilhelm Fliess read the proofs of *The Interpretation of Dreams* in 1899 and complained that the dreams were full of jokes, Freud responded immediately with an explanation inserted into the book.

13. Freud, *Jokes*, 103. "It [the joke] will further bribe the hearer with its yield of pleasure into taking sides with us without any very close investigation, just as on other occasions we ourselves have often been bribed by an innocent joke into over-estimating the substance of a statement expressed jokingly. This is brought out with perfect aptitude in the common phrase 'die Lacher auf seine Seite ziehen.'"

14. Ibid., 200–201. "Caricature, as is well known, brings about degradation by emphasizing in the general impression given by the exalted object a single trait which is comic in itself but was bound to be overlooked so long as it was only perceivable in the general picture. By isolating this, a comic effect can be attained which extends in our memory over the whole object . . . If a comic trait of this kind that has been overlooked is lacking in reality, a caricature will unhesitatingly create it by exaggerating one that is not comic in itself; and the fact that the effect of the caricature is not essentially diminished by this falsification of reality is once again an indication of the origin of comic pleasure."

15. Ibid., 171–73. Freud summarizes the differences between joke-work and dream-work, despite the features they share in common—indirect representation, displacement, and allusion—and their similar methods of operation. "For jokes do not, like dreams, create compromises; they do not evade the inhibition, but they insist on maintaining play with words or with nonsense unaltered. They restrict themselves, however, to a choice of occasions in which this play or this nonsense can at the same time appear allowable (in jests) or sensible (in jokes), thanks to the ambiguity of words and the multiplicity of conceptual relations" (172). Jokes are bound by certain conditions that do not apply to dreams, especially the social context of jokes and the completely asocial mental production of dreams.

16. Carl Schorske, "Politics and Patricide in Freud's *Interpretation of Dreams*," in *Fin-de-siècle Vienna* (New York: Alfred E. Knopf, 1980), 181–82, cites both Goethe's observation on the satirist J. G. Lichtenberg and Freud's addition.

17. Wolf, *Briefe an Emil Kauffmann*, ed. Edmund von Hellmer (Berlin: S. Fischer, 1903), 104, letter of 5 August 1893. In this letter, Wolf speaks of Beethoven's music as "heavenly air and forest breezes" to counteract the "bewitching drug" of Wagner's music. Then he hastily adds that he has not joined the camp of the anti-Wagnerites. "Wagner is and remains the greatest god, even though he perhaps inspires more fear, or if you like, reverential fear than love in his worshipers."

18. Wolf sketched the setting of the "Gesellenlied" (the sketch is Ms. 19, 550 in the collection of the Austrian National Library) on 24 January 1888. The conjunction of this composer and this poem in January 1888 seems symbolic and premonitory. Each of the four stanzas of Reinick's poem begins with an apprentice repeating a proverblike refrain, "Kein Meister fällt vom Himmel!" (Masters don't grow on trees—the saying has clearly been repeated often by his own master) and then reinterpreting it in light of his desire to be out on his own, freed from all masters and masters' wives, at liberty to find a bride and be a master himself. Wolf was only three weeks away from the mastery evident in the outpouring of Mörike songs; his own apprenticeship period was almost over.

19. The occasion for imprecation was the notorious performance of *Penthesilea* by Hans Richter and the Vienna Philharmonic in 1886. See Walker, *Hugo Wolf*, 182–83.

20. Consulting Ernst Challier, *Grosser Lieder-Katalog: Ein alphabetisch geordnetes Verzeichniss sämmtlicher Einstimmiger Lieder* (Berlin: privately published, 1885),

one discovers that of the texts Wolf chose from the *Italienisches Liederbuch*, only two had been previously set to music: "Wie lange schon" by both Hermann Goetz, op. 4, no. 6 (Wolf liked Goetz's operatic setting of "The Taming of the Shrew") and Hans Huber (1852–1921), op. 72, no. 7 (974), and "Ein Ständchen Euch zu bringen" by the Viennese operetta composer Richard Heuberger, op. 15, no. 1 (211).

21. It is difficult to imagine Wolf setting poems such as "Ich sprach den Papst in Rom und fragt' ihn frei, / Ob denn das Lieben eine Sünde sei. / Er sagte: Nein! Liebt nur in Gottes Namen, / Doch wohl gemerkt: nur schöne Mädchen! Amen" (I spoke to the pope in Rome and asked him outright if love is a sin. He said: No! Love in God's name, but only beautiful maidens! Amen), or "Ich war in Rome. Den Papst hab' ich gefragt, / Ob der denn sündigt, der zu lieben wagt. / Ein Cardinal, uralt, hat mir entgegnet: / Liebt, Kinder, immerzu und seid gesegnet!" (I was in Rome and asked the pope if one who chances love is a sinner. An age-old cardinal answered me: Child, be always in love and be blessed!).

Paul Heyse's *Italienisches Liederbuch* (Berlin: Wilhelm Hertz, 1860) includes 135 *rispetti*, divided into sections by region (the majority Tuscan); 54 Venetian *vilote*; 127 *ritornelle*; 24 folk ballads; 23 folk songs; and 12 Corsican works of varying kinds, mostly laments. In German translation, the ritornelle are equivalent to *Sprüche* or epigrams, only two or three lines long and therefore not amenable to musical setting. Most of the *vilote* are quite brief as well, usually no more than four lines; Wolf could not have set them to music without repeating much of the text, a practice of which he disapproved. He *did* set all but a few of the longer ones (no. 1, "Gesegnet sei das Grün"; no. 16, "Geselle, woll'n wir uns in Kutten hüllen"; no. 38, "O wüßtest du, wie viel ich deinetwegen"; no. 41, "Ich liess mir sagen"; and no. 45, "Mein Liebster hat zu Tische mich geladen"). The ballades and Corsican laments, both very lengthy, seem not to have attracted Wolf at all. All but six of the thirty-three Italian songs are taken from the *rispetti*, which range from a mere two lines to twelve, the majority eight lines long. His choices from among the *rispetti* are indicative of his customary discrimination: he passes by poems that celebrate a place ("Erst schien mir Cevoli ein Paradies") and dialogue poems, including one between a reluctant novice and the abbess who blocks her access to the hidden sweetheart. He does not set a poem (no. 46) in which a suitor pleads with his beloved to set the wedding day, nor does he set the most bitter of the male complaints against a cruel sweetheart (no. 37), a fantasy set in hell. Heyse disposes many of the poems in thematic clusters, and it is interesting to note Wolf's choice of the best works within each group. For example, of the three serenades nos. 76, 77, and 79, Wolf set "Ein Ständchen Euch zu bringen" and "Nicht länger kann ich singen," but omitted the one that begins, "So dringe denn mein Lied ins Haus hinein" and ends, "Statt alles Trostes starr' ich auf die Mauer."

22. Hugo Wolf, *Sämtliche Werke*, vol. 5: *Italienisches Liederbuch I und II*, ed. Hans Jancik (Vienna: Musikwissenschaftlicher Verlag, 1972), 54–55.

23. Mörike, *Gedichte*, 221.

24. Hugo Wolf, *Sämtliche Werke*, vol. 1: *Gedichte von Eduard Mörike*, ed. Hans Jancik (Vienna: Musikwissenschaftlicher Verlag, 1963), 203–4.

25. Walker, *Hugo Wolf*, 238.

26. Aristophanes, *Plays*, trans. Patric Dickinson (Oxford: Oxford University Press, 1970), 214.

27. Heinrich Werner, *Hugo Wolf in Perchtoldsdorf* (Regensburg: Gustav Bosse

Verlag, 1925), 35, letter from 22 February 1888. In Hugo Wolf, *Briefe an Oskar Grohe*, ed. Heinrich Werner (Berlin: S. Fischer, 1905), 23, letter of 1 June 1890, Wolf rejoiced over the advent of a new song, writing "Also this time the Muse, on her first entrance into the house, has given me a rare and wonderful song: it resounds like a 'Welcome!' The poem is by Gottfried Keller and begins: 'Tretet ein, hoher Krieger.' "

28. Ibid., 90, letter of 14 September 1892.

29. Hugo Wolf, *Briefe an Frieda Zerny*, ed. Ernst Hilmar and Walter Obermaier (Vienna: Musikwissenschaftlicher Verlag, 1978), 11–13. Also Walker, *Hugo Wolf*, 353–54.

30. Werner, *Wolf in Perchtoldsdorf*, 94.

31. Mörike, *Gedichte*, 87.

32. Quoted in Walker, *Hugo Wolf*, 467. Walker also cites the letter to Frieda Zerny in which Wolf writes, "As you know, the spring of my creative work has been practically dried up for several years. What this appalling realization means to me is quite indescribable. Since then I have led, truly, the existence of a frog and not even that of a living one, but that of a galvanized frog" (361). See Wolf, *Briefe an Frieda Zerny*, 36.

33. See Hermann Bahr, *Selbstbildnis* (Berlin: S. Fischer, 1923), 153–56 for Bahr's reminiscences of Wolf, whom he compares to E.T.A. Hoffmann's Kapellmeister Kreisler, also 166 for the anecdote of Wolf's late-night readings of Kleist and Grabbe.

34. Christian Dietrich Grabbe, *Werke*, vol. 1, ed. Alfred Bergmann (Emsdetten: Verlag Lechte, 1960), 239–46.

35. Mörike, *Gedichte*, 227–28.

36. Peter Lahnstein, *Eduard Mörike: Leben und Milieu eines Dichters* (Munich: Paul List Verlag, 1986), 104–5. Mörike, at first exhilarated by the offer of a yearly stipend from the publisher Franck, soon became anxious at the prospect, describing himself as similar to a cat not wishing to wet its feet in the rain.

37. Thomas Mann would later use the contrast between chromaticism and dissonance on one hand, consonance and stable tonality on the other as a principal symbol of paradox in *Doktor Faustus*, in which the composer Adrian Leverkühn is modeled in part on Wolf. In Leverkühn's fictive oratorio *Apocalypsis cum figuris*, "dissonance stands for the expression of everything lofty, solemn, pious, everything of the spirit; while consonance and firm tonality are reserved for the world of hell, in this context, a world of banality and the commonplace." Thomas Mann, *Doktor Faustus*, vol. 6 of the *Gesammelte Werke* (Frankfurt: S. Fischer, 1960), 498.

38. Wolf, *Briefe an Kauffmann*, 8.

39. Wolf, *Sämtliche Werke*, vol. 1: *Gedichte von Mörike*, 195–98.

40. Heinrich Werner, *Wolf in Perchtoldsdorf*, letter of 25 February 1888, cited in Walker, *Hugo Wolf*, 204.

41. Rudolf Louis and Ludwig Thuille, in their well-known *Harmonielehre*, 3d ed. (Stuttgart: Carl Grüninger, 1910), cite Wolf's 1888 Heine song "Wo wird einst" in their "Literaturbeispiele" (Musical examples), 369, and their discussions of fin-de-siècle chromatic practices reflect Wolf's usages in many instances. On 349–50, they cite Palestrina's "Stabat Mater" as a model from which later composers derived their "grenzenlos" (boundless) passages "to illustrate musically the removal from all earthly bonds."

42. Ibid., 217.

43. Eric Sams, *The Songs of Hugo Wolf*, 2d ed., rev. and enlarged (London: Eulenburg Books, 1983), 143. Sams also suggests that the introduction may have been designed to recall Beckmesser's Merker motif and chromatically pathetic state at the beginning of act 3, scene 3 and that the "lachrymose poets" at the end could come from *Tannhäuser*.

44. Wolf, *Sämtliche Werke*, vol. 1: *Gedichte von Mörike*, 207–12.

45. Wolf had little use for critics. In *Briefe an Faisst*, 124, letter of 25 October 1895, he scornfully compares critics who talk about music to the blind discoursing on color. "They are all more or less ignoramuses," he concludes. Paul Müller had sent him a sheaf of articles on *Der Corregidor*, thus provoking the brief outburst.

46. Mörike, *Gedichte*, 232–33. Mörike wrote another poem, also in dialogue but much shorter, about a poet and a self-appointed critic:

> "Recht hübsche Poesie; nein, ohne Schmeichelei!
> Aber eins vermiss' ich an Ihren Sachen."—
> "Nämlich?"—"Eine Tendenz."—"Tendenz! Ei, meiner Treu'!"—
> "Die kriegen Sie sich ja, mein Besser!"—"Bleib's dabei!
> Will mir gleich einen Knopf an mein Sacktuch machen!"

("Very nice poetry; no, no flattery! But one thing I do miss in your material"— "And that is?"—"A focus."—"Focus! Oh, my word!"—"You'll certainly get it, my good fellow!"—"Stick with it! I'll tie a knot in my handkerchief right away!")

As in "Zur Warnung," the poetic "I" pretends wholehearted agreement with the nonsensical criticism that his poetry lacks "focus" or "direction."

47. It is interesting to compare the end of "Abschied" with bona fide waltzes, such as the fifth waltz in the set entitled "Hoffnungs-Strahlen," op. 158, by Josef Lanner, from *Josef Lanner's Wälzer. Neue Gesammtausgabe nach den Originalen*, vol. 4, ed. Eduard Kremer (Leipzig: Breitkopf and Härtel, n.d.), 37. Wolf exaggerates the melodic and tonal simplicities of the Viennese waltz in order to underscore the childish-malicious glee. Lanner's decorative melodic variations and profuse accents—he was especially fond of Scotch-snap figures—are more elaborate than in "Abschied." The Viennese waltz as a genre is notable for its off-beat accents, grace notes, trills, and staccato markings; the various means of emphasis lend themselves well to mockery, as in Adèle's Laughing Song, "Mein Herr Marquis," from *Die Fledermaus*.

48. Freud, *Jokes*, 222–28.

49. The definition of *Rollengedichte* is taken from Jürgen Thym, "The Solo Song Settings of Eichendorff's Poems by Schumann and Wolf" (Ph.D. dissertation, Case Western Reserve University, 1974), 254. Thym furthermore points out that these poems reveal character traits and show people in their social context. Unlike the undefined poetic personas who speak in the *Stimmungsgedichte*, their identity blurred or lost altogether in the merger with Nature, these characters are sharply drawn.

50. Wolf made occasional exceptions to his rule of avoiding previously composed poems. Schumann set "Waldmädchen" (Forest maiden) in 1849 for two women's voices in his op. 69; Wolf may have felt that the single poetic persona in the poem deserved a solo setting.

51. None of the role poems with a humorous or demonic element (Wolf called "Die Zigeunerin" a "wild exotic piece") were set by previous composers. In Challier, *Grosser Lieder-Katalog*, one finds listed a setting of "Der Musikant" by Friedrich Kiel, 606; settings of "Das Ständchen" by the Liszt epigone Eduard Lassen and by H. Marschall and E. Klitzsch, 793; and settings of "Verschwiegene Liebe" by Wilhelm Freudenberg and A. Holländer, 878.

52. The letter of 12 March 1891 is cited in Ernst Decsey, *Hugo Wolf*, vol. 2, 92–93.

53. Did Wolf perhaps already have in mind a setting of Goethe's "Der Rattenfänger" when he passed up Eichendorff's "Der neue Rattenfänger"? Mahler might have been attracted to "Auf der Feldwacht" ("Holding my weapon, I stand here forlorn at my watch"), but not Wolf. The role poems he chose not to set, such as "Der Poet," are as indicative of his personal tastes in verse for music as those he *did* select.

54. Wolf used either the second edition of Eichendorff's collected works, edited by the poet's son Hermann and published under the title *Joseph Freiherrn von Eichendorffs sämmtliche Werke*, 6 vols. (Leipzig: Voigt and Günther, 1864), or one of the editions based upon it. In this edition, the poems appear emended, rearranged, and retitled. Wolf could not have known the texts were inauthentic. The most obvious alterations are the titles: Eichendorff's "Der wandernde Musikant" is changed to "Der Musikant," "Der wandernde Student" to "Der Scholar," "Der Glückliche" to "Liebesglück," "Steckbrief" to "Erwartung," "Die Nachtblume" to "Die Nacht," and "Der verliebte Reisende" to "In der Fremde." The fact that the poetic persona of "Der Landreiter" is a gendarme in Eichendorff's original title adds to the element of comic reversal of what is usual in life. Policemen usually have the upper hand in confrontations, but here, the enforcer of law and order is victim rather than victor.

55. See Marina Warner, *Monuments and Maidens: The Allegory of the Female Form* (New York: Atheneum, 1985) for a discussion of the aesthetic and symbolic meanings of the female form in the arts.

56. In "Erstes Liebeslied eines Mädchens" (A maiden's first love song), the poetic persona is a fisher-girl who describes the first act of intercourse as she experiences it. It is an amazingly subversive poem. Unlike most of the eighteenth- and nineteenth-century erotic poetry written by men and purporting to describe female eroticism (Friedrich von Schlegel wrote an entire cycle of such poems), the speaker is by stages curious, repelled, and then terrified by what happens to her. She does not worship the male half of this duo; he is no more than an "eel" leaping about within her and, she fears, tearing her to pieces. Pain and fear are not succeeded by the obligatory rapture and gratitude of most erotic literature. Wolf himself characterized this poem as an example of the "demonic truth," that is, the heightened psychological (not social) realism, that he sought in poetry.

57. To cite only a few examples listed in Ernst Challier's *Grosser Lieder-Katalog*, one finds that "Der neue Amadis" (The new Amadis) was set by Johann Friedrich Reichardt, J. A. Wendt, and Petersen Grönlad (1760 or 1761–1834), 142; "Ritter Kurts Brautfahrt" by Reichardt and Grönlad, 698; "Gleich und gleich" by Robert Franz, Karl Anton Florian Ecker, Albert Hahn (1828–80), Johann Peter Emilius Hartmann, Friedrich Gustav Jansen, Wilhelm Langhans (1832–92), Otto Scherzer (1821–86), and Oscar Weil (1839?–1921), 315. "Epiphanias" had been set previously by Carl Friedrich Zelter and Beethoven.

58. Walker, *Hugo Wolf*, 249.

59. Wolf, *Briefe an Kauffmann*, 25, letter of 22 December 1890. "What you have written to me about 'Prometheus' and 'Ganymed' deeply delighted me. I am also of the opinion that Schubert did not succeed with the composition of these two poems and that these great poems had to await the post-Wagnerian era before they could be set to music in a truly Goethean spirit."

60. From Victor Luithlen, "Hugo Wolfs Goethelieder," in *Chronik des Wiener Goethe Vereins* 42 (1937): 12–13. Also Wolfgang Leppmann, *The German Image of Goethe* (Oxford: Oxford University Press, 1961), 99. Wolf had performed six of his Goethe songs for the Society on 20 March 1890.

61. The only earlier setting of the "Cophtisches Lied I" is the op. 6, no. 2 lied by the minor composer Leo Grill, published by Kistner in Leipzig. See Challier, *Grosser Lieder-Katalog*, 142.

62. Johann Wolfgang von Goethe, *Gedenkausgabe der Werke, Briefe und Gespräche*, vol. 1: *Sämtlicher Gedichte*, ed. Ernst Beutler (Zürich: Artemis-Verlag, 1950), 91.

63. The cause célèbre known as the Necklace Affair began with a plot devised by Jeanne de Saint-Rémy de Valois, Comtesse de La Motte. Her accused fellow conspirator was Cardinal Prince Louis de Rohan, or "la Belle Éminence," of Strasbourg, who had sought out Cagliostro for counsel. The Cardinal was persona non grata with the Austrian Empress Maria Theresa and her daughter Marie Antoinette, the Queen of France; the Countess pretended to have privileged access to the Queen and therefore the means to restore the Cardinal to royal favor. She duped the gullible prelate into signing a contract for the diamond necklace, designed for Louis XV's mistress Madame du Barry and then valued at 1,800,000 francs, supposedly on behalf of the Queen, who would receive and pay for them. When the Byzantine plot erupted into public scandal, the Cardinal and Countess were arrested and tried before the Parliament of Paris, the Cardinal to be acquitted and the Countess declared guilty. Cagliostro was put in the Bastille for six months and then exiled from France by the King. See Frances Mossiker, *The Queen's Necklace* (New York: Simon and Schuster, 1961). Goethe saw in the scandal the prologue to the Revolution and the end of any last remnants of dignity for the House of Capet.

64. C.A.H. Burckhardt, *Goethe und der Komponist Philipp Christoph Kayser* (Leipzig: Verlag von Friedrich Wilhelm Grünow, 1879), 21, letter of 28 June 1784. Goethe writes, "I greatly admire Italian opera buffa and would like to collaborate with you on a small work of this nature." A year and a half later, in a letter from Weimar dated 28 February 1786, Goethe tells the composer that their collaborative venture will, he believes, be best modeled after Metastasio (ibid., 34).

65. Ibid., 69–72, letter of 14 August 1787. "Now a word about the new opera. I have in mind nothing less than to make an opera buffa of the famous Necklace Affair."

66. Both the first outline in Italian and the second in German, as well as the subsequent fragments—mostly the beginnings of scenes, followed by a sentence or two summarizing what the scene would later contain—were not published until 1894 in the "Paralipomena" to "Der Gross-Cophta" in *Goethes Werke*, vol. 17 (Weimar: Hermann Bohlau, 1894), 369–94. What later became the two Coptic songs were originally intended to be the Graf's third and second arias respectively.

67. Numerous biographies, from Giovanni Barberi's work of 1791 to the present, attest to the fascination of charlatanry on such a scale. See Grete de Francesco, *The*

Power of the Charlatan (New Haven: Yale University Press, 1939), 209–26; Johannes von Guenther, *Cagliostro* (New York, 1929); Harry Schnur, *Mystic Rebels: Apollonius Tyaneus, Jan van Leyden, Sabbatai Zevi, Cagliostro* (New York: Beechhurst Press, 1949); and Roberto Gervaso's *Cagliostro: A Biography*, trans. Cormac Ó Cuilleanàin (London: Victor Gollancz, 1974). The "Quack of Quacks" (Thomas Carlyle's designation) also inspired numerous literary works, including Friedrich Schiller's novella *Der Geisterseher*; Alexandre Dumas père's drama "L'Alchimiste," written in 1839 in collaboration with Gérard de Nerval; and large portions of the Marie Antoinette romances, also by Dumas. Of the five novels in that series, one is entitled *Joseph Balsamo: Mémoirs d'un médicin*.

68. See François Ribadeau Dumas, *Cagliostro* (London: Allen and Unwin, 1967), trans. Elizabeth Abbott; also Elise von der Recke, *Nachricht von des berüchtigen Cagliostro Aufenthalte in Mitau im Jahre 1779 und von dessen dortigen magischen Operationen* (Berlin: F. Nicolai, 1787), and Thomas Carlyle's 1833 essay "The Count Cagliostro," later published in the *Critical and Miscellaneous Essays*, vol. 2 (London: Chapman and Hall, 1887), 520.

69. See Johann Wolfgang von Goethe, *Italienische Reise*, or *Autobiographische Schriften*, vol. 3 of *Goethes Werke* (Zürich: Artemis-Verlag, 1954), 253–56.

70. Wolf, *Sämtliche Werke*, vol. 3: *Gedichte von Johann Wolfgang von Goethe*, ed. Hans Jancik (Vienna: Musikwissenschaftlicher Verlag, 1978), 83–86.

71. Eric Sams, *The Songs of Hugo Wolf*, 28.

72. Walker, *Hugo Wolf*, 251.

73. Joseph von Hammer-Purgstall, *Der Diwan von Mohammed Schemsed-din Hafis*, 2 vols. (Stuttgart and Tübingen: J. G. Cotta, 1812–13). A *Diwan* or *Divan* is an anthology or collection of poems.

74. Goethe had company in his Orientalizing interests. Poets as diverse in their abilities as August von Platen-Hallermünde, Friedrich Rückert, Friedrich Bodenstedt, and Heinrich Stieglitz, whose *Bilder des Orients* (Images of the East) of 1831 attracted a swarm of composers, looked to the romanticized East for inspiration. Not everyone agreed with the enthusiasm newly kindled by Hammer-Purgstall, however: Wilhelm Müller, the poet of the Schubert song cycles, criticized Rückert's *Östliche Rosen* (Oriental roses) and the search for poetry in such distant places as antithetical to true poetry, which should be, in his opinion, characterized by an emotional immediacy only derived from one's native language and habits of thought. See Wilhelm Müller, "Östliche Rosen. Von Friedrich Rückert," in *Vermischte Schriften von Wilhelm Müller*, vol. 5: *Kritische Arbeiten*, ed. Gustav Schwab (Leipzig: F. A. Brockhaus, 1830), 290–313.

75. Cited in *Goethes Werke*, ed. Erich Trunz, vol. 2 of *Gedichte und Epen* (Munich: Verlag C. H. Beck, 1978), 656. In the same letter, Goethe comments approvingly on the Viennese composer Karl Eberwein's (1786–1868) *Lieder aus Goethes west-östlichem Divan* (Hamburg: Böhme [1820]); Eberwein's music is, he says, like the gas that lifts the balloon of his verse into the heights.

76. Goethe found his subject and several key words and images in three poems from the Hafiz-Hammer-Purgstall *Diwan*. In *Der Diwan von Mohammed Schemsed-din Hafis*, vol. 1, 106, poem no. 40, the poet writes, "Es ward mein Staub am Schöpfungstag / Mit Wein geknätet" (My dust was kneaded with wine on the day of my creation). In ibid., 234, Hafiz takes up the theme again, writing, "Die Säuerung von

Adams Stoff, / Nichts anders ist der Trinker Thun" (Only the drinker's deed can leaven the stuff of which Adam is made); Hammer-Purgstall adds in a footnote to those lines, "Without this leavening, Man remains an insipid, unfermented clump." Again, in ibid., vol. 2, 182, Hafiz-Hammer-Purgstall writes, "Einstens ward der Staub des Körpers / Abgeknettet mit dem Wein."

77. Wolf often expressed his love of Mörike's works in letters to his friends, especially the music professor and composer Emil Kauffmann (1836–1909). Kauffmann was the son of the Swabian composer Ernst Friedrich Kauffmann (1803–56), who had been a childhood friend of Mörike's; upon discovering Wolf's *Gedichte von Mörike*, Emil Kauffmann wrote to Wolf of his admiration and sent a treasure as a token of his appreciation: the autograph manuscript of Mörike's "An Longus," which had been in his father's possession. In the *Briefe an Kauffmann*, letter of 5 June 1890, Wolf protests Kauffmann's good opinion of Brahms by first stating his [Wolf's] own artistic credo ("rigorous, harsh, inexorable truth") and then listing those who represent a similar aesthetic, including Mörike. "And Mörike himself, beloved of the Graces! To what excesses his Muse transported him, when the demonic side of truth showed its face to him! The 'Erste Liebeslied eines Mädchens' offers a striking example of this. And what convulsive sincerity, what intimate knowledge of that which is painful speaks from these inimitable lines: 'Erinn'rung reicht mit Lächeln die verbittert / Bis zur Betäubung süßen Zauberschalen; / So trink' ich gierig die entzückten Qualen" (Besuch in Urach). That is written with blood, and such tones only strike fire with him who passionately feels, from his inmost being, a deep and true sensibility of like degree." Kauffman also sent Wolf books on Mörike, to which Wolf responded with lively commentary; for example, in a letter of 24 November 1893, he was delighted to discover, in one J. von Günthert's *Mörike und Notter*, the genesis of "Auf eine Christblume I" and protested the author's misunderstanding, according to Wolf, of "Auf einer Wanderung." In *Briefe an Faisst*, 113, letter of 24 July 1896, Wolf writes, "I'm sending you enclosed Nietzsche's expectorations on Mörike. As in so many things (for example, Wagner), this mighty spirit misunderstood Mörike as well. One can't believe one's eyes. Grohe sent me this selection as a curiosity. Curious indeed!" Shortly thereafter in the same letter, he adds, "Today I have decorated my lodgings with an outstanding picture of Mörike (unfortunately from his last years)."

78. As usual, Wolf the omnivorous reader explored Heyse's other works but found nothing to his taste, neither the poetry nor the prose. In a letter to Melanie Köchert from Windischgraz on 6 October 1893, Wolf tells Melanie that he has been tippling his mother's mediocre wine from sheer boredom, thus becoming accustomed to poor-quality merchandise (all, of course, tongue-in-cheek). "Only in the case of the moralist novellas of Heyse have I been unable to accustom my particular taste . . . I much prefer the 'red' [his mother's wine] to this insipid Heyse-lemonade." See Hugo Wolf, *Letters to Melanie Köchert*, 78–79.

79. Selected poems, novellas, and letters by members of the society are reprinted in *Die Krokodile: Ein Münchener Dichterkreis*, ed. Johannes Mahr (Stuttgart: Reclam, 1987), including "Das Lied vom Crocodil" for barbershop quartet and chorus to words by Emanuel Geibel (82–83).

80. Eduard Mörike, *Briefe*, vol. 3 of the *Sämtliche Werke*, ed. Gerhart Baumann and Siegfried Grosse (Stuttgart: J. G. Cotta, 1959), 751–52.

81. In Mörike, *Briefe*, 743–44, one finds Mörike in 1855 advising Heyse to shun drama, which he believed was not the younger writer's forte. The next year, Mörike praised him warmly for his prose (750).

82. See Cecilia Baumann, *Wilhelm Müller, the Poet of the Schubert Song Cycles: His Life and Works* (University Park: Pennsylvania State University Press, 1981), chap. 5, "The Promulgator of Folk Songs," 91–97.

83. In the foreword to his *Agrumi* translations, Kopisch acknowledges his debt to Müller and to Herder. His volume, unlike the Müller and Heyse anthologies, is in parallel-text format, the Italian on the left and his translation on the right. In the preface to the *Italienisches Liederbuch*, in which Heyse pays tribute to his predecessors, he has particular words of praise for Kopisch's mastery of comic moods, although the sweeter accents of love poetry often escape him. (Heyse reprinted the poems of the *Italienisches Liederbuch* in his series *Italienische Dichter seit der Mitte des 18ten Jahrhunderts*, vol. 4: *Lyriker und Volksgesang* [Berlin: Wilhelm Hertz, 1889], 175–348.)

84. Niccolò Tommaseo (1802–74) was a distinguished Dante scholar and editor of *La divina commedia*, whose other published works included a dictionary of synonyms, colloquies with Alessandro Manzoni, novels, poems, short stories, memoirs, and works on morals, education, and aesthetics.

85. Heyse, *Italienisches Liederbuch*, xii.

86. Ibid., xxxvi.

87. Giuseppe Tigri, *Canti Popolari Toscani* (Florence: Barbera, Bianchi, and Co., 1860), 280. The *rispetto* and the Venetian equivalent, the *vilota*, usually consist of a single stanza, most often eight end-stopped lines, less often of six and occasionally ten, twelve, fourteen or even seventeen lines. Each line contains ten or eleven syllables, and the rhyme scheme in the eight-line poems is *a b a b c c d d*. "Rispetto" means an elegant compliment from a lover to the beloved, with the same conceit varied and rephrased two or three times; in Heyse's artful German translations, the homage—or taunt, sarcastic complaint, what have you—is intensified with each repetition.

88. Wolf, *Briefe an Kauffmann*, 81.

89. Heyse, *Italienisches Liederbuch*, 16.

90. Wolf, *Sämtliche Werke*, vol. 5: *Italienisches Liederbuch*, 31–33.

91. Angelo Dalmedico, *Canti del Popolo Veneziano* (Venice: Andrea Santini e Figlio, 1848), 141.

92. Heyse, *Italienisches Liederbuch*, 82.

93. Wolf, *Sämtliche Werke*, vol. 5: *Italienisches Liederbuch*, 56–57.

94. Niccolò Tommaseo, *Canti Popolari Toscani Corsi Illirici Greci* (Venice, 1841), 273.

95. Heyse, *Italienisches Liederbuch*, 55.

96. Wolf, *Sämtliche Werke*, vol. 5: *Italienisches Liederbuch*, 20–21.

97. Tigri, *Canti Popolari*, 179.

98. Heyse, *Italienisches Liederbuch*, 24.

99. Wolf, *Sämtliche Werke*, vol. 5: *Italienisches Liederbuch*, 102–3.

100. The first of Wolf's Eichendorff serenades is "Rückkehr" (The return), composed on 12 January 1883 and first published posthumously in 1936 by the Musikwissenschaftlicher Verlag of Leipzig and Vienna in a volume edited by Helmut Schultz. Schultz, in his foreword to the original edition, points out that "there are consecutive

octaves and fifths, and clashes between a gentle melodic line and daring harmonies, that he would never have allowed himself in later years. He also keeps closer to the strophe than in Lieder written ten years later." In retrospect, "Rückkehr" seems a preliminary study for the later, mature lied "Das Ständchen" (The serenade), among the loveliest of the Eichendorff songs. The milieu for "Rückkehr" is almost the same as that of "Das Ständchen": either the wanderer-singer's native town or else a place where he used to live. It is night, with all of its Eichendorffian resonances of spiritual darkness, and the wanderer roams through the deserted streets. He had thought that he would be welcomed home by those who had known him in the past, but his expectations are disappointed. When he hears music played by "strange, merry folk," he is impelled out into the world again, a saddened and unresolved return followed by continued quest onward. The older man who speaks in "Das Ständchen" sees and hears a young serenader and remembers when he too wooed a beloved woman with songs of a summer night, remembers too her premature death. In both songs, the instrumental music by poetic personas other than the singer is represented in the piano, Self and Other differentiated in both songs and by the same mechanism. When Wolf in 1889 published the *Gedichte von Eichendorff*, he deemed only two settings composed before 1886 worthy of publication, "Erwartung" and "Die Nacht." He did not choose "Rückkehr," although he did preserve the manuscript.

101. Giuseppe Tigri, *Canti Popolari*, 2. In the 2d augmented ed. of 1860, the rispetto appears on p. 3 in a section entitled "Il Canto." Tigri organizes his collection of Tuscan folk poems by themes: "Innamoramento," "Bontà e Bellezza di Donna," "Amore Sfortunato," etc.

102. Heyse, *Italienisches Liederbuch*, 17.

103. Wolf's friend Heinrich Potpeschnigg arranged a performance of "Wie lange schon war immer mein Verlangen" in which a violinist presumably played the soprano line of the postlude from behind a curtain. See Hugo Wolf, *Briefe an Heinrich Potpeschnigg*, ed. Heinz Nonveiller (Stuttgart: Union Deutsche Verlagsgesellschaft, 1923), 65, letter written 16 December 1894. Wolf teases his friend gently about the ad hoc addition to his score: "The participation of a violinist must have been delightful— and this from behind the curtain! What a refined fellow you are!"

104. Wolf, *Sämtliche Werke*, vol. 5: *Italienisches Liederbuch*, 94–95.

105. *Briefe an Melanie Köchert*, 172, and *Letters to Melanie Köchert*, 200.

106. Tommaseo, *Canti Popolari*, no. 16 of the "Serenate," 120.

107. Heyse, *Italienisches Liederbuch*, 38.

108. Sams, *The Songs of Hugo Wolf*, 12–13, writes that Wolf, like Schubert and Schumann, seems to have associated certain keys with particular poetic themes. "Der Soldat I," "Gesellenlied," and "Königlich Gebet" are also set in C major.

109. Wolf's term, in *Briefe an Grohe*, 30–32, letter of 28 June 1890, also Walker, *Hugo Wolf*, 268.

110. Friedrich Eckstein, *Alte unnennbare Tage: Erinnerungen aus siebzig Lehr-und Wanderjahren* (Vienna: Herbert Reichner Verlag, 1936), 197–98. Peter Gast was the pseudonym of Johann Heinrich Koselitz (1854–1918), whom Nietzsche once praised as "a new Mozart." Eckstein had obtained the overture and a duet from the opera *Der Loewe von Venedig*. I surmise that he had a manuscript copy, as the opera was first performed in 1891 and not published until 1901.

Chapter 3

1. Henry Pleasants, trans. and ed., *The Music Criticism of Hugo Wolf* (New York and London: Holmes and Meier Publishers, 1978), 277. Paul Bulss was a Viennese singer known for his interpretations of Loewe.

2. Edmund von Hellmer, *Hugo Wolf: Erlebtes und Erlauschtes* (Vienna and Leipzig: Wiener Literarischer Anstalt, 1921), 137. "One day in company, after Wolf had played some of his Goethe songs for us, the conversation turned to the 'Erlkönig' and its many composers. Schubert und Loewe were among others named and praised. Hugo Wolf was in favor of Loewe and his setting, without being able to give any explanation other than his preference. 'To me, the Loewe "Erlkönig" is—better,' he said." Carl Loewe, in *Dr. Carl Loewe's Selbstbiographie*, ed. C. H. Bitter (Berlin: Wilhelm Müller, 1870), 345, writes of his stay in Vienna on 27 July 1837, when he sang his "Erlkönig," "Die Glocken zu Speier," "Prinz Eugen," and "Der Schatzgräber." According to his report, "They were all beside themselves with rapture. I can be not a little proud that my 'Erlkönig' gives such pleasure here, that the Viennese public esteem it as highly as Schubert's."

3. Heinrich Werner, ed., *Hugo Wolf in Maierling: Eine Idylle, mit Briefen, Gedichten, Noten, Bildern und Faksimiles* (Leipzig: Breitkopf and Hartel, 1913), 17. Wolf became a friend of the Werner family when Heinrich Werner was very young; after Wolf's collapse and death, he devoted much of his life to the cause of Wolf's music. After recalling that one of Wolf's favorite operas during the Maierling idyll had been Heinrich Marschner's *Hans Heiling*, he writes, "Also Loewe's master-ballad 'Archibald Douglas' was a favorite of his, one that he sang over and over again." Gustav Schur, in *Erinnerungen an Hugo Wolf*, ed. Heinrich Werner (Regensburg: Gustav Bosse Verlag, 1922), 37, also confirmed Wolf's love of the Loewe setting of "Der Erlkönig": "He placed the Erlkönig of Carl Loewe high above Schubert's."

Mörike, who loved music, knew Schubert's setting of "Erlkönig" and told his pianist-friend Wilhelm Hartlaub how impressed he was with the composition. See *Freundeslieb' und Treu' : 250 Briefe Eduard Mörikes an Wilhelm Hartlaub*, ed. Gotthilf Renz (Leipzig: Leopold Klotz Verlag, 1938), 194. He called it a "Prachtierstück," a glorious piece, and wrote that the child's cries could break mirrors and windows ("die Spiegel und Fenster zersprengen").

4. *Hugo Wolfs Briefe an Hugo Faisst*, ed. Michael Haberlandt (Stuttgart and Leipzig: Deutsche Verlags-Anstalt, 1904), 37, a letter from Vienna, 17 July 1894. "I am delighted to acquaint you with a Loewe ballad that is just made for you [die Dir auf den Leib geschnitten ist]. But for this, you must come to Traunkirchen, or it won't be possible. The ballad is entitled: The long [*sic*] Christoph. This is signified in the unbelievable length; one might believe the piece will never finish, so unending is the river of music through which this long Christopher wades. But this is a heavenly length . . . Yes, you'll soon see."

Loewe's *Legende* "Der große Christoph" is included in Runze's edition, vol. 13, 26–50. The text of "Der große Christoph" was written in 1807 by Friedrich Kind (1768–1843) and based upon the account of Offerus, who became Christophorus after his conversion to Christianity, in Jacobus de Voragine's *Legenda aurea*.

5. In Maximilian Runze's *Loewe redivivus*, vol. 2 of the *Schriften zur Balladen-Forschung* (Berlin: Carl Duncker's Verlag, 1888), Loewe's editor chronicles the con-

certs presented by the Berlin Loewe Society, praises at length the singers and organizations he designates as Loewe's "saviors," and discusses the ballad aesthetic and Loewe's life and works. In the "Bausteine zur Balladen-Aesthetik" (53–58), Runze cites Schopenhauer to bolster his claim that Loewe disdains word-by-word, phrase-by-phrase textual nuances in order to achieve a truly tragic essence in ballads such as "Edward" and "Erlkönig."

6. Philipp Spitta, "Die Ballade," in *Musikgeschichtliche Aufsätze* (Berlin: Verlag von Gebrüder Paetel, 1894), 405–61.

7. Ibid., 406–7.

8. Ironically, Loewe had earlier been among the few composers of vocal music to win Schumann's approval. In the *Neue Zeitschrift für Musik* 5, no. 36 (1 November 1836), in a review of Loewe's "Esther, ein Liederkreis in Balladenform" (Esther, a song cycle in ballad form) to a text by Ludwig Giesebrecht, Schumann praised Loewe for his ability to create paintings, or images, in music.

9. Spitta, "Die Ballade," 408, points out that the ballad in poetry and the ballad in music (*Kunstballade*) are not the same. In his essay "Ballade, Betrachtung und Auslegung" of 1821, Goethe formulated his famous definition of the literary ballad as the *Ur-Ei* of poetry, a primordial egg containing in undifferentiated unity the lyric, epic, and dramatic strains later separated into different genres and verse types, with the story-telling function as the fundamental characteristic; it was, he believed, a Northern poetic art, the awakening of a "clouded, dark, and nocturnal world" in which the irrational operates powerfully on human fate. See *Goethes Werke: Hamburger Ausgabe in 14 Bänden*, vol. 1, ed. Erich Trunz (Hamburg: Christian Wegner, 1965–67, first published in 1948), 400. For more on the ballad in music, see C. David Ossenkopf, "The Earliest Settings of German Ballads for Voice and Clavier" (Ph.D. dissertation, Columbia University, 1968), and Edward F. Kravitt, "The Ballad as Conceived by Germanic Composers of the Late Romantic Period," in *Studies in Romanticism* 12, no. 2 (Spring 1973): 499–515. For more on the German literary ballad, see Winfried Freund, *Die deutsche Ballade. Theorie, Analysen, Didaktik* (Paderborn: Ferdinand Schöningh, 1978); Christian Freitag, ed., *Ballade* (Bamberg: C. C. Buchners Verlag, 1986); Walter Hinck, *Die deutsche Ballade von Bürger bis Brecht. Kritik und Versuch einer Neuorientierung*, 3d ed. (Göttingen: Vandenhoeck and Ruprecht, 1978); Wolfgang Kayser, *Geschichte der deutschen Ballade*, 2d ed. (Berlin: Junker and Dünnhaupt, 1936); Hartmut Laufhütte, *Die deutsche Kunstballade: Grundlegung einer Gattungsgeschichte* (Heidelberg: C. Winter, 1979); Gottfried Weissert, *Ballade* (Stuttgart: Metzler, 1980); and Otto Holzapfel's discussions of five German ballads in *The Ballad as Narrative: Studies in the Ballad Traditions of England, Scotland, Germany and Denmark* (Odense, Denmark: Odense University Press, 1982).

10. Spitta, "Die Ballade," 407.

11. Leopold Hirschberg, in *Reitmotiv: Ein Kapitel vorwagnerischer Charakterisierungskunst* (Langensalza: Hermann Beyer and Söhne, 1911). Runze and others also claimed Loewe for the Wagnerites.

12. From the foreword to Max Runze, ed., *Carl Loewes Werke: Gesamtausgabe der Balladen, Legenden, Lieder und Gesänge*, vol. 8: *Geisterballaden und Gesichte, Todes- und Kirchhofs-Bilder* (Leipzig: Breitkopf and Härtel, 1900), viii–ix. Lilli Lehmann wrote in a letter to Runze on 10 December 1897 of her Bayreuth memoirs, *Auf der Festbühne (1875–1876)*, published in Berlin by Raabe and Plothow, and her

reminiscences of Wagner and "Walpurgisnacht." Lehmann told Runze that Wagner particularly prized the ballad and lamented the fact that it was no longer performed. "Richard Wagner held the 'Walpurgisnacht' in quite singular esteem and thought it a shame that the ballad was not performed any more, [that] it was masterfully worked out and one of Loewe's best compositions. How often he spoke of him!"

13. Eugen Gura's account is found in Runze, *Carl Loewes Werke*, vol. 3: *Schottische, englische und nordische Balladen*, vi, from a letter to Runze of 22 September 1897 about his reminiscences of Bayreuth and Wagner in the summer of 1875. A conversation about musical declamation led to mention of Loewe, on which Wagner retrieved his personal copy of the early opuses. "After a time, a conversation about musical declamation developed, the talk turning to Weber and Marschner. He [Wagner] referred to Carl Loewe as a particular master in that regard. As he told the others present that I had sung Loewe's ballads since 1870 in Leipzig, he hurried to his library . . . and brought out a beautifully bound folio volume of Loewe's ballads from his earliest period, from 'Edward' on. Wagner placed the volume on the piano-stand and spoke with zeal and in detail of several ballads. 'Edward,' he said, was a masterpiece." Gura sang the ballad, with Josef Rubinstein accompanying; upon Gura's observation that the repeated exclamations of "Oh!" might be wearying for the listener, Wagner vehemently objected and told him not a single one could be omitted.

14. Ludwig Schemann, *Martin Plüddemann und die deutsche Ballade* (Regensburg: Gustav Bosse Verlag, 1930), 44. According to Plüddemann, Wagner is credited with saying, "The ballad remains, despite its inner kinship with music drama, only a pencil sketch. Music drama alone is an oil painting in full, richly colored glory."

15. Hanslick wrote of "Des Glockenthürmers Töchterlein" (The tower bell–ringer's daughter) in the *Wiener Neue Freie Presse* for 4 November 1887, cited in Loewe-Runze, *Carl Loewes Werke*, vol. 10, iv, of the preface.

16. The recital, *À la Recherche de la Musique perdue, or From the Sublime to the Ridiculous*, was recorded for RCA Records LRL 1-5007 (1974).

17. Schemann, *Martin Plüddemann*, 25.

18. See Karl Heckel, *Hugo Wolf in seinem Verhältnis zu Richard Wagner* (Munich, 1905). See also Frank Walker, *Hugo Wolf: A Biography*, 2d ed. (London: Dent, 1968), 26–30.

19. Ibid., 250.

20. Loewe, *Selbstbiographie*. "The music of this old, unjustly neglected master [Zumsteeg] deeply moved me. His motives are lively and depictive; he follows the text with complete fidelity." Loewe then points out the "highly aphoristic nature" of Zumsteeg's figures and writes, "It seemed to me that music, to be dramatic, must be shaped from broader, more developed motives, and just so have I sought to do in my ballads. And yet Zumsteeg's merit as a ballad composer is indisputable."

21. Forty-eight Loewe settings of Goethe's poems are printed in Runze, *Carl Loewes Werke*, vol. 11: *Lieder und Balladen*, and vol. 12: *Gesänge im grossen Stil und Oden, Grosslegenden und Grossballaden*. Loewe knew Zelter and met Goethe himself shortly before the elderly poet's death (vol. 11, v–vi). On that occasion, according to his own account, he told Goethe of his (Loewe's) special affinity for the ballad above all other kinds of poetry and praised "Erlkönig" as "the best German ballad."

22. Walker, *Hugo Wolf*, 36–37. Walker quotes Wolf's diary: "Monday, 13th February 1876. Saw the main stream of the Danube and the Imperial Bridge for the first time, on the occasion of wishing to compose the *Raubschütz*. As however I could not go into

the little wood, owing to the snow being too deep, nothing occurred to me and I went home."

23. "Der Raubschütz" in the Vienna City Library is actually a little collection of manuscripts and sketches in both ink and pencil, ranging from the most hurried slap-dash notation in pencil of a tentative vocal line to a single leaf in brownish ink, the beginnings of a fair copy. There are also four entire folio leaves in pencil, the first leaf of which bears the heading "Allegro con spirito. Gedicht v. Lenau. Der Raubschütz." They are, if possible, more amateurish than the ink study. The sketches will be published in the forthcoming Hugo Wolf, *Sämtliche Werke*, vol. 19: *Unvollständige Kompositionen, Entwürfe, Skizzen*, ed. Hans Jancik (in press).

24. Wolf's three Eichendorff ballads, "Der Kehraus" (The last dance), "Das zerbrochene Ringlein" (The broken ring), and "Der traurige Jäger" (The sorrowful hunter) were composed circa 1878 and subsequently lost. Perhaps the eight songs from *Des Knaben Wunderhorn* (The youth's magic horn), also composed circa 1878 and also lost, included ballad texts as well, but we do not know which poems he chose from this famous anthology. This is the only occasion he ever had recourse to it for song composition.

25. This set is already indicative of Wolf's later tastes and methods in the constant search for poetry apt for music. Hebbel (1813–63) spent the last nearly twenty years of his life in Vienna and is best known, then and now, for his dramas: *Judith, Genoveva, Maria Magdalene, Herodes und Mariamne, Michel Angelo* (dedicated to Schumann), *Die Nibelungen, Agnes Bernauer*, and others; he wrote poetry on occasion throughout his life, much of it filled with the largely pessimistic ethical-philosophical-moral preoccupations that one finds in the plays. During the single decade of his compositional maturity, Wolf was typically drawn to earlier-nineteenth-century works, to major writers rather than poetasters, and to repertoires less thoroughly picked over by his predecessors. Hebbel qualifies on all three counts.

26. Wolf would presumably have known Schumann's settings of Hebbel's "Schön Hedwig," op. 106 (1849) and the "Ballade vom Haideknaben," op. 122, no. 1 (1852) as melodramas to be declaimed against the background of a piano accompaniment. Did his lost setting of the ballad of "beautiful Hedwig" owe anything, I wonder, to Schumann's prior composition?

27. Spitta, "Die Ballade," 427. Schubert did of course write true ballads after the model provided by Johann Rudolf Zumsteeg (1760–1802) in such works as "Colma, ein Gesang Ossians," Gottfried August Bürger's "Lenore" (the ne plus ultra of ballad composers), and "Hagars Klage in der Wüste Bersaba." Schubert, interestingly, stayed away from the mammoth ballads of Bürger, preferring those by Schiller, James Macpherson's Ossian hoaxes, and others. See Gunter Maier, *Die Lieder Johann Rudolf Zumsteegs und ihr Verhältnis zu Schubert* (Göppingen: Alfred Kümmerle, 1971).

28. Loewe designated his "Geisterleben," op. 9, no. 4, to a text by Ludwig Uhland (Runze edition, vol. 8, 11–14) as a ballad in lied form because it is unified throughout by a motivic figure consisting of tapping repeated pitches and a scalewise minor-third figure and because it lacks action.

29. Edward Kravitt, "The Ballad as Conceived by Germanic Composers of the Late Romantic Period," 507.

30. See also Richard Batka, *Martin Plüddemann und seine Balladen* (Prague, 1896). Plüddemann's second volume of ballads in 1891 was dedicated to the same Kammersänger, Paul Bulss, whom Wolf had earlier both praised for his singing and

criticized for his neglect of Loewe ballads. Plüddemann was born 29 September 1854 in Kolberg and later became a singer who taught voice in Graz and Berlin. He was a convinced Wagnerite, who wrote, "Die Bühnenfestspiele in Bayreuth, ihre Gegner und ihre Zukunft," and who sought out Wagner's acquaintance on several occasions: he spent a week in the summer of 1878 at Bayreuth and celebrated Wagner's birthday on 22 May 1880 with the composer in Naples.

31. Edward Kravitt, "The Ballad as Conceived by Germanic Composers of the Late Romantic Period," 505, calls for a renewed consideration of Plüddemann and writes that "Plüddemann was the only late romantic composer to be thoroughly faithful in his music to the intrinsic nature of the traditional literary ballad."

32. Schemann, *Martin Plüddemann*, 61, originally from Plüddemann, "Stille Betrachtungen eines Musikers," in the *Rundschau der Deutschen Zeitung* for September 1897. "Even as poetry, the ballad is sharply differentiated from song and all other poetic genres. To recount the past prevails over mere emotional content. This must naturally be defined in the music as well. How difficult it is to hit the mark with the singularity of story-telling melody is evident in the scarcity of ballad composers."

33. Schemann, *Martin Plüddemann*, 62, originally the afterword to the first volume of ballades.

34. Plüddemann, *Balladen und Gesänge für Baryton mit Pianoforte*, vol. 2 (Munich: Alfred Schmidt, 1891), foreword, iv. Plüddemann presents himself as a singer writing for other singers and therefore knowledgeable about singers' needs. "There I always strove for the most singable and declamatory working-out, for the most concise, clear, and and distinctly ordered form and development, for harmonic neatness, not so much for musical originality." (He then points out exceptions.) "Overall, however . . . I have not sought after oddities and singularities, but made use of the simplest harmonies, unlike the prevailing practice of my contemporaries, who fill the simplest song or piano piece with harmonic curiosities, a practice that to me seemed very unnatural. It has become the mode to begin and end with dissonances."

35. Martin Plüddemann, *Balladen und Gesänge*, 3d ed., vol. 1 (Nuremberg and Leipzig: Wilhelm Schmid, 1892), iv.

36. Plüddemann, ibid., ii.

37. Even so, Plüddemann emphasizes the traditional roots of his motivic practices. Zumsteeg, Plüddemann states in the introduction to the first volume, used recurring motives before Loewe's more systematic and complex motivic development and well before his own ballads. Schemann, *Martin Plüddemann*, 65, again from the afterword to the first volume of ballads.

38. See Plüddemann, the foreword to vol. 3, ii. He includes a "period-piece" account of composing the ballad in a white-hot fever of creativity while staying at a hotel in Capri.

39. Spitta, "Die Ballade," 443.

40. Schemann, *Martin Plüddemann*, 63.

41. Martin Plüddemann, *Balladen und Gesänge für eine Singstimme mit Klavierbegleitung*, 3d ed., vol. 1 (Nuremberg: Wilhelm Schmid, 1892), afterword, i–iii. Plüddemann criticizes publishers for their lack of courage and their refusal to publish ballads by anyone other than Loewe; the critics for their lack of perception; performers for their inattention to the modern ballad (he castigates Eugen Gura by name in this regard); and the public for a lack of imagination required to hear and appreciate ballads properly.

42. Schemann, *Martin Plüddemann*, 62–63. "This somewhat remote realm [of the ballad] stands in relationship to the vast heights of music perhaps like a microcosm to a macrocosm. The microcosm is the smaller mirror image of the macrocosm; it includes everything that the larger realm includes but in small dimensions."

43. Schubert's setting in 1815 of Friedrich Anton Bertrand's "Minona, oder Die Kunde der Dogge," D. 152, in which the poetic voice of the narrator alternates with that of the young woman whose mastiff leads her to her fiancé's dead body, has recently been recorded by Elly Ameling (with Graham Johnson, piano) for the Hyperion Schubert Edition, vol. 7). The convention that has Minona, deprived by Edgar's death of all reason for living, commit suicide with the self-same arrow that killed him is clearly male.

44. For his "great ballad" setting of Goethe's "Die erste Walpurgisnacht," op. 25, Loewe directs that the work can be performed by one singer or, "according to the various characters in the piece, by many." Presumably, the accompanist would take over the four-part harmonization he gives for the final Great Chorus of watchmen, women, and the assembled heathen folk.

45. Plüddeman the Wagnerite might have noticed the kinship between Schiller's German bards mocking the tyranny of rules and Wagner's later drama of German art, *Die Meistersinger von Nürnberg*.

46. Perhaps to prove he could master both lied and ballad, perhaps to demonstrate the differences to an ill-informed public, Plüddemann included a group of outright lieder in his second volume—three of the Hafis paraphrases of Daumer and Goethe's early Anacreontic poem "Ihr verblühet, süsse Rosen," all four composed in 1879 well before his ballad crusade reached its apogee. He was following Loewe's model in this respect as well, since Loewe composed both sacred and secular lieder, including chorale harmonizations, children's songs, folk song–imitations, and drinking songs. Runze's vol. 16 (1903) is entitled *Das Loewesche Lied*, vol. 17 (1904) , *Liederkreise*.

47. The poem comes from Platen's *Geschichte und Sage*, which includes the text of Loewe's "Der Pilgrim vor St. Just." See *August Graf von Platens Sämtliche Werke*, ed. Max Koch and Erich Petzet, 12 vols. (Leipzig: Hesse and Becker, 1910).

48. C. W. Previté-Orton, *The Shorter Cambridge Medieval History*, vol. 1: *The Later Roman Empire to the Twelfth Century* (Cambridge: Cambridge University Press, 1971), 85.

49. Max Runze, in his notes to Loewe's historical ballads, does little beyond identifying the principal personages as briefly as possible and citing a relevant date or two. For example, in the notes for the popular ballad "Die Glocken zu Speier," op. 67, no. 2 to a text by Max von Oër (1806–46) from his *Balladen und Romanzen* of 1837 (Loewe apparently composed the musical setting that same year), Runze indicates that the tale has to do with Henry IV, deposed by his son, banned by the pope, who died 7 August 1106 and was buried in Speier in 1111. See Runze's vol. 4, *Die deutschen Kaiserballaden* (1900), vii.

50. Spitta, in "Die Ballade," mentions Plüddemann (454), but refuses to comment on developments in his own day. The latest composer of whom he writes is Brahms (453–54), and then only to point out briefly that Brahms did not set those ballad texts he *did* select after the pattern established by Loewe; for example, Eichendorff's "Nonne und Ritter" becomes a duet in Brahms's hands.

51. *Hugo Wolf: Letters to Melanie Köchert*, ed. Franz Grasberger, trans. Louise McClelland Urban (New York: Schirmer Books, 1991), 80.

52. Here again, there seems to be a conflict between his prose pronouncements and the actual music. The vocal lines of his ballads are liberally sprinkled with directives to the singer, often requiring a new inflection or change of vocal color every few measures: "sweetly," "dying away, almost spoken," "strongly," "mysteriously," "whispering," "very legato," "somewhat more quickly," "tearfully," "scornful," "shrieking," "merrily," "with disguised voice, dissembling . . . with the natural voice," and so on.

53. Henry Pleasants, trans. and ed., *The Music Criticism of Hugo Wolf*, 260, 268, and 274 respectively.

54. *Dr. Carl Loewe's Selbstbiographie*, 339. The incident occurred in July 1837.

55. From the *Neue Zeitschrift für Musik* 11, no. 24 (20 September 1839): 93–94.

56. Three of Kopisch's poems—"Die Notglocke," "Maley und Malone," and "Die Heinzelmännchen"—are included in the anthology *Deutsche Balladen*, ed. Harald Haselbach (Klagenfurt: Neuer Kaiser Verlag, 1978), 224–29.

57. See Lee B. Jennings, "Mörike's Grotesquery: A Post-Romantic Phenomenon," in *Journal of English and Germanic Philology* 59 (1960): 600–616.

58. One example is the character Agnes in Mörike's novel *Maler Nolten* (Nolten the artist), the first version published in 1832, a second revised version completed by a friend after Mörike's death in 1875. Agnes is a case study in the gradual onset of insanity that she herself foresees in the song "Rosenzeit! wie schnell vorbei," set to music by Robert Franz in his *Sechs Lieder von Eduard Mörike*, op. 27; by Brahms, op. 59, no. 5; and by Wolf in 1888. See S. Youens, "Madness in Music: Agnes' Song" in *Journal of Research in Singing* 11, no. 1 (December 1987): 29–46.

59. The two poets despised each other's work. Heine remarked in 1838, shortly before the appearance of the first edition of Mörike's collected poems later that same year: "People assure me that a most excellent poet of the Swabian school is Herr Mörike, who recently came to light, but who hasn't appeared yet (in print, that is). I am told that he sings not only of maybugs, but even of larks and thrushes, which is, to be sure, most praiseworthy." See *Heines Werke*, ed. E. Elster (Leipzig: Meyers Klassiker-Ausgaben, n.d.), vol. 7, 328. Eight years earlier, Mörike had written to his friend Johannes Mährlen in 1830: "The parcel you sent me contained packing paper with some of Heine's wishy-washy political stuff printed on it. A great disgust took hold of me." See Mörike, *Briefe*, ed. Friedrich Seebaß (Tübingen, n.d.), 189. In 1855, Mörike told the writer Theodor Storm in the course of a conversation that Heine was a poet to his fingertips, but that he could not tolerate him for fifteen minutes "because his whole being is a lie." See Christopher Middleton, trans., *Friedrich Hölderlin, Eduard Mörike: Selected Poems* (Chicago: University of Chicago Press, 1972), xli.

60. Harry Maync, ed., *Mörikes Werke*, 2d ed. (Leipzig: Bibliographisches Institut, 1914), vol. 1, 23–24.

61. Spitta's opinion in "Die Ballade," 434, is reinforced by the popularity of such works as "Die nächtliche Heerschau," op. 23; "Herr Oluf," op. 2, no. 2; "Odins Meeresritt," op. 118; and "Edward," op. 1, no. 1, none of them among the gigantic ballads.

62. Loewe's longer introductions often have an overt story-telling purpose; they establish, in advance of the words, something essential about the mood and milieu of the tale. For example, the contrast of V/C minor and V/C♯ major at the beginning of "Das Ständchen" (1826) to a text by Ludwig Uhland, an introduction rendered additionally mysterious by the unison texture and una corda indication, symbolizes the opposing worlds of the mother and the mortally ill child serenaded by the angels of death.

63. Unlike Loewe and Plüddemann, however, Wolf does not use any derivative of the word "erzählen" in the performance directives for his ballads.

64. The German term *Schauerballaden* begins with the word "Schauer," a favorite term in the ballad repertoire because it simultaneously describes an event in the natural world, something done by wind or rain; a human being's physical reaction to the event; and the feeling of awe before invisible and intangible forces. Poets seized upon signs and symbols drawn from Nature in order to convey by analogy their recognition of transpersonal and transcendant forces, whether holy or demonic. The etymological kinship with the word "schaudernd" (shuddering) is obvious. See Siegbert Salomon Prawer, "Reflections on the Numinous and the Uncanny in German Poetry," in *Reality and Creative Vision in German Lyrical Poetry*, ed. A. Closs (London: Butterworths, 1963), 153–72.

65. Sigmund Freud, in his essay "Das Unheimliche," argues that supernatural beings are sinister or uncanny when they intrude into human lives, representations, he believed, of repressed fears and their sudden, disorienting incursions into everyday thought. See Freud, *Studienausgabe*, vol. 4 (Frankfurt: Fischer Taschenbuch Verlag, 1982), 243–74.

66. Ibid., vol. 9, iii–iv. "I often gazed out the window of our house at an old ruined churchyard, over the disintegrating mounds and crumbling crosses . . . The shadowy figure of my mother seemed, in the moonlight on the grave-mounds, as if moving about. She wandered over to me and, half anxiously, half longingly, I clung to her. When Mother was finally still and held me closely on her knees, then I begged her: 'Mama, now play something.' Laughingly, she took the violin with which my father led his school-classes in song, and played the most beautiful melodies. Oh, how these melodies delighted me, out there in the moonlight! She never had any instruction in violin playing, but her music sang to me deep within my heart!" Loewe would later compose a ballad about a mother's ghost returning from the dead to protect a child mistreated by a cruel stepmother, a ballad entitled "Der Mutter Geist," op. 8, no. 2 (The mother's ghost; 1824).

67. Ibid., vol. 8, vii–viii, cites the passage from Spohr's "Chorus of Witches," which Loewe varied in appropriating it for his own ballad.

68. Wolf might well have known Brahms's duet setting of the same text, op. 75, no. 4 of 1877–78.

69. Goethe's poem had been taken over as a folk song soon after its publication. In addition to Schubert's setting, Challier's *Grosser Lieder-Katalog* lists settings by Louis Schlottmann (1826–1905), op. 45, no. 2; Emil Naumann (1827–88); Viktor Ernst Nessler (1841–90); Wenzel Johann (Václav Jan) Tomaschek (1774–1850); Nicolaus von Kraft, and M. Vogl. Nessler also composed a five-act opera entitled *Der Rattenfänger von Hameln* to a libretto by Friedrich Hofmann.

70. See Walker, *Hugo Wolf*, 368. Hanslick's review of 5 December 1894 for the *Neue Freie Presse* is cited in Decsey, *Hugo Wolf*, vol. 2: *Hugo Wolfs Schaffen*, 55, and printed in full in Eduard Hanslick, *Fünf Jahre Musik (1891–1895). Der "Modernen Oper*," vol. 7 (Berlin: Allgemeiner Verein für Deutsche Litteratur, 1896), 270–71. Wolf's arrangement of the Shakespeare "Elfenlied" for soprano solo, women's chorus, and orchestra was also performed at this concert, with Wilhelm Gericke conducting and Sophie Chotek as the soprano soloist. Because the majority of Hanslick's writings are long out of print and because Henry Pleasant's selected translations from *Hanslick's*

Music Criticisms (New York: Dover Publications, 1950; reprint, 1978) do not include this review, I reproduce it here:

> Two choruses with orchestral accompaniment, "Elfenlied" and "Der Feuerreiter," have met with great success and are the best works I know from this unendingly prolific composer in a narrowly confined realm of composition. Hugo Wolf pursues song compositions in large volumes, not sets, rivaling the ballad-manufacturer Martin Plüddemann of Graz, who railed against the evil publishers whose caution compelled him, for his next large volume of ballads, to initiate a subscription. Hugo Wolf composes not merely poems but, so to speak, entire poets. A volume of Goethe songs, 51 poems (costing 25 marks); a volume of Mörike songs, 53 poems (25 marks) and so on. Our composer greatly loves to make the vocal part an appendage to his main concern—the piano accompaniment, which is a sort of sarcastic opponent to the singer's part. Like every self-conscious and revolutionary young talent, Wolf—the ostensible founder of the "symphonic song"—has a small, enthusiastic band of adherents at his disposal. They perceive the Richard Wagner of song in Hugo Wolf, just as they see the Richard Wagner of the symphony in Bruckner. The acclaim for both men, if one understands it correctly, lies in the fact that both make something of their artistic genres (song, symphony) that they shouldn't be. With these two above-named choral compositions, Wolf has taken the first step, if not to larger forms (both pieces were originally published for solo voice and piano), then to richer means. He succeeded in his attempt. Both works belong to the depictive, descriptive species which this composer's gifts most readily meet halfway. The choral parts, for the most part well-suited to the voice and with good text declamation, sound above brilliant, refined orchestral music. In the "Elfenlied," the subtlest refinements, in the "Feuerreiter" the most strident effects of modern instrumentation are successfully deployed. At many places in the "Feuerreiter," unfortunately, the orchestral clamor was so loud that one could not understand a single word, not a matter for indifference in the ballad genre. At this concert, Hugo Wolf for the first time presented himself well to a large, not exclusively Wolfian public. Undoubtedly a man of spirit and talent, who need only beware of arrogance and "good friends."

The orchestrated version of "Der Feuerreiter" has been published in Hugo Wolf, *Chöre mit Orchesterbegleitung*, ed. Hans Jancik, vol. 11 of the Wolf *Sämtliche Werke* (Vienna: Musikwissenschaftlicher Verlag, 1986). The orchestration and the choral writing are indeed effective. The orchestra is somewhat large: piccolo, two flutes, two oboes, two clarinets, three bassoons, four horns, three trumpets, three trombones, bass tuba, timpani, tamtam, strings, and SATB chorus. Wolf's instrumentation at the beginning of the ballad is typical of the colorful, well-balanced orchestration he had finally learned to produce. The unison figure in the piano accompaniment at the start is assigned complete to the cellos and violas, with the first and second bassoons reinforcing the outlined third G–E; the second clarinet doubling only the semitone figures at midmeasure and at the beginning of the measure; and the transition upward to the next leg of the sequence assigned to the second clarinet and third bassoon, with the double bass and cello playing the scalewise ascent G–A–B♭ in the low bass. The refrain is first sung by a three-part female chorus SAA, followed by the men "wie aus weiter Ferne" (as if in the far distance), pianissimo and accompanied only by muted horns doubling the choral parts, with tremolando second violins and violas and flutter-tonguing flutes. The instrumental writing for the "dying away" effects after the crowd has all departed in measure 95 is particularly delicate, and the choral and orchestral writing at the end are especially effective, as Hans Jancik points out in his edition.

71. Heinrich Heine, "The Romantic School," trans. Helen Mustard, in *The Romantic School and Other Essays*, ed. Jost Hermand and Robert C. Holub (New York: Continuum Publishing, 1985). Heine makes fun of his youthful enthusiasm for the poetry of Ludwig Uhland; now, he writes, "What seemed to me so splendid, that chivalrous, Catholic world, those knights who cut and thrust at each other in aristocratic tournaments, those gentle squires and well-bred noble ladies, those Nordic heroes and Minnesingers, those monks and nuns, those ancestral vaults and awesome shudders, those pallid sentiments of renunciation to the accompaniment of bell-ringing, and the everlasting melancholy wailing—how bitterly it has been spoiled for me since then!"

72. Harry Maync, *Mörikes Werke*, 62–63.

73. Maync, an unabashed Wolf enthusiast, writes in his notes to the poetry (*Mörikes Werke*, 422): "One of the surpassingly beautiful compositions by Hugo Wolf." For more on the Orplid mythology that Mörike and his circle of Tübingen friends invented, see Jeffrey Todd Adams, *Eduard Mörike's "Orplid": Myth and the Poetic Mind* (Hildesheim: Georg Olms Verlag, 1984), and Lee B. Jennings, "Suckelborst, Wispel, and Mörike's Mythopoeia," in *Euphorion* 69 (1975): 320–32.

74. Sigmund Freud, "Das Unheimliche." Freud analyzes E.T.A. Hoffmann's tale "Der Sandmann" (238–42) to exemplify his argument that the uncanny has to do centrally with the recurrence of childhood trauma.

75. Joseph Schalk, "Neue Lieder, neues Leben," in the *Allgemeine Zeitung* for Wednesday, 22 January 1890 (Stuttgart and Munich: J. G. Cotta). Schalk observes that there must be a deep affinity between Wolf and Mörike, that he was ashamed to have been part of the general neglect of the "half-forgotten Swabian poet" with so "rich and deep a poetic nature." When one reads "Das erste Liebeslied eines Mädchens," he writes, one marvels at its audacity, far oustripping the narrower bounds of Uhland and his imitators. An "elemental power" resides in this verse and in the music to which Wolf set Mörike.

Schalk exaggerated somewhat when he characterized Mörike as "half-forgotten." When Nietzsche wrote in 1875 that Mörike lacked lucidity, his "music" trivial in nature, he was objecting to current claims that Mörike was the greatest German lyric poet—hardly evidence of oblivion. See Nietzsche, *Werke: Kritische Gesamtausgabe*, vol. 1, ed. Giorgio Colli and Mazzino Montinari (Berlin: Walter de Gruyter, 1967), 204.

76. The letter is cited in Rainer Pohl, "Zur Textgeschichte von Mörikes 'Feuerreiter,'" in *Eduard Mörike*, ed. Victor G. Doerksen (Darmstadt: Wissenschaftliche Buchgesellschaft, 1975), 336.

77. *Des Knaben Wunderhorn: Alte deutsche Lieder*, ed. Achim von Arnim and Clemens Brentano, facsimile of the Heidelberg (Mohr, 1819) 2d ed. (Meersburg: F. W. Hendel, 1928), "Das Feuerbesprecher," 21–22.

78. Maync, *Mörikes Werke*, 419, cites Kerner's journal of the occult, vol. 5 of the *Magikon* for 1853 (300), about fire-seers who could pinpoint the location of distant fires.

79. Mörike recruited his older brother Karl Eberhard (1797–1847) and a friend, Karl Ludwig Friedrich Hetsch (1806–92) to compose the *Musikbeilage zu* MALER NOLTEN / von / Eduard Mörike / Stuttgart / F. Schweizerbart's Verlag, the little collection of six songs lithographed in facsimile. On 22 February 1832, Mörike sent an urgent express letter to his brother—"A musical plea!"—asking for a setting of a Latin religious poem he translated as "Seufzer" and which appears near the end of *Maler Nolten* as part of its tragic dénouement. The *Musikbeilage* includes:

1–12 [in *Querformat*]. "Romanze, vom wahnsinnigen Feuerreiter"—Karl Ludwig Friedrich Hetsch
13–14. "Lied der Feenkinder" ("Die Geister am Mummelsee")—composer not indicated, probably Karl Mörike
15–20. "Elfenlied"—Hetsch
21–24. "Lied" ("Das verlassene Mägdlein")—Hetsch
25–26. JESU BENIGNE ("Seufzer")—Karl Mörike
27–32. No title given ("Agnes")—Hetsch

None of the six is more than competently "gemörikelt," Wolf's neologism for musical settings of this poet. A modern facsimile of the Hetsch and Karl Mörike songs can be found in Eduard Mörike, *Werke und Briefe*, vol. 5: *Maler Nolten: Lesarten und Erläuterungen* (Stuttgart: Ernst Klett Verlag, 1971), 259–75.

80. Maync, *Mörikes Werke*, 56–57.

81. Winfried Freund, "Eduard Mörike: Der Feuerreiter," in *Die deutsche Ballade: Theorie, Analysen, Didaktik* (Paderborn: Ferdinand Schöningh, 1978), 66–72.

82. Consulting Challier's song catalog, one finds only a single setting of "Die Geister am Mummelsee"—by one H. v. Eyken, no opus or publisher given, listed in the *Neunter Nachtrag . . . enthaltend die neuen Erscheinungen vom Juli 1900 bis Juli 1902* (Berlin, 1902), from 1715—and two other settings of "Der Feuerreiter" (Challier, *Großer Lieder-Katalog*, 263). One of those settings was composed by Wolf's friend Emil Kauffmann, brought up from childhood to be familiar with Mörike's name and works. Numerous minor composers were attracted to such poems as "Frühling, läßt sein blaues Band"—there had always been a following for "Das verlassene Mägdlein"—but not the ballads.

Chapter 4

1. *The Music Criticism of Hugo Wolf*, trans. and ed. Henry Pleasants (New York and London: Holmes and Meier Publishers, 1978), 224 and 190.

2. Ibid., 101.

3. Ibid., 273–75, an article written 3 April 1887; and 278–80, an article written 17 April 1887.

4. Ignaz Brüll (1846–1907) was a pianist, composer, and teacher who composed ten operas; Eduard Schütt (1856–1913) was a pianist, composer, and conductor who was director for a time of the Academic Wagner Society; Carl Goldmark (1830–1915) is now remembered only for his opera *The Queen of Sheba* and the *Sakuntala* Overture. Johannes Hager was a pseudonym for Johann Hasslinger (1822–98), an official in the Imperial Foreign Office, and Karl Schön (1885–?) was director of the Vienna Singakademie.

5. Goldschmidt's (1851–1906) "Lehre," marked "Neckisch und zierlich" (Teasing and dainty) is a brief and insipid waltz song in the simplest of diatonic styles. There is none of the turgid, Lisztian chromaticism that marks Goldschmidt's oratorio *Die sieben Todsünden* (The seven deadly sins).

6. *The Music Criticism of Hugo Wolf*, 279. Richard Heuberger's "Herzenbeklemmung" (Heart's anguish) provoked the charge.

7. Hans von Bülow, *Ausgewählte Schriften 1850–1892*, vol. 1 (*Briefe und Schriften*, vol. 3) (Leipzig: Breitkopf and Härtel, 1911), 347, asks whether song in the wake of Schubert (the "lyrical house-god"), Schumann, and Robert Franz "has not reached its end as a genre, with no new realms left." The context is a review in 1860 of Eduard Lassen's *Acht Lieder von Hoffmann von Fallersleben*, op. 4.

8. Peter Cornelius, *Literarische Werke*, in 4 vols. (Leipzig: Breitkopf and Härtel, 1904; reprint, New York: Johnson Reprint Corporation, 1970), vol. 2, 646, also cited in Magda Marx-Weber, "Cornelius' Kritik des Liedes," in *Peter Cornelius als Komponist, Dichter, Kritiker und Essayist*, ed. Hellmut Federhofer and Kurt Oehl (Regensburg: Gustav Bosse Verlag, 1977), 172–73. "Are not Heine's poems somewhat tempo passato? [Cornelius characterizes Heine's preoccupation with "pale dead bodies" and writes that these were the sensitivities of the best poetic genius in "the sleeping years after the War of Liberation."] But today? Today, in my opinion, a healthier poetry seems advisable, something founded in the real and material world, something along the lines of Goethe and Bürger, in which one touches what one knows, like children newly come into the world."

9. Cornelius, *Literarische Werke*, vol. 2, 646. "Don't you shrink when you read the thousand names whose 'three songs' are announced over and over again as novelties in the newspapers? Today Müller—tomorrow Schmidt—but they are always the same old three songs. I can't help when I say 'Lied' thinking of Schubert, Schumann, and Franz; if I cannot see something in my works that does not assert itself next to and in spite of these great masters, I'd rather let the matter rest there."

10. The *Spanisches Liederbuch* was published by Hertz of Berlin in 1852, with a frontispiece by Heyse's friend Adolf Menzel, depicting lovers in Spanish dress against a backdrop of Moorish arches and greenery. An admonishing mother, a horror-struck priest clutching at his endangered lectern, and a winged Cupid round out the cast of traditional characters.

11. In October 1890, Wolf visited Munich and made the acquaintance of one Michael Georg Conrad, who later sent his reminiscences of conversations with Wolf to Ernst Decsey. Wolf spoke heatedly of the ten years that elapsed between the publication of the first and second editions of Mörike's collected poetry and of critics' preference for the likes of Otto Roquette or Friedrich Bodenstedt over Mörike. "What miserable weeds the critics have used to heat their stoves!" he exclaimed. See Ernst Decsey, *Hugo Wolf*, vol. 3: *Der Künstler und die Welt 1892–1895* (Berlin and Leipzig: Schuster and Loeffler, 1904), 39.

12. Ernst Challier, *Grosser Lieder-Katalog: Ein alphabetisch geordnetes Verzeichniss sämmtlicher Einstimmiger Lieder* (Berlin: privately published, 1885), 320, lists 78 different settings of Geibel's "Gondoliera (O komm' zu mir, wenn durch die Nacht)" and later cited 163 settings in *Börsenblatt für den deutschen Buchhandel*, no. 174 (1912), quoted by Friedrich Düsel in his edition of Geibel's *Werke: Auswahl in zwei Teilen* (Berlin: Bong [1920]), vol. 1, 7. In the *Lieder-Katalog*, 856, he cites 74 settings

of Heine's "Und wüssten's die Blumen, die kleinen," ranging from Alberti to Zenger. The final tally is undoubtedly much larger.

13. Challier cites only the composer's last name and first initial, the opus number, the publisher, and the price. Where I have cited composers in the main text without dates or a full name, I have been unable to locate further information about them.

14. The religious poems were less popular with composers than the secular works, although a now-forgotten composer named George Flügel set six of the *Geistliche Lieder* as his op. 43, and a few other earlier settings can be traced as well. Ferdinand Hiller set the Nicolas Nuñez poem, "Die du Gott gebarst," and "Die ihr schwebet," in his op. 100. Max Bruch set "Nun bin ich dein," "Nun wandre, Maria," and "Ach, des Knaben Augen" in op. 17. "Die ihr schwebet" was also set by W. Voullaire as op. 4; by Hermann Wichmann as op. 28, no. 2; by F. Gernsheim as op. 34, no. 4; by Georg Flügel; and by Johannes Brahms. Wichmann also set "Ach, des Knaben Augen" as op. 31, no. 5.

15. Cited in Decsey, *Hugo Wolf*, vol. 3: *Der Künstler und die Welt*, 31, letter to Gustav Schur, 16 June 1890. "Enclose in your answer to Schott that it is at my discretion and not the publisher's to select poetry. That is all we need . . . ! A whole series of uncomposable poems! O thou Caliban, since I composed them, they were composable."

16. Bad poetry was epitomized for Wolf in the person of a contemporaneous writer, the philosopher-medievalist-poet Richard Kralik von Meyrswalden (1852–1934). Walker, in *Hugo Wolf: A Biography*, 2d ed. (London: Dent, 1968), 142–43, cites an amusing anecdote about Wolf in a comical rage over poetry he guessed to be Kralik's, as Wolf continually savaged the fellow in his Salonblatt articles. "The useful and agreeable occupation of writing bad verses has for some time now, fortunately, been a monopoly enjoyed by Herr R. K.," he wrote in January of 1885. See Henry Pleasants, *The Music Criticism of Hugo Wolf*, 104.

17. Ernst Decsey, *Hugo Wolf*, vol. 2: *Hugo Wolfs Schaffen* (Berlin and Leipzig: Schuster and Loeffler, 1904), 77.

18. Ibid., 33.

19. Cited in Carl Conrad Theodor Litzmann, *Emanuel Geibel. Aus Erinnerungen, Briefen und Tagebüchern* (Berlin: Wilhelm Hertz, 1887), 49–50.

20. Karl Theodor Gaedertz, *Emanuel Geibel, Sänger der Liebe, Herold des Reiches* (Leipzig: Georg Wigand, 1897), 178–92 for an account of Geibel's stay at Escheberg. See also *Emanuel Geibel's Briefe an Karl Freiherrn von der Malsburg und Mitglieder seiner Familie*, ed. Albert Duncker (Berlin: Verlag von Gebrüder Paetel, 1885).

21. Heinrich Heine, *Voyage en Espagne*, rev. and aug. ed. (Paris, 1870), 17. First published as *Tra los Montes*, 2 vols. (Paris, 1843). Cited in Margaret Sleeman and Gareth Davies, "Variations on Spanish Themes: The *Spanisches Liederbuch* of Emanuel Geibel and Paul Heyse and Its Reflection in the Songs of Hugo Wolf," in *Proceedings of the Leeds Philosophical and Literary Society: Literary and Historical Section 18* (1982), 164.

22. *Der Briefwechsel von Emanuel Geibel und Paul Heyse*, ed. Erich Petzet (Munich: J. F. Lehmanns Verlag, 1922), 65–84, letters 17–30.

23. See Sleeman and Davies, "Variations on Spanish Themes," 155–274.

24. The seguidillas, a poetic form of popular origin favored by eighteenth-century poets, and the gypsy songs are very brief, and Wolf did not set any of them to music.

25. Ibid., 303–4.

26. "In dem Schatten meiner Locken" was translated by Heyse and is the twenty-fifth poem in the "Weltliche Lieder," in *Spanisches Liederbuch*, 58. "À la sombra de mis cabellos" is found in Böhl, vol. 1, 293, no. 248; and also in Ochoa, 293–94; Duràn, 114; and Huber, 575–76.

27. "Herr, was trägt der Boden hier" was translated by Heyse and is the tenth poem in the "Geistliche Lieder," in *Spanisches Liederbuch*, 18. Its source, "Qué producirá mi Dios" is in Böhl, vol. 1, 31, no. 49, who attributes the work to an anonymous poem in a manuscript cancionero "A."

28. "Komm, o Tod, von Nacht umgeben" was translated by Geibel and is the thirty-fourth poem in the "Weltliche Lieder," in *Spanisches Liederbuch*, 70. It is found in Böhl, vol. 1, 268, no. 184; Ochoa, 244; Duràn, 64–65; and Huber, 572.

29. See Barbara K. Sable, "The Translation Chain in Some of the Hugo Wolf Settings of the *Spanisches Liederbuch*," in *Journal of Musicological Research* 5 (1984): 213–35.

30. See Paul Kuczinsky, ed., *Aus Briefen Adolf Jensens* (Berlin, 1879); Arnold Niggli, *Adolf Jensen* (Berlin: "Harmonie" Verlagsgesellschaft für Literatur und Kunst, 1900); A. Pohl, ed., "Unbekannte Jensenbriefe," in *Die Musik* 29, no. 1 (1936–37): 44–46; and Gottfried Schweizer, *Das Liedschaffen Adolf Jensens* (Giessen: H. L. Brönner, 1933).

31. From the introduction by William Foster Apthorp to *Forty Songs by Adolf Jensen*, ed. William Foster Apthorp (Boston: Oliver Ditson, 1913), xxi. Jensen's acquaintance with Brahms and Hans von Bülow occurred in Baden-Baden in 1876; other visits followed in 1877. Apthorp's source was Arnold Niggli, *Adolf Jensen*, 96–97.

32. Jensen's first set of six songs, published in Königsberg in 1849, was later withdrawn by the composer. The six songs of his 1859 op. 1 include poems by Heine, Heyse, and Eichendorff and were followed by the *7 Gesänge aus dem Spanischen Liederbuch*, op. 4, published in Hamburg by Friedrich Schuberth in 1860. The op. 21 Spanish songbook settings were first published by the same firm in 1865. Jensen was quite partial to Geibel and Heyse, and his oeuvre considerably swells the roll call of their musical settings. The six *Minneweisen* of op. 6 (Leipzig, 1862) to texts by Geibel; the opp. 4 and 21 Spanish songbook settings; the op. 22 set of twelve songs to texts by Heyse; the *Acht Lieder von Emanuel Geibel für Sopran, Alt, Tenor u[nd] Bass*, op. 28; and the *Zwei Marienlieder (aus dem Spanischen) von Paul Heyse*, op. 64 of 1881, settings of "An die Jungfrau Maria" and "Nun wandre, Maria" for tenor, violas, cellos, double basses, and timpani, are the groups entirely devoted to these two poets. His other song sets and cycles include the seven *Lieder des Hafis* in Georg Daumer's translations, op. 11 (Hamburg, 1863); the six songs of *Dolorosa* by Adalbert von Chamisso, op. 30 (Leipzig, 1868); the *12 Lieder aus Scheffels Gaudeamus*, op. 40 (Dresden, 1870); the seven Robert Burns songs of op. 49 (Breslau, 1875); the six Walter Scott songs of op. 52 (Breslau, 1875); and *4 Gesänge aus [Herder's] Stimmen der Völker*, op. 58 (Breslau, 1877).

33. William Foster Apthorp, *Forty Songs*, xix.

34. Ibid., xix; and Arnold Niggli, *Adolf Jensen*, 65.

35. Hans von Bülow, "Adolf Jensen. Einige Worte als Nachtrag zu den Schumanniana," in *Ausgewählte Schriften 1850–1892*, vol. 2, 34–45. The article was first published in the *Neue Zeitschrift für Musik* 59, no. 18 (30 October 1863).

36. William Foster Apthorpe, *Forty Songs*, xxii.

37. Hermann Kretzschmar, *Gesammelte Aufsätze über Musik und Anderes aus den Grenzboten* (Leipzig: Breitkopf and Härtel, 1911), 19–21. In his 1898 essay "Das deutsche Lied seit dem Tode Richard Wagners," in ibid., 287, Kretzschmar pairs Jensen and Brahms as masters of the lied and prophesies that "Jensen will disappear, but Brahms's songs, as with his other works, will remain."

38. In Decsey, *Hugo Wolf*, vol. 2: *Hugo Wolfs Schaffen*, 59–62, the author compares Wolf's and Jensen's settings of "Klinge, klinge, mein Pandero." Jensen's E-minor melody is attractive, Decsey observes, but the melodic phrase structure destroys the syntax of the poetry, creates false emphases on words undeserving of emphasis, and separates clauses that should be joined. Nor did Jensen think to set the words "Doch an Andres denkt mein Herz" as a short-lived modulation to *another* tonality, nor to reflect the seriousness of those thoughts by an abruptly slower rhythmic pace in the vocal line, nor to make of the word "Qual" a stylized cry—a descending leap of a ninth.

39. *7 Songs aus dem Spanischen Liederbuche. With English and German Words and Pianoforte Accompaniment, by Adolf Jensen*, op. 21 (London: Augener [1889?]). Jensen is also, to my knowledge, the only composer before Wolf to set "Mein Liebster singt am Haus im Mondenscheine," which he entitled "Toscanischer Rispetto," from the *Italienisches Liederbuch*.

40. Niggli, *Arnold Jensen*, 96.

41. Hugo Wolf, *Sämtliche Werke*, vol. 4: *Spanisches Liederbuch*, ed. Hans Jancik (Vienna: Musikwissenschaftlicher Verlag, 1967), 49–52.

42. "En campaña, madre" appears in Böhl, vol. 1, 300, no. 264; also in Ochoa, 321. The translation by Paul Heyse is no. 84 in the *Spanisches Liederbuch*, 148–49.

43. Wolf, *Sämtliche Werke*, vol. 4: *Spanisches Liederbuch*, 138–40.

44. Ibid., 131–32.

45. See Hanslick's review of 5 December 1894 cited in chap. 3, n. 70.

46. Eduard Hanslick, *Die moderne Oper: Kritiken und Studien* (Berlin: Allgemeiner Verein für Deutsche Literatur, 1885), 332. Despite Hanslick's qualified approbation, Rubinstein was disappointed in the work's reception and wrote to the librettist Rodenburg, saying, "The Wagner clique set up hostile demonstrations . . . In addition, the public is now so led astray by brochures on Opera, Drama, New Paths and the Future that a harmless, purely lyrical, specifically musical composition—moreover a Russo-Jewish composition—must leave the people cold." Cited in Catherine Drinker Bowen, *"Free Artist": The Story of Anton and Nicholas Rubinstein* (New York: Random House, 1939), 223–24.

47. Hanslick, *Musikalische Stationen. Der "Modernen Oper,"* vol. 2 (Berlin: Allgemeiner Verein für Deutsche Literatur, 1885), 325.

48. From *Musikalisches Skizzenbuch. Der "Modernen Oper,"* vol. 4 (Berlin: Allgemeiner Verein für Deutsche Litteratur, 1896), 76. Here, Hanslick praises a minor composer named Viktor Nessler (1841–90) for his un-Wagnerian choice of subject matter. "Nessler has put into practice a fortunate thought at the right time: the return to subjects that are simply human, with gravity and gaiety intertwined; the return to the reign of melody, to unpretentious and merry expression. The public, tired of prehistoric, mythic, and Oriental opera subjects, crushed by the taxing voluptuousness of Wagnerian gigantic opera, longs for musical repose on German soil."

49. Hermann Kretzschmar, "Das deutsche Lied seit Robert Schumann," 5.

50. Wolf reviewed Rubinstein's Violin Sonata, op. 19, saying, "It is a piece like so many others from the pen of this composer, that promises well in the beginning and finally produces nothing of any account." See *The Music Criticism of Hugo Wolf*, 27, review of 23 March 1884. In this instance, Wolf and Brahms agreed with each other. Brahms told the critic and composer Richard Heuberger (who knew Wolf as well) in 1894 that he was delighted with one of Rubinstein's concerts and could listen to him play all night, especially as he had performed that evening with greater accuracy than usual. Asked what he thought of Rubinstein's compositions, Brahms was not so complimentary, condemning his works as rubbish. See Richard Heuberger, *Erinnerungen an Johannes Brahms*, 2d rev. ed., ed. Kurt Hofmann (Tutzing: Hans Schneider Verlag, 1976), 65.

51. Wolf, *Sämtliche Werke*, vol. 4: *Spanisches Liederbuch*, 133–35.

52. *Preciosens Sprüchlein gegen Kopfweh (Cabezita, cabezita). Nach dem Spanischen des Cervantes von Paul Heyse. Frau Hofrat Schöll zu freundlicher Erinnerung von Peter Cornelius* (Leipzig: E. W. Fritzsch, 1888). See Peter Cornelius, *Musikalische Werke*, vol. 1, ed. Max Hasse (Leipzig: Breitkopf and Härtel, n.d.; reprint, Farnsborough, England: Gregg International Publishers, 1971), 83–85.

53. *Briefe an Melanie Köchert*, ed. Franz Grasberger (Tutzing: Hans Schneider Verlag, 1964), letter of 14 April 1891. Cornelius was prone to short lines in varying meters and rhythms. "Ich ersehnt' ein Lied," in Peter Cornelius, *Literarische Werke*, vol. 4: *Gedichte*, ed. Adolf Stern (Leipzig: Breitkopf and Härtel, 1905), 44, is typical:

> Ich ersehnt' ein Lied
> Wie die Blume den Tau,
> Wie Tränen lau
> Ein Augenlid.
> Und wie Tau so klar
> Und wie Tränen sacht
> Bot das Lied sich dar
> Eh' ich's gedacht.

54. *Briefe an Grohe*, 86–87, letter of 9 May 1892.

55. Peter Cornelius, "Autobiographische Skizze" (1874), in *Literarische Werke*, vol. 3: *Aufsätze über Musik und Kunst*, ed. Edgar Istel (Leipzig: Breitkopf and Härtel, 1904), 2–3.

56. The phrase occurs in a letter sent from Munich in June 1866 to his bride and written shortly after Wagner's departure. Cornelius tells his wife that at last he can breathe, can begin to find himself once more, and observes that his best work was created away from the influence of Liszt and Wagner. See Peter Cornelius, *Ausgewählte Schriften und Briefe*, ed. Paul Egert (Berlin, 1938), 402. The letter is cited in Christoph-Hellmut Mahling, "'. . . in Dichtung und Komposition auf eigenem Boden gewachsen': Cornelius und sein Verhältnis zur 'Neudeutschen Schule,'" in *Peter Cornelius als Komponist, Dichter, Kritiker und Essayist*, ed. Hellmut Federhofer and Kurt Oehl (Regensburg: Gustave Bosse Verlag, 1977), 106–7. The struggle for musical independence is a leitmotif of Cornelius's life and one he invokes many times in his diary and letters. In a letter written in 1865 to his sister, he tells her that he did not compose a note while staying with Wagner; he is now a free man, he writes, and realizes that he cannot pursue greater musical accomplishments in Liszt's company, "as

friendly as he is," nor in the grasp of Wagner's tyrannical friendship, but only by himself. See Carl Maria Cornelius, *Peter Cornelius. Der Wort- und Tondichter* (Regensburg: Gustav Bosse, 1925), vol. 1, 412. The examples multiply: Cornelius's resolve to write comic opera within the bounds of pre-Wagnerite opera was formed in conscious opposition to Wagner's influence, a foreshadowing of Wolf's later resolution to do likewise. For more about Cornelius's life and his troubled relationship with Wagner, see Walter Jacob, *Der beschwerliche Weg des Peter Cornelius zu Liszt und Wagner* (Mainz: H. Krach, 1974); Barbara Glauert, *Spuren eines bewegten Lebens: Verschollenes und Unveröffentliches von Peter Cornelius* (Mainz: H. Krach, 1974); Volker Hoffmann, "Leben und Werk des Peter Cornelius zu seiner und in unserer Zeit," in *Peter Cornelius als Komponist, Dichter, Kritiker und Essayist*, 9–18; and Hans-Joachim Bauer, "Cornelius und Richard Wagner" in ibid., 93–104.

57. Kretzschmar, "Das deutsche Lied seit Robert Schumann," 27.

58. Peter Cornelius, "Das Fest des 'Allgemeinen deutschen Musikvereins' in Meiningen," in *Literarische Werke*, vol. 3, 122–23. Cornelius was later to revise his opinion of Lassen downward.

59. Peter Cornelius, "Richard Würst, Preis-symphonie in F-Dur," in *Neue Zeitschrift für Musik* 41, no. 24 (8 December 1854): 257–59, reprinted in *Literarische Werke*, vol. 3, 45.

60. Miguel de Cervantes, *Novelas ejemplares* (Madrid: Clasicos Castalia, 1982), vol. 1.

61. *Spanisches Liederbuch*, 158, no. 90.

62. Kretzschmar, "Das deutsche Lied seit Robert Schumann," 28.

63. Wolf, *Sämtliche Werke*, vol. 4: *Spanisches Liederbuch*, 94–95.

64. Leopold Damrosch, *Collected Songs*, ed. Frank Damrosch (New York: G. Schirmer, 1903).

65. The critic for the *Deutsche Musikzeitung* in 1860 was hitting two birds with one stone by pairing Lassen and Damrosch as equivalent miscreants. Cited in Magda Marx-Weber, "Cornelius' Kritik des Liedes," 176.

66. Kretzschmar, "Das deutsche Lied seit Robert Schumann," 31.

67. Eric Sams, *The Songs of Hugo Wolf*, 2d ed., rev. and enlarged (London: Eulenberg Books, 1983), 300.

68.   Willst du feste Wurzel fassen,
                     Liebster, hier an meiner Brust,
                     Ohne daß der Neider Hassen
                     Stürmisch uns verstört die Lust;
                     Willst du, daß zu tausendmalen
                     Ich wie heut dich sehen mag,
                     Und dir stets auf Sicht bezahlen
                     Unserer Liebe Schuldbetrag:

                     Geh', Geliebter . . .

(Will you take firm root, beloved, here in my breast, without the hatred of envious people destroying our pleasure; will you have me, for the thousandth time, look at you the way I do today, and always pay you on sight the debt of our love. Go beloved . . .)

69. "Geh', Geliebter" was translated by Geibel and is the fifty-fourth poem in the "Weltliche Lieder," 101–3. The Spanish source, "Vete amor, y vete, / mira que amanece," was attributed to the ubiquitous "Anonymous" in the *Romancero general* (Madrid, 1604), fols. 363r–v and is also found in Ochoa, 494–95; and Huber, 563.

70. Wolf, *Sämtliche Werke*, vol. 4: *Spanisches Liederbuch*, 159–65.

71. Decsey, *Hugo Wolf*, vol. 3: *Der Künstler und die Welt*, 8. Decsey was quoting from a newspaper article written on 1 December 1889 by a critic for *Vaterland*.

72. Richard Batka, "Zur Würdigung Hugo Wolfs," in *Kranz: Gesammelte Blätter über Musik* (Leipzig: Lauterbach und Kuhn, 1903). In Hugo Wolf, *Briefe an Heinrich Potpeschnigg*, ed. Heinz Nonveiller (Stuttgart: Union Deutsche Verlagsgesellschaft, 1923), letter of 19 May 1892, Wolf told Potpeschnigg, "I am currently orchestrating 'Geh' Geliebter.' " When Siegfried Ochs, the director of the Berlin Philharmonic and a member of the so-called Berlin "Informals" (Berlin Wolfianer), wanted orchestrated versions of some of Wolf's songs for performance in Berlin, Wolf wrote to Grohe on 19 October 1895, saying, "I have proposed the Mignon song, Ganymed, or Geh' Geliebter." On 17 November, he wrote that he had orchestrated five songs—"the two already chosen," as well as "Ganymed," "Geh', Geliebter," and "Er ist's"—but had carelessly left the rolled-up manuscripts in a tram car. After Wolf's death, the Hugo-Wolf-Verein in Vienna came into possession of "Mignon" and "Er ist's," but the others remain lost.

73. *Des jungen Kreislers Schatzkästlein. Aussprüche von Dichtern, Philosophen und Künstlern*, ed. Carl Krebs. (Berlin: Deutsch Brahms-Gesellschaft, 1909).

74. The song was first published in the *Sechs Gesänge für eine Sopran- oder Tenor*, op. 6 (Leipzig: Verlag von Bartolf Senff, 1853). It is an attractive strophic song, but those accustomed to Wolf's more finely tuned declamation (Brahms begins the vocal part with a downbeat stress on the relatively unimportant preposition "In [dem Schatten]") and contrasting mediant tonalities might find that Brahms's song suffers by comparison.

75. See Walker, *Hugo Wolf*, 83–87 for an account of the incident. Kalbeck's description can be found in his review of *Ein Musikbuch aus Österreich*, ed. Richard Heuberger (Vienna, 1904), a review printed in the *Neues Wiener Tagblatt* for 9 March 1904. In *Johannes Brahms III: Zweiter Halbband 1881–85* (Berlin: Deutsch Brahms-Gesellschaft, 1912), 410–12, Kalbeck again described the incident in terms only slightly less offensive than the earlier review.

76. *The Music Criticism of Hugo Wolf*, 27–28 and 274. Wolf characterizes "Von ewiger Liebe" as "deeply felt and deeply expressive," "the best thing Brahms has accomplished in this genre," but immediately follows the words of praise with the observation "It is hard to believe that the same composer who wrote this splendid song could also write four symphonies whose ludicrous solemnity, a model of involuntary humor, deserves preservation as a droll souvenir of the promised messiah."

77. Decsey, *Hugo Wolf*, vol. 3: *Der Künstler und die Welt*, 76–77, recounts an anecdote of Wolf's visit to Germany in April 1891 and the composer's disagreement with Wilhelm Schmid, a classics professor at Tübingen University and Emil Kauffmann's son-in-law. Schmid, who later wrote a preparatory article in the *Tübingen Chronik* for the Wolf concert of 31 October 1893, could not accept Wolf's harsh attitude toward Brahms's music. Wolf defensively insisted that his sentiments regarding

Brahms were entirely impersonal, that he had even praised the *Magelone* cycle, and that his criticisms sprang from the "untruth" of Brahms's music. Wolf had earlier, in June of 1890, shortly after making Emil Kauffmann's acquaintance, disagreed with him as well on the same subject, using Nietzsche's phrase "the melancholy of impotence" to characterize Brahms. See *Briefe an Emil Kauffmann*, ed. Edmund von Hellmer (Berlin: S. Fischer, 1903), 13–14. Wolf would later express his displeasure with Paul Müller, a gymnasium teacher and founder of the Berlin Wolf Society, after a visit in 1897 because Müller would not condemn Brahms.

78. It is interesting to observe that Brahms was far more open in his avowals of admiration for Schubert's lieder than Wolf was, at least, on one level—Brahms, one notices, largely shunned Goethe's poetry for his solo lieder, and the single exception is a poem not set by Schubert: "Dämmrung senkte sich von oben," op. 59, no. 1, published in 1873. In a letter of 1887, Brahms writes:

> The true successor to Beethoven is not Mendelssohn, also not Schumann, but Schubert. It is unbelievable, how much music he put into his songs. No other composer understands correct declamation as well as he does. The best comes from him in so obvious a manner that it could not be otherwise. For example, the beginning of *Winterreise*: "Fremd bin ich eingezogen." Such as we would stress the second syllable; in Schubert, it flows by beautifully. How he ennobled not only older verse but the newest poetry, that of Platen, Rückert, and Heine. He rightly found subjects for music in poems by Schlegel that other composers had disregarded. The way he set a ghasel by Platen is simply marvelous. We have also tried to do likewise, but measured against Schubert, it's all bungling. How wonderful the setting of the final stanza of the poem "Ach, um deine feuchten Schwingen" [Suleika I] from the Divan is!

See Max Kalbeck, *Johannes Brahms I: Erster Halbband 1833–1856* (Berlin: Deutsch Brahms-Gesellschaft, 1912), 220. Elsewhere, he observed that "There is no song by Schubert from which one cannot learn something." The homage occasionally imprints itself on Brahms's own music, as in the citation from "Der Doppelgänger" (the setting of the last words of Heine's poem, "in alter Zeit") at the final vocal phrase of Brahms's "Herbstgefühl," op. 48, no. 7 ("bald stirbst sie auch"), to a poem by Adolf Friedrich von Schack. The link between the two songs is obvious: to see one's ghostly double in German Romantic literature was a presage of imminent death.

Brahms also liked Loewe, especially the ballads and the Serbian songs, but did not fall into the trap of overestimating him. In Vienna, according to Brahms, Loewe was wrongly esteemed as a genius of equal caliber with Schubert (Kalbeck, *Johannes Brahms III*, 85). See also Christiane Jacobsen, *Das Verhältnis von Sprache und Musik in ausgewählten Liedern von Johannes Brahms, dargestellt an Parallelvertonungen* (Hamburg: Verlag der Musikalienhandlung Karl Dieter Wagner, 1975).

79. Richard Heuberger, *Erinnerungen an Johannes Brahms: Tagebuchnotizen aus den Jahren 1875 bis 1897*, 2d rev. ed., ed. Kurt Hofmann (Tutzing: Hans Schneider Verlag, 1976). When Heuberger in 1895 spoke to Brahms of the Mandyczewski Schubert edition and said that the Vienna Conservatory should arrange performances of Schubert, Brahms replied, "They would rather have Hugo Wolf" (166). The anecdote about the Richter-Brahms discussion of Wolf is from ibid., 45. Both items are misper-

ceptions, ones Wolf would never have endorsed. Brahms and Richter were probably repeating the incorrect designation of "symphonic lied composer" from Hanslick.

80. *Briefe an Melanie Köchert*, 11–12, letter of 20 August 1890. Wolf could not resist quoting an example of Brahms's "quite peculiar original declamation"—the sarcasm in the adjective "original" laid on with a trowel—in the phrase "O ihr Jungfraun im Land von dem Berg und über See" from "Singt mein Schatz wie ein Fink."

81. Florence May, *The Life of Johannes Brahms*, 2d rev. ed. (reprint; Neptune City, N.J.: Paganiniana Publications, 1981), vol. 1.

82. See Imogen Fellinger, "Brahms's 'Way': A Composer's Self-View," in *Brahms 2: Biographical, Documentary, and Analytical Studies*, ed. Michael Musgrave (Cambridge: Cambridge University Press, 1987), 53.

83. An anecdote may perhaps help to confirm Brahms's need to place his chosen texts at a distance, that is, to classify them with the elements of music. When the poet Klaus Groth asked Brahms why he did not set his (Groth's) Plattdeutsch poems to music, the composer responded that the dialect was "too close" to him, that it signified something other than language and therefore he could not compose songs in it. See Heinrich Miesner, ed., *Klaus Groth und die Musik: Erinnerungen an Johannes Brahms* (Heide in Holstein, 1933), 64.

84. Richard Heuberger, *Erinnerungen an Johannes Brahms*, 41. The anecdote Heuberger cites occurred on 28 March 1889. Brahms continued: "Besides, we see what a cultured, intelligent, polite man he is!"

85. *Johannes Brahms and Theodor Billroth: Letters from a Musical Friendship*, trans. and ed. Hans Barkan (Norman: University of Oklahoma Press, 1957), 121. See also *Billroth-Brahms im Briefwechsel* (Vienna: Urban and Schwartzenberg, 1935).

86. *Spanisches Liederbuch*, 10–11. Böhl, vol. 3, 13, at the end of the romance "La niña á quien dijo el Angel."

87. *Johannes Brahms Briefwechsel V: Johannes Brahms im Briefwechsel mit Joseph Joachim*, ed. Andreas Moser (Berlin, 1921), and *Briefwechsel IX: Johannes Brahms Briefe an P. J. Simrock und Fritz Simrock*, ed. Max Kalbeck (Berlin, 1917).

88. Brahms indicates the German text of the carol in parentheses beneath the viola part in measures 1–10.

> Josef, lieber Josef mein,
> Hilf mir wiegn mein Kindlein fein,
> Gott der wird dein Lohner sein,
> Im Himmelreich der Jungfrau Sohn,
> Maria, Maria.

(Joseph, my beloved Joseph, help me cradle my lovely little child. God will reward you, in the paradise of the Virgin's Son, Mary, Mary.)

A five-voice setting of the melody appears in Johann Walter's *Geistliches Gesangbüchlein* (Wittenberg, 1551); see Johann Walter, *Sämtliche Werke*, ed. Otto Schröder (Kassel and Basel: Bärenreiter, 1953), vol. 1, 81–83. Reger's treatment of the melody in his "Mariä Wiegenlied" (text by Martin Boelitz), the first of the *Neun Kinderlieder aus Christa's und Lotti's Kinderleben* in the mammoth op. 76, is perhaps the most popular of his many songs. Boelitz's words, "Maria sitzt am Rosenhag und wiegt ihr Jesuskind, / Durch die Blätter leise weht der warme Sommerwind," would naturally recall the traditional melody. See Max Reger, *Sämtliche Werke*, ed. Fritz Stein (Wiesbaden: Breitkopf and Härtel [1959]), vol. 33, 141–42.

89. Eric Sams, *Brahms's Songs* (London: British Broadcasting Corporation, 1972), 53.

90. *Hugo Wolf. Eine Persönlichkeit in Briefen. Familienbriefe*, ed. Edmund von Hellmer (Leipzig: Breitkopf and Härtel, 1912), 91–92.

91. It is tempting to connect Wolf's tirade against pro forma prayers with the lesser level of musical inspiration in his earlier setting of Mörike's "Gebet." Poems such as "Seufzer" elicited a much deeper musical response.

92. Wolf, *Sämtliche Werke*, vol. 4: *Spanisches Liederbuch*, 14–21.

93. Cited in Decsey, *Hugo Wolf*, vol. 2: *Hugo Wolfs Schaffen*, 31.

94. Ibid., 31, letter of 23 March 1890. In the same letter, he tells Strasser that these are the best songs since Schubert and Schumann.

95. Kretzschmar, "Das deutsche Lied seit dem Tode Richard Wagners," 299–300. Kretzschmar admired Brahms and wrote a lengthy essay on the composer in 1884 (*Gesammelte Aufsätze über Musik*, 151–207), but he considered Brahms's songs representative of subjective Romanticism and therefore an unfruitful model.

Chapter 5

1. *Hugo Wolfs Briefe an Oskar Grohe*, ed. Heinrich Werner (Berlin: S. Fischer, 1905), 174–75. See also Peter Cook, *Hugo Wolf's Corregidor: A Study of the Opera and Its Origins* (London: privately published, 1976), 45. Cook cites passages from Wolf's correspondence regarding the opera in his third chapter, "The Composition of the Opera Illustrated by Hugo Wolf's Letters," on 43–80.

2. In an unpublished letter to Josef Strasser, dated 10 September 1888, Wolf mentioned his intention of writing his own libretto for an opera based on *Der Dreispitz*.

3. Pedro Antonio de Alarcón, *Der Dreispitz*, trans. Hulda Meister (Leipzig: Reclam, 1886).

4. Bruckner never set the text, which came complete with hunting scenes and organ music. Dr. Max Vancsa, in an article on the opera in the *Neue Musikalische Presse* of Vienna for 19 March 1904, discussed the Schaumann libretto and summarized its three-act construction. According to Ernst Decsey (only Decsey, Gustav Schur, Max Vancsa, and Joseph Schalk saw the libretto, and only Schalk liked it), Wolf was unhappy with the coarseness of the language and with what he perceived as an overemphasis on action at the expense of character development.

5. Cook, *Hugo Wolf's Corregidor*, 45.

6. Wolf, *Briefe an Grohe*, 177, letter of 10 February 1895. "Think a little more about a suitable title. 'Der Dreispitz' doesn't please us, nor 'Der Corregidor.' 'Frasquita' has been proposed, but that title doesn't represent enough of the content. A joker suggested 'Caballero and Love' as a free paraphrase of Schiller [referring to Schiller's drama *Kabale und Liebe*]. What do you propose?" See also Cook, *Hugo Wolf's Corregidor*, 45–46.

7. Heinrich Werner, *Hugo Wolf in Perchtoldsdorf: Persönliche Erinnerungen, nebst den Briefen des Meisters an seine Freunde Dr. Michael Haberlandt, Rudolf von*

Larisch und andere (Regensburg: Gustav Bosse Verlag, 1925); also Cook, *Hugo Wolf's Corregidor*, 46–47.

8. See Susan Youens, "Hugo Wolf and the Operatic Grail: The Search for a Libretto," in *The Cambridge Opera Journal* 1, no. 3 (November 1989): 277–98.

9. The only music Wolf ever wrote on commission was his incidental music to Ibsen's *Das Fest auf Solhaug* for Max Burckhard, the director of the Vienna Burgtheater. Wolf had at first liked the drama and even considered it operatic material, but changed his mind quickly. On 11 November 1890, he wrote to the composer Engelbert Humperdinck about his misery concerning the project, saying, "The Devil should set this to music." See Ernst Decsey, *Hugo Wolf*, vol. 3: *Der Künstler und die Welt* (Berlin and Leipzig: Schuster and Loeffler, 1904), 59. In *Briefe an Grohe*, 47, letter of 14 November 1890, Wolf writes, "The Ibsen play pleases me less and less each day. It is a bungling, shoddy piece with damnably little poetry in it." The requirement that his opera text be "poetic" in the larger sense of that word was established early in his search for a text.

10. Wolf, *Briefe an Emil Kauffmann*, ed. Edmund von Hellmer (Berlin: S. Fischer, 1903), 43–44.

11. Ibid., 55–56, letter of 12 October 1891.

12. Ibid., 53, letter of 6 August 1891. Wolf then goes on to say that he is currently reading the plays of Aristophanes, "this richest and wittiest of all poets," in the hopes of finding material for a comic opera—but he does not ever bring the subject up again.

13. Ibid., 49.

14. Wolf, *Briefe an Grohe*, 80, letter of 9 January 1892.

15. Ibid., 95, letter of 22 December 1892. "Recently I have been fortunate enough to escape from several so-called professional librettists. This is a type who proceeds, so to speak, by means of robbery. The fundamental concept underlying their thought and poetry is always success at the box office."

16. Ibid., 116–17, letter of 30 July 1893.

17. Ibid., 39–40, letter of 25 September 1890.

18. Frank Walker, *Hugo Wolf: A Biography*, 2d ed. (London: Dent, 1968), 412.

19. Wolf, *Briefe an Rosa Mayreder, mit einem Nachwort der Dichterin des Corregidor*, ed. Heinrich Werner (Vienna: Rikola, 1921), 60, letter of 24 November 95. The couplet from Heine is: "Schade, daß ich ihn nicht küssen kann, / Denn ich selbst bin dieser braver Mann."

20. Both Gustav Mahler in Vienna and Bruno Walter in Munich compressed the composer's four acts into three by, first, omitting the Bishop's music at the end of act 1 and adding the first scene of act 2 to the first act. The second act consisted of three scenes: the scene in the Mayor's house, the nocturnal meeting between Repela and Frasquita, and the Jealousy monologue of Tio Lukas, the Corregidor only emerging from the bedroom at the start of act 3. After the street scene of act 4, everything else was considerably cut.

21. Grohe had doubts about the Mayreder libretto from the beginning. When Grohe conveyed his criticisms of the text to Wolf, the composer replied on 30 March 1895, "I find the greater part of your negative remarks about the opera text unjustified. Since Herr Heckel seems to share your opinion you will understand that I don't care to be informed of this by a series of letters from another person. I will leave the text to be judged by a specialist because I cannot deny that some matters do need the experienced

hand of a stage specialist." Cook, *Hugo Wolf's Corregidor*, 47, surmises that the reference is perhaps to the Stuttgart Kapellmeister and composer Hermann Zumpe whom Wolf mentioned in a letter to Emil Kauffmann of 11 February 1895. See *Briefe an Kauffmann*, 149–50.

22. In *Gustav Mahler: Memories and Letters*, ed. Donald Mitchell, trans. Basil Creighton (London: John Murray, 1986), 64–65, Alma Mahler gives a questionable account of the Mahler-Wolf negotiations regarding *Der Corregidor*.

23. Walker, *Hugo Wolf*, 415 and 421. On 18 August 1897, Wolf wrote Heinrich Potpeschnigg to say that Mahler doubted the work could be produced in Vienna. Wolf's bitterness and sense of betrayal are evident in the angry phrase "Mahler, dem ich das Messer an die Kehle setzte . . ." See Hugo Wolf, *Briefe an Heinrich Potpeschnigg*, ed. Heinz Nonveiller (Stuttgart: Union Deutsche Verlagsgesellschaft, 1923), 202. On 1 September, however, he wrote Paul Müller to say that the opera would be produced in January or February.

24. Wolf, *Briefe an Rosa Mayreder*, 92, letter of 7 September 1897.

25. "Ein Opernplan Hugo Wolfs. Mit ungedruckten Briefen," in *Der Merker* 4 (1 March 1913): 173–77. Dr. Winter's letters are no longer extant. When he evidently responded to Wolf's initial inquiry of 23 May with more information on Ilse and her legendary transmutations than expected, Wolf wrote back enthusiastically on 3 June, saying that he had already sketched a scenario in his head and would send his benefactor an outline in his next letter. Winter had apparently written to say that he believed Heine's source was a work by Philipp Georg August Wilhelm Blumenhagen, *Wanderung durch den Harz*. Wolf had tried to find a copy of the work but was unsuccessful; as he tells Winter in his inimitable way, though dust had only gathered for a mere thirty years over Blumenhagen's works (the author died in 1839), the chap was in danger of becoming a fossil. Could Winter, he asks, summarize as much of Blumenhagen as he can remember, preferably in comfort with coffee and a pipe at hand? In the third and last letter of 21 June, Wolf again marvels at Blumenhagen's disappearance into "Egyptian darkness" and recounts his trips to antiquarian booksellers in hopes of locating the volume.

26. Ibid., 176–77.

27. Wolf, *Briefe an Kauffmann*, 128–29.

28. Friedrich Nietzsche, *The Birth of Tragedy and The Case of Wagner*, trans. Walter Kaufmann (New York: Vintage Books, 1967), 172.

29. Eduard Hanslick's career as a music critic in Vienna was launched when he published an analysis and critique of *Tannhäuser* in the *Wiener Musikzeitung* in 1846 in which he lauded Wagner as "the greatest dramatic talent among all contemporary composers." By the time of Hanslick's November 1858 review of *Lohengrin*, however, he had come to find Wagner dangerous, although his criticisms are tempered by the observation of what Wagner does well. In *Hanslick's Music Criticisms*, trans. and ed. Henry Pleasants (New York: Dover Publications, 1950; reprint, 1978), 61, Hanslick points out that "this knack of Wagner's for building groups and introducing situations which cannot fail of pictorial effect is perhaps the most characteristic facet of his talent and the aspect most deserving of closer analytical examination." The intent of such statements is denigration of Wagner as a graphic and decorative artist rather than an inspired true musician, but nevertheless Hanslick concedes at every turn that Wagner is "an inspired genius" (ibid., 152, from Hanslick's article "Richard Wagner's Stage

Festival in Bayreuth") and measures everyone else's operas against the Wagnerian standard. For example, he criticizes Humperdinck for having no personality of his own—his music, he complains, all stems from "Wagner the Father and Wagner the Son." More of Hanslick's criticisms should be translated and published, including the reviews of works by lesser lights. It is interesting that Wolf's recorded moments of rebellion against Wagner often take the form of statements similar to Hanslick's objections.

30. Wolf, *Briefe an Grohe*, 30–31; and Walker, *Hugo Wolf*, 268.

31. Wolf, *Briefe an Grohe*, 33. "Not a single ray of sunshine, not even a rousing storm with thunder and lightning. Nowadays people want change, especially the theatergoing public, and therefore merry and pleasing subjects have the greatest longevity."

32. Three years earlier, Wolf had asked in a review published on 10 April 1887 in the *Salonblatt*, "Is there any need to spell out the fate of Wagner's many successors in the field of opera, the still white-hot *Armins, Kunihilds Sakuntalas, Urvasis* and however—God knows—they are all called?" See *The Music Criticism of Hugo Wolf*, 275.

33. Wolf, *Briefe an Rosa Mayreder*, 23.

34. Ibid., 25–26. "I am so happy to have this wretched piece finally behind me. You can't imagine how much mental anguish I have suffered for it. Some days I went about like a desperate man and cursed myself and composing and opera and the entire world. For three days I crucified my poor brain to find the right musical expression for 'Wenn es Gott gefallen hätte, mich durch schlimmen Schein zu prüfen.' I was as if woodenheaded; I couldn't do it. Every attempt failed: nothing can be achieved by force in art. What to do? I wrote immediately to my friend Larisch to send me the full score of 'Meistersinger' to give me the inspiration to orchestrate the first act of Corregidor. The score arrived, but by then the mood to compose had returned, and so I haven't done the instrumentation. Thank God! Superstitious as I am, I interpreted this particular passage in Lukas's monologue as reflective of my condition, as if all existing creativity showed me the unworthiness of the opera through a sudden interruption. What could I have done with half an opera? Such dreadful notions make me feel even worse and to escape such terrible imaginings I wanted to regain my sanity with the orchestration of the first act of the Corregidor.

Today I am so happy and so optimistic that I could embrace the world. What I have done with this scene!—when I played it for myself, I was so moved I had to stop."

35. Eduard Hanslick, "Die Meistersinger von Richard Wagner," reprinted in *Die moderne Oper: Kritiken und Studien* (Berlin: Allgemeiner Verein für Deutsche Literatur, 1885), 300–302. According to Hanslick, Wagnerian declamation and the composer's propensity for pathos at the high points of his dramas, such as the third-act quintet in *Die Meistersinger*, inveigh against true comedy, while Beckmesser's dissonances belong, he felt, more to *Schauerdrama*, or tales of horror, than to comedy.

36. Wolf, *Briefe an Rosa Mayreder*, 55, letter of 4 November 1895.

37. Ibid., letter of 27 October 1895.

38. Ibid., 55, letter of 4 November 1895.

39. See *Aufbruch in das Jahrhundert der Frau? Rosa Mayreder und der Feminismus in Wien um 1900. 125. Sonderausstellung des Historischen Museums der Stadt Wien, 21. September 1989 bis 21. Jänner 1990*. See in particular, the following essays in the exhibition catalog: Edith Prost, "Individualisten-Bürgerliche-Feministin. Biographische Notizen zu Rosa Mayreder," 59–66; Leopold Spitzer, "Rosa Mayreder und

Hugo Wolf," 73–78; and Andrea Dopplinger-Loebenstein, "'Die tanzende Seele'—Rosa Mayreders literarisches Schaffen," 79–83. See also Rosa Mayreder, *Mein Pantheon. Lebenserinnerungen*, ed. Susanne Kerkovius (Dornach: Philosophisch-Anthroposophischer Verlag am Goetheanum, R. Geering, 1988) and *Tagebücher 1873–1937*, ed. Harriet Anderson (Frankfurt: Insel Verlag, 1988); Harriet Anderson, "Zwischen Modernismus und Sozialreform: Rosa Mayreder und die Kultur der Wiener Jahrhundertwende," in *Rosa Mayreder 1858–1939*, Mitteilungen des Instituts für Wissenschaft und Kunst 44, no. 1 (Vienna 1989): 6–12; Harriet Anderson, "Beyond a Critique of Femininity: The Thought of Rosa Mayreder 1858–1938" (Ph.D. dissertation, University of London, 1985); Edith Prost, "Weiblichkeit und bürgerliche Kultur am Beispiel Rosa Mayreder-Obermayer" (Ph.D. dissertation, University of Vienna, 1983); Hertha Dworschak, "Rosa Obermayer-Mayreder" (Ph.D. dissertation, University of Vienna, 1949); and Hanna Bubenicek, ed., *Rosa Mayreder oder Wider die Tyrannei der Norm* (Vienna: Böhlau, 1986).

40. Rosa Mayreder, "Richard Wagner, der Heide" and "Richard Wagner, der Christ," in *Magazin für Litteratur* 66 (1897): 1333–38 and 1367–73, respectively.

41. Wolf, *Briefe an Grohe*, 35, letter of 11 August 1890.

42. Arthur Groos, "Appropriation in Wagner's Tristan Libretto," in *Reading Opera*, ed. Arthur Groos and Roger Parker (Princeton: Princeton University Press, 1988), 12.

43. Pedro Antonio de Alarcón, *The Three-Cornered Hat*, trans. Jacob S. Fassett, Jr. (New York: Alfred A. Knopf, 1929), 23–33.

44. There is no precise English equivalent for this word, used to designate a gathering of close friends in which the chief activity is meeting for conversation.

45. Alarcón, *The Three-Cornered Hat*, 35–36.

46. Ibid., 40–42.

47. Walker, *Hugo Wolf*, 388.

48. Alarcón, *The Three-Cornered Hat*, 47–48.

49. Carl Dahlhaus, *Richard Wagner's Music Dramas*, trans. Mary Whittall (Cambridge: Cambridge University Press, 1979), 65.

50. Alarcón, *The Three-Cornered Hat*, 52–53.

51. Ibid., chap. 30, "A Lady of Distinction," 166–67.

52. Ibid., 71.

53. "The Case of Wagner," in *The Works of Friedrich Nietzsche*, ed. Alexander Tille, trans. Thomas Common (New York: Macmillan, 1896), vol. 11, 8.

54. Alarcón, *The Three-Cornered Hat*, 196–97.

55. Ibid., 54–55.

56. Ibid., chap. 17, "A Country Alcalde [Mayor]," 106.

57. Karl Grunsky, *Hugo Wolf* (Leipzig: Kistner and Siegel, 1928), 74.

58. Alarcón, *The Three-Cornered Hat*, chap. 15, "A Prosaic Farewell," 101.

59. Eduard Hanslick quotes an unnamed critic for the Berlin newspaper *Die Zeit* in an article entitled "Gelegentliches über Zemlinsky und Richard Strauss," reprinted in *Aus neuer und neuester Zeit. "Der modernen oper*," vol. 9: *Musikalische Kritiken und Schilderungen* (Berlin: Allgemeiner Verein für Deutsche Litteratur, 1900), 44.

60. Wolf, *Briefe an Rosa Mayreder*, 26–27.

61. Margarethe Saary, in ibid., 368–69, speculates that Frasquita may resemble Wolf's first love, Vally Franck.

62. Ibid., 378.

63. Ibid., 380.

64. Wolf, *Briefe an Melanie Köchert*, 130–31.

65. Edgar Istel, *Das Libretto: Wesen, Aufbau und Wirkung des Opernbuchs* (Berlin and Leipzig: Schuster and Loeffler, 1914), 95–104.

66. Wolf, *Briefe an Melanie Köchert*, 129, letter of 13 April 1895.

67. Alarcón, *The Three-Cornered Hat*, chap. 23, "Once More the Wilderness and the Aforesaid Voices," 142–43. In his orchestral *Verwandlung*, Wolf incorporates brassy allusions to the donkeys braying, Alarcón's "Voces clamantes in deserto." The beasts recognize one another, but the human beings on their backs fail to do likewise.

68. Walker, *Hugo Wolf*, 409. "The songs are fitted cleverly enough into their places in the text, but the procedure is a sufficiently desperate one, and indicative of Wolf's need of a succession of brief lyrical opportunities rather than a properly cumulative dramatic action." The first song in particular is indeed cleverly fitted into its new operatic context. A song whose persona sings of lying next to her sleeping lover functions as erotic incitement for the Corregidor, who responds, "Lass ihn schlafen, lass ihn ruh'n!" (Let him sleep! Let him rest!) to variations of the song's principal motive, shading into the Corregidor's Authority theme, with which it shares a similar dotted rhythmic pattern.

69. Edgar Istel, *Das Libretto*, 73.

70. Walker, *Hugo Wolf*, 390–91. Walker complains first of the "excessive rapidity of his stage action, leading to effects of restlessness and the failure to establish firmly the atmosphere of the different scenes." Shortly thereafter, he writes that "the time factor in opera was new to him and brought with it problems that he did not solve."

71. Humperdinck wrote an approving review of Wolf's setting for chorus, soloists, and orchestra of Count August von Platen-Hallermünde's "Christnacht" in an article for the *Frankfurter Zeitung* of 10 April 1891, an article reprinted two weeks later on 23 April in the *Wiener Fremdenblatt*. Later, when his malady had rendered Wolf even more ungenerous to friends and allies, he had harsh words for Humperdinck and his *Märchenoper*, with its interpolated folk songs, but the libretto (written by his sister Adelheid Wette, with the participation of the entire family—Humperdinck called it "the family headache") is more creditably constructed by far than the Mayreder libretto. Humperdinck, Wagner's choice as *répétiteur* for the first performance of *Parsifal*, set the libretto that finally emerged with ample length and breadth for each episode and without the temporal discrepancies that so mar Wolf's opera.

72. Wolf, *Briefe an Mayreder*, 32.

73. Ibid., 37–38, 19 July 1895.

74. Ibid., 58, letter of 8 November 1895. "An epic element cannot be avoided in the treatment of this subject, and therefore no one shall take away from us the right to expand the drama because of traditional school-rules and regulations. Many such conventions have already been done away with, such as the well-known Aristotelian unity of time and place—in short and to the good, the entire tale stays, and let that be an end to this." A *Mastersinger*-inspired rebuke? The next day, he wrote to Grohe in annoyance, complaining that Frau Mayreder was pestering him with all sorts of questions about changes in the text.

75. Ibid., 34, letter of 18 June 1895.

76. *The Portable Nietzsche*, trans. and ed. Walter Kaufmann (New York: Penguin Books, 1959; reprint, 1982), 665–66.

77. Dahlhaus, *Richard Wagner's Music Dramas*, 65.

78. Eduard Hanslick, *Fünf Jahre Musik (1891–1895). Der "Modernen Oper*," vol. 7 (Berlin: Allgemeiner Verein für Deutsche Litteratur, 1896), a review from 1892 of Eduard Schütt's *Signor Formica*, 48.

79. Margarete Saary, *Persönlichkeit und Musikdramatisches Kreativität Hugo Wolfs* (Tutzing: Hans Schneider Verlag, 1984), 397.

80. *Briefe an Melanie Köchert*, 77, letter of 8 January 1894; and *Letters to Melanie Köchert*, 87–88. Cited also in translation in Walker, *Hugo Wolf*, 333.

81. Ernst Otto Nodnagel, *Jenseits von Wagner und Liszt: Profile und Perspektiven, Op. 35* (Königsberg: Ostpreußischen Druckerei und Verlagsanstalt, 1902), the profile of Wolf, 21–36. Wolf, of course, had not yet died, and Nodnagel's essay begins, "The musical world sorrows for a living man."

82. Ernst Otto Nodnagel, *Käthe Elsinger: Bericht über Leo Borgs Liebe und Tod* (Berlin: "Harmonie" Verlagsgesellschaft für Literatur und Kunst, 1905), 61–62.

83. Wolf, *Briefe an Melanie Köchert*, 144, letter of 12 June 1895; and *Letters to Melanie Köchert*, 163–64.

84. Wolf, *Briefe an Grohe*, 83.

85. Ibid., 122 and 132, letters of 19 October 1893 and 20 December 1893, respectively. The latter includes another of Wolf's brief outbursts of longing for an opera text; telling Grohe that he has enclosed a review of *Hanneles Himmelfahrt*, he then writes, "That the poetic drama be suitable for music—Oh, if only the dramatic speech can in general be adaptable for music . . ." He says nothing more about the play, not surprisingly; Wolf disliked sentimentality (he would later dismiss Hauptmann's poem, "'s ist ein stiller, heiliger Tag" as too sentimental—see Wolf, *Briefe an Grohe*, 250), and he was not religious; the child Hannele's vision of heaven as compensation for a short, brutal life would not have suited him.

86. Wolf asked his friend Paul Müller, a gymnasium teacher and the founder of the Hugo Wolf Society in Berlin, to act as an intermediary in negotiations with Hauptmann. Rosa Mayreder, who knew that Müller was a friend of the poet Richard Dehmel, a member of Hauptmann's inner circle, suggested that Müller might approach Hauptmann through Dehmel. By the end of January 1897, so Wolf tells Grohe, both Wolf's patron Baron Franz Lipperheide and Müller had told him that knowledgeable sources (friends of Hauptmann) had declared the collaboration unworkable. See Hugo Wolf, "Ungedruckte Briefe von Hugo Wolf an Paul Müller," in *Jahrbuch der Musikbibliothek Peters für 1904* (Leipzig: Edition Peters, 1905), 86; and *Briefe an Grohe*, 252.

87. Franz Rudolf Eyßenhardt, *Manuel Venegas* (Stuttgart: W. Spemann [1882?]).

88. *Briefe an Grohe*, 81, undated letter written between 13 February and 20 April 1892.

89. See Walker, *Hugo Wolf*, 312–16; Hugo Wolf, *Sämtliche Werke*, vol. 13: *Manuel Venegas: Opernfragment*, ed. Leopold Spitzer (Vienna: Musikwissenschaftlicher Verlag, 1975), foreword, vii–xiv; and Saary, *Persönlichkeit und Musikdramatisches Kreativität Hugo Wolfs*, 427–42, for other accounts of the opera.

90. *Briefe an Grohe*, 84, letter of 20 April 1892.

91. Rosa Mayreder, "Hugo Wolfs zweite Oper," in *Deutsche Musiker-Zeitung* 59, no. 27 (7 July 1928): 584.

92. Wolf, *Briefe an Heinrich Potpeschnigg*, 185, letter of 20 March 1897; and *Briefe an Grohe*, 260, letter of 24 March 1897.

93. Wolf, *Briefe an Grohe*, 262.

94. Ibid., 267. Rosa Mayreder was indeed hurt when Wolf rejected her libretto. When Decsey wrote her a letter requesting material for his biography, she recorded, with difficult honesty, in her diary on 19 February 1905 that Wolf's descent into madness had not affected her as deeply as his rejection of her text for *Manuel Venegas*, that she had indeed felt a kind of satisfaction in knowing that he could not ever compose "das fremde Textbuch." Although the memory of their estrangement had become less painful in the interim, she still counted it a malignity of fate that the great sorrow of his insanity and death was thus poisoned for her. See Mayreder, *Tagebücher 1873–1937*, 91–92.

95. Leopold Spitzer, who edited *Manuel Venegas* for the *Hugo Wolf Gesamtausgabe* (vol. 13; 1975), has written an informative article, "Rosa Mayreders Textbuch zu Hugo Wolfs 'Manuel Venegas,'" in *Österreichische Musikzeitschrift* 18, no. 10 (1973): 443–51. See also Spitzer, "Hugo Wolfs 'Manuel Venegas': Ein Beitrag zur Genese," in ibid., 32 (1977): 66–74.

96. From Michael Haberlandt, *Hugo Wolf, Erinnerungen und Gedanken* (Darmstadt: A. Bergsträssers Hofbuchhandlung [W. Kleinschmidt], 1911), 47.

97. Wolf's letters to Mayr are a fascinating source of information about the genesis of *Manuel Venegas*. The letters of 21 June and 10 July have been published in Richard Schaal, "Ungedruckte Briefe von Hugo Wolf," in *Deutsches Jahrbuch der Musikwissenschaft für 1968*, ed. Rudolf Eller (Leipzig: Edition Peters, 1969): 125–26. The letters to Mayr about the second Alarcón opera are found on 122–30. The letters end with Joseph Schalk's postcard to Mayr of 2 October 1897, telling him of Wolf's collapse.

98. Spitzer, "Hugo Wolfs 'Manuel Venegas': Ein Beitrag zur Genese," 69, compares ten lines of poetry Hoernes had assigned Vitriolo in act 1, scene 1 with Wolf's compression into six lines.

99. Mayreder, "Wolfs zweite Oper," 604.

100. Walker, *Hugo Wolf*, 426.

101. Thomas Mann, *Die Entstehung des Doktor Faustus* (Amsterdam: Bermann-Fischer Verlag, 1949), 25. Saary, in *Persönlichkeit und Musikdramatische Kreativität Hugo Wolfs*, 86–87, discusses the elements of Wolf's life and creation that Mann incorporated into the figure of Adrian Leverkühn, including the composer's attraction to vocal music, the opinion that lieder were merely preparations for the larger work of opera, possibly even the late notion to marry (the Frieda Zerny episode in Wolf's life), and the onset of insanity.

Adams, Jeffrey Todd. *Eduard Mörike's "Orplid": Myth and the Poetic Mind*. Hildesheim: Georg Olms Verlag, 1984.

Bach, Albert B. *The Art-Ballad: Loewe and Schubert*. 3d ed. London: Kegan Paul, Trench, Trübner, 1987.

Bahr, Hermann. "Erinnerungen an Hugo Wolf." In *Buch der Jugend*. Vienna: K. Heller, 1908.

Batka, Richard. *Martin Plüddemann und seine Balladen*. Prague, 1896.

Bitter, Werner. *Studien zur Entwicklung der deutschen komischen Oper im 20. Jahrhundert*. Halle: Otto-Hendel-Druckerei, 1932.

Brahms, Johannes. *Johannes Brahms Briefwechsel V: Johannes Brahms im Briefwechsel mit Joseph Joachim*. Ed. Andreas Moser. Berlin, 1921.

——. *Briefwechsel IX: Johannes Brahms Briefe an P. J. Simrock und Fritz Simrock*. Ed. Max Kalbeck. Berlin, 1917.

——. *Johannes Brahms and Theodor Billroth: Letters from a Musical Friendship*. Trans. and ed. Hans Barken. Norman, Okla.: University of Oklahoma Press, 1957.

Bülow, Hans von. *Ausgewählte Schriften 1850–1892*, vol. 1 (*Briefe und Schriften*, vol. 3). Leipzig: Breitkopf and Härtel, 1911.

Busse, Eckart. *Die Eichendorff-Rezeption im Kunstlied: Versuch einer Typologie anhand von Kompositionen Schumanns, Wolfs und Pfitzners*. Würzburg: Eichendorff Gesellschaft, 1975.

Challier, Ernst. *Grosser Lieder-Katalog: Ein alphabetisch geordnetes Verzeichniss sämmtlicher einstimmiger Lieder*. Berlin: privately published, 1885.

Chamisso, Adalbert von. *Chamissos Werke*, vol. 1. Ed. Hermann Tardel. Leipzig and Vienna: Bibliographisches Institut, 1907.

Cook, Peter. *Hugo Wolf's Corregidor: A Study of the Opera and Its Origins*. London: privately published, 1976.

Cornelius, Carl Maria. *Peter Cornelius. Der Wort- und Tondichter*, vol. 1. Regensburg: Gustav Bosse Verlag, 1925.

Cornelius, Peter. *Literarische Werke*, vol. 3: *Aufsätze über Musik und Kunst*. Ed. Edgar Istel. Leipzig: Breitkopf and Härtel, 1904.

——. *Musikalische Werke*, vol. 1. Ed. Max Hasse. Leipzig: Breitkopf and Härtel, 1905–06. Reprint. Farnsborough, England: Gregg International Publishers, 1971.

Dahlhaus, Carl. "Ein Dilemma der Verskomposition." In *Melos/Neue Zeitschrift für Musik* 3 (January 1977): 15–18.

Dalmedico, Angelo. *Canti del Popolo Veneziano*. Venice: Andrea Santini e Figlio, 1848.

Damrosch, Leopold. *Collected Songs*. Ed. Frank Damrosch. New York: G. Schirmer, 1903.

Decsey, Ernst. *Hugo Wolf*. 4 vols. Berlin and Leipzig: Schuster and Loeffler, 1903–06.

Dümmling, Albrecht, ed. *Gottfried Keller, vertont von Johannes Brahms, Hans Pfitzner, Hugo Wolf*. Lied und Lyrik, no. 3. Munich: Kindler, 1981.

Dworshak, Herta. "Rosa Obermayer-Mayreder: Leben und Werk." Ph.D. dissertation, University of Vienna, 1949.

Eckstein, Friedrich. *Alte unnennbare Tage: Erinnerungen aus siebzig Lehr- und Wanderjahren*. Vienna: Herbert Reichner Verlag, 1936.

Egger, Rita. *Die Deklamationsrhythmik Hugo Wolfs in historischer Sicht*. Tutzing: Hans Schneider Verlag, 1963.

Engel, Hans. *Carl Loewe: Überblick und Würdigung seines Schaffens*. Greifswald: Bamberg, 1934.

Eppstein, Hans. "Entwicklungszüge in Hugo Wolfs frühen Liedkompositionen." In *Svensk tidskrift för musikforskning* 66 (1984): 43–58.

———. "Zu Hugo Wolfs Liedskizzen." In *Österreichische Musikzeitschrift* 39 (December 1984): 645–56.

———. "Zum Schaffensprozess bei Hugo Wolf." In *Die Musikforschung* 32 (January–March 1984): 4–20.

Fellinger, Imogen. "Brahms's 'Way': A Composer's Self-View." In *Brahms 2: Biographical, Documentary, and Analytical Studies*. Ed. Michael Musgrave. Cambridge: Cambridge University Press, 1987.

———. "Die Oper im kompositorischen Schaffen von Hugo Wolf." In *Jahrbuch des Staatlichen Instituts für Musikforschung Preussischer Kulturbesitz* 5 (1972): 87–99.

Freud, Sigmund. *The Standard Edition of the Complete Psychological Works of Sigmund Freud*, vol. 8: *Jokes and Their Relationship to the Unconscious*. Trans. James Strachey, Anna Freud, Alix Strachey, and Alan Tyson. London: Hogarth Press, 1960.

Freund, Winfried. "Eduard Mörike: Der Feuerreiter." In *Die deutsche Ballade: Theorie, Analysen, Didaktik*. Paderborn: Ferdinand Schöningh, 1978.

Gaedertz, Karl Theodor. *Emanuel Geibel, Sänger der Liebe, Herold des Reiches*. Leipzig: Georg Wigand, 1897.

Geibel, Emanuel, and Paul Heyse. *Der Briefwechsel von Emanuel Geibel und Paul Heyse*. Ed. Erich Petzet. Munich: J. F. Lehmanns Verlag, 1922.

———. *Spanisches Liederbuch*. Berlin: Wilhelm Hertz, 1852.

Geiringer, Karl. "Hugo Wolf und Frida von Lipperheide: Some Unpublished Letters." In *Musical Times* 77 (August–September 1936): 701–2, 793–97.

Grasberger, Franz. "Johannes Brahms und Hugo Wolf." In *Österreichische Musikzeitschrift* 15 (February 1960): 67–69.

Grunsky, Karl. *Hugo Wolf*. Leipzig: Kistner and Siegel, 1928.

Gülke, Peter. "Sterb' ich, so hüllt in Blumen meine Glieder . . . : zu einem Lied von Hugo Wolf." In *Musica* (Kassel) 33 (March–April 1979): 132–40.

Hanslick, Eduard. *Aus meinem Leben*, ed. Peter Wapnewski. Kassel and Basel: Bärenreiter, 1987.

———. *Concerte, Componisten und Virtuosen der letzten fünfzehn Jahre 1870–1885*. Berlin: Allgemeiner Verein für Deutsche Literatur, 1886.

———. *Fünf Jahre Musik (1891–1895). Der "Modernen Oper,"* vol. 7. Berlin: Allgemeiner Verein für Deutsche Literatur, 1896.

———. *Die moderne Oper: Kritiken und Studien*. Berlin: Allgemeiner Verein für Deutsche Literatur, 1885.

————. *Musikalische Stationen. Der "Modernen Oper,"* vol. 2. Berlin: Allgemeiner Verein für Deutsche Literatur, 1885.

————. *Musikalisches Skizzenbuch. Der "Modernen Oper,"* vol. 4. Berlin: Allgemeiner Verein für Deutsche Literatur, 1896.

Hatch, Christopher. "Tradition and Creation: Hugo Wolf's 'Fussreise.'" In *College Music Symposium* 28 (1988): 70–84.

Heckel, Karl. *Hugo Wolf in seinem Verhältnis zu Richard Wagner.* Munich and Leipzig: Georg Müller, 1905.

Heine, Heinrich. *Historisch-Kritische Gesamtausgabe der Werke.* Ed. Manfred Windführ. Vol. 1, part 1: *Buch der Lieder.* Ed. Pierre Grappin. Hamburg: Hoffmann and Campe Verlag, 1975.

Hellmer, Edmund von. *Hugo Wolf: Erlebtes und Erlauschtes.* Vienna and Leipzig: Wiener Literarische Anstalt, 1921.

Heuberger, Richard. *Erinnerungen an Johannes Brahms: Tagebuchnotizen aus den Jahren 1875 bis 1897.* 2d rev. ed. Ed. Kurt Hofmann. Tutzing: Hans Schneider Verlag, 1976.

Heuss, Alfred. "Mörikes 'Das verlassene Mägdlein' in verschiedenen musikalischen Fassungen." In *Neue Zeitschrift für Musik* (March–May 1926): 140–44.

Heyse, Paul. *Italienisches Liederbuch.* Berlin: Wilhelm Hertz, 1860.

Hofrichter, Laura. *Heinrich Heine.* Trans. Barker Fairley. Oxford: Oxford University Press, 1963.

Holde, Artur. "A Little-Known Letter by Berlioz and Unpublished Letters by Cherubini, Leoncavallo, and Hugo Wolf." In *Musical Quarterly* 37 (July 1951): 340–53.

Jancik, Hans. "Die Hugo Wolf-Autographen in der Musiksammlung der Österreichischen Nationalbibliothek." In *Beiträge zur Dokumentation: Franz Grasberger zum 60. Geburtstag.* Ed. Günter Brosche. Tutzing: Hans Schneider Verlag, 1975.

Jennings, Lee B. "Mörike's Grotesquery: A Post-Romantic Phenomenon." In *Journal of English and Germanic Philology* 59 (1960): 600–616.

Jensen, Adolf. *Forty Songs by Adolf Jensen.* Ed. William Foster Apthorp. Boston: Oliver Ditson, 1913.

————. *7 Gesänge aus dem Spanischen Liederbuch,* op. 4. Hamburg: Friedrich Schuberth, 1860.

Kalbeck, Max. *Johannes Brahms I: Erster Halbband 1833–1856.* 3d ed. Berlin: Deutsch Brahms-Gesellschaft, 1912.

Karpath, Ludwig. *Begegnung mit dem Genius.* 2d ed. Vienna and Leipzig: Fiba, 1934.

Kienzl, Wilhelm. "Der Corregidor." In *Aus Kunst und Leben: Gesammelte Aufsätze.* Berlin: Allgemeiner Verein für Deutsche Literatur, 1904.

Kneisel, Jessie Hoskam. *Mörike and Music.* Ph.D. dissertation, Columbia University, 1949.

Kramer, Lawrence. "Decadence and Desire: The *Wilhelm Meister* Songs of Wolf and Schubert." In *19th-Century Music* 10, no. 3 (Spring 1987): 229–42.

Kravitt, Edward F. "The Ballad as Conceived by Germanic Composers of the Late Romantic Period." In *Studies in Romanticism* 12, no. 2 (Spring 1973): 499–515.

————. "The Late Romantic Lied: Performance, the Literary Approach, and the Naturalistic Movement." Ph.D. dissertation, New York University, 1961.

————. "The Orchestral Lied: An Inquiry into Its Style and Unexpected Flowering Around 1900." In *Music Review* 37 (August 1976): 209–26.

Kretzschmar, Hermann. "Das deutsche Lied seit dem Tode Richard Wagners." In *Jahrbuch der Musikbibliothek Peters* 4 (1898): 45–60. (Also in *Gesammelte Aufsätze über Musik und Anderes aus den Grenzboten*, 284–300.) Leipzig: Breitkopf and Härtel, 1910.

Lahnstein, Peter. *Eduard Mörike: Leben und Milieu eines Dichters*. Munich: Paul List Verlag, 1986.

Lindner, Dolf. "Hugo Wolf an sein Schwester Katharina: ein unveröffentlicher Brief." In *Österreichische Musikzeitschrift* 15 (February 1960): 100–103.

Litzmann, Carl Conrad Theodor. *Emanuel Geibel. Aus Erinnerungen, Briefen und Tagebüchern*. Berlin: Wilhelm Hertz, 1887.

Loewe, Carl. *Dr. Carl Loewe's Selbstbiographie*. Ed. C. H. Bitter. Berlin: Wilhelm Müller, 1870.

Mahler, Alma. *Gustav Mahler: Erinnerungen und Briefe*. Amsterdam: Albert de Lange, 1940.

Mann, Thomas. *Die Entstehung der Doktor Faustus: Roman eines Romans*. Amsterdam: Bermann-Fischer Verlag, 1949.

Marx-Weber, Magda. "Cornelius' Kritik des Liedes." In *Peter Cornelius als Komponist, Dichter, Kritiker und Essayist*. Ed. Hellmut Federhofer and Kurt Oehl. Regensburg: Gustav Bosse Verlag, 1977.

Mayreder, Rosa. "Hugo Wolfs zweite Oper." In *Deutsche Musiker-Zeitung* 59 (7 July, 17 July, and 21 July 1928): 584–85; 604–6; 628–30.

———. *Tagebücher 1873–1937*, ed. Harriet Anderson. Frankfurt am Main: Insel Verlag, 1988.

———. "Über Hugo Wolf und seine Oper. Erinnerungen." In *"Der Corregidor" von Hugo Wolf. Kritische und biographische Beiträge zu seiner Würdigung*. Ed. Edmund von Hellmer. Berlin: S. Fischer, 1900.

———. "Über die Operndichtung 'Der Corregidor.'" In *Die Glocke. Wiener Blätter für Kunst und geistiges Leben* 2, nos. 29–30 (1936): 3–8.

———. "Zur Entstehung von Hugo Wolfs zweiter Oper 'Manuel Venegas.'" In *Die Glocke. Wiener Blätter für Kunst und geistiges Leben* 1, no. 5 (1935): 3–8.

Mörike, Eduard. *Sämtliche Werke, Briefe*. 3 vols. 2d aug. ed. Ed. Gerhart Baumann and Siegfried Grosse. Stuttgart: J. G. Cotta, 1959–61.

Müller, Gerhard. *Heinrich Heine und die Musik*. Leipzig: Reclam, 1987.

Müller, Paul. "Ungedruckte Briefe von Hugo Wolf an Paul Müller aus den Jahren 1896–1898." In *Jahrbuch der Musikbibliothek Peters* 10 (1904): 69–100.

Newman, Ernest. *Hugo Wolf*. London: Methuen, 1907.

———. *Hugo Wolf*. Trans. Hermann von Hase. Leipzig: Breitkopf and Härtel, 1910.

Niggli, Arnold. *Adolf Jensen*. Berlin: "Harmonie" Verlagsgesellschaft für Literatur und Kunst, 1900.

Nodnagel, Ernst Otto. "Hugo Wolf." In *Jenseits von Wagner und Liszt: Profile und Perspektiven, Op. 35*. Königsberg: Ostpreußische Druckerei und Verlagsanstalt, 1902.

"Ein Opernplan Hugo Wolfs. Mit ungedruckten Briefen." In *Wiener Zeitschrift für Musik* 1 (January–February 1908): 21–24. Reprinted in *Der Merker* 4 (1 March 1913): 173–77.

Ossenkopf, C. David. "The Earliest Settings of German Ballads for Voice and Clavier." Ph.D. dissertation, Columbia University, 1968.

──────. *Hugo Wolf: A Guide to Research.* New York and London: Garland Publishing, 1988.

Pohl, Rainer. "Zur Textgeschichte von Mörikes 'Feuerreiter.'" In *Eduard Mörike.* Ed. Victor G. Doerksen. Darmstadt: Wissenschaftliche Buchgesellschaft, 1975.

Plüddemann, Martin. *Balladen und Gesänge für eine Singstimme mit Klavierbegleitung.* 3d ed. 8 vols. Nuremberg: Wilhelm Schmid, 1892–98.

Prawer, Siegbert Salomon. *Heine: Buch der Lieder.* London: Edward Arnold, 1960.

──────. *Mörike und seine Leser: Versuch einer Wirkungsgeschichte.* Veröffentlichungen der Deutschen Schillergesellschaft, no. 23. Stuttgart: Klett, 1960.

Radner, Lawrence. *Eichendorff: The Spiritual Geometer.* Lafayette, Ind.: Purdue University Press, 1970.

Rolland, Romain. "Hugo Wolf." In *Musiciens d'aujourd'hui.* Paris: Hachette, 1908.

Rosen, Waldemar. "Hugo Wolfs musikalischer Nachlass." In *Allgemeine Musik-Zeitung* 64 (30 April and 7 May 1937): 261–63, 277–79.

Rostand, Claude. *Hugo Wolf: L'homme et son oeuvre.* Paris: Seghers, 1967, Reprint. Geneva: Slatkine Reprints, 1982.

Runze, Maximilian. *Carl Loewe.* Leipzig: Reclam, 1905.

──────. "Carl Loewe, eine ästhetische Beurtheilung." In *Sammlung musikalischer Vorträge.* Ed. Paul Graf Waldersee and V. Reihe. Leipzig: Breitkopf and Härtel, 1884.

Saary, Margarete. *Persönlichkeit und musikdramatische Kreativität Hugo Wolfs.* Wiener Veröffentlichungen zur Musikwissenschaft, no. 26. Tutzing: Hans Schneider Verlag, 1984.

Sable, Barbara K. "The Translation Chain in Some of the Hugo Wolf Settings of the *Spanisches Liederbuch.*" In *Journal of Musicological Research* 5 (1984): 213–35.

Sammons, Jeffrey L. *Heinrich Heine, The Elusive Poet.* New Haven: Yale University Press, 1969.

Sams, Eric. *The Songs of Hugo Wolf.* 2d ed., rev. and enlarged. London: Eulenburg Books, 1983.

Sarchet, William. "The *Hugo Wolf* of Ernst Decsey." Ph.D. dissertation, Indiana University, 1974.

Schaal, Richard. "Ungedruckte Briefe von Hugo Wolf." In *Deutsches Jahrbuch für Musikwissenschaft* 13 (1968): 115–31.

Schalk, Joseph. "Neue Lieder, neues Leben." In *Gesammelte Aufsätze über Hugo Wolf,* vol. 1. Berlin: S. Fischer, 1898–99.

Schemann, Ludwig. *Martin Plüddemann und die deutsche Ballade.* Regensburg: Gustav Bosse Verlag, 1930.

Schmalzriedt, Siegfried. "Hugo Wolfs Vertonung von Moerikes Gedicht *Karwoche*: realistische Züge im spätromantischen Lied." In *Archiv für Musikwissenschaft* 41 (1984): 42–53.

Schmitz, Eugen. "Hugo Wolfs Opernfragment 'Manuel Venegas.'" In *Neue Zeitschrift für Musik* 72 (15 November 1905): 943–46.

Schur, Gustav. *Erinnerungen an Hugo Wolf, nebst Hugo Wolfs Briefen an Gustav Schur.* Ed. Heinrich Werner. Regensburg: Gustav Bosse Verlag, 1922.

Schwartz, Egon. *Joseph von Eichendorff.* New York: Twayne Publishers, 1974.

Seelig, Harry E. "Goethe's 'Buch Suleika' and Hugo Wolf: A Musico-Literary Study." Ph.D. dissertation, University of Kansas, 1969.

Seidlin, Oskar. *Versuche über Eichendorff.* Göttingen: Vandenhoeck and Ruprecht, 1965.

Serauky, Walter. "Zu Carl Loewes Biographie und musikalischem Schaffen." In *Festschrift Arnold Schering zum sechzigsten Geburtstag.* Ed. Helmuth Osthoff, Walter Serauky, and Adam Adrio, in collaboration with Max Schneider and Gotthold Frotscher. Berlin: Glas, 1937.

Spitta, Philipp. "Die Ballade." In *Musikgeschichtliche Aufsätze.* Berlin: Verlag von Gebrüder Paetel, 1894.

Spitzer, Leopold. "Hugo Wolfs 'Manuel Venegas': Ein Beitrag zur Genese." In *Österreichische Musikzeitschrift* 32 (February 1977): 68–74.

———. "Rosa Mayreders Textbuch zu Hugo Wolfs 'Manuel Venegas.'" In *Österreichische Musikzeitschrift* 28 (October 1973): 443–51.

Steglich, Rudolf. "Zum Kontrastproblem Johannes Brahms und Hugo Wolf." In *Kongress-Bericht der Gesellschaft für Musikforschung Lüneberg 1950.* Ed. Hans Albrecht, Helmuth Osthoff, and Walter Wiora. Kassel and Basel: Bärenreiter, 1952.

Stein, Deborah. *Hugo Wolf's Lieder and Extensions of Tonality.* Studies in Musicology no. 72. Ann Arbor: UMI Research Press, 1985.

Strehl, Reinhard. "Die musikalische Form bei Hugo Wolf." Ph.D. dissertation, University of Göttingen, 1964.

Suppan, Wolfgang. "Wolfiana in der 'Sammlung Wamlek,' Graz." In *Österreichische Musikzeitschrift* 15 (February 1960): 103–6.

Tausche, Anton. "'An eine Aeolsharfe': die Vertonungen von Eduard Mörikes Gedicht durch Brahms und Hugo Wolf." In *Österreichische Musikzeitschrift* 3 (February 1948): 47–48.

Thiessen, Karl. "Johannes Brahms und Hugo Wolf als Lieder-Komponisten. Eine vergleichende Studie." In *Neue Musik-Zeitung* 27 (4 January 1906): 145–49.

Thym, Jürgen. "The Solo Song Settings of Eichendorff's Poems by Schumann and Wolf." Ph.D. dissertation, Case Western Reserve University, 1974.

Tigri, Giuseppe. *Canti Popolari Toscani.* Florence: Barbera, Bianchi, and Co., 1860.

Tommaseo, Niccoló. *Canti Popolari Toscani Corsi Illirici Greci.* Venice, 1841.

Walker, Frank. *Hugo Wolf: A Biography.* 2d ed. London: Dent, 1968.

———. *Hugo Wolf: Eine Biographie.* Trans. Witold Schey. Graz: Styria, 1953.

Waters, Edward N. "Musical Vienna in the Library of Congress." Intro. by L. Quincy Mumford. In *Festschrift Josef Stummvoll.* Ed. Joseph Mayrhofer and Walter Ritzer. Vienna: Brüder Hollinek, 1970.

Werner, Heinrich. "Hugo Wolf in Maierling: zwei ungedruckte Briefe Wolfs aus dem Jahr 1881." In *Almanach der deutschen Musikbücherei auf das Jahr 1922.* Regensburg: Gustav Bosse Verlag, 1921.

———. *Hugo Wolf in Maierling: Eine Idylle.* Leipzig: Breitkopf and Härtel, 1913.

———. *Hugo Wolf in Perchtoldsdorf: Persönliche Erinnerungen, nebst den Briefen des Meisters an seine Freunde Dr. Michael Haberlandt, Rudolf von Larisch und andere.* Regensburg: Gustav Bosse Verlag, 1925.

———. "Some Unpublished Letters of Hugo Wolf." Trans. Marie Boileau. In *Monthly Musical Record* 57 (1 August 1924): 226–28.

Wolf, Hugo. *Briefe an Emil Kauffmann.* Ed. Edmund von Hellmer. Berlin: S. Fischer, 1903.

————. *Briefe an Frieda Zerny*. Ed. Ernst Hilmar and Walter Obermaier. Vienna: Musikwissenschaftlicher Verlag, 1978.

————. *Briefe an Heinrich Potpeschnigg*. Ed. Heinz Nonveiller. Stuttgart: Union Deutsche Verlagsgesellschaft, 1923.

————. *Briefe an Henriette Lang, nebst den Briefen an deren Gatten Prof. Joseph Freiherr von Schey*. Ed. Heinrich Werner. Regensburg: Gustav Bosse Verlag, 1923.

————. *Briefe an Hugo Faisst*. Ed. Michael Haberlandt. Stuttgart and Leipzig: Deutsche Verlags-Anstalt, 1904.

————. *Briefe an Melanie Köchert*. Ed. Franz Grasberger. Tutzing: Hans Schneider Verlag, 1964. English translation, *Letters to Melanie Köchert*. Trans. Louise McClelland Urban. New York: Schirmer Books, 1991.

————. *Briefe an Oskar Grohe*. Ed. Heinrich Werner. Berlin: S. Fischer, 1905.

————. *Briefe an Rosa Mayreder, mit einem Nachwort der Dichterin des Corregidor*. Ed. Heinrich Werner. Vienna: Rikola, 1921.

————. *Hugo Wolf: Ein Persönlichkeit in Briefen*. Ed. Edmund von Hellmer. Leipzig: Breitkopf and Härtel, 1912.

————. "Daten aus meinen Leben." In *Österreichische Musikzeitschrift* 15 (February 1960): 49–50.

————. *Der Corregidor: Oper in vier Acten. Text nach einer Novelle des Alarcon von Rosa Mayreder-Obermayer*. Mannheim: K. Ferdinand Heckel, 1896.

————. *Der Corregidor: Oper in vier Acten* [orchestral score]. Mannheim: K. Ferdinand Heckel, 1904.

————. *The Music Criticism of Hugo Wolf*. Trans. and ed. Henry Pleasants. New York and London: Holmes and Meier Publishers, 1978.

————. *Hugo Wolfs musikalische Kritiken*. Ed. Richard Batka and Heinrich Werner. Leipzig: Breitkopf and Härtel, 1911.

————. *Sämtliche Werke*, vols. 1–20. Ed. Hans Jancik and Leopold Spitzer. Vienna: Musikwissenschaftlicher Verlag, 1963–87.

Vol. 1. *Gedichte von Eduard Mörike*. Ed. Hans Jancik. 1963.

Vol. 2. *Gedichte von Josef von Eichendorff*. Ed. Hans Jancik. 1970.

Vol. 3, Parts 1 and 2. *Gedichte von J. W. von Goethe*. Ed. Hans Jancik. 1978.

Vol. 4. *Spanisches Liederbuch*. Ed. Hans Jancik. 1967.

Vol. 5. *Italienisches Liederbuch I und II*. Ed. Hans Jancik. 1972.

Vol. 6. *Lieder nach verschiedenen Dichtern*. Ed. Hans Jancik. 1981.

Vol. 7. *Nachgelassene Lieder*.

Part 1. *Liederstrauss; Lieder aus der Jugendzeit*. Ed. Hans Jancik. 1980.

Part 2. Lieder first published in *Nachgelassene Werke. 1. Folge*. Ed. Hans Jancik. 1969.

Part 3. Nineteen previously unpublished lieder. Ed. Hans Jancik. 1976.

Vol. 8. *Lieder mit Orchesterbegleitung I: J. W. Goethe*. Ed. Hans Jancik. 1982.

Vol. 9. *Lieder mit Orchesterbegleitung II: Eduard Mörike; Spanisches Liederbuch*. Ed. Hans Jancik. 1983.

Vol. 11. *Chöre mit Orchesterbegleitung*. Ed. Hans Jancik. 1986.

Vol. 13. *Manuel Venegas*. Ed. Leopold Spitzer. 1975.

Youens, Susan. "'Alles endet, was entstehet': The Second of Hugo Wolf's *Michelangelo-Lieder*." In *Studies in Music* (University of Western Australia) 14 (1980): 87–103.

————. "Charlatans, Pedants, and Fools: Hugo Wolf's 'Cophtisches Lied I.'" In *Studies in Music* (University of Western Ontario) 8 (1983): 77–92.

————. "Drama in the Lied: Piano vs. Voice in Wolf's Serenades." In *Studies in Music* (University of Western Australia) 23 (1989): 61–87.

————. "Hugo Wolf and Gottfried Keller: 'Wie glänzt der helle Mond.'" In *NATS Bulletin* 41, no. 1 (September–October 1984): 15–20.

————. "The Song Sketches of Hugo Wolf." In *Current Musicology* 44 (1990): 5–37.

Index